Manchester:
Looking for the Light
through the Pouring Rain

Manchester:
Looking for the Light
through the Pouring Rain

Kevin Cummins

ff

faber and faber

First published in 2009
by Faber and Faber Limited
Bloomsbury House,
74–77 Great Russell Street,
London WC1B 3DA
This paperback edition first published 2012

Design by Wallzo
Printed in China by C&C Offset Printing Co. Ltd

A CIP record for this book
is available from the British Library

ISBN 978–0–571–28338–5

10 9 8 7 6 5 4 3 2 1

The only band which got going at
all was The Saints from Manchester.
Their success was, I suspect, due to the
fact that the Royal Family are based
in London. Like all Mancunians they
were in a state of constant irritation
that so much went on in the capital,
whereas anyone could see that
Manchester was in every way superior.

[*George Melly*]

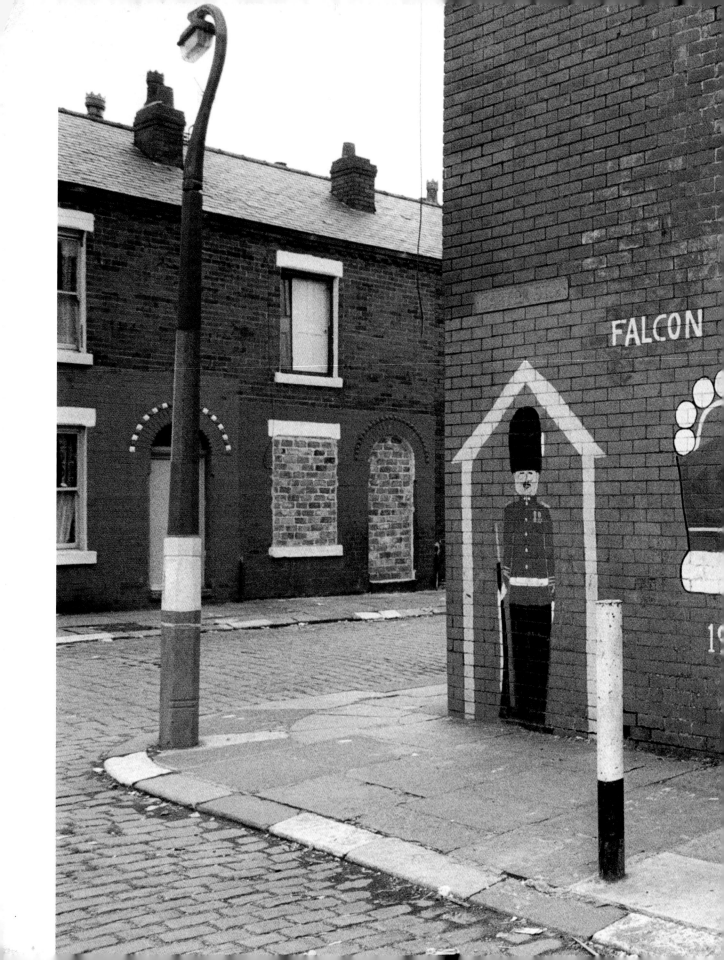

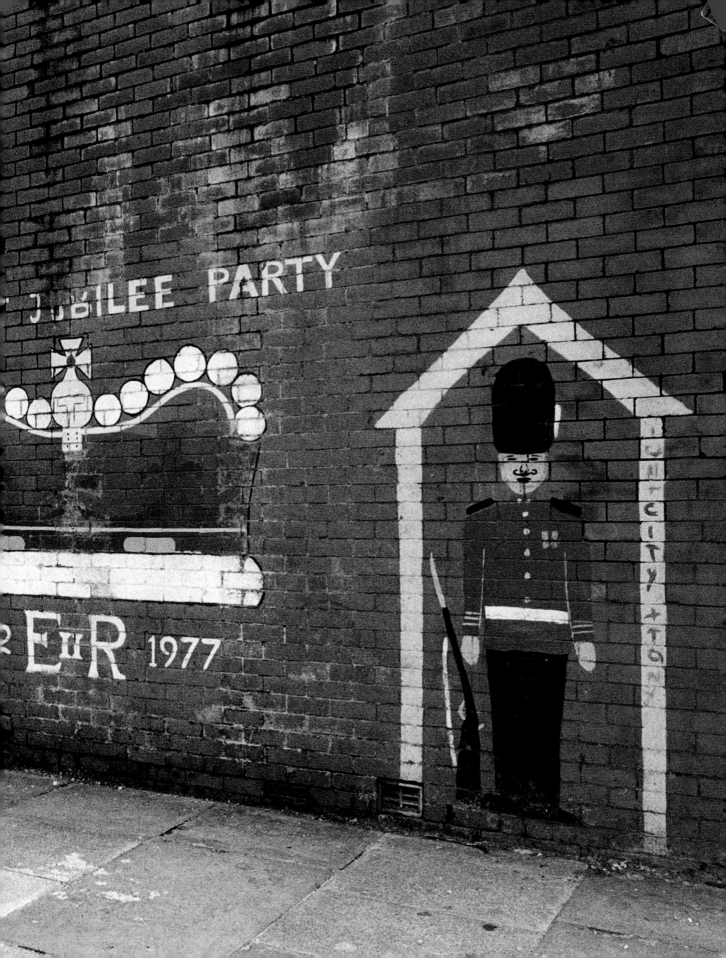

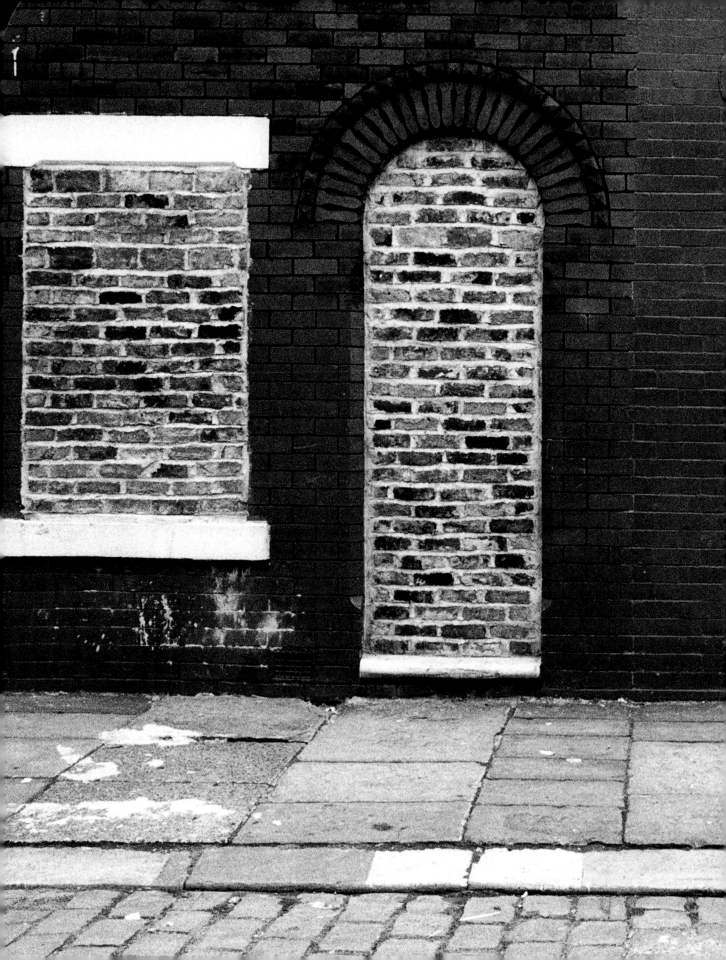

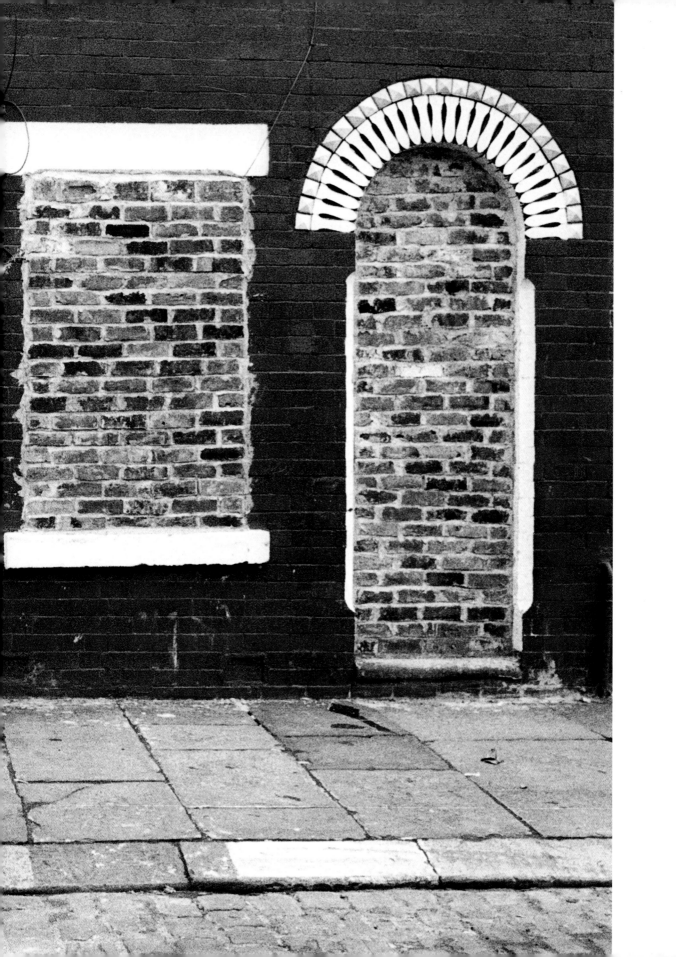

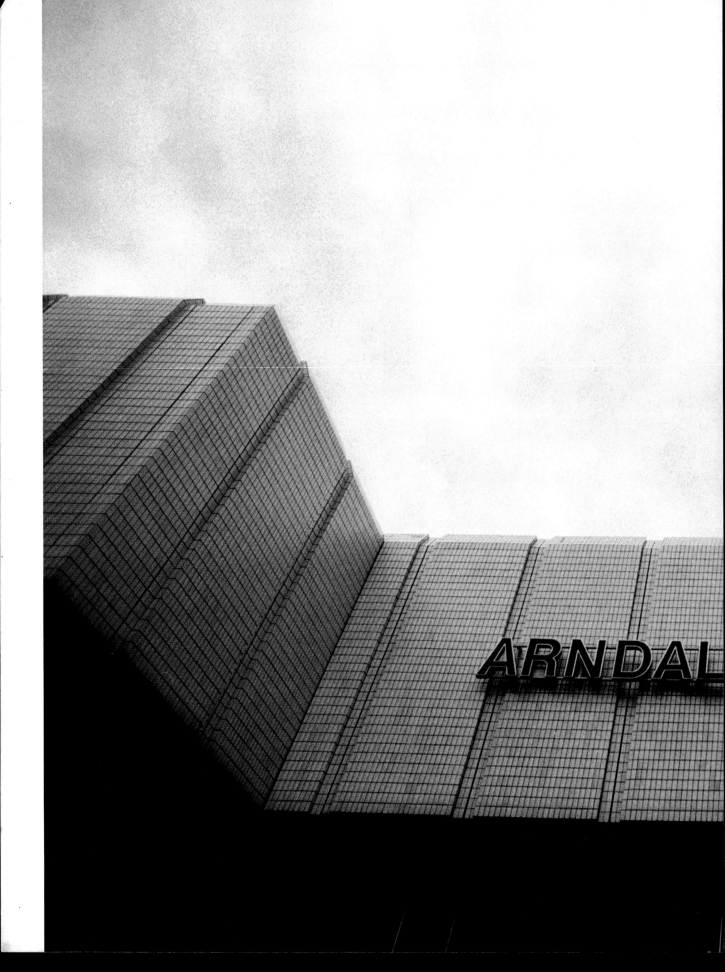

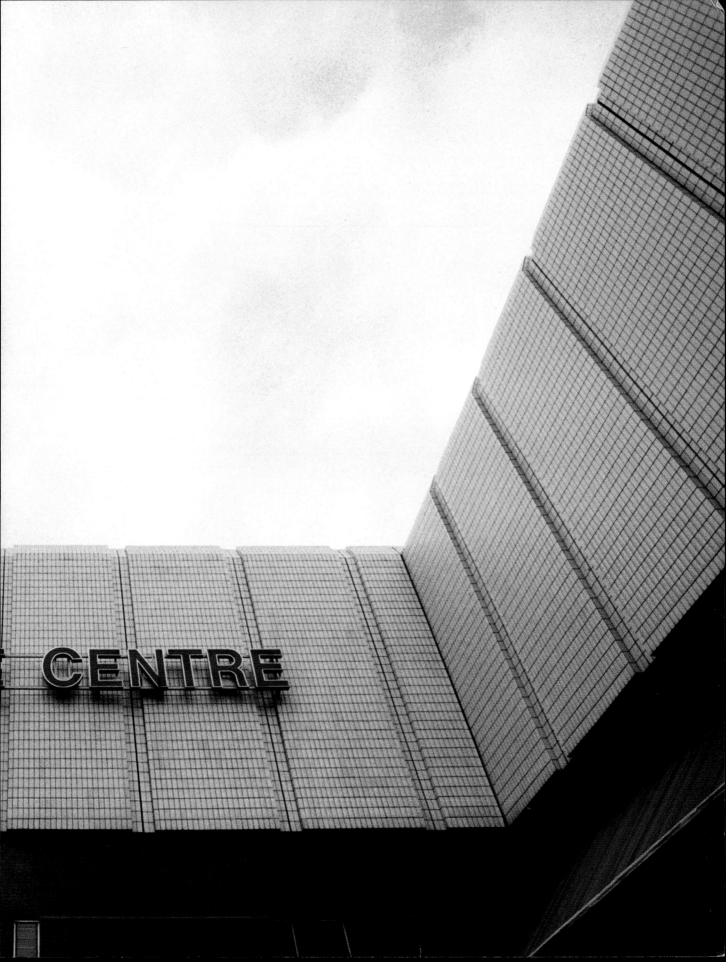

Contents

Is that Parker out of *Thunderbirds* in a Man City top, getting battered?

The first time I came across Kevin Cummins' photographs, I was ten years old and greedily perusing one of the tabloids. It was the first time I'd seen two Man City fans trying to knock each other out. Or rather, one minute they're trying to knock each other out, the next minute they're on each other's backs, absolutely beaming. They looked funny, those shady Gallagher siblings – like a pair of flower-power footy hooligans. It's a great set of pictures – still evoking in me this strange, sunny sense of glee. I missed the first two Summers of Love, but for me 1994 was special. Britpop marked my awakening as a music fanatic – I was the first to get *Definitely Maybe* in my class, and definitely maybe the only one still sleeping in my first Oasis T-shirt. It's full of holes now. And it's still miles too big for me.

It's a shame not to see the Gallagher brothers any more in their Brother shirts, with their gegs on, mucking about. I'm not a Manchester City fan, but those photos marked the first time I relished having their colours pasted on my wall.

Suddenly the Rainy City seemed incredibly romantic, like Paris or Berlin, except with more sportswear and more Eccles cakes. Aside from the music itself, Kevin Cummins is – in part – responsible for that romance for me. From Madchester and Shaun Ryder with his great big E, to Sadchester and Ian Curtis shuffling through the snow, Kevin has captured the spirit of many of my all-time heroes and heroines, like precious bugs in amber. In fact, from my formative years, fingering the *NME*, I discovered all my favourite musical Mancunians have, at some point, been caught by the Midas touch of Kevin's trigger finger – look, there's cheery, sneery Mark E. Smith in his argyle jumper; and over there, Morrissey's lounging about, lamenting the death of a bunch of flowers.

The other night, I was lucky enough to attend a Kevin Cummins exhibition. Of all the places, it was held in my mates' front room – they just weren't aware of it. Over in the corner, Liam stares you out, languidly clinging to his mike. Elsewhere, The Stone Roses emerge from painty, Pollocky sludge, like mad sun-hatted mermen.

For years now, Kevin's photographs have watched over me and my pals, like debauched religious figures, inspiring us to get intoxicated, wear parkas, pick flowers and listen to records. Their familiarity is blissful. Most of the time, they just eyeball us nonchalantly. But now and then, if the mood and the drugs are right, they dance about.

I've seen many more mini Kevin Cummins exhibitions, in countless other houses down countless other streets in Britain. It's not hard to see why. Kevin creates rock 'n' roll art, you see; not cock-and-bull journalism.

Time after time, Kevin's work makes me wish I was in a band. He also makes me wish I was in Manchester in the late eighties, sucking a Day-Glo dummy, instead of in the northeast, in a nappy. And, occasionally, he very nearly makes me wish I was a Man City supporter. With a mop-top, and gegs, getting battered by my brother.

You and I aren't gonna live forever, but you can bet your bottom dollar Kevin's photographs are.

Introduction – Kevin Cummins

1973: I was nineteen years old, studying photography in Salford, and had an unhealthy obsession with David Bowie. I'd already seen the *Ziggy Stardust* tour at Manchester's Free Trade Hall, and taken some photos from the stalls – as a fan – but I wanted to take a shot of Bowie that would capture the essence of the show. I managed to get a ticket for a rescheduled gig towards the end of the tour and on 29 June 1973 I finally took a shot (p. 5) which I still think of as one of my finest live photographs. I remember the excitement of capturing the decisive moment, the nervous anticipation of processing the film and the relief of seeing the image perfectly exposed. I decided that night that I wanted to photograph rock 'n' roll for a living.

I had no idea how to go about it though. I took my camera with me when I went to see Bryan Ferry at the Royal Albert Hall on 19 December 1974. I thought that if I walked down to the front and spoke to another photographer, the security guys would think I must be there officially too. I spoke to a woman who told me she was Pennie Smith. Pennie Smith, the great *NME* photographer. I smiled at her and told her that one day I was going to be her. She has no memory of this momentous occasion. I thought of nothing else for weeks.

I occasionally took shots of my favourite bands in concert but, like several people featured in this book, the Sex Pistols at the Free Trade Hall in Manchester was my epiphany. I'd already photographed Slaughter and the Dogs and Rockslide (quickly reborn as The Drones). I was soon to photograph Buzzcocks and anyone else who was forming a band, however slight. In April 1977 I went to London to meet up with Neil Spencer, features editor at the *NME*, who told me I should seek out Paul Morley – a writer from Stockport – who they'd just taken on. He gave me my first commission: photographing all the bands from Manchester to accompany a feature by Paul. My first *NME* feature and it was a double-page spread. I told everyone I knew. I was waiting outside the newsagent's an hour before he opened in order to buy several copies to leave lying casually around the house. I took one straight round to show my parents at 6 a.m. 'They've spelt your name wrong,' my father said, taking a cursory glance at the

NME before picking up his *Daily Mirror*. Paul and I were inseparable that summer of '77. I'd finally found my niche and I loved it. I was Kevin Cummins of the *NME*. I quickly realised that in order to really be Kevin Cummins of the *NME* I was going to have to move to London, so after several false starts I finally took the plunge in 1987. Yes, 1987, just as Madchester was beginning to gather momentum. I spent a large part of the following two years going back to Manchester and wondering why I'd bothered moving.

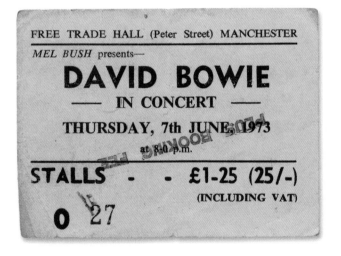

FREE TRADE HALL (Peter Street) MANCHESTER

MEL BUSH presents—

DAVID BOWIE
—— IN CONCERT ——

THURSDAY, 7th JUNE, 1973
at 8.0 p.m.

STALLS - - £1-25 (25/-)
                    (INCLUDING VAT)
0 27

This book is a retrospective of my time photographing Manchester bands and musicians. It covers the period from 1976 to date. To help contextualise the different eras, I commissioned writers I'd worked closely with at the *NME* who became intrinsically linked with those periods of musical history. Paul Morley has written about punk and the aftermath. Gavin Martin interviewed Johnny Marr, Peter Hook and Mark E. Smith to shed some light on why they each wanted to form a band. Stuart Maconie dons his Joe Bloggs flares again and takes us back on a trip to the Summer of Love, and John Harris explains the phenomenon of Oasis and tells us why it can never happen again.

The photographs tell their own stories. From Buzzcocks standing on a motorway bridge for my first *NME* cover (and theirs) to Joy Division in the bleak snow-covered cityscape on another bridge to The Smiths in the park to New Order's shadowplay to Shaun Ryder on a massive E and The Stone Roses covered in paint and Liam Gallagher looking as Cool as Fuck in the Oasis bar. These are photographs that not only captured the zeitgeist but have become iconic images, helping to shape the way these bands and musicians are perceived. When I started shooting bands I was shooting for the moment. I rarely shot more than one roll of film. I couldn't really afford to. However, I quickly learnt that I was also working my way into the mythology of rock 'n' roll.

According to Jake Kennedy in his book *Joy Division: The Making of Unknown Pleasures* (MQ Publications, 2006), 'Joy Division's identity was established – and fixed in time forever – by Kevin Cummins' famous January 1979 *NME* cover shot. In it, Curtis leans against a wall* in his military overcoat, Red Star badge on his lapel smoking a cigarette and gazing out at us.'

Referring to my Smiths photographs in Tatton Park (which Mike Joyce assures me was actually Dunham Massey), Sean O'Hagan in the *Observer* said: 'Kevin Cummins, a fellow Mancunian, came to The Smiths early in their career, and it would not be overstating the case to suggest that he was the first to see that the group, for all their Oxfam chic and resolute ordinariness, had tapped into something timeless and resonant.'

Both Richard Ashcroft and Liam Gallagher – when choosing their favourite *NME* covers of all time – picked my photograph of Shaun Ryder on the E and my Stone Roses paint shot as the most defining images of their generation.

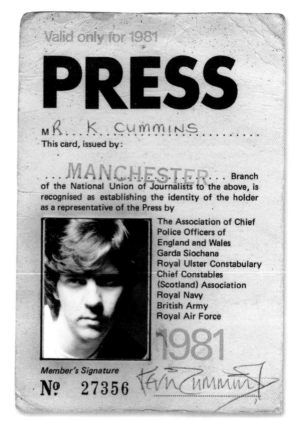

As Roland Barthes said in *Camera Lucida*, 'Every photograph is a certificate of presence.' The fact that I was there for many defining rock 'n' roll moments is a great testimony to the power back then of the *NME*.

Rock 'n' roll photography has been unfairly denigrated over the past few years. Many art critics dismiss it as juvenilia. However in my opinion the way we perceive our bands is often formed by the images we remember of them. Sure, the music is why we like them, but I always think of Pennie Smith's photos when I think of The Clash; of Gered Mankowitz's photos of Hendrix; of Bob Gruen's photos of John Lennon; and of Mick Rock's photos of Bowie.

In the same way I hope that my images will define Manchester for you . . .

A photograph can be reproduced to infinity but the image has occurred only once. I often felt when I was photographing bands that I shouldn't be there. That it was a rather perverse way of earning a living. My photograph of Joy Division on the bridge in Hulme, Manchester, captures this idea perfectly. It was ostensibly a landscape in which four figures become part of that composition. It broke all the rules (if there are any) in the *Rock Photographer's Manual*. In truth it was because I was slightly nervous in their company and shooting from a distance was easier.

I soon got the hang of it though.

---

* It's a lamp post.

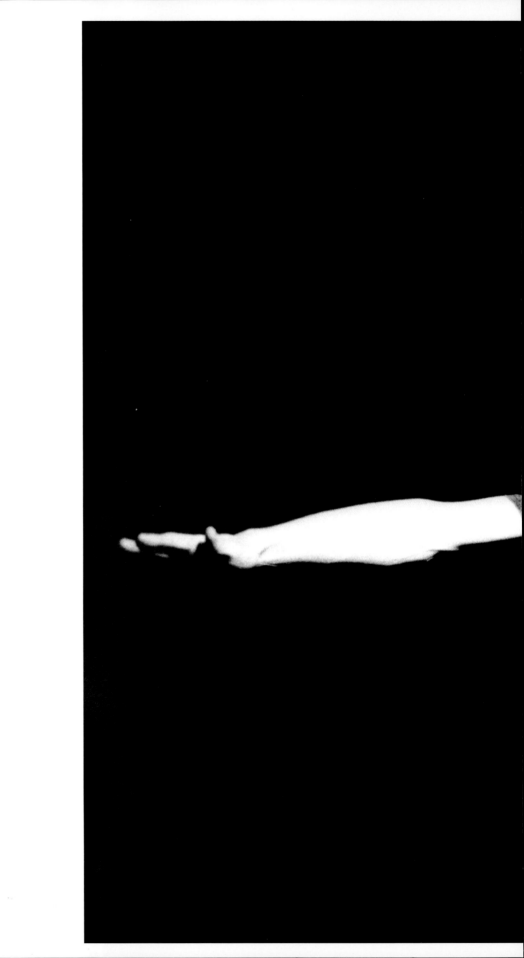

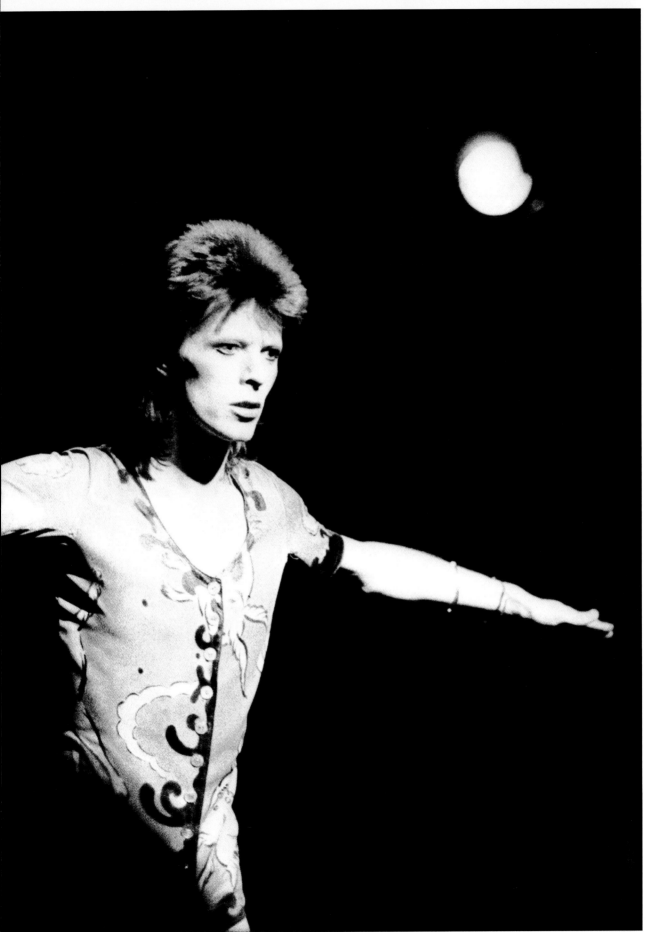

By the way, as this is the start of it all, the start of this particular story of Manchester music, a story filled with characters, songs and stories that might not have revealed themselves but for what happened, because there was an actual beginning, a zero moment, a bang, some chords, some words, a look, a floor, a wall, the best place to begin, to some extent, would be at what has been described, by people like me at the beginning of stories like this, as the beginning, as if you can ever accurately locate a beginning, but in this case, where everything that follows happened, more or less, because there was a beginning, a place, a date, a time, an event, a haircut, a look in the eye, a building, an entrance, a way in, and a stage.

There are now hundreds of photographs to look at from across thirty years of post-punk Manchester-related pop history. In a way all of those photographs are of what happened on that stage, in the middle of Peter Street, just along the road from the Midland Hotel, a hundred yards from Deansgate, a short walk from the ongoing reality of *Coronation Street*, under the stark grey northwest sky. There are moving, edgy photographs of distinctive Manchester faces, the faces of those bussing into Manchester from those towns historically placed all around the compressed city centre, faces shining in the dark, faces disappearing into the dark, faces belonging to those who had been inspired, directly or indirectly, because of what happened on a stage in Peter Street in June 1976. The photographs are of faces that only existed for sudden moments, before their time was up. Romantic, startling photographs of rebels, dreamers, thinkers, workers, posers, loners, losers, lovers and legends, of pop stars, voyeurs and rejects exist because there was a way in to a building, and a small stage, and then some action, action that was all guitar, nerve and thought, action that rhymed, and didn't, action that didn't make sense, and then did.

What happened on that stage would lead to lives being changed, books being written and photographs being taken. All of those photographs of Manchester musicians, technicians, talkers, schemers, mischief-makers and miscellaneous passers-by exist because of the bitter, aroused, pissed-off and jubilant faces the people on that stage pulled, the way they moved, how they taunted, delighted and abused their audience, and how they walked off, job done. They walked off into their own history, but also they trailed ahead of them the history of a new city. The people on that stage, four rough, swaggering Londoners who'd travelled up to Manchester as if they were invading a foreign territory, taking charge of local sensibilities, walked off as if they'd fulfilled their mission – a sort of snotty, puffed-up conquering – and left the stage as abruptly, and as indifferently, as they had arrived. They left as if they might never be back again, these slouchy conspirators, a bunch of kids more teen than twenty holding stolen instruments the way they'd learned from The Stooges, The Who, The Monkees, the New York Dolls, Mick Ronson, Keith Richards. They left as if their destiny was to leave nothing behind but this memory of energy that at the time it was happening didn't necessarily seem to be something that would ultimately alter the entire metaphysical, and to some extent physical, landscape of the city.

You found the stage where these four people acted out extreme local drama at the top of some ordinary stairs, stairs the neutral colour of a hospital waiting room, and inside a brown, faded room filled with polite rows of seats. It was a still, small theatre space that might have reminded you of school and a tedious history lesson. The stairs and the room in that building do not exist any more, you cannot find them any more, because walls move, floors fall away, ceilings disappear, moods evaporate, things change.

In a way, because of what happened in that fusty, dusty room, at the top of those anonymous, slightly creepy stairs, on 4 June 1976, things would never be the same again, and the building itself would be a casualty of that change.

That stage would be engulfed by a brand-new hotel that would mention this historic day in its in-room literature, as if it added to the lustre of the luxury five-star Radisson. Its location was once the Free Trade Hall, home of the Hallé Orchestra, a proud, sturdy theatre built out of bold sandy stone that established itself in the sixties and seventies as

Manchester's main rock venue. Attached to the Free Trade Hall was a smaller theatre, the Lesser Free Trade Hall. On 4 June 1976, the Sex Pistols, a punk rock group in their own universe, a place stamped inside mid-seventies London, performed there, in front of about forty people who had got the tickets that took them up the stairs and through the door and – look – into the future. A future that would end up being photographed as it happened, as if history was being made.

Where Manchester is now was originally a dense forest. This is one way that this story begins, a tall tale which led to the flowers of Morrissey, the brain of Devoto, E. Smith's concentration zone, the Kim Philby bar at the Haçienda Club, John Cooper Clarke's specs, vowels, hair and knees and Damon Gough's woolly hat. A Celtic tribe, called the Setantii or Sistuntii, took possession of this dark, tangled forest about 500 years BC and remained unmolested on it for about five centuries, until they were suddenly invaded by the tribe of Brigantes from Yorkshire.

This Manchester story, that led to characters with ordinary names and their own approach to life, that led to Ian Brown's brow, Mick Hucknall's funk, Johnny Marr's fingers, Peter Hook's persistence, Martin Hannett's heart and Liam Gallagher's swagger, that led to photographs of snow, nightclubs and northern light, might have begun two thousand years ago, when a Roman army subdued the Brigantes and built a wooden fort on a small hill about a mile south of where the Cathedral is now. The Romans named this fort Mamucium, Latinising the Celtic words for 'breast-shaped hill', because of the distinctive shape of the plateau.

Photographs of angry, happy, driven young people, finding themselves in an industrial cityscape that was opening up around them, as if they had something to do with it, exist because a few people had tickets to an event that seemed as avant-garde as Artaud, Cage or Hell, that seemed for those few the only place to be when there was nothing else to do. What else was there to do if at home you'd been playing the first albums by Patti Smith and the Ramones, the second albums by New York Dolls and Burning Spear, and had tried out the cryptic, glorious *Faust Tapes* that had cost a mere forty-eight pence – a quarter of the full price of an album – because Richard Branson of Virgin Records had decided as soothsayer salesman that the only way to sell such scraping, chewed-up noise was at a massive discount.

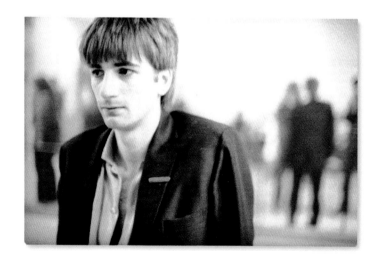

These tickets to the Lesser Free Trade Hall were bought by people who mostly became teenagers in an early seventies Manchester city centre yet to shake off ancient soot, all cobbles and alleyways, backstreets and shadows, manly history and furtive business, and a place ruined by the merciless attention of a wartime enemy.

During the Second World War, large areas of the city centre had been destroyed by German bombing, and hasty attempts by 1960s urban planners to rebuild the city had led to such bland architectural blight as the Arndale Shopping Centre, which blotted out Manchester atmosphere instead of updating it. All Arndale Centres the world over are the same. The shopping centre could have been in the centre of anywhere.

In the cramped centre of the city, around Piccadilly Gardens, the old Manchester

Infirmary was replaced by the blank concrete presence of Piccadilly Plaza, which seemed instantly shabby. The city centre, trapped between wrecked grandeur and the abortive modernisation, was a compact, almost collapsed space littered with sly corners and abrupt cul-de-sacs, disturbing bricked-up doorways and truncated secret alleyways decorated with rust and decay, filled with ghosts and shadows devoted to blocking progress and trapping souls.

The final disfigured, sighing remnants of the mighty industrial past had yet to be completely demolished, the statuesque warehouses and factories that had survived yet to be postmodernised as part of a glossy revitalisation of Manchester's historical enterprise. It all seemed more nineteenth century than twentieth, as if the twenty-first century would never arrive, scared off by the bones and smoke, the bomb sites and the dire new buildings, the dead ends and the receding energy.

Dank dreamless canals seemed to worm their way through the city like black channels of ancient poison, stranger than Martian canals, the home of foraging rats and lost drunks. The canals seeped out of Friedrich Engels' mean, cluttered Manchester slums, swampy emblems of a great, brutal Victorian city's grimy decline. There seemed no possibility that they would become an integral part of any groovy urban resurgence. As you walked with your ticket towards the Lesser Free Trade Hall, desolate canal water would make you think of what was over, not what was to come.

Within a matter of three slow, quick years, a group called Joy Division, pushed and pulled into being because the Sex Pistols walked on and off the stage at the Lesser Free Trade Hall, would somehow transfer the uncanny ache that cries out from the silence of solid things into music. The stubborn, miserable, crumbling brick walls and the bleak city pavements would be turned into sound, the derelict old buildings bisected by the sweeping Ballardian motorways would mutate into rhythm, as if the soot and ash and dust, the sinister accumulated weight of history, the dead grandness and the brutal, neutral new skyscrapers could be cleared away by dreams, and nightmares, and a certain kind of serious, dynamic song.

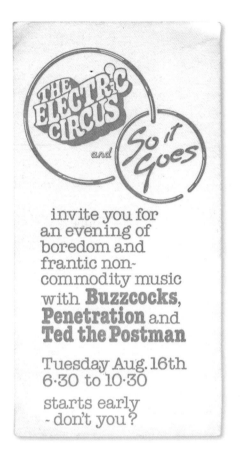

THE ELECTRIC CIRCUS and So it Goes invite you for an evening of boredom and frantic non-commodity music with **Buzzcocks, Penetration** and **Ted the Postman**

Tuesday Aug. 16th 6·30 to 10·30 starts early - don't you?

The story that leads down solid roads and across millions of scattered memories to New Order's sybaritic electronics, to Mark E. Smith's psykick dance hall, to Morrissey's miserable, magnificent mind, to the tense self-control of The Passage and the lethal, choppy loneliness of the Blue Orchids, might even begin when the Roman army finally leave in disarray in AD 400. They had established the trade routes the city would follow. Or in the seventh century when the Saxons create a small village, after struggles with the Angles and Danes for control. Or in 1086 when what is in this place that was once Mamucium is now Mameceaster.

More possible points of departure that would lead to Howard Devoto singing about the ladies who put the little plastic robins on the Christmas cake, to The Worst in their oily overalls singing aggressively abbreviated garage folk songs about police oppression: the thirteenth century when the village is officially recognised; the fourteenth century when Manchester becomes home to a community of Flemish weavers; 1515 when Manchester Grammar School is founded. The sixteenth century when there are four thousand people living in the area, the seventeenth century when there are five thousand . . .

. . . 1603, when Manchester suffers a bout of the plague, killing over one quarter of the population. Manchester fared better economically than many devastated English cities, as there were always people from the surrounding countryside coming to find work in the mills. The eighteenth century when Manchester is described as a thriving place and the population grows to over seventy thousand. The first newspaper is published in 1719 – a century before the *Manchester Guardian*; an infirmary opens in 1752, followed a year later by a theatre.

Perhaps the journey to A Certain Ratio's sulky sunken punk funk, to the sensual chaos of Ludus and John Cooper Clarke's tense splitting vowels began in the nightmarish nineteenth-century slums, in the way a city emerged out of a shitty crowded hell.

A city somehow slowly took shape. In 1816, a water company began to pump water through iron pipes to those who could afford it. In the 1820s, parts of the city were illuminated with gas lights. In 1829, the Royal Institute for the Promotion of Literature, Science and Art was built.

The population grew to 185,000 by the 1820s, and in 1830 a railway linked Manchester with Liverpool. The prime minister and a large number of important people attended the opening ceremony. Crowds assembled along the line and when the train entered Manchester, weavers remembering the Peterloo Massacre pelted the carriages with stones.

According to the historian Asa Briggs, by the time of the Reform Bill of 1832, 'Manchester enhanced its national reputation as a centre of social disturbances, even as a possible cradle of revolution.'

On 14 June 1974, one Steven Morrissey, a melancholy, bullied but athletic lad with strange, horrid and sublime fascinations ranging from *Coronation Street* to the Moors Murders via James Dean and Cilla Black, son of hospital porter Peter and librarian Elizabeth, of King's Road, Stretford, Manchester, who'd bought his first pop record, 'Come and Stay With Me' by Marianne Faithfull, when he was six years old, had a letter published in the *NME*:

> Today I bought the album of the year, I feel I can say this without expecting several letters saying I'm talking rubbish. The album is Kimono My House by Sparks. I bought it on the strength of the single. Every track is brilliant – although I must name 'Equator', 'Complaints', 'Amateur Hour' and 'Here in Heaven' as the best tracks and in that order.

The Peterloo Massacre of 16 August 1819 was the result of a cavalry charge into the huge crowd at a public meeting in Manchester. It is also called the Manchester Massacre. A meeting planned for 9 August to elect Henry Hunt as the working man's representative for Lancashire and to demand reform was cancelled, declared an illegal gathering. The meeting was reorganised for 16 August and held on St Peter's Field. The magistrates brought in the Cheshire Yeomanry to control the crowd of up to sixty thousand people. The JPs decided to arrest Hunt. The crowd moved in, the Yeomanry drew their sabres and panic ensued. Eleven died. Over five hundred others, including many women and children, were injured. It became known as Peterloo, the poor man's Waterloo.

In 1838, near the site of the Peterloo Massacre, on the corner of St Peter's Field and Southmill Street, a temporary wooden hall was constructed to hold protest meetings against the 1815 Corn Laws. The repeal of these laws in 1846 reduced the political power that land ownership had represented. It also led to the fall of the government and the split of the traditional Conservative Party into two, the more radical side forming the Liberal Party.

The Victorian architect Edward Walters completed the stone building of the Free Trade Hall in 1856, three years after Manchester was made a city, to commemorate the tenth anniversary of the repeal of the Corn Laws and honour the dead in the struggle for democratic freedom.

The driven northerner Tony Wilson, who would eventually want to be known as

Anthony H. Wilson, if only to wind up his enemies and amuse his comrades, was born in Salford on 20 February 1950. He studied English at Cambridge University, and then returned to Manchester to work as a journalist and broadcaster at Granada Television, the local ITV company founded on the principle that its onscreen representatives would speak in local accents without that leading to a loss of authority or articulacy. Unusually for a local newsreader/correspondent, Wilson's inspirations were the language of Shakespeare and the various improvised theories of the argumentative post-surrealists known as the Situationists.

The Sex Pistols were visually caked in imagery and energy lifted from Situationist theories. Wilson too would luxuriate in the Situationists' subversive slogans and radical agitating playfulness and based his dreams for a local community, a local record label, a local system of dreamers and doers, around their principles. In a way, because of Shakespeare, Situationism and the Sex Pistols, Tony Wilson, whatever else he seemed to be, was a cerebral city planner devoted to ensuring Manchester's radical history didn't just fade away.

Perhaps it all happened, these musical events organised by people with ideas to share that could be photographed just as they started to matter, because Manchester is a city of libraries, the first free public library in Britain opening there in 1852.

Perhaps there was The Fall starting as they meant to carry on, provisionally magnificent, crashing through their own staggering ideas, staining the pure rush of their exciting times, making immediate sense to themselves, and one or two others, because the Manchester Ship Canal opened in 1894, turning the city into an inland port. Ocean-going ships could sail all the way into Salford, as if the world had turned inside out and Lancashire was somehow itself part of an ocean, marvellously, mysteriously, opened up to the whole world, and completely cut off from it.

Perhaps it all happened, as it happened, a thinking Manchester, a Manchester mind, a Manchester, as it turned out, in photographs that appeared to tap into some truth or another, that featured faces that were dead sure of their history, and their place, and their future, because the philosopher Ludwig Wittgenstein lived around Manchester between 1908 and 1911. From Wittgenstein to A Certain Ratio's second single, 'Flight', down a Manchester road in ways you wouldn't believe.

Another story leading, somewhat, somehow, to the triangles, cubes, beats, circles and bounce of 808 State, Manchester's most wired pop group, begins somewhere, somehow, with the shy, awkward, chess-loving, long-distance-running atheist Alan Turing, who accidentally, incidentally, definitely dreamt up the blueprint of what eventually became the electronic digital computer.

He argued passionately with Wittgenstein at Cambridge lectures in 1939, one of the few who'd dare to challenge the Master's visions. You can plot a move from such rigorous, reality-challenging debates to the early stages of Factory Records.

Factory were a record label that could only have happened in and after a Manchester history of ideas and intrigue that followed the gravity-defying words of Wittgenstein and the testing truth of Turing, although it needed a little Marx, Engels and the Sex Pistols as well. It may not be unconnected that the item allocated the catalogue number Fac 1 was not a record but a poster designed by local design student Peter Saville. It was commissioned by Factory to draw attention to the first gigs they promoted at a working men's club they found buried in Hulme. The poster was printed in yellow on black and on first sight seemed to be advertising not rock or pop music but perhaps an art exhibition, or a philosophical investigation of the relationship between the concrete and the abstract, between love and sex, between buildings and brilliance. Saville's poster arrived after the first show had actually happened, but even though it was late, the show still went ahead and the poster still existed. The poster seemed to belong to the future, one that was already happening, even though no one had yet caught up. It was a poster that would never have looked the way it looked and said the things it said unless the Sex Pistols had visited Manchester. Someone had to make that happen, so that Peter Saville could position type, and speak his secretive mind, as if his life depended on getting it right.

Peter Saville, stealing ideas from his own future as much as from the past, was responsible for Factory's design. He was jealous that his former classmate Malcolm Garratt was designing record sleeves for Buzzcocks that looked like fearless Manchester modern art, having fun with the idea of product, commodity and advertising, leaving him behind as mere boyish student.

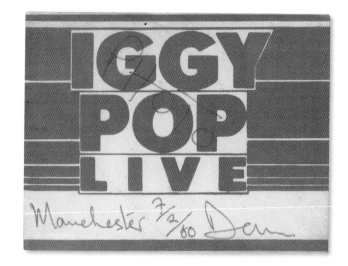

The second item allocated a Factory catalogue number would actually be a record, *A Factory Sample*, released in late 1978, a seven-inch EP featuring the music of Joy Division, Durutti Column, John Dowie and Cabaret Voltaire. Five thousand copies were pressed in a sleeve that seemed to be constructed out of silver liquid.

Saville had decided that records should be intelligently packaged as mysteries, as secrets, as an evanescent series of codes and signals that could change the shape of reality. He created solutions to problems of packaging and presentation that didn't exist for most people. He used Factory to tell a preposterous, enthralling history of twentieth-century graphic design, and in doing so helped Wilson and co.'s movement appear a real movement with surreal potential. In the end, how Saville visualised their presumptuous mock-movement using type, colour and space helped alter the appearance – both the surface and the shadows – of the entire world.

Before he could do that, the Sex Pistols would have to turn up in town, to explain, as riff-carrying ruffians, as romantic modernists committed to making the mind reel and time tumble, that in order for Manchester to develop, things must be abstract, they must change, and they must give pleasure.

In 1949, Alan Turing became deputy director of the computing laboratory at Manchester University. He lived in Manchester until his death, by self-administered poison, on 7 June 1954. Some say he killed himself accidentally, experimenting with various chemicals and eating a cyanide-laced apple. Others suggest he was hounded to death as a shamed homosexual who'd been compelled to lead a fragile, secret life.

In one of his papers, which led to the famous Turing test for evaluating whether a computer is intelligent, he wrote, 'We can only see a short distance ahead, but we can see plenty that needs to be done.'

Eight days after the Sex Pistols played their first public date, supporting Eddie and the Hot Rods at the London Marquee on 12 February 1976, two college friends from the North, the bony, opaque Howard Trafford and the friendly, curious Pete McNeish, borrowed a car and drove down south to High Wycombe. They had both joined the electronic music society at the college, and had tried to form a group playing cover versions of Eno and so on.

The Sex Pistols were playing a show at the College of Further Education, supporting Screaming Lord Sutch, as if what they did was a kind of comedy, a novelty act. Howard and Pete wanted to see and hear for themselves this new thing that according to early reports promised 'chaos' and not 'music', implying that whatever music there was, it was worth driving hundreds of miles to experience. After all, these two friends from the Bolton Institute of Technology had been drawn together because of their love for Captain Beefheart and Iggy Pop, and the understanding that if you formed a band you should know your way around the Velvets' 'Sister Ray' inside and out, and have something to say not just about love, and sex, but also light, and darkness, and the background noise of existence.

They liked what they discovered in High Wycombe so much that not only did it abruptly reveal a sudden welcome contemporary relevance for what they might get up to, but it inspired them to change their own names. New names meant new life, new ideas, new force. You could change your name and then perhaps change the world. The unashamedly intellectual Trafford would become Devoto – Latin for 'I bewitch' – and McNeish would become, romantically, Shelley – the name he would have had if he'd been born a girl. They would become Buzzcocks, a made-up name that sounded a little rude, a little inexplicable, a shade glamorous, the answer to a question that hadn't yet been asked.

Struck by the Pistols' angle of attack, which at the beginning of 1976, and for a few more months, seemed just about the newest thing on the planet, they had the unusual desire to bring the Sex Pistols up to Manchester. Howard Devoto, already shrewdly noticing that the Pistols' singer was more poet than hooligan, or at least that their thuggishness had a cerebral side, actually put that dream, part nerdy, part philanthropic, part bureaucratic, into practice.

And so a little over ten years after Bob Dylan played the Manchester Free Trade Hall, when his new electric approach to folk provoked a certain John Cordwell to brand him a 'Judas', the Sex Pistols played the smaller annexe theatre, mysteriously tucked into the wings of the building. Dylan's historic appearance was on 17 May 1966; for a time the Judas incident appeared on a famous bootleg album mistakenly entitled *Live at the Albert Hall,* its Manchester roots suspiciously shrouded.

You can read all about that concert in a book written by local historian C. P. Lee, who by the time the Pistols travelled north for their date with destiny at the Lesser Free Trade Hall on 4 June 1976 was a member of a local psychedelic comedy revue troupe, Alberto y Lost Trios Paranoias, sort of the Bonzos dipped in Zappa with a side order of the Firesign Theatre. For a while, just before the Sex Pistols turned up in the early summer, it seemed as if the Albertos were the only truly Manchester band around. The problem was, the Albertos were not the band to influence the local teenagers who were into the music of Can, Roxy Music, David Bowie, Patti Smith and The Velvet Underground. There was a gap in that market.

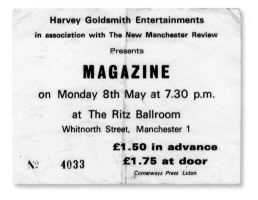

Harvey Goldsmith Entertainments
in association with The New Manchester Review
Presents

MAGAZINE

on Monday 8th May at 7.30 p.m.

at The Ritz Ballroom
Whitnorth Street, Manchester 1

£1.50 in advance
£1.75 at door

№ 4033

Cornerways Press Luton

If you lived in a city like Manchester, in the mid-seventies, you didn't really think of forming a band unless that band sounded like it was from London, or even Los Angeles. There was nothing around to show you how to do it. Bands came to Manchester, but not from Manchester. The sound and content of those that did, like the Bee Gees, Barclay James Harvest, The Hollies, 10cc and Sad Café, didn't seem to have much to do with Manchester, or the North. They did not sing with northern accents, they didn't open their albums, as The Fall did, with paranoid songs about running away from faeces, they didn't begin songs by asking questions – eh, what's this song about? – and answering – er, nothing. Therefore, they didn't connect with the music of Bob Dylan and Captain Beefheart, Frank Zappa and Kraftwerk – when you first heard The Fall, from the very first second matching words and noise with a kind of desperate, terrifying crudity that was also somehow defiantly sophisticated, it seemed instantly connected to the difficult, wonderful music you had heard John Peel play, to the world-shattering confidence of Dylan, the supernatural deviousness of Beefheart, the space, rage and drum that connected Lee Scratch Perry with Henry Cow.

Local Manchester bands had previously just seemed like decorators making rooms pretty with decent harmonies and familiar, heartwarming guitar playing. Buzzcocks, with their surreal, self-centred love songs made out of spite and bite, The Fall, with their brainy hate songs built out of snarl and mettle, Magazine, with their epic explorations of love and hate and a shifting self, it all seemed to be a genuine part of an adventurous musical world that stretched between Ornette Coleman and Roxy Music, between Jimi Hendrix and Robert Wyatt.

The Free Trade Hall was the best local venue for any music fan living in Manchester throughout the late sixties and early seventies. Whatever music you liked, eventually it, or something very like it, would arrive in this grand hall, decorated with figures and symbols that seemed to stretch back to Roman influences, even into the darkness of the dense forest. The Free Trade Hall was something special, somewhere intimidating, and grown-up, and intimate, especially if you had managed to get a seat in the prized front-row stalls that ran from AA to JJ. Sat there you could seem so close to Bowie and Bolan it was like they were breathing on you, whispering magic spells in your ear. Every visit would become an adventure, whether you were seeing Little Feat, or Wings, or Fanny, or Rory Gallagher, or Graham Central Station, and soon, in the new post-punk world, Television. It was the world beyond Manchester, connected to the city centre by train, bus or second-hand car, a world that visited, and then went away.

I saw my first ever pop concert at the Free Trade Hall in 1971. The folk-tongued wizards of weird Tyrannosaurus Rex had just shape shifted into the spectacularly glamorous T. Rex and were having hits where eerie white swans throbbed with erotic promise and hot love rained from the sky, and an audience of bewildered hobbity hairy hippies were being rudely shoved out of the way by screaming teenage girls with glitter under their eyes waving luminous satin scarves. I was on my own in row HH. My ticket cost 60p, because the country had just gone decimal, but it also cost twelve shillings, because the country was still arranged around a system where there were twenty shillings to the pound and twelve pennies to a shilling. I imagine a skinny twelve-year-old Morrissey in National Health specs also on his own sat breathless and moist near by, destined to be stunned, and vaguely thrilled, that he was entering a world where the pennies were new and there were only one hundred of them to a pound.

Bowie visited for an early first blistering showing of his brand-new horny space-age Ziggy in front of one of the smallest audiences I'd ever seen there. By the time he came back as Aladdin Sane, just over a year later, the hall was packed, for two nights. Roxy Music beamed in, out of a world where Dr Who would be played by Duchamp, with both Brian Eno and Bryan Ferry as the potential Doctors, as friends of Dalí, supported by a ludicrous Leo Sayer. Mott the Hoople's equipment failed to arrive and an embarrassed Ian Hunter played an acoustic set. Tangerine Dream sent the theatre into space. Black Sabbath dragged it back down to earth and buried it. A hooded, magnificent John Cale and a sleazy, terrifying Lou Reed passed through, bringing tantalising hints and threats of a New York that made Manchester seem a little . . . provincial. A few weeks after Japanese classically-inspired prog-electro wizard Tomita played – in Quadraphonic – at the Free Trade Hall, on 28 March 1976, a very typical mid-seventies Free Trade Hall show, Devoto and colleagues arranged for the Sex Pistols to make their appearance next door.

The decision to have the Sex Pistols play a rather posh little theatre instead of a squalid cramped dump was inspired, although largely economically driven as it only cost £25 to hire. Devoto may well have planned it this way not just because it was cheap enough, but because of the radical history that connected the building with authentically revolutionary atmosphere. Perhaps he had no idea, and the way this show would eventually fit into history as if it was planned all along was just one of those accidents of fate that only makes sense once the dust, the facts and the associated gossip have settled. The photographs in this book in a way monitor the settling of the dust, facts and gossip, the history taking shape, as reflected in the faces of those who found themselves near by as if it was meant all along, as if it was not just luck but wild, glorious fate.

The Sex Pistols show at the miniature Lesser version of the main Free Trade Hall has now entered music history, and a wider historical context, as much as the Dylan 'Judas' concert. Documentaries have been made about it, whole books have been written about it. It featured in Michael Winterbottom's potty, profound film about Factory Records, *24 Hour Party People*, a true story based on lies, or a made-up story based on truth. The film reflected twenty-five years after the fact and the fiction that history had already made its mind up that the Pistols at the Lesser Free Trade Hall was the start of something.

The book about the show is called *I Swear I Was There*, because only between about forty-one and 103 actually attended, but in hindsight thousands of people felt that they should have spotted the signs and been there. By early June, this group, with a singer called Johnny Rotten, had been openly hating hippies and pub-rock bands and playing at least a dozen intimidating, incendiary gigs, all of them closely covered in the music magazines quickly sensing a vital new scene. Here was a group whose singer was actually sending the vague young people wherever they happened to be in the dead decaying nation a direct internal message – 'I want people to see us and start something, or I'm just wasting my time.'

I swear I was there, 4 June 1976, and my memory, challenged over the years now that the gig has been enshrined as one of the greatest of all time, was that there were closer to forty people there than a hundred, and most of them were male music fans far too young to have seen the electric '66 Dylan. Howard Devoto, the surreal promoter, likes to push the estimate up to about a hundred, and he should know as he presumably counted the cash, but even if you count the startling entourage of freshly painted and punctured proto-punks that accompanied the Pistols as if they'd tumbled out of an imaginary Jean Cocteau's Alice in Wonderland, making it seem as if us locals were actually wearing clogs and flat caps, there weren't enough people in the small theatre to make it seem more full than empty.

I had gone on my own, making my usual anxious, excited leap from bedroom to venue, from music-fuelled daydreaming to approximate real-life experience. A lot of other people seemed to be on their own as well, not talking to their neighbours, who looked a little strange, if not downright sad and peculiar. We now know enough about the others present to be able to name almost everyone else, because in an abrupt instant a Manchester scene was created. The members of the groups that were to become Joy Division, The Fall, The Smiths and of course Buzzcocks and then Magazine were there, the singers-to-be Mark E. Smith, Devoto, Morrissey and Ian Curtis. (Buzzcocks guitarist Steve Diggle was mistakenly directed towards Devoto and Shelley by Pistols manager Malcolm McLaren, who was outside the hall hawking the gig to passers-by. Diggle was looking for someone else, but McLaren thought his face fitted with Shelley and Devoto's. He was correct, in the way that Harrison's face fitted with Lennon and McCartney, or Reed's with Cale.)

A few weeks later, on 20 July, the Pistols returned to the same venue, and this time it was sold out. The rumours had spread around town and into the grey, green counties beyond. Even though I was at both performances, and had very different experiences at the two separate shows, it would be years before I could accurately recall how the

Pistols came twice, turning up again just to make sure we were paying attention. The two shows were bent into one for a time, until history required that they be split apart into the actual truth.

The man who would go on to produce some of the greatest new Manchester music, Martin Hannett, was there, surely, at the first show, along with other curious people, including smiling, near naff, warm-hearted TV presenter Tony Wilson. Wilson made the second show, if not the first, although history requires that he was one of the very first few. He was famous enough, though, that his presence at the first show, as if Quentin Crisp had attended an early Clash show, would have been hard to forget. What is not in dispute is that Wilson would quickly invite the Sex Pistols on to the music show that he had developed at Granada Television as an instant punk-inspired retort to the slow-moving, genteel *Old Grey Whistle Test*. Wilson's *So It Goes* was the first to feature the Sex Pistols playing live their lurid new music.

Mick Hucknall was there, oddly enough, at the first show, considering that once he had got the new ideas out of his system with his early punk group the Frantic Elevators, his Simply Red combo seemed to have emerged out of the Manchester scene that existed before the Pistols turned up.

An intense young musical fan we would know as John the Postman, who had extraordinary knowledge of cult American psychedelic music, was there – eventually no Manchester gig would be complete without a mass stage invasion begun by the twenty-one-year-old real-life postman. Sweating out the pints of Boddingtons bitter that had given him the drive to perform, his swollen head red with effort, as soon as a group had finished their set he would grab the mike and snort out an extended a cappella improvisation based around a version of 'Louie Louie' that made it sound like some kind of demonic Lancastrian voodoo. Others would join in, so that sometimes he would be surrounded by Shelley, Smith and Curtis – or so it seemed – and even one day, I swear, Morrissey. The first time you would hear Mark E. Smith at a gig, apart from when he heckled Paul Weller at an early Jam show for being a Tory, was when he disharmonised with the Postman on 'Louie Louie' after a show by Buzzcocks. His introduction to the Postman's recorded version would also be his first appearance on record, appearing a few months before his band The Fall's debut single in August 1978.

At the first Pistols show the support band was Solstice, a long-haired group in flared jeans and cheesecloth shirts looking twice their early-twenties age. Devoto and Shelley's group was not yet fully formed, certainly not ready to make any kind of history, and Devoto asked a group from his college in Bolton to fill in. They played cover versions of rambling jam-songs by the Welsh Grateful Dead, Man. The difference between their take on rock music and the Pistols' was like the difference between the theatre of Agatha Christie and the theatre of Samuel Beckett. It made the moment of shock even more pronounced, to watch the frankly amateur example of the typical local group for whom music was a kind of trainspotting hobby and then to witness the future as a group who clearly knew their way around 'Search and Destroy' and, it seemed, even *Trout Mask Replica* snarled at us through pop songs that there was no future as if in fact there really was. More than anything political, more than anything that was to do with fashion, this was a private gathering of the most avant-garde Manchester fans of music, who suddenly found a focus for how to exploit their knowledge of strange cult sounds. It was the equivalent of a lecture by Charles Darwin. Suddenly the rules of the world, the laws of your entire existence, were rewritten. Local limits were shattered. Minds were blasted open.

We all sat in our seats, as if it really was a lecture, marvelling at the supple, mocking face of Rotten as he marvelled at us pale, shy northerners who hadn't yet worked out how to open our mouths and use our eyes and ears just like him. He stared at us like he hated us, but could grow to love us, although that love would pretty soon grow into disgust, so he might as well just hate us, and get it over with, but even though he hated, he was going to entertain us, just to show us what a wonderful mind he had, and what great taste in music. The ticket price was just 50p, which a few years before would have been a cheap ten shillings. Even at that price, just a matter of summery

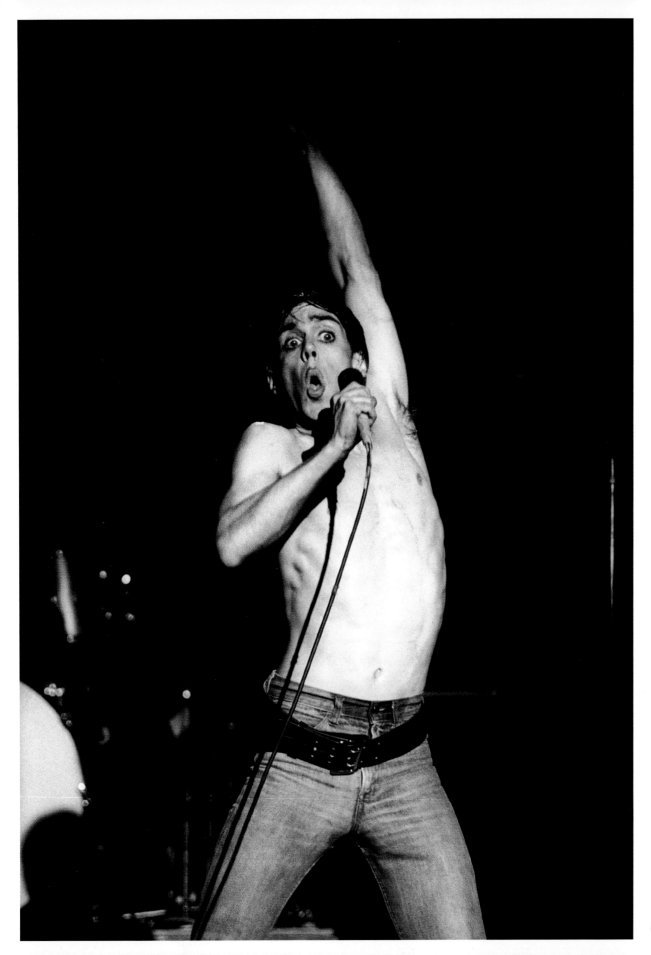

weeks before punk became a fashionable movement, only a few adventurous souls were tempted.

Steven Morrissey, from another bedroom in another house within seven or eight bus stops of Manchester city centre, wrote a review of the first Sex Pistols show, which appeared as a letter in the 18 June edition of the *NME*. I have vague memories, possibly made up after the event, of a stringy young man, some kind of orphan, a fussy, frayed strangeling, all quiff and elbows, with soft, sad eyes and a tough chin, bristling with shyness and pent-up vanity, hovering at the edge of my vision as I made my way to some show or another that had also tempted this lonely boy whose only friends at the time, it turned out, were James Dean and the New York Dolls.

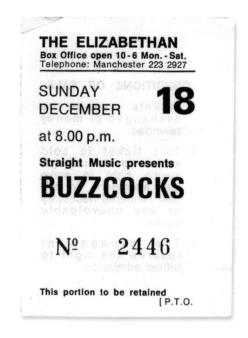

I wonder if these memories of a Morrissey-like figure appearing at the same gigs as me, watching from afar, learning how to speak, are made up because surely I must remember this creature, heading slowly but surely for queer fame, who always seemed to be where things were happening, and recorded his feelings like some mad, panting diarist, even though he was so withdrawn, to the point of invisibility.

He talked to the world through the letters pages of the music papers, clearly already convinced that he was right about most things, and would in the end be so much more than just an obsessive letter-writer. The letters helped him plot and plan the very discriminating moves that would eventually see him leave behind his bedroom and his Basildon Bond stationery and unleash his vanity. 'I pen this epistle,' he began, using one of his favourite words at the time, so much the son of a librarian,

> *after witnessing the infamous Sex Pistols in concert at the Manchester Lesser Free Trade Hall. The bumptious Pistols in jumble sale attire had those few that attended dancing in the aisles despite their discordant music and barely audible lyrics . . . the Sex Pistols are very New York and it's nice to see that the British have produced a band capable of producing atmosphere created by the New York Dolls and their imitators, although it may be too late. I'd love to see the Pistols make it. Maybe then they will be able to afford some clothes which don't look as though they've been slept in.*

The music the Pistols played then was still not really called punk – definitely not at the first show, possibly provisionally at the second. I was to make my own stab at identifying this nameless music that was soon being followed by tribes of fans emerging out of their own shadows dressed in anti-hippy Oxfam grey (male) or post-glam dole-queue erotica (female), quickly connecting with its attack and language that seemed to surge out of their very own environment. Guitars, suddenly, could sound northern, just as they could sound LA or New York or Chicago.

During 1976, working in a Stockport bookshop just a couple of hundred yards down the hill from 10cc's Strawberry recording studios, where Joy Division would soon make up their *Unknown Pleasures* with Martin Hannett's deliberate, eccentric assistance, I prepared the publication of *Out There*, the fanzine that was my reaction to what was happening. The Pistols' show focused my desire to be a writer, and gave me a subject that seemed to belong to me and just a few others.

For the second show, Solstice could stay at home. Manchester's very own new music ensemble with shorn hair, nervous energy and narrow trousers was ready. Devoto and Shelley had taped the Pistols' High Wycombe show, and they'd studied it extremely closely, like a scripture to decipher and turn into their own series of cryptic signals. The

Pistols played giddy sixties songs by The Who and the Small Faces. Buzzcocks played The Troggs' 'I Can't Control Myself'. Rotten's edgy Holloway Road Englishness was sucked into an American sneer following years of exposure to Iggy Pop. Devoto's Leeds/Bolton/Trafford northernness snapped around Rotten's north London Iggyism, and he sneered too, so that if you didn't listen carefully you would not notice that his lyrics were teeming with literate wit, dazzling wordplay and knowing urgency. He had this look in his eye which suggested:

a) He had a paranoid perception of reality, and was locating the enemy outside himself, which brought him relief, for he now knew exactly what it was he wanted. I loved the idea that here was someone, dressed in cheap, drably seductive second-hand clothes that didn't flap around the calves, who sang pop songs in the manner of someone fighting an enemy. It was clearly important that this enemy be destroyed.
b) Whatever he had to say, he wanted to say it quickly now just in case he never got another chance.
c) He did not expect a reward of any kind.
d) Self-criticism was good, and self-discipline as well.
e) He had just that year read Dostoyevsky's *Notes from Underground*, and although he found the protagonist unlikeable, he had been influenced, or induced, to sink to his level, and give everyone a slap in the face. He appeared to be singing pop songs, because they lasted about three minutes, and resembled to a very small degree the Ramones, if also the free jazz of Anthony Braxton and the drone metal of The Stooges, but he somehow communicated that he valued himself highly, and had rather an attractive contempt for humanity.
f) He didn't necessarily want to change the world for the better, just demonstrate his dissatisfaction.
g) He had an empty stomach.

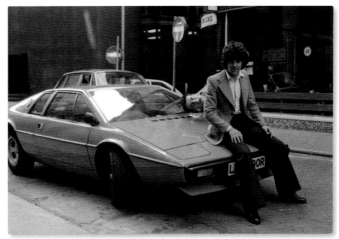

Perhaps because of the recent arrival of Johnny Rotten and Patti Smith, and the way they dragged the mind, mood and body of Iggy, Dylan, Reed and Bowie into specific English districts, into tiny Manchester terraces and distant, cloudy Lancastrian outskirts, all this seemed to be totally appropriate. When, in time, Mark E. Smith turned up just round the corner with a look in his eye that suggested impressions were positively rushing into his head and it was no use smiling, and Ian Curtis strolled along cold narrow roads with a look in his eye that said it is horrible to me that this damned life and the world around me will remain incomprehensible, and then Morrissey came out of a desolate rain-soaked park with a look in his eye that made it clear he had decided just how frank you can be with other people, it simply seemed to be what happened because Devoto found himself on that stage in Manchester, which was once a dense forest, and then a seething, defiant soot-frosted city, a few weeks after Rotten had stood on that stage and, to some extent, quickened his step to see who could keep up.

At the second Pistols Lesser Free Trade Hall show, Buzzcocks were bottom of the bill and went on first. Wythenshawe's mouthy, ragged Slaughter and the Dogs, three months old, had chatted up rabble-rousing ringleader McLaren, boasting that their apparent following would help sell out the show. Their manager, Ray Rossi, was the older brother of the guitar player. His day job was manager of an off-licence. Their shouty, snotty punk revealed they hadn't studied the Pistols' ways and means as ruthlessly as Devoto and Shelley. They'd just heard dogged riffs, fucking swearing and thick attack. They knew their way around Slade's 'Cum On Feel the Noize' and Gary Glitter's 'Do You Want to Be in My Gang?'. (The Fall would also take into their mutant music a sense of Glitter's glitter drum pop and Slade's skinhead metal boogie, but mix it up more articulately with dub, rockabilly, garage rock and a skewed idea about soul music that was somewhere between white working-class northern and psychedelically fraught.) The Dogs' cocksure singer had bad blue hair like he hadn't yet fully made the move from nightclub glam boy to rebel punk rocker. A bandwagon had already started, and Slaughter and the Dogs had hungrily bounded on to it. Their music really did bark, their songs foaming at the mouth, whereas Buzzcocks made up a whole new language. Their songs foamed with terrific feeling and featured lyrics that knew all about the way Shakespeare mixed the Latin with the Anglo-Saxon. They sang fast songs loaded with words that appreciated the importance in terms of pause and effect of the semi-colon. Slaughter and the Dogs were more taken with the exclamation mark. Their roadie for the night had been Ed Garrity, a member of another Wythenshawe rock group suddenly turned punk, Wild Ram. They didn't make it on to the bill. After the show, Ed got into a fight, and was hit over the head with a bottle. Blood poured out of his skull. A friend of his was hit in the face, and suffered a nosebleed. Wild Ram would become Ed Banger and the Nosebleeds.

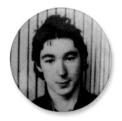

It took a little time for things to settle after the visits by the Pistols. The various inspired witnesses spent the remainder of 1976 working out what their response would be. Buzzcocks would be drawn into the heart of the new punk movement, supporting the Pistols, becoming a major name alongside the Sex Pistols, The Clash, The Damned, The Slits, Subway Sect and Siouxsie and the Banshees. They were the first sign that whatever this new music was, wherever it was heading, it was not going to just be from and about London. Punk-rock package tours containing the fired-up English pioneers and the delirious New York theorists began to travel around the country, dragging an incredible message all over the nation much to the horror of those who heard no tunes, saw no smiles and felt no safety.

By the end of 1976, the controversial *Anarchy* package tour led by the Pistols and The Clash visited Manchester twice, when most town councils were refusing to allow the tour to play. Buzzcocks became part of it, replacing the fuming, exclaiming Damned. The tour visited a crumbling old bingo hall at the centre of some waste land in Collyhurst called the Electric Circus. The Circus, previously just an ordinary venue for ordinary bands, quickly became the first and best known of the venues about to host the new local bands that were beginning to work out what they should be called.

Just after Christmas 1976, Buzzcocks borrowed £250 from Pete Shelley's father and inside six hours recorded four tracks with Martin Hannett aka Zero. (That there happened to be a producer in town with the necessary skills, experience and perception to usher Buzzcocks, and then Joy Division, and so on, into the recording studio was one of those things that suggested all was as it was always destined to be, magically, technically, emotionally, in terms of right place, right time.)

This was traditional northwestern enterprise. Industrial workers producing material unique to themselves using methods they alone had sourced. They could share their craft with others, for a small price, and perhaps make enough profit to develop their product range. These first tracks, 'Boredom', 'Breakdown', 'Friends of Mine' and 'Time's Up', would become the *Spiral Scratch* EP, released on the group's own New Hormones label at the end of January 1977 in an edition of one thousand copies. The minimal record sleeve was degraded newspaper black and white, featuring a foggy Polaroid photograph of the four members packed together as if cornered in a dense forest or imprisoned in a cellar slum. They looked at the camera as if, yes, they might be a kind of pop group, although not one you'd bump into on *Top of the Pops*, but mostly they were just four young men who for a moment happened to know each other and had bonded like men sometimes do. They didn't look like punks or anything, not the ones being written about in national newspapers as if it was a terrible and rather stupid shame. Shelley, Diggle and John Maher looked close to cute, damned near clean-cut and humane. They all looked a bit thoughtful – especially Devoto, on the right as you looked, wearing what could have been a country-and-western tie, looking as if he was thinking that despite all appearances he had real reasons to feel mysterious. The receding hairline placed him somewhere between Brian Eno and Noël Coward.

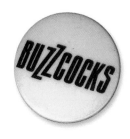

They each had a skill that helped the others with their particular skill achieve their task, which was to communicate something about how they were feeling, or what they were doing, at the exact moment they were feeling and doing it. In the 5 February 1977 edition of the *NME*, I wrote a feature about Buzzcocks – my first for the *NME*, their first in any national publication. I wrote it as if I had something very important to say, something that seemed significant enough to change minds and lives and the very history of rock, but also as if I must hide my excitement, just in case no one believed that something so influential could be produced by an odd-looking group of quite small men who had just played a handful of gigs and then released a self-financed EP that looked and sounded so handmade. The headline to the piece was 'Teen rebel scores £250 from Dad', the *NME* itself not really believing that this odd-looking northern group whose music apparently sounded like 78 rpm Ramones could be anything other than a quaint passing fad.

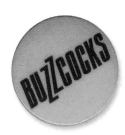

The group were photographed for the article looking less than menacing. Shelley's funny feet stuck out at ridiculous angles as he concentrated on playing a sawn-off guitar he had bought at Woolworths. Devoto wore loose trousers, a worn-out shirt and house slippers, or something like that. Certainly none of the Westwood/McLaren material that it was assumed punks would be wearing, or the Clash military paraphernalia. He wrapped himself around a microphone stand as if he meant some kind of intense rock business, but there was something about him that seemed more Bertrand Russell than Iggy Pop. The way they looked, though, extraordinarily ordinary, was as much a reaction against rock's preposterous indulgences as the Pistols' and The Clash's specific costumes, which would soon become tribal uniforms. Buzzcocks dressed up for action by dressing down, with mere theatrical traces of some kind of otherness to express their keen resistance to the everyday.

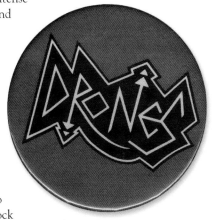

Shelley explained to me in the interview that his favourite guitar player was the vacantly vivid Michael Karoli from Can, and he loved the splintered guitar of John Lennon playing on Yoko Ono's *Fly* album. Emerging from this love for a way of playing the guitar that rejected rock conventions, he played a two-note guitar solo on 'Boredom' that seemed at the time the most exciting guitar-playing since Hendrix. The solo seemed to be a glorious minimal assault on rock excess, an abrupt antidote to prog-rock nonsense, a way of halting in its tracks the absurd stuffy gigantism of Yes and ELP, the flowery theatrics of Genesis. Perhaps this new Manchester began with this comically precise, seriously dramatic repetition of two notes. And then there was the exact moment during the song that Devoto slyly lets slip the words 'Ber-dum ber-dum'. Sometimes in live performances there would be a number of seconds between the 'ber' and the 'dum', or between the two 'ber-dums'. Sometimes there were so many seconds it would seem like minutes, and this would be another space and time that could be defined as the start of it all, a hole inside which you might discover the beginning of a new Manchester.

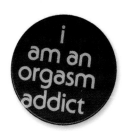

To some extent, *Spiral Scratch* was meant merely as a Manchester memento of a movement that might not necessarily go anywhere, a personal souvenir of the journey in their own minds from High Wycombe to nationwide Anarchy, from north to south and back again. Devoto sings that he's come from nowhere and he's going straight back there, not really knowing, or knowing only too well, that this would be totally true, and not true at all.

The seven-inch vinyl EP is in many ways the first genuine British punk record, and so in many ways the start of it all, the all that is something, which leads to something else. It is the very beginning of alternative indie culture, it is a basic blueprint of how a group transformed their influences – Can, Eno, Iggy, the Velvets, Dylan, Beefheart, Beckett, Bolan – into fast furious artful punk songs that were of brilliant pop length and which told vivid stories about action and inaction, about lust and longing, about what it is to do something, and then describe it, and then move on. It might be the very beginning of the Manchester that would eventually become thousands of photographs of faces colluding in scenes, collaborating in mischief, a Manchester where Devoto and Shelley, Curtis and co., Smith and himself, Morrissey and Marr, Ryder and Bez, Brown and Squire, and Gallagher and Gallagher added sound to history.

At the end of 1976, the faint, foolhardy Steven Morrissey living in some back-to-back house squeezed into some low row of terraces where the streetlights seemed to intensify not diminish the surrounding darkness placed an ad in *Sounds*. 'Dolls/Patti fans wanted for Manchester based punk band.' He thought that many of those who answered the ad seemed capable of murder. This didn't necessarily put him off as much as their choice of shoe.

Manchester, as a place, a landscape, a series of dates, a sequence of opportunities, a progression of minds, a rich collection of greys, as photographed over thirty catalogued years between the Lesser Free Trade Hall and the Manchester Evening News Arena, between 'Boredom' and 'Wonderwall', between 'Repetition' and 'Catch the Sun', between 'Hand in Glove' and 'You Have Killed Me', began in 1977, began with *Spiral Scratch*. Four tracks, four ways, four quick starts, quick middles, quick ends, as if life was a matter of quickly in and quickly out, with nothing but quickness in between, life broken up into outbursts, into abrupt blasts of trembling, caustic interference and scratched flashes of articulacy.

At the start of 1977, in and around the city of Manchester, there was Buzzcocks, out there alongside the Pistols and The Clash, weathering the storm on our behalf, and a few clumsy, determined newcomers practising in large, empty rehearsal spaces dotted around a city that was as much slum as up-to-date, not quite sure in their minds how to sound. There was Slaughter and the Dogs, and a couple of other groups making a punk that scrapped its way out of local estates, cribbing the energy of punk from the Pistols and The Clash, but lacking the cultural vision, any knowledge of Situationism, Burroughs and Warhol, ignorant of the names and songs that would plunge them into history.

APOLLO THEATRE, MANCHESTER

CLASH

Plus FULL SUPPORT

SATURDAY	SATURDAY
29th Oct., 1977	29th Oct., 1977
7-30 p.m.	7-30 p.m.
STALLS £2.50	STALLS £2.50

L 47   L 47

OFFICIAL PROGRAMMES ONLY ON SALE IN THE THEATRE
Tickets cannot be exchanged nor money refunded
TO BE GIVEN UP   TO BE RETAINED

Their records would be released by Rabid Records, a quickly formed independent label formed by energetic local music business tyrant Tosh Ryan. He had assembled a group of local disc jockeys, promoters, technicians and hustlers to capitalise on this new energy. These would include Rob Gretton, initially the manager of Slaughter and the Dogs, and Martin Hannett, promoter turned producer and music-equipment obsessive.

Rabid was like a pub-rock Factory, a slapdash rehearsal for the idea of a pioneering local label run by local people wanting to make local music a widespread phenomenon.

Rabid seemed to be all mouth and ambition, but in the end they were a quaint example of a well-intentioned pre-punk local label that was doomed to stay local, and then disintegrate. They were the past. Factory, for all their discreet artwork and cryptic mutterings, actually had the bigger mouth, and a better understanding of how the future could emerge out of an apparently mismatched combination of influences and styles. Rabid was a novelty label that told its story as if it was a comic. Their big hit would be a lovesick *Coronation Street* plotline set to fast, punk-like music performed by a character called Jilted John. It was produced with bizarre lightweight vitality by Martin Hannett. Factory was a novelty label that told its own story as if it was an experimental novel looking back on its own future before it had even happened. Factory's big group, Joy Division, would play semi-apocalyptic self-dramatising post-punk music, songs that seemed inspired, appalled and shattered by the human condition. They would be produced with tenacious, nervous subtlety by Martin Hannett.

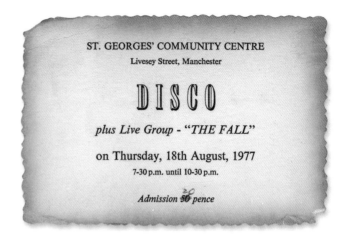

Week by week through 1977, Manchester changed, smoke cleared, doors opened, stages appeared or were built from scratch. A scene started, a scene taking shape because there were new places to be seen, clubs, pubs, rooms and derelict spaces where gigs by the new, driven, protesting bands would abruptly take place, without much planning, just enough time for a leaflet, a phone call, just enough time to find a drummer and think of a name, just a slight sense that this was the start, the start of it all, the start of something that might only last the week, might just make the weekend, might go nowhere beyond the blank Manchester walls that suddenly held noise with a mind all of its own, the start of something that might just finish before it had started.

The Manchester that would become famous as Madchester, with the famous Haçienda, its very own postmodern Cavern, with Tony Wilson as a hybrid of reforming mayor, gaudy, seedy pop impresario, wild-eyed heretic, cheery feelgood host, insistent propagandist and shoddy local celebrity, that would lead to suicide, romance, adventure and a few millionaires, to hits and misses, heroes and failures, poets and vandals, that would lead to Selfridges, Harvey Nichols and boutique hotels, to canalside apartments and a miraculous kind of soot-free, illuminated self-confidence, perhaps really began at some scrappy point in 1977.

Elsewhere everything in the music world was carrying on as if the Sex Pistols had never made it out of London, to Manchester and beyond. Abba appeared at the Free Trade Hall on 11 February 1977, just days after the release of *Spiral Scratch*. It's not clear whether this concert had anything to do with it, but as if he'd done it all by promoting the Pistols and releasing *Spiral Scratch*, Devoto left his group. Buzzcocks carried on, with Shelley singing, so that the hard edges to the group, the epic panic, the gripping nervous anxiety shifted into a softer, odder kind of panic, and their songs became poppier, if still prickly and considerably bothered by life, love and the commitment required to live, and love, in some kind of decent, dignified way.

Devoto explained to me after he had left Buzzcocks – I was now officially the *NME*'s northwest correspondent, solemnly transmitting messages from this small community quickly taking shape – that his reasons for leaving Buzzcocks had something to do with the amount of breath in his body, and his annoyance at having to jam so many words into short songs in order to get across all the things he felt compelled to say. 'I'm not stupid,' he told me. 'And I refuse to pretend to be.' He described himself as an intelligentleman, in the manner of e e cummings. I'm not ashamed to say that such talk took my breath away as much as the glitter under Marc Bolan's eyes did and the arm David Bowie had draped around Mick Ronson's shoulder on *Top of the Pops*.

His official notice to whoever cared at the time was:

I don't like most of this new wave music. I don't like music. I don't like movements. Despite all that – things still have to be said. But I am not confident of Buzzcocks' intention to get out of the dry land of new waveness to a place from which these things could be said. What was once unhealthily fresh is now a clean old hat.

He immediately began planning a new group, using the local Virgin Records shop to advertise for members who must be able to play fast and slow music. (The Virgin shop's manager, Jon Webster, had helped finance a new pressing of *Spiral Scratch*.) It was as if he had already noticed, before there was anything to notice, that the punk-rock groups were becoming clones of The Clash, and that by staying inside Buzzcocks he was in danger of becoming the kind of comforting cliché he felt the Pistols, and his songs, were committed to destroying. By seeking musicians that could play slow as well as fast, at just the time when everyone was forming groups to play fast, he was already working out the more adventurous sound and style of what would become post-punk. His dramatic resignation, dramatic to the few hundred it instantly affected, plus the decision of The Clash to sign to CBS Records in early 1977, described by the founder of *Sniffin' Glue* fanzine as the death of punk, were early signs that what was now definitively called punk rock was already over. It was as if the very act of naming this movement had halted the momentum, fixed something in place that worked best when it was out of reach of those that wish to tame new energy by labelling it. What came next, what was after punk, and therefore post-punk, was already in their air in the first part of 1977, and it was hanging low over Manchester.

Everything associated with the Manchester contained in photographs that capture an attitude that is local, contemporary and individual began during 1977, when one thing ended, quickly, in quick out quick as quick as possible, and another thing started. In a way, Devoto's grand resignation, and the kind of ambitious, analytical group he formed next, with a name, Magazine, that seemed all metaphor and mirrors, had as much direct and indirect impact on the kind of music that would start to emerge as the Pistols' shows and *Spiral Scratch*. His influence was as someone who dared to think, about music, and why it sounded the way it did, and how you could use songs to explore the very idea of being alive, and the absurd pressure, and miracle, of being able to think. He took the Pistols as a kind of elastic starting point, and looked forward as if the end point was to equal, even outmanoeuvre the outlaw ideas and genius of not just Bob Dylan, Lou Reed, David Bowie, Captain Beefheart and Brian Eno, but also, why not, of Camus, Joyce, Beckett, Genet and Kafka.

By the time Mark E. Smith, Morrissey and Ian Curtis – who would have noted well the humorous but serious tone of Devoto's resignation note as they were writing their first post-Pistols songs – were ready to sing their words, they were already exploring subjects, coming to conclusions and using language that set them well outside ranting punk obviousness. Not long after Devoto left Buzzcocks, instantly creating two Manchester groups, other groups and individuals found their names and things to sing about and places to play. By June 1977, there was something that you can call a scene, just about a year after the Sex Pistols first appeared.

I can now piece together what happened during 1977, almost day by day. This is because of the internet, and the faithful recording of the year on various websites dedicated to gathering information about the development of punk, how it went from obscure cult during 1976 to fast-moving phenomenon during 1977. These sites help create some kind of pattern to those years, even though the events were calculated to disrupt pattern.

I lost the idea of 1977, even as I knew that I had been right in it, and so much happened during it, because my father committed suicide that year. His sudden death meant that I lost my memory, or at least that part of my memory that had anything to do with dates, and family life, and him. His death meant that 1977 collapsed, fused into one lump of time. I knew Marc Bolan died that year. I know Elvis Presley died that year. I shoved my father's death behind those deaths, and it seems behind what was happening to me, as a writer for the *NME* in a Manchester that was fast becoming something, the something that leads to something else, a something that was taking all my concentration, and all my time. I obviously needed something to do, something to take my mind off what was about to happen, and then what happened. Luckily, given the circumstances, he decided to kill himself at just the time there was plenty for me to see and do within a bus ride, within a brisk, thoughtful walk, of my house in Heaton Moor, up the hill from Stockport town centre on the way to Manchester. While he was planning how to disappear for ever, I would be thinking about this thing that we could now call the Manchester punk scene. The Fall and Warsaw went into studios to record their first songs. Buzzcocks recorded their first songs without Devoto. Devoto had decided to involve a keyboard player in his new group, which seemed about as rational under the fashionable circumstances as the use of a string quartet and oboe.

I wrote a book about my father's suicide, and it was during the writing of this that I finally found out the year that he died. 1977. I didn't understand this. It made no sense. Piecing the year together, and combining it with memories I had that were never date-specific, I can see that while he was preoccupied with his own unbelievable demise, I was otherwise engaged. Otherwise engaged as northwest punk rocker with part-time job as *NME* writer spending most days making sure I was totally up to date with what was happening in the immediate vicinity of my life as music fan, which was changing by the day.

In May 1977, I saw the powdered, lipsticked Siouxsie and the Banshees play like a corroded Velvet Underground and Nico at the Oaks pub in Chorlton, a gig promoted by Rob Gretton and pal Vini Faal. The Oaks was near where Steven Morrissey was living at the time, and within half an hour's walk of my house. I saw the viciously innocent Slits there, four baby-faced girls with hair wilder than John Cooper Clarke, fantastically not knowing their place, eyes wilder than Iggy, and clothes in rags falling off their bodies. Their version of punk rock was savage, sensual and deliciously random. Neither group could as such play their instruments, but made a harsh, alluring noise, a shadowy reflection of pop, somehow just in sight of rock, that created a map that clearly led towards a future that had to happen.

I saw the first gig by a pale, unfocused Warsaw, who clearly knew their Banshees, as well as their Iggy, and their Low, even if they didn't yet know what to do with the information. This might have been because their drummer wasn't yet Stephen Morris, whose timing and almost autistic concentration would soon transform their sound. They supported Buzzcocks and Penetration at the end of May at the Electric Circus, and seemed in their own serious, tentative way to belong, to know what to do next. The bassist wore a leather cap and the guitarist had a spidery moustache, but somehow this seemed more impressive than if they'd appeared with their hair spiked and their lips punched with safety pins.

I saw the first, or the second, or the third, or all three, of the first shows by The Fall. There was nothing pretty about The Fall from the very first second they made noise in public, as if they were on the run, as if they were in hiding. You could see all the Mark E. Smiths and all The Falls that were to come as soon as they got up and played in front of five, ten, fifteen people, as soon as they began to drive with maniacal battered monotony towards a single point of deafness, of nothingness, of futility, as soon as

Smith wrenched open his wretched, wonderful mouth and attempted to find immunity from the chaotic cruelty of an unfair world. They would repeat themselves, repeat that opening sequence of noise and confession, repeat their birthing noise their living unease their deathbed rattle, repeat themselves again and again without ever sounding the same twice.

They had played their first show on a Monday in May, the 23rd, in a low-ceilinged café at the North West Arts office. The gig was promoted by the Manchester Musicians' Collective, an organisation run by Dick Witts (later of The Passage) and Trevor Wishart, who had quickly noted the connection there was between the new freer punk music and the more traditional experimental and improvised music. The Fall were presented as if

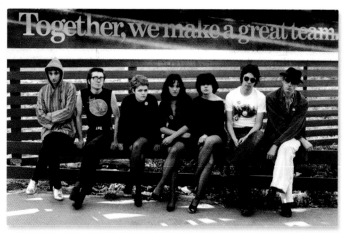

they existed as much because of the British free jazz of Derek Bailey and Evan Parker as Lenny Kaye's *Nuggets* collection. They sounded not as such like a post-Pistols band but a version of Van der Graaf Generator made out of needles, pins and elastic bands. They sounded as if the source of the blues was the Manchester Ship Canal, as if Captain Beefheart was born in Bury. The music used cracked, creased and rattling pop songs to closely examine the structure of reality and report back numerous suspicions.

Mark E. Smith was bent at the shoulders because of the low ceiling, and to some extent he would never straighten his posture. Smith was within inches of the brain of Howard Devoto as he sang savagely nitpicking songs about fascism, race, random terror and monotony with such absorbed drastic rage he seemed on the verge of plunging his hands straight into Devoto's exposed skull. The audience was possibly entirely made up of members of Buzzcocks and the Manchester Musicians' Collective. They applauded politely, because this was a recital as much as a rant. They must have felt they were drowning in the fluid of Smith's concentrated despair as it streamed out his of nose, a torrent of snot and consciousness.

He sang a song called 'Industrial Estate', and as far as I could hear, as he flatly, irritably chanted the chorus, as if he had found it on the ground, sounding just like himself even though there wasn't yet a himself to sound like, he was singing 'God, oh, you're all a state.' He would add a sudden snarling sound, a dingy extra syllable, a kind of trapped cackle, a yelp of relief, of darkened joy, to the end of some of his words, opening them up to the elements, rolling a damned hostile thought around his dry wet mouth.

I saw John Cooper Clarke, lanky Lanc lapsed comedian turned knobbly new wave poet, legs like shoelaces, eyes dragged miles and miles behind Dylan '66 shades, voice pressed into cheery, sneery misshape by Salford, cigs, self-consciousness and speed. He had been around for years, somewhere, perhaps when Wittgenstein was around, perhaps a drinking pal of Turing, or Dylan Thomas, a drug chum of William Burroughs, a dream acquaintance of John Cale, looking like *Blonde on Blonde* Dylan before Dylan did. Eventually he would link up with Warhol's Nico in far-fetched Manchester surroundings as if in another life they had talked beauty and brains with Paul Verlaine. I saw him on a train once travelling from Manchester to Stockport, sat upright in his seat, looking a little nineteenth-century, dazed, ropey and dandyish and wearing sunglasses even in the rain, looking like he'd just had gin-spiked tea with the Brontës and Philip K. Dick.

He read poems, as if it was entirely natural that poems would be read at punk gigs, before the Buzzcocks played, in March, April, May, June without Devoto, who was up to something. Afterwards the pissed, frenetic John the Postman would moan, rant, snort all over 'Louie Louie', making it last ten, fifteen, twenty minutes, as if that was entirely natural. I saw Magazine's first gig, Howard Devoto embracing change and making it clear through song, and near dance, how today's reality is very different from yesterday's reality. He still had things to say that he could not satisfactorily do in conversation, things about himself, if not the world, that he wanted to fix, and he was doing it as the singer in a band that was to Buzzcocks what Roxy Music was to The Monkees.

I saw The Worst get up and play for the first time, three hardcore punk fans from Preston move from audience to stage to play scuffed neo songs that lasted about a raucous minute, and that weren't Buzzcocks, or Slaughter and the Dogs, not subtle or unsubtle, not thuggish or cerebral, just something pure and madly actual. Every second they played carried with it a menace that rivalled the early Sex Pistols. They would wear the smeared overalls they wore as car mechanics. They lived inside slashed, blasted leather jackets stained with graffiti and accumulated waste product. Ian the drummer played a tiny toy drum kit with a bass drum weighed down with a brick. Alan the guitarist played a paint-splattered guitar as if it was something you hit to make a noise. Woody the bass player never had his lead plugged in, so it was just stomping drums, fuzzy guitar and rasping voice, a primitive prehistoric hint of White Stripes. They made The Fall seem smooth and positively symphonic. The Worst would never record. If it wasn't for the photographs, and the occasional confirmation from those that were there at the time, I would think I'd made them up as some pure example of the punk rock that never was.

I even played useless guitar as a non-musician in a group, the Negatives, a new-wave novelty group, or a punk Portsmouth Sinfonia, full of non-musicians non-playing non-music as if that was beautiful, or a Dadaist expression of the excitement that was in the air, as new groups kept coming, filling out the scene, and it seemed anyone could get on the stage and act as if they had their own equivalent of Shelley's two-note solo and Devoto's astounding perception. The Negatives featured Buzzcocks' watchful, bookish manager Richard Boon on saxophone and photographer Kevin Cummins on drums. Kevin was photographing everything that was happening as if he knew that one day it would all be in a book that explained what happened even as we were getting up to the kind of things you often forget in the years to come, because you were so excited, because you forgot to remember, because it seemed the moment was far more important than doing anything so sentimental as making sure it became a clean, tidy memory. He even photographed himself playing the drums, setting the camera on timer and then racing back behind his kit so that he was sat down crashing cymbals when the shutter clicked.

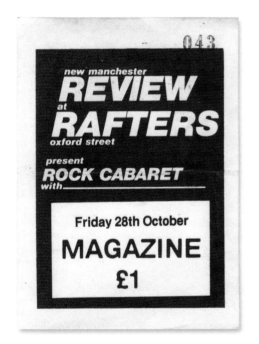

Warsaw's second gig, which seemed to be The Fall's second gig, and also The Worst's, also featured the Negatives. It was probably our second gig. Shamefully we may well have topped the bill, above Warsaw, above The Fall, above a band I'm told I managed, The Drones, hearty mainstream punk rockers who were more Slaughter and the Dogs than The Fall. Because the Queen had been Queen for twenty-five years and there was something of a civil war between the royal loyalists keen to celebrate the occasion and those that agreed with the Sex Pistols that she ain't no human being, this was a Stuff the Jubilee festival. Those of us who felt we were in on something new, cropping our hair and leaping around as if we'd found the future, relished the supreme irony, the glorious inevitability, that the year of the Jubilee was becoming the year of punk. Our very own anti-royalist fete took place on 3 June 1977 at the Squat. It seemed of vital importance. I may well have had something to do with organising it. I don't remember much about what happened, or I remember things but I don't know if that is me remembering what actually happened or what I believe must have happened, because of what happened later.

I think that the audience was mostly made up of the people playing at the event, plus, perhaps, John the Postman and posse, and eventually he would have jumped on to the stage as well. There would have been Denise and Joan, the female equivalent of The Worst's Ian and Alan, the first girls to tear their tights, spike their hair and darken their eyes. There would have been Dave Bentley, the first to bootleg The Clash and the Pistols, as inspired by the local uprising as Tosh Ryan or Tony Wilson, the long-haired enthusiast I thought was the manager of The Drones, even though somewhere along the line, people kept saying, I had volunteered.

The Drones played like skilled entertainers fast, sure and melodic punk-pop attacking the monarchy a little too glibly, looking, too much, the fashionable punk part. Their singer couldn't quite disguise his natural politeness and the fact he was craving a conventional, instant kind of success. The Fall, dressed in shapeless clothes that had little life left in them, didn't as such want to please anyone with melody or message. They were still piecing and piercing their music together, concocting an eccentric formula, working out how to come to the correct skinned, infinite sound using influences that included the Groundhogs, Henry Cow, Siouxsie and the Banshees, Captain Beefheart, Can and Gene Vincent. Their slouching, slurring lead singer had no intention of asking for any kind of help, and was already resigned to the idea of singing his burnt, buoyant songs for thirty, forty, fifty years without ever as such having a hit.

Warsaw at the Stuff the Jubilee Squat would seem a solemn, almost transparent version of what they would become, a tentative boyish hint of a momentous Joy Division, still struggling to work out where to put their fingers and legs, how to hold their instruments, how to move, lost in thought, as if they were trying to hide even as they stood on stage. Next to The Worst they looked neat, and a bit fey. The frivolously passionate Negatives were nothing other than a joke plus noise without much of a punchline, but played their part in what in the end was a sincere post-Pistols variety show as if they had as much of a future as Warsaw, or The Fall, or The Drones, or The Worst. I gave myself a quite good review, but not the band I apparently managed for a few weeks.

Now that I know what I know, I know that after the Stuff the Jubilee concert, my father had three weeks to live. Piecing together the month from online records, I can now see that about a week before he died, I went to see the Ramones and Talking Heads play together on the same bill at the Electric Circus, as if New York was now just down the road. I stood next to Morrissey in the queue waiting to get in. He was wearing odd shoes. I was now writing for the *New Musical Express* and he was just writing letters to the letters page. He had plans, though, to turn the letter-writing into songs sung as if they were letters to secret loved ones. He was looking for people to help him, but there didn't seem to be anyone in the world who would be prepared to help this weird, withdrawn loner who seemed so full of himself and so cut off from reality.

There will have been much that was separating the mental state of myself from my father, who was busy emptying himself of himself. Our ages, the way I had faith in music and he had faith in nothing, the fact that he was severely depressed and unemployed, but one of the most profound differences must have been the way I would be leaving the house to head off to music venues spread around Manchester where I could see the future take shape. He would be leaving the house thinking about never returning, less and less able to find anything that resembled the future. It is no wonder that we could find very little to talk about in those final few weeks. He knew that he was about to disappear, but he must have felt that I was disappearing as well.

I remember when I heard that he had killed himself how angry and disappointed I was that I wouldn't be able to travel on the coach that had been arranged to take a group of local fans down to London to see Buzzcocks play. Missing a Buzzcocks show seemed to me a terrible betrayal, of something, I wasn't sure what, like I was letting people down. It was as if when I missed a show I needed a note from my parents to explain my absence, or perhaps a note from John the Postman. I do remember, I think the day or the day after we had found out the news about my father, Richard Boon had called my house to check on the arrangements for the trip to London. In the most sane way I could imagine, which must have sounded terrifying, I informed him that I wouldn't be able to come. My father had killed himself. There was a silence at the other end of the line. My worst fears were confirmed. I was letting down Richard and the group. I just hoped my excuse was good enough. Richard said goodbye without saying anything at all. God only knows what he did next after that phone call.

I now know, because all of this has made it into history, that the Buzzcocks gig that I couldn't go to, which now clashed with the date of my father's funeral, was on Monday 4 July, and it was the opening night of the Vortex club. The Fall and John Cooper Clarke supported Buzzcocks, and how Manchester would that have been. About a year after the Sex Pistols had asked some questions of a small Lesser Free Trade Hall audience, London heard some of the answers, and they could only have come from the North.

The first thing I did after my father's funeral was sit down cross-legged in the front room of a now officially darkened house in Heaton Moor and write an article for the *New Musical Express* about the new Manchester music scene. I suppose this was a part of my answer to the Pistols' questions. It took my mind off the immediate hell of my devastated mind, and what had just happened in my house infected the writing with a certain desperate, grateful intensity, and a bias towards the local music that seemed to me more art than entertainment.

There was something about the piece that implied lives could be saved because suddenly local to where I lived, and around the corner from where Morrissey lived and damply breathed over his pet obsessions, from where John the Postman delivered letters, probably to Tony Wilson, Rob Gretton, Linder, Martin Hannett, Richard Boon and John Cooper Clarke, there were groups with names like Buzzcocks, The Fall, Warsaw and The Worst, and new, new-wave venues like Rafters, the Squat and the Electric Circus. There were some groups that seemed lost, but were quickly finding themselves, and there were groups that seemed like losers, and would stay lost. The names alone of the good, bad or ugly bands seemed to say that they could not have come from London, Liverpool or Leeds. The clubs they played in were so Manchester, too.

The Ranch, a tiny club, a sort of exotic public toilet with bar and seats, situated through a dubious door down steep, menacing stairs, was where Buzzcocks played their second show, a month after they'd supported the Sex Pistols. Devoto and Shelley went dirty blond for this performance, they painted their nails, Devoto looking like an East European exile who read the *Dalí Express*, Shelley looking like he was already getting ready for the abrupt departure of Devoto in about, oh, eleven shows.

It seemed the perfect place for this new scene to head after the Lesser Free Trade Hall, into a dark underground cave that seemed to exist only at night, past threatening doormen, into a thrillingly seedy Manchester, an outsider Manchester, a world frequented with shadowy grown-ups who were clearly up to no good. It was from such places, you felt, places on the edge of the law, or reason, out of sight of the everyday, dedicated to pleasure, alive after midnight, that new ideas emerged. This was where you could find the hidden energy of the city on the verge of leaking into the future, moving out from anonymous rooms, some private, some public, from bedrooms, living rooms, television studios, pubs, clubs, laboratories, lecture rooms, classrooms, discotheques, recording studios and libraries.

There was no stage at the Ranch, and I remember The Fall playing in the middle of their audience, which numbered not more than twenty, as if they weren't so much performing as simply hanging out at the club. Everybody knew everybody else even if they didn't say much to each other. One wrong, or right, move and you could have found yourself playing in The Fall, getting a little too close to Smith's mind, his baggy trousers, his hellhole of a navel, for comfort.

Halfway through a creamy pint of Boddingtons, midway through a violent smoke, Mark E. Smith suddenly started making a noise with his twisted mouth and the still, frowning members of The Fall that surrounded him took very seriously the whole idea of ending the song they were playing at about the same time. They never quite made it, but their sense of timing seemed brutally logical. I seem to remember that every time I left the Ranch it would be dawn, a Fall fracas would be lingering in my ears, and Pete Shelley would also be leaving, along with various girls and boys wrapped in each other's arms as if they were forming bands and swapping dreams, and John the Postman looked a little worse for wear, and the world seemed stranger, and Manchester had moved a little further into its future.

As I wrote the piece for the *NME*, mid '77, post death in the family, there was enough happening in Manchester, for real and almost for real, for me to write about Howard Devoto as if he was the local bard, laureate, Ferry, Beckett, Dylan, Iggy, genius. The new group with the inexplicably glossy name he was in the process of forming seemed crammed with existential promise, and I couldn't stop myself from getting excited.

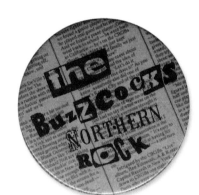

The article was illustrated with a large Kevin Cummins photo of a pert, possibly quite pious Devoto, sat with his then girlfriend, the mysterious artist Linder, as if Manchester was now continentally exotic and much more mysterious than it had been a year ago. The expression on his face was itself a picture. The piece was published in the *NME* on 30 July 1977. There is a world, even if it is just my world, where you could mark the beginning of the Manchester that was to become the subject of histories like this the week the *NME* published that photo of the thin, thinking Devoto representing, as he was, the different northern mind.

Manchester kept starting during 1977. It started up so much that by 1978 there was no end to all these starts, none of which were false, all of which could be pinpointed as the place where the story began.

By early October, the city's liveliest venue, the Electric Circus, managed by Allan Robinson and Graham Brooks, had to close down. It began hosting punk concerts at the end of 1976 when the Sex Pistols' *Anarchy* tour visited. Since then, at least every weekend there would be 'new wave' shows, a focus for the expanding community of post-Buzzcocks bands and fans, which seemed to trouble local officials more than the mainstream rock shows they hosted. Local health and safety officials suddenly decided that the venue's capacity must be 280, to satisfy fire regulations. If you try to look for it now, a hint of where it was, a big old bingo hall slap bang in the middle of Collyhurst, on the road to Oldham and Rochdale, you'll find nothing to help you. The Circus got swallowed up, leaving nothing behind but photographs and a few stories, none of which seem quite real.

The club closed down with a protest, a weekend festival that reflected the changing shape of Manchester music. Buzzcocks would top the bill, playing fast, bright pop for desperate romantics. You could see how important the venue had become during 1977, because this was where Buzzcocks signed their recording contract with United Artists – not in a London office, but in the bar of the Electric Circus. Richard Boon, their prudent, thoughtful manager, grinned as he ushered his pop-art boys forward in their career, everything going according to plan, everything leading to a debut album that would be called with abstract militancy *Another Music in a Different Kitchen*.

Devoto's Magazine would play their first show on the Circus's last night, a trio of surreal pop songs delivered with knotty, swift and vivaciously matter-of-fact precision. They now had their keyboard player.

There was The Fall, still hiding out, who also had a keyboard player, in a manner of speaking, and had been playing at least twice a week since their first show. Singer

Smith seemed to know already he would be falling forever into a falling world, and sang with deranged, authoritative indifference as if he'd been doing it since the early 1900s. They had become, as if it mattered, one of the most experienced new groups, already sounding as rancorous and stormy as any rock group ever had and ever would. Warsaw, The Worst, the Negatives, Slaughter and the Dogs, The Drones and newcomers such as Ed Banger and the Nosebleeds and The Distractions were on the bill, and one of those groups had their eyes and ears on turning out as bold and permanent as the leading lights.

John Cooper Clarke turned up to lash together some rhymes of wisdom as if he'd just stepped out of the Tardis. Funnily enough, after years of being what he was, radical novelty act, semi-pro eccentric, and just letting the world around him change until eventually he made a kind of temporary sense, he would sign a record deal with a major label, Epic. This meant he would be a labelmate of Judas Priest and Meatloaf. How Manchester was that.

Major labels were beginning to sign anything possibly punk-ish, just in case it gave them a Strummer, a Rotten, a way in to this music the music papers were raving about like it might not just matter but actually make money. Perhaps Epic thought they were getting a northern Ian Dury, or a milder, sweeter, more controllable Mark E. Smith. Martin Hannett would produce Cooper Clarke's debut Epic album, funny, peculiar down-to-earth poems set to pastoral post-punk muzak, as if he couldn't believe his luck.

Virgin Records decided to record the last two nights of the Electric Circus, adding a couple of suggestions of their own to the bill, slightly ruining it as a purely local occasion, as if they were using it as some kind of non-London A&R audition. They were already in the process of signing Magazine, led by a singer someone in the *NME* that I have to admit was me had called the most important man alive.

Two groups from Birmingham were added, the reggae band Steel Pulse, who didn't fit at all, and The Prefects, who did. They played a ten-second version of Queen's 'Bohemian Rhapsody' and their songs were somewhere murkily brash between The Fall and The Worst.

The weekend seemed to be about the end of something, and the Electric Circus would indeed be torn down, as if certain conservative forces felt demolishing the building might halt the potent accelerating energy that they would prefer pop music didn't have. Virgin packaged the souvenir of the weekend as a rather quaint ten-inch blue vinyl album. They messed up an attempt to properly capture a rapidly coalescing scene, but the little blue LP offers a vague glimpse, because of the damp, cramped Fall and the grinding, flowering Warsaw, if not Buzzcocks and Magazine, who didn't fit contractually or conceptually into this scrapbook, of a new Manchester. By the time the *Short Circuit* albumette was released in June 1978, Warsaw would be known as Joy Division, and even though they sounded more Warsaw than Joy Division, more dirty and needy than divine, that's how they were credited.

———————————————

Warsaw became Joy Division at the end of 1977, changing their name because of a group called Warsaw Pakt. Warsaw were Warsaw more because of the David Bowie *Low* album and the 'Warsawza' track than any direct fascination with Poland. The name seemed too grey and obvious, more Slaughter and the Dogs naive than Magazine, more dead punk than living, seething post-punk. They changed their name to Joy Division, and this move somehow signalled a determination not to flinch from the Mancunian chasm of possibility that had opened up around them. They suddenly became serious, as if they were not now mere fans of Bowie, Kraftwerk, Eno and Can, but musicians determined to make music that belonged in the same universe. Their first show as Joy Division would be in the same month, January 1978, that Magazine released their debut single, 'Shot by Both Sides', and Johnny Rotten left the Sex Pistols.

On 24 January 1978, a determined Tony Wilson decided he was going to significantly add to his CV. The kind of local television personality who inspired giggles when he arrived at a Manchester punk gig swathed in minor celebrity clothing with middle-of-the-road hippy hair, no one really took him or his idea seriously. With friend Alan Erasmus, a Manchester actor once spotted in an episode of *The Liver Birds* as a doctor with one line, Wilson formed the Movement of 24 January, after the Situationist International Movement of 22 March. They formed an imaginary band that the pair of them could manage. Eventually, they would make up a record label that would transform their ideas into sound, vision and, eventually, urban planning. They would call this label Factory, because of the northern industrial history piled up behind them, and Andy Warhol's New York studio, both places where things happened because circumstances led to their happening.

The band Wilson and Erasmus dreamed up from stoned scratch was called The Durutti Column, a name inspired by the Spanish Civil War anarchist Buenaventura Durruti and a Situationist International comic strip of the sixties. Wilson asked an old friend, Vini Reilly, a frail, exotic-looking guitarist so far associated with the unfocused Rabid class, to become a part of the group. During 1977 he had been a member of Wild Ram, who had become Ed Banger and the Nosebleeds.

The Durutti Column were put together as a kind of avant-garde boy band, featuring musicians who would eventually join Mick Hucknall in Simply Red, but it quickly became the solo project of Reilly. Reilly's ancient, modern guitar-playing sounded as if it belonged with the sweetest melodies of Erik Satie, the most minimalist music of Miles Davis, the chamber jazz of Jimmy Giuffre, the tentative post-rock of Talk Talk and the fully abstracted post-rock of Sigur Rós. Reilly's distressed delicacy would be an essential element of the sound of Factory, even if it was a million sound years away from what Erasmus and Wilson originally imagined. Reilly, meanwhile, passed on his pasty face and post-mod hair to Smiths guitarist Johnny Marr who would pass it on to Ian Brown and the Gallaghers, and eventually he would play for the solo Morrissey, someone else who had passed in some hopeful confusion through Ed Banger and the Nosebleeds. Wilson and Erasmus's second experimental boy band designed for their theoretical record label was called A Certain Ratio, this group taking their name from a jaunty, jagged unpop song by Brian Eno, who had probably written it for just that reason.

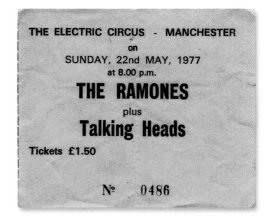

THE ELECTRIC CIRCUS - MANCHESTER
on
SUNDAY, 22nd MAY, 1977
at 8.00 p.m.
THE RAMONES
plus
Talking Heads
Tickets £1.50
Nº   0486

Compulsive, stillborn letter-writing New York Dolls-mad James Dean-sad Steven Morrissey had yet to find his dream boy band, and time was passing. Action was in motion since the Pistols, freedom was in the drizzly air, but where was he, nowhere to be seen, the other side of the door, muttering to himself, the decaying loser awaiting a random injection of significance, trapped in a circular cell with the infinite wall closing in, somewhere over there, bearing a marked physical resemblance to an unlikely eighties pop star who had a touching provincial aspiration to material comfort, but who knew, who could have predicted, what kind of miracle would need to occur in the curious grey area between fact and fiction.

A sudden change in personnel within the scrambling, fumbling Ed Banger and the Nosebleeds saw a 1978 version two of the group feature Morrissey on vocals and Billy Duffy on guitar. Somewhere else, Duffy had been showing a friend of a friend called Johnny Maher how to play the guitar. Somehow, in this story, because it was 1978, somewhere between January and December, and according to the narrative it just wasn't time, Morrissey never met Marr, or if they did, across a crowded room, at a gig, possibly by Patti Smith, at the Apollo, where there was no time to talk, or to listen, Maher thought Morrissey was a little reticent, and Morrissey thought Maher was a little benign. Perhaps he was perturbed that this John shared the same surname with the drumming John from Buzzcocks. Maher needed to be Marr before Morrissey could really look him in the eye and be satisfied with the reflection.

I was pleased that the Nosebleeds now had a new singer, not least because their last singer, the bloody bandaged Ed, had once leapt off the stage at the Electric Circus and tried to stab me, before jumping back on stage and carrying on singing, probably a rotten song called 'Ain't Bin to No Music School'.

Morrissey's Nosebleed songs included one that was called '(I Think) I'm Ready for the Electric Chair', which was wrong with wit, and one called 'I Get Nervous', which was almost Devoto queasy. I reported in the *NME* that the Nosebleeds had resurfaced boasting, and I must have had a glimpse of some unlikely future where Morrissey was a successful self-made man, because I made the line stand out in black-and-white print using capital letters, 'A Front Man with Charisma'. Only the Nosebleeds' name, I concluded, could stop them from being that year's surprise.

Because nothing was fixed, and the news was yet to happen, I got the new singer's name wrong. At the time, as far as I knew, he was Steven Morrisson, the not particularly numinous, pretty mute friend of the glamorous girl who went out with Billy Duffy. His name and presence had not yet rearranged itself into Morrissey. He was out of focus. I called him a minor local legend, but I might have been poking fun. He was to leave the Nosebleeds, to be stupidly replaced by Ed, the original singer. He flirted with joining Slaughter and the Dogs. In the end, he was too much of a gentleman.

Middleton Civic Hall · Nº 000110

THE DAMNED

On SATURDAY, 14th MAY, 1977 at 7.30 p.m.

Tickets £1 in advance   £1.25 at the door
Tickets not returnable or refundable

He hung around a city-centre office maintained by Richard Boon and Buzzcocks, vaguely looking to be discovered and swept from his feet into a pop movie of his life. He struck up a tender, unlikely relationship with Devoto's captivating surrealist girlfriend Linder. He gave up on his dream of writing for the *NME* after persistent rejections – there was I, in his way – and accepted third best, writing live reviews for the *Record Mirror*. In his big head, where you could find an imagination vainly plotting how to gain the cheers and thanks of posterity, it just wasn't good enough.

He almost headed for a career writing scripts for *Coronation Street*. He might have been the man to bring gay love and men kissing to the *Street* twenty-five years before it happened – Jimmy kissing Dean to the sound of Sandie Shaw's 'Heaven Knows I'm Kissing Him Now'.

Duffy would later play rocking guitar like a glam-rock star in Theatre of Hate and The Cult. Maher/Marr would be in rock bands with plain, obvious names like Sister Ray, Freaky Part, Paris Valentine, each of which lacked as singer and lyricist a bitter, dubious self-centred dreamer with strange appetites and limited awareness of the actual mechanics of sexual intercourse and who preferred to hide behind his surname, because his first name was too Christian, and too soft.

A day after Wilson and Erasmus's flash movement moment, so it goes, on 25 January 1978, Joy Division played the Pips nightclub, their first show as Joy Division. The story surely starts here, because now the story keeps beginning, all the way through 1978, as Joy Division gathered the active members of the local community around them who would make them just that, just themselves, completely Joy Division.

Their third show was in April at Rafters on Oxford Street in Manchester, where Rob Gretton was the disc jockey. The London record labels Stiff and Chiswick had organised a battle of the bands evening, essentially a talent competition to trawl through local bands. The silly ungroup I was part of with Kevin Cummins and Richard Boon applied to take part, as did a dozen other groups, including Joy Division.

There were too many groups jammed into the evening. There was pressure for some groups to drop out. The Negatives, not taking things very seriously, refused to drop out. Joy Division, taking things very seriously, perhaps seeing a way out of a Manchester which at that point didn't seem to care about them, refused to drop out. Joy Division members were appalled that the pointless Negatives were stubbornly determined to hold on to their performance slot. Words were exchanged. It was pointed out by worked-up Joy Division members that the Negatives were not even a real band and that they were just getting in the way of a proper group with proper musicians and proper songs. As far as Joy Division were concerned, I had a job. I wrote for the *New Musical Express*. They needed this break. I'd had mine, and it was pointed out to me years later that in their eyes I was part of the local elite, which hadn't occurred to me at the time, and they were pissed off that they weren't. Joy Division were not happy. To some extent, faced with such righteous fury, it was right that the Negatives were never heard of again.

Joy Division finally went on in the early hours of the morning, driven by such authentically alienated anger and frustration that they combined their fierce, fretful music with the attack of Led Zeppelin and the careering discipline of Jimi Hendrix. They jumped forward in time, left behind their boyish earnestness and crashed through doorways, over roofs and down deep, dark tunnels into a sudden mesmerising special-ness. The help and attention they needed inevitably soon followed.

Rafters DJ Rob Gretton knew that he had found his group. They had played as if they were the greatest group in the world, and Rob knew instantly that, in real terms, they actually could be the greatest group in the world. The funny thing about Rob was that even though he looked a little funny, a tough but nervous little big bear of a man in camp glasses who laughed his way through life, he loved and knew music as much as anyone in the city at the time.

He'd been operating out of the ragged Wythenshawe Rabid world, devoting his time and energy to Slaughter and the Dogs, who could never be great. He wanted some-thing great, because he was the kind of man who would give his life to something if he believed in it. And there in front of him was something great.

He took over Joy Division. There was never any doubt. In the films and books of this story he did so almost as soon as they left the stage because the story of Manchester started when Gretton said, in his slow, emotional way, to Joy Division, who stared at this grinning man as if he might be dangerous, might be serious, might be simply stoned, as if he might be as reasonable and unreasonable as they were, that he was going to make them stars. It was good old-fashioned northern showbusiness. He was to some extent, although some of us would fight over it, especially those of us there that night at Rafters, the first utterly convinced Joy Division fan. Their first fan became as great managers often do a member of the group, an essential part of the spirit that set out to make everyone notice.

After that it was like he never left their side. If you happened to interview the group, Gretton would be part of the arrangement, always sat with you around pub tables, as if he just couldn't take his eyes off them, or remove his proud, protective arms from around their shoulders. No one in the group had much to say, not for a while, not until the situation was too catastrophic to talk about, and interviews with Joy Division would be a series of shy mumbles as the group made it quietly clear, using few words, that they were on a mission, or something, and had some gigs lined up, and were making a record. Gretton grinned, and grinned, and eventually pulled them out of interviews, deciding their silence would seem more mysterious, and winning, than their stilted pause-packed conversation.

After a few false starts and business mistakes, a few deals that were a little post-Rabid clumsy, a bit Warsaw crude, Joy Division, drifting in from the wilderness, finding them-selves loved and wanted at the centre of the city, became a Factory band. Wilson, also at Rafters at two in the morning as the newly extreme Joy Division screamed across Manchester history, invited them on to one of his Granada shows.

Gretton, now a man with a plan, became a Factory director, at the home of dreamy planning. With the arrival of Martin Hannett, another Rabid exile, and the shy, cock-sure design graduate Peter Saville, the Factory family was complete. Manchester made the considerable move to be the Manchester that it became because of this roman-tic, damaged family, a tragi-comic dissenting collective of bolshy brotherly secure and insecure talents, of princes and peasants, of historians and futurists, where boast-ful Wilson was the brains, silent Erasmus the soul, humble Gretton the conscience, uncompromising Hannett the ears and fanciful Saville the eyes. Heads banged together, Manchester through and through, they erratically, idealistically made up a Manchester that would not have existed without them.

The story can be written based around what The Fall got up to over the next few decades, from 1978 to some point in the future, always starting an adventure, always finishing themselves off, making enormous changes at the last minute, pleasing the apprehensive middle-aged and the astonished young. After a delay, due to circumstances within their control, sometimes due to the fact no one would lend them five shillings, or that they were bored and lazy, by the end of 1978 they started releasing records, and then they never stopped, from illegitimate album to earth-shattering album, two in 1979, when Smith was but a blurred hallucinating boy, and the Manchester that had now begun began again, and again, wrapped in the scarred, seething flesh of The Fall. There would never again be such a delay, they would take the law into their own smutty hands, stop-start relatively speaking time, sarcastically reflect on their own bad-tempered boredom, hurtle through a text backwards, jumble up catchphrases that say it all as if it is nothing, a way of life, laughter and consolation, what's so great about all of this gloomy tune crap, it's filthy work but someone's got to do it, and the raw and real caterwauling Fall, feckless wrinkled working Smith in psychic uniform, in V-neck sweater, anorak and old-man pants, poet of those exiled from poetry, pickled in the sour brine of poverty, condemned to a lifetime of affliction and addiction, ferreting for droning gold, singing the bedevilled scrutable blues, demonstrating dream terror vagueness, coming to terms with the specific, approxi-mately competent, sticking to his own legend, focusing his beady eye, clearing his brain, sharpening his knife, scuffing

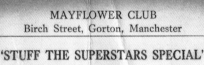

MAYFLOWER CLUB
Birch Street, Gorton, Manchester

'STUFF THE SUPERSTARS SPECIAL'

on SATURDAY, 28th JULY, 1979
2 pm till Late (Doors open 1-30)

The Fall, Joy Division, The Distractions
Jon the Postmans, Psychedelic, 5 Skinners
Frantic Elevators, Armed Force, Elti Fits
The Liggers, The Hamsters

Compere: Gordon the Moron

Tickets £1-50

his throat, cutting his teeth, breaking his neck, quickening his pulse, flipping his pain, sniffing out clues, rummaging through discarded boxes, bugger it, as he finds it, at the drop of a hat, from phantom song to acid song, so that when you patched together the thousands of songs they/he/it sang that were one song smashed into pieces, you would end up with a map that took you from Manchester to a metaphysical Manchester an hallucinated Manchester a chosen Manchester a universe of stacked Manchesters where whatever happens next, no choice, gets on with it.

There is a world that probably never existed where Steven Morrissey noticed the developing status of The Fall, loved by John Peel as potentially the greatest of all time, admired by critics as potentially fabled, and thought, it might suit my rough aching needs to be a Smith.

The story can be written based around what Magazine got up to over the next few years, once they'd burst into glittering, fruitful real life, praised to the skies, in the fine, fatal grip of their singer's obsessions, before the apocalyptically optimistic Devoto finally used up his words, and his curiosity, or found too many words and had too much curiosity to carry on.

He attracted attention to himself, and then walked away. He slipped through the holes of a Manchester he'd invented, and disappeared. He went on to *Top of the Pops* to sing Magazine's self-consciously brilliant, ferociously indifferent 'Shot by Both Sides' and performed it with a frozen-faced set-piece oddness that was so subtle he might as well have been invisible. He tossed himself away, choosing *Top of the Pops* as the place to perform his act of self-destruction, as if to say, ludicrously surrounded by the glossy palaver of pop, life is too heavy for me to lift. How Manchester was that.

In a locked room to the north or south or east or west of Manchester, Steven Morrissey saw that performance, and it made him think.

He would still be thinking as 1978 turned into 1979, and then as the eighties began, a decade that would lead to the full-colour TV of MTV and the scandalous national rip-off of Thatcher and Duran Duran. In his bedroom, deep inside a turn-of-the-decade, damp, cramped Manchester that still looked the same but now felt different, he imagined a world where people made a song and dance of his thoughts, as if they hung low and lovely over the universe in the shape of melodies. There is a world that probably didn't happen where he looked at Devoto turn to smoke watched by Tony Blackburn and thought, if I get there, if I make it to *Top of the Pops*, I won't let the occasion slip my mind, I'll make sure I turn up with a gift. I'll take flowers.

Magazine never had hit singles after their first and farewell appearance on *Top of the Pops*, after Devoto's grand act of self-immolation, and between 1978 and 1981 released a series of exposed, exultant, powerfully bitter long-playing albums demonstrating that you could sing pop songs about absolutely anything – attraction and repulsion, reason and energy, dinner and survival, hindsight and self-righteousness, insects and angels, crime and crucifixion, pity and terror, guilt and havoc, weather and worry – and then slowly, calmly, with exquisite purpose, they let the energy flag, because in the end, everything comes to a bad end. Morrissey took notes. It seemed being in a group like Magazine was better than being in a group like Ed Banger and the Nosebleeds or Slaughter and the Dogs.

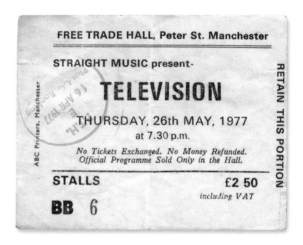

Buzzcocks had the stimulating and precise, frank and clear hits about sexual tension and making up your mind using their very own post-Devoto language of passion. They had the *Top of the Pops* appearances that Magazine never had, singing sing-songs about love and hate as if life was a) a never-ending carnival, b) a rush of sexual gossip, c) no laughing matter, and d) a very Manchester condition. Morrissey took notes.

Factory started to explain itself through a neurotic, charming ordering system that never quite wanted to make sense. Fac 3 was a black-and-white poster designed by a naturally solemn Peter Saville advertising a gig at the Factory Club on 20 October 1980 featuring Cabaret Voltaire, The Tiller Boys and Joy Division. Fac 5 was 'All Night Party', the debut single by a drumless A Certain Ratio, Factory's slum-funking hope for a bright tomorrow. Fac 6 was a nervously optimistic pop song about energy inspired by the synthesisers of Kraftwerk and the wit of Eno, 'Electricity', by a group from Liverpool who possibly attracted Tony Wilson because they were called Orchestral Manoeuvres in the Dark. This bundle of words and images had to mean something, if only that a new Liverpool was sick and tired of pop as dominated by The Beatles. The Factory stationery was given a catalogue number (Fac 7), just in case there were never enough records to get a pleasing system up and running.

Fac 8 was a one-off piece by Linder, a menstrual abacus or egg-timer that never went into production. Manchester was a bit boys' world, but there was always Linder with the art, and the anti-art, and the unsettling conceptual jokes, sailing near to the wind, close to the bone, to remind the men that it wasn't all about their minds and their fantasies.

Always ahead of the more acclaimed Manchester men when it came to exploring and explaining life's secret fears and anxieties, Linder had created the hard-edged dreamlike cover art forms for Buzzcocks' debut single on United Artists, 'Orgasm Addict', and for Magazine's debut album on Virgin Records, *Real Life*. She had formed the aggressively aesthetic, genuinely strange pop group Ludus in late 1978. Morrissey took notes and he reserved one of his most effusive, infatuated reviews in *Record Mirror* for Ludus. Linder would make cameo appearances in his songs, just as she had in the songs of Devoto and Shelley, but it would be Linder and Morrissey's relationship that would last. In the privacy of his fame, the extraordinary place he escaped to after Manchester, as his mad, damaged life spiralled downwards through success, acclaim and derision, like anyone saw that coming, she was one of the few people he would trust.

Fac 10 was Joy Division's *Unknown Pleasures*, released in June 1979, in an ominous, blank, vivid, spatial, compressed, somehow austerely jewelled black-and-white sleeve designed by Peter Saville. It announced both that something is happening somewhere all the time, and that some things are best kept secret.

The list kept revealing itself, as if the Factory collective actually had a destination in mind. Fac 12 was a gorgeous post-Buzzcocks pop song set in Manchester by a Stockport group called The Distractions, 'Time Goes By So Slow'. In October 1979, Fac 13 – should there have been a number 13? – was Joy Division's 'Transmission', a song on its own, because it didn't quite fit on *Unknown Pleasures*, where it would have seemed a little . . . explosive, and notice how when Ian Curtis starts to sing, there seems to be a drop in temperature, which Peter Hook's bass confirms, and exploits.

Fac 14 was *The Return of the Durutti Column*, where soft vinyl containing tender music was slipped inside a harsh sandpaper sleeve. It was produced by a surreally clear-headed Martin Hannett, paying special attention to questions of structure, as if he never doubted the existence of the Moors on the edge of Manchester, where thin, slate-coloured clouds sometimes let through flat blades of sun.

Factory groups now included Crawling Chaos and Section 25, and Fac 21 was a maroon metal badge containing a Peter Saville *f*, presented as a logo, a very small poem, and something to admire. Fac 22, A Certain Ratio's 'Flight', was released after Fac 23, Joy Division's 'Love Will Tear Us Apart', an intimate pop song which was a little too . . . deadly to appear on Fac 25, which was the second and final Joy Division album, *Closer*, somewhere between a masterpiece of gothic sentimentality and insanely tender. It was produced by Martin Hannett with a passion for precision and a certain moody spaciousness that suggested he was very keen people take this record seriously.

In May 1980, Ian Curtis, Joy Division's obsessive singer, exhausted by the business of being Ian Curtis, which was leading to emotional chaos, a sheer dishevelment of the mind, had killed himself, because he wanted to bring everything, including Manchester, to an end. At the time, faced with such an abrupt act of nihilism, no one knew what to say, although over the years, responses to what this actually meant have led to books, films, articles, an accumulation of anniversaries, reminiscences and analysis, making it hard to recall that at the time, no one really knew what to say.

Morrissey must have been taking notes, lightly appalled, perhaps envious that someone had actually pulled the suicide carpet from under his feet before he'd had a chance to position himself under the spotlight and make such an abdication have an impact beyond the merely local. He might have been so lost inside the details of his own quest that he barely noticed.

The rest of Joy Division and their manager Rob Gretton thought about Ian's death for a few days, wondering what the hell it meant. Their first tour of American had to be hastily cancelled. 'Love Will Tear Us Apart', a flowing, lyrical pop song, sounded spookily separate and beautiful even before Ian's suicide. It would have been a hit without the suicide. Now it was to be the kind of hit that for all its occult seriousness might just seem a little staged. *Closer* was about to be released, with a statuesque sleeve by Peter Saville that seemed to morbidly illustrate the tragedy, even though it had been finalised in the strange days before Curtis's death.

The practical Gretton and band decided what it all meant was that they should carry on as another Manchester group, one that sounded just like Joy Division would have sounded if the lead singer had killed himself and they decided to carry on. After a lively chat about a possible new name, and a little hesitancy about who should now sing, they changed their name to New Order. They became a four-piece again by the simple act of asking drummer Steven Morris's girlfriend Gillian to join the group, a marvellous decision brokered by Gretton that kept things in the family, and that seemed profoundly to rearrange the dynamic of the group. In the middle of pressing darkness, they found a way to get on with the details of becoming a new group, which would involve being constantly shadowed by their past, whatever they did, and acting as if they weren't.

They could now head into the eighties, where things would be different.

The Factory catalogue kept flowing forward, perhaps towards something solid and even sensible. A Joy Division flexidisc containing songs from the *Closer* session was given away free of charge at record shops, which was either post-Marxist or just mad. Factory groups had names like Stockholm Monsters, Swamp Children, Crispy Ambulance, and The Royal Family and the Poor. Fac 33 was the New Order debut single, released in January 1981. The song, 'Ceremony', written by Joy Division, with lyrics by Curtis that may have been about his baby daughter Natalie, sounded like Joy Division melting, like a broken heart in slow motion, and now there was something dark and damaged about Factory, for all Saville's play, Hannett's drums and Wilson's talk.

Fac 50 was the debut New Order album, *Movement*, released in November 1981, which sounded like Joy Division in shock, like an abandoned, messed-up, intimately apprehensive family putting a brave face on things. It was produced by Martin Hannett as if his hands were tied and his mind was tired. New Order had not yet found their sound, one that would use electronic pulse, frayed nerves and melancholy brightness, and because of the way things turned out, this meant Manchester, as represented by Factory, did not have its new sound. New Manchester groups didn't know which way to turn. Morrissey, lost in a Manchester that was in danger of losing itself after its incredible recovery, was festering.

Wilson, Erasmus and Gretton held meetings about what we may now call the future of Manchester, many of which deserved their own catalogue numbers. Gretton, perhaps because he had been a DJ in Manchester clubs, perhaps because he didn't want his boys, and now girls, to be spoiled by royalties, perhaps because he was a punk show-business stylist, thought it would be a good idea if Factory put something back into the community, now that they were, to all extents and purposes, a going concern. It seemed only right.

It might have been something Erasmus said that got Gretton musing. It may be that only Gretton ever understood what Erasmus was saying, although Wilson pretended to. It may have been that Erasmus was the most important Factory mind, but we will never know, because as much as Wilson talks, about ideas and how to come up with them, Erasmus does not talk. He might have been the Factory Ringo, just turning up for tea and cakes. He might have been the Factory Engels, creating the circumstances where others might have the freedom to think how they could make things happen. He might represent the Manchester spirit, more than Mark E. Smith, as being a kind of incandescent laziness, which involves a lot of hard work.

It might have been Wilson's infatuation with the Situationists and their theories of urbanism and architecture that inspired Gretton unexpectedly to conclude that what Manchester needed was a club run by people like Factory. Wilson had read an essay the French theorist Ivan Chtcheglov had written as a nineteen-year-old in 1953 called 'Formulary for a New Urbanism': 'We are bored in the city, everybody is bored, there is no longer any temple to the sun . . . You never see the Haçienda,' he wrote. 'It doesn't exist. The Haçienda must be built.'

The essay is the missing link between the appearance by the Sex Pistols in early June 1976 and the opening of the Haçienda nightclub on 21 May 1982 on Whitworth Street West, a short walk around the corner from the Free Trade Hall. Absurdly, gloriously, stupidly, Factory, using money made by New Order, or perhaps Joy Division, built the Haçienda where they felt it belonged, in Manchester, home of knowledge and adventure, on a lost street corner, just near Oxford Road train station, in sight of canals, motorways, office buildings and derelict spaces, as if a building could give people an insight into the consciousness of the cosmic as much as music. The Haçienda, built on the site of an old yacht showroom, a joke in itself, was Fac 51: you could see the construction of the Haçienda on a video given the catalogue number Fac 54.

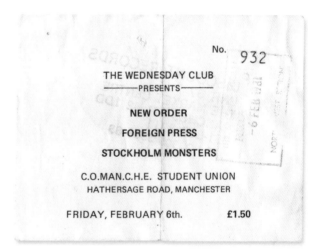

Gretton, loving the showbusiness of it all, had his club, a playground for fun and games and, perhaps, money-making. His band were bemused, but, still in a kind of shock, went along with what seemed to be a fiasco. Saville had in abstract building form, as conceived by the architect Ben Kelly, a version of one of his sleeves and posters. Erasmus thought it was all a dream, as if stars and rain could be seen through a glass ceiling. Hannett was furious, thinking it a complete waste of money. His way of spending the money that may or may not have existed because of Factory record sales was to invest it in new recording technology, feeling that a Fairlight computer, the newest technological tool to be of great benefit to the likes of Michael Jackson's Quincy Jones and Frankie Goes to Hollywood's Trevor Horn, would lead to better-sounding records, not understanding this busybody concern with the welfare of the local community. He just wanted to produce great records. Wilson may well have believed that this was the first step – the final beginning – on a journey that would make Manchester the intellectual capital of the world.

You would never have guessed this from the raucous opening night, which seemed like a Dada working men's club celebration of Bertolt Brecht's life and death, or as the club limped through its first few years as rock venue folly, as Wilson's Church of Ego, sort of a pop-funded post-punk Millennium Dome. Eventually, Bizarre Quarter – sometimes Sad, even Sinister Quarter – turned into Happy Quarter, and darkness and obscurity would be banished by artificial lighting and the distracting dance music ultimately required in a nightclub. By the end of the 1980s, visitors to the Haçienda would have their moods and perceptions altered, just as Ivan's essay had predicted. It was as though it had been planned all along.

The same month that the Haçienda opened its doors, Johnny Marr bravely knocked on the Stretford door of Steven Morrissey. Imagine how sick with worry Morrissey must have been waiting for that knock, any knock, the knock that might wake up the sleeping monster that was his destiny. Imagine the door of the bleak little terrace house creaking as Morrissey opened it, and the boy looked at Johnny. Morrissey, no longer a teenager, on the verge of having never really existed, so wanted to be left alone, and so wanted to be kissed on the mouth by a million fans, and then left alone, and then kissed.

Marr thought that Morrissey was exceptionally considerate, as though he wanted to apologise for something. Perhaps by now Morrissey, who had met his fair share of losers, time-wasters and what he called sluts, was prepared to let anyone into his house, especially someone with a haircut like Marr's, which showed promise. He had nothing to lose. Morrissey had long established a kind of application test, to check out the credentials of those that had ventured to where he had settled in desperate exile. He showed visitors a shoebox crammed with treasured seven-inch singles and asked them if they wanted to put a record on. He took a sneak peek at his visitor's shoes, and wasn't totally appalled.

Marr, silently marvelling at the carpet on the floor, at the wallpaper, at smells he didn't quite recognise, at the tenant's quiff, the stiffest thing about him, chose a Marvelettes single on Tamla Motown, an American ex-jukebox copy with the central hole extracted, and possibly won Morrissey's heart, for as long as it would take, by playing 'Paper Boy', the B-side of 'You're the One'. Marr was impressed that Morrissey had all The Marvelettes' singles. Morrissey was impressed that Marr knew enough to be impressed. These two intensely pseudy music fans were snobbishly unswayed by the then current fascination with cold, mechanical synths and brittle electro-pop, but willingly intoxicated by the fragrance of sixties girl pop groups wafting across time from the days before punk. At the time, this seemed both a little quaint, a bit backward, and a little daring.

Both music addicts were fully aware of how Patti Smith had covered the Marvelettes' 'The Hunter Gets Captured by the Game' as if she was pulling the skin away from reality. Both could probably discuss in intimate detail the bootleg recording of her 30 January 1976 Los Angeles Roxy concert. It was called *Teenage Perversity and Ships in the Night* and featured a surprise appearance by Iggy Pop. How Manchester was that.

There was an instant attraction between these two Mancunian exiles as they bonded over wonderful, wounding pop songs about sexual attraction and solitude. Both had found their way to Phil Spector and his supple, gaudy girl singers through the recommendations of the New York Dolls' lead singer David Johansen. They fell into each other's arms, saving each other's souls, and set to work. In a way, they formed a post-punk sixties girl group, styled by Edith Sitwell, Elsie Tanner, Gene Pitney and Billy Liar, having songs written for them by Marvin Gaye and Joe Orton, with a backing band of ex-members of Buffalo Springfield, The Velvet Underground and Sparks. The menaced, cheated, vengeful Morrissey, almost paralysed with fear that all his rich human knowledge would never leave his head, or his bedroom, burst into torrid, confessional life, and Marr was able to turn that life, the howling hilarious hopelessness, that sad crawling intimacy, into heady song.

By October 1982, they were ready to go on stage, wearing shoes that almost matched, supporting silly cocktail-loving London pop group Blue Rondo A La Turk at the Ritz. As a terse, aloof reaction against groups with names like Orchestral Manoeuvres in the Dark, or perhaps in opposition to plain, ugly names like Ed Banger and the Nosebleeds, White Dice and Slaughter and the Dogs, Morrissey and Marr called themselves The

Smiths. In surprising ways, these incredibly white northerners were the Blacksmiths, playing music that was, in its own pale, blasted way, soul.

They played four songs, including their own gothic Moors Murders lament 'Suffer Little Children' and a cover of black girl trio The Cookies' 'I Want a Boy for My Birthday'. Here was an ostentatious all-male girl group singing traumatic songs about the Moors Murders, about the death of children who would never dream. Here was a group, in love with pop, Manchester through and through, Hulme and Wythenshawe and Salford and Ardwick all mixed up with Detroit and New York and the middle of nowhere, a group spilling out of a dream Manchester was having about its own history, a group crawling out of a certain amount of emotional wreckage, balancing beauty and brains, good and evil in a way no one else could have done.

The Smiths' second performance was at a gay bar called Manhattan. Their third show, on 4 February 1983, was at Factory's Haçienda Club. Morrissey decorated the club with flowers, because it looked a bit drab. The Smiths wouldn't sign to Factory Records, because Morrissey didn't want to, or because Wilson didn't want them to. It worked better that way. They both came from Manchester, but not in the same way. For Morrissey, the city was behind him, frozen in time, seared into his imagination. For Wilson, it had only just started, and he'd always have plans.

On 13 March 1984, The Smiths, a sudden success, adored for their ecstatic despair, their plain, potent flamboyance, played the Manchester Free Trade Hall, eight years after the Sex Pistols had shown up. Manchester was now somewhere else, closer to now than it had ever been, and there was no going back.

Exceptional patience, and infernal impatience, seemed folded into Morrissey and Marr's insistent, sombre, homesick melodies. Nothing brings the past back like a tune.

'Oh, Manchester,' sang Morrissey, about the myth of the place and the resounding truth, finding a clearing in the dense forest, sure of his calculations, making sense of his inheritance, as his hair flopped over his long, grave face, as he found himself, after being lost in endless narrow streets, relieved of a certain amount of pressure, and burdened with succulent new concerns. The last one in line was finally on his way, his oddly beautiful voice sinking into our hearts like a sad grey rain into already wet soil. He posed like a scapegoat, like a mentally ill genius, like an aroused glam rocker, like a fantasist accused of unspeakable crimes. 'Oh, Manchester . . . so much to answer for.'

By no stretch of the imagination is Manchester a picturesque city. It is however, emphatically if unconventionally beautiful. In common with all things beautiful . . . it is fundamentally flawed. It has a compulsion to preen and show off. It is narcissistic, contrary and wayward, and yet you cannot help but love it. It is both admirable and maddening.

Chris Lethbridge

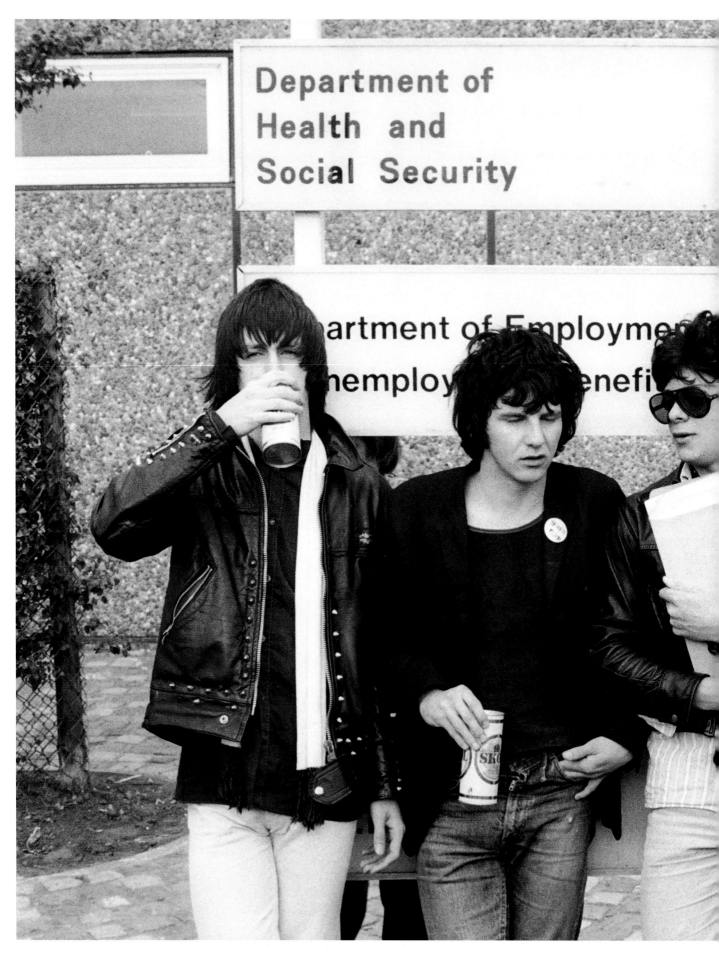

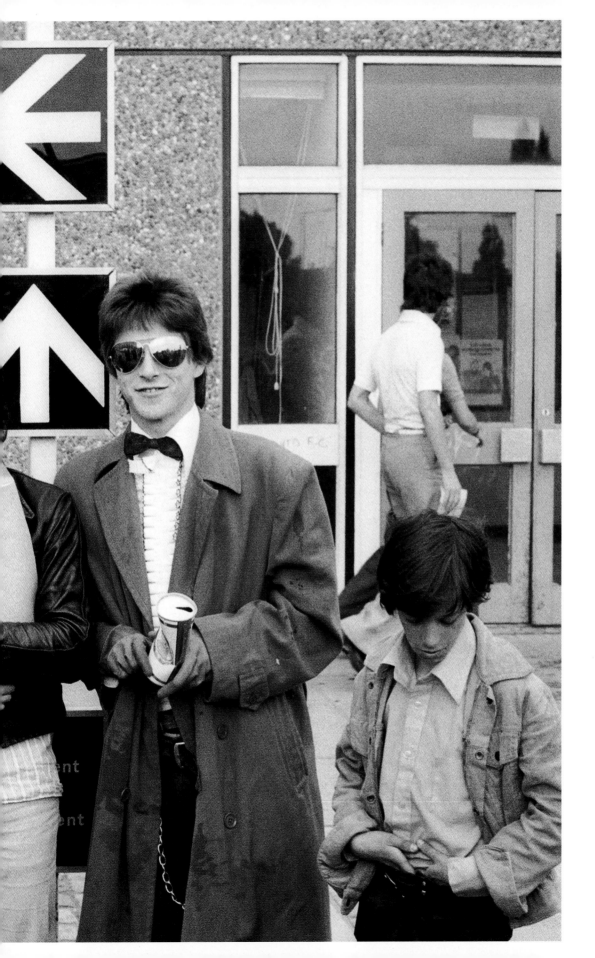

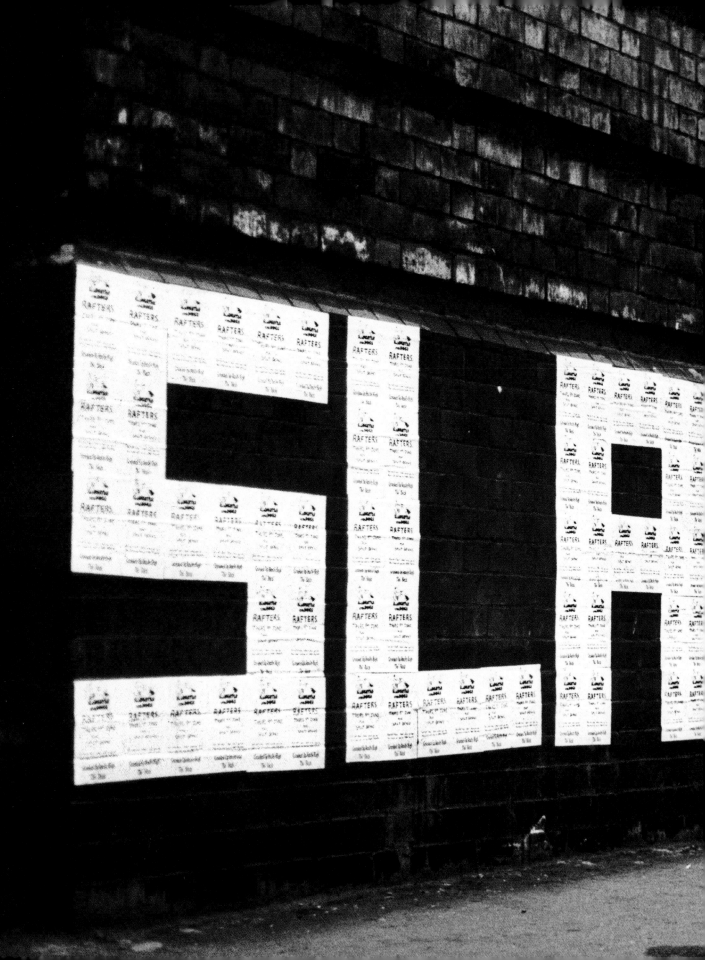

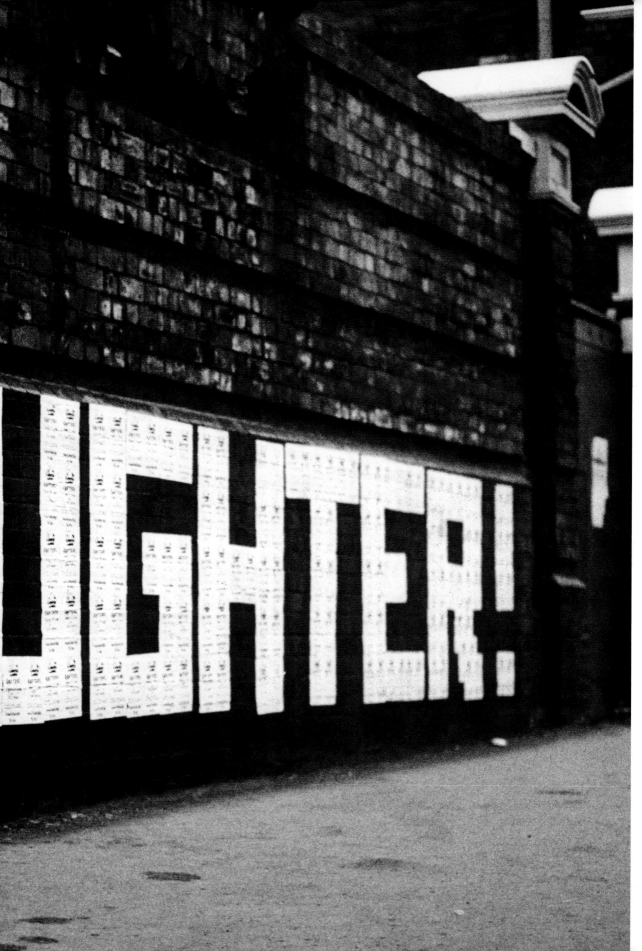

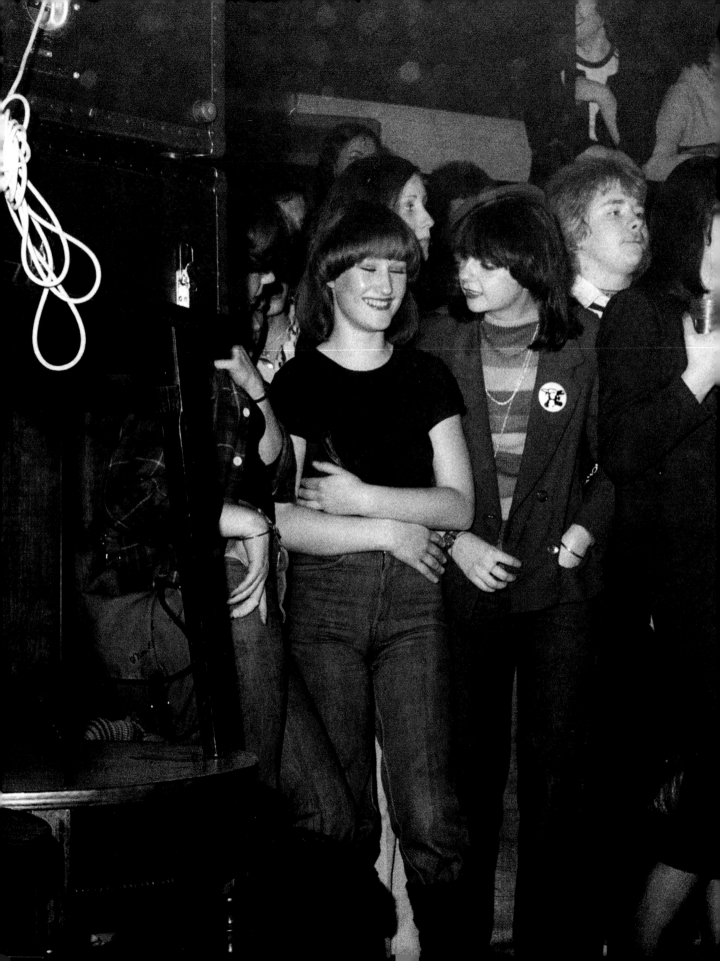

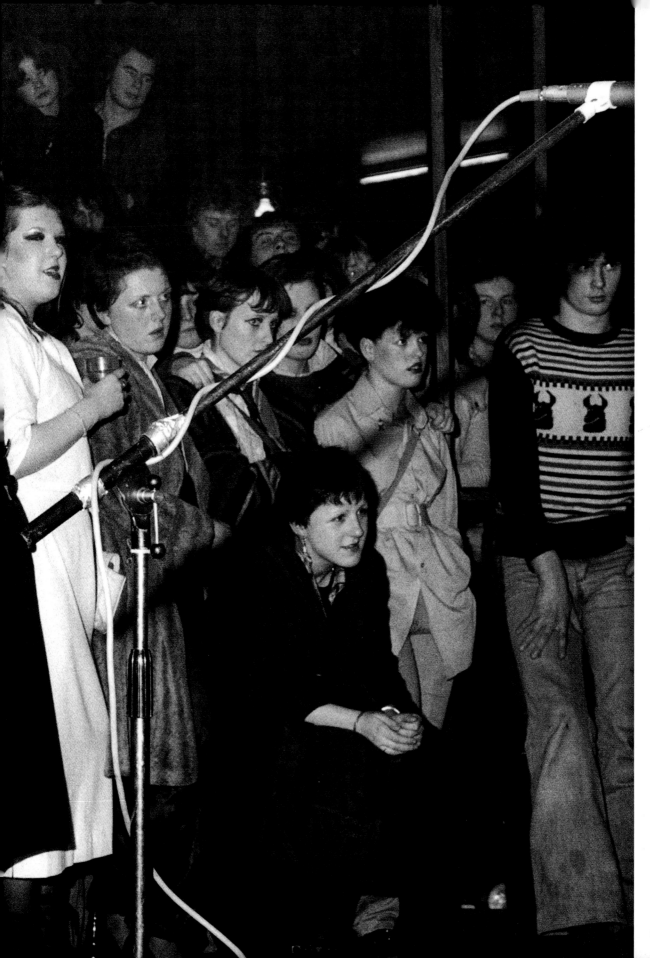

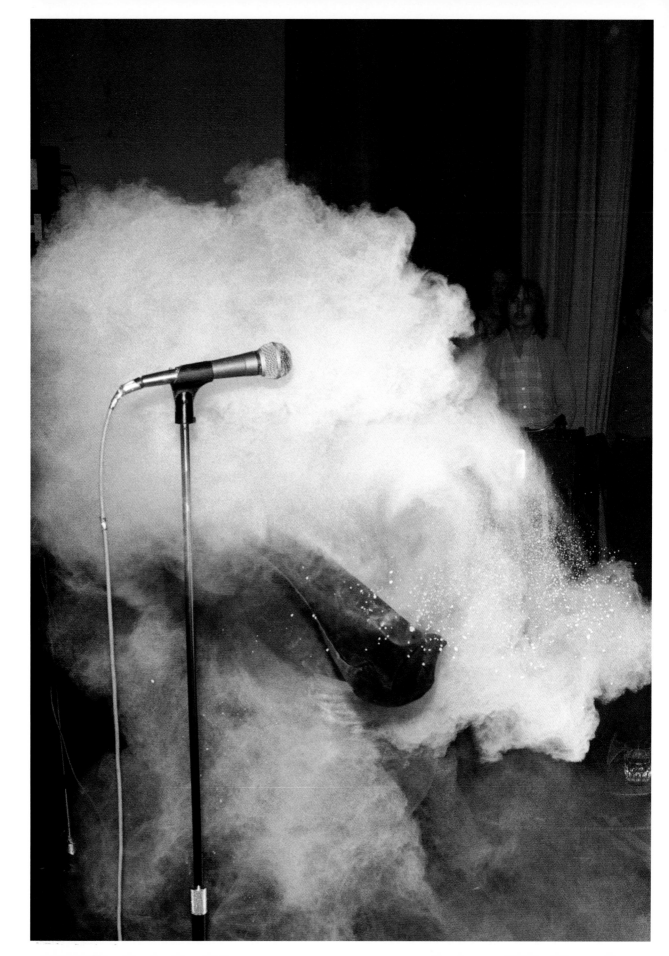

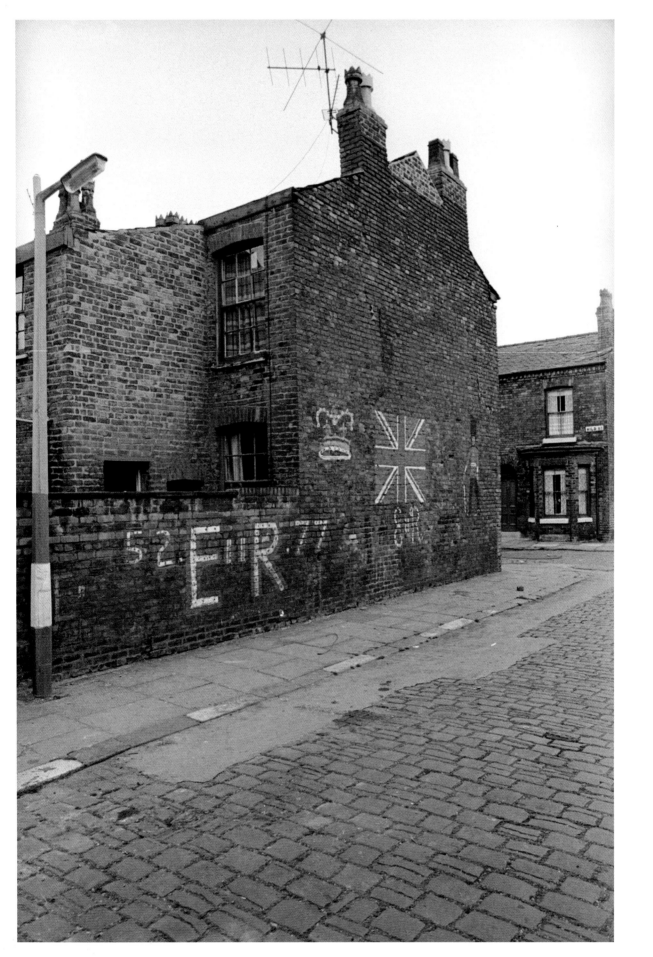

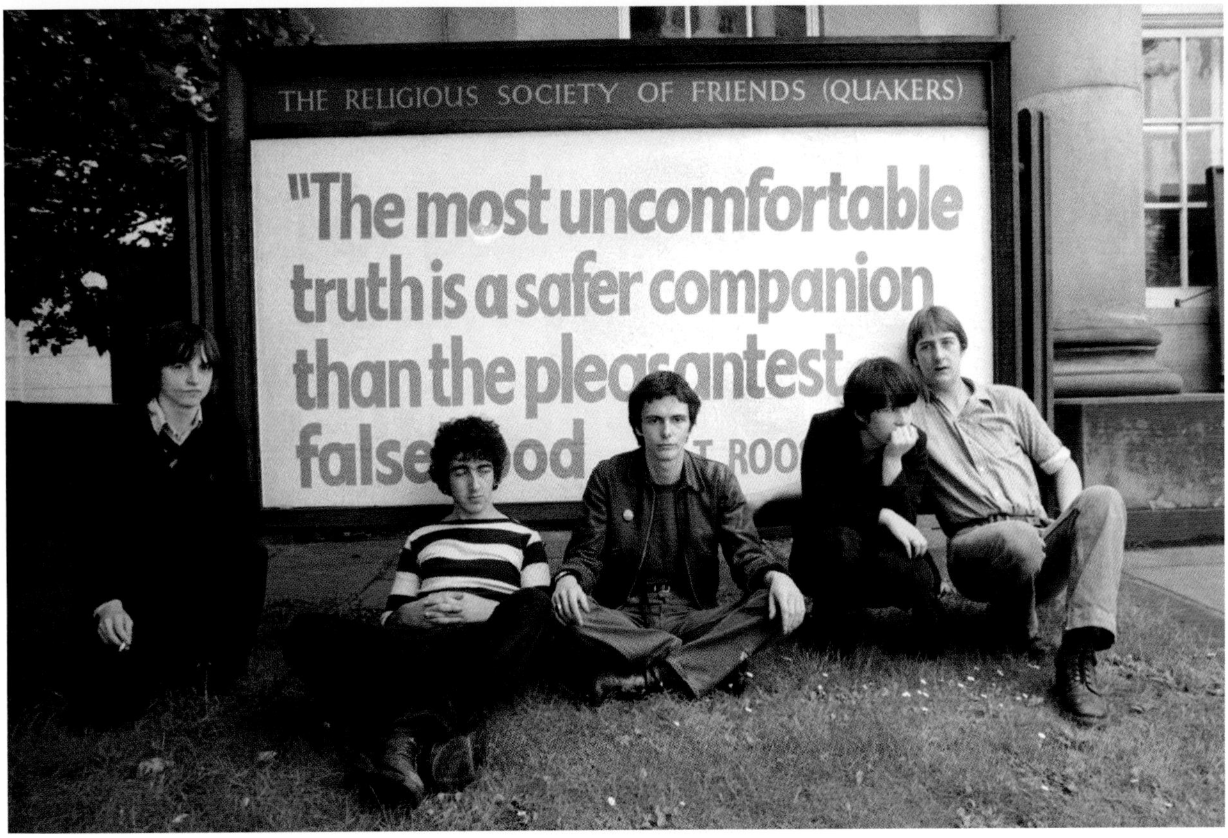
THE RELIGIOUS SOCIETY OF FRIENDS (QUAKERS)
"The most uncomfortable
truth is a safer companion

The Fall
Mount Street, Manchester
1978

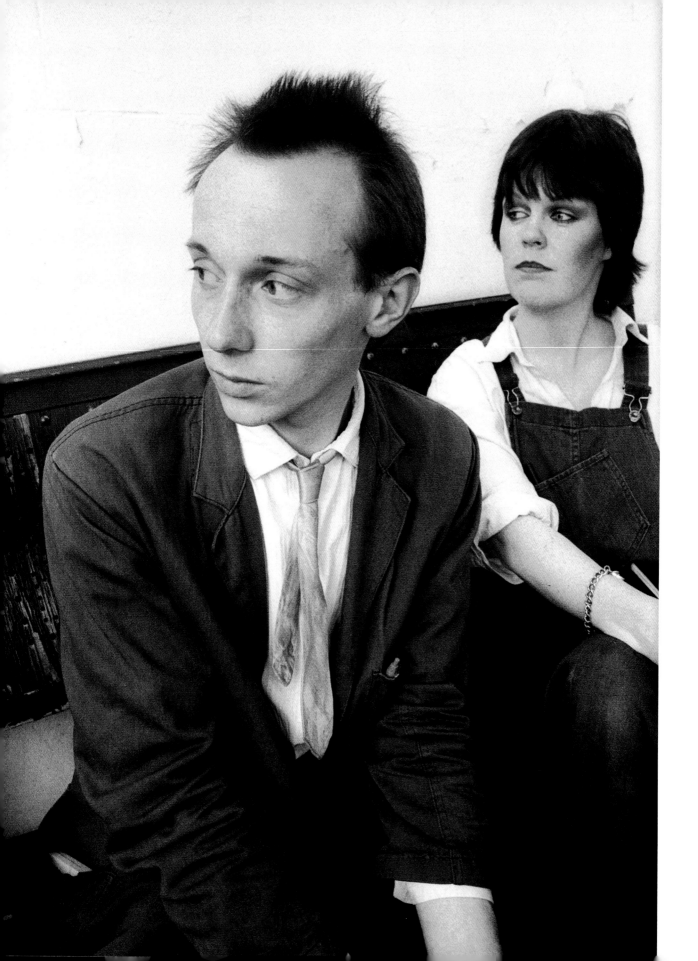

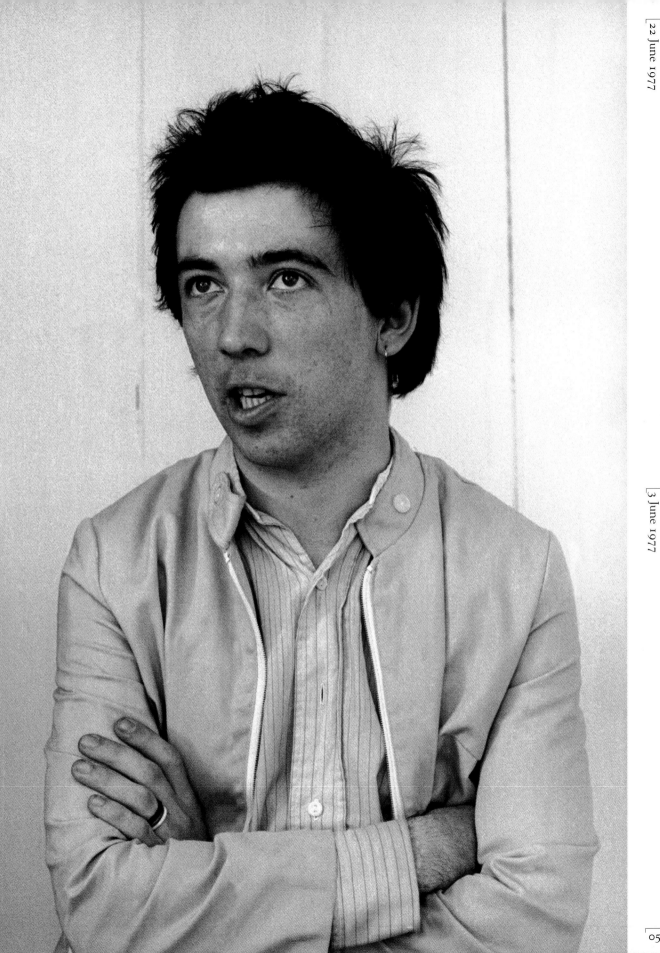

Howard Devoto and Linder Sterling
The Priory, Lower Broughton, Salford
22 June 1977

Pete Shelley
Manchester
3 June 1977

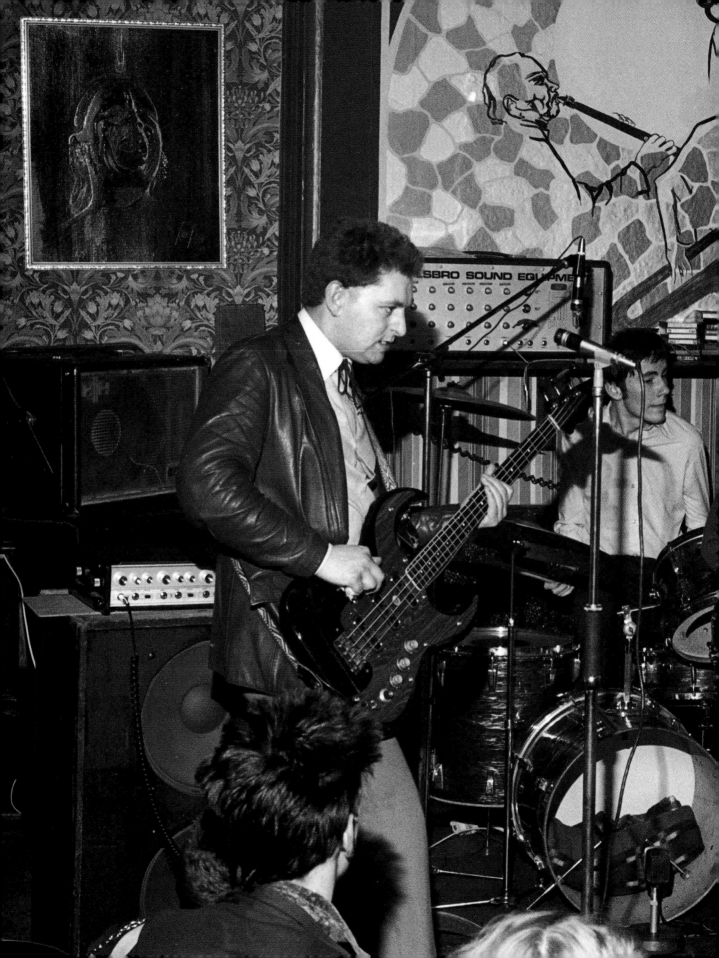

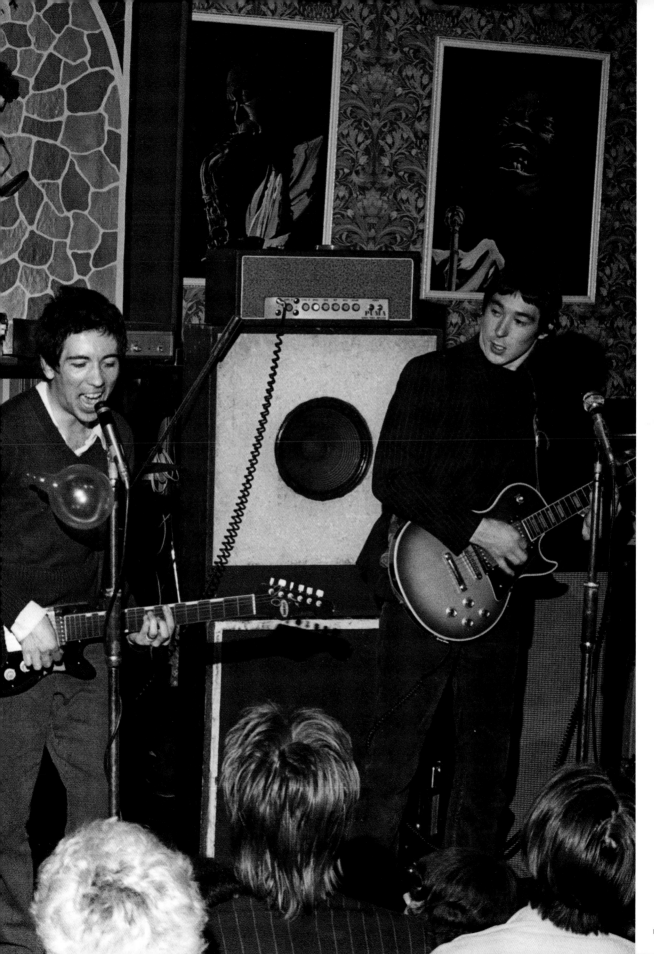

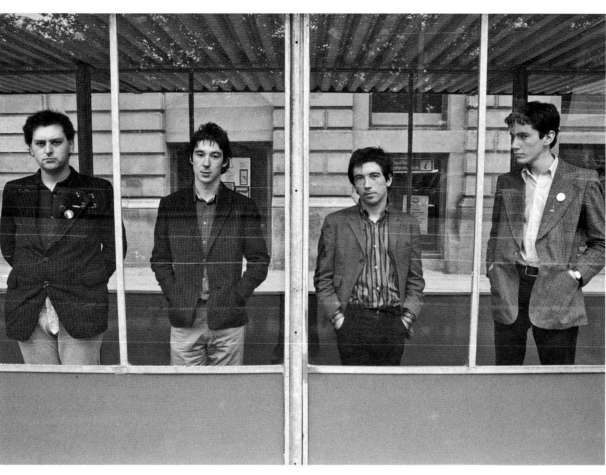

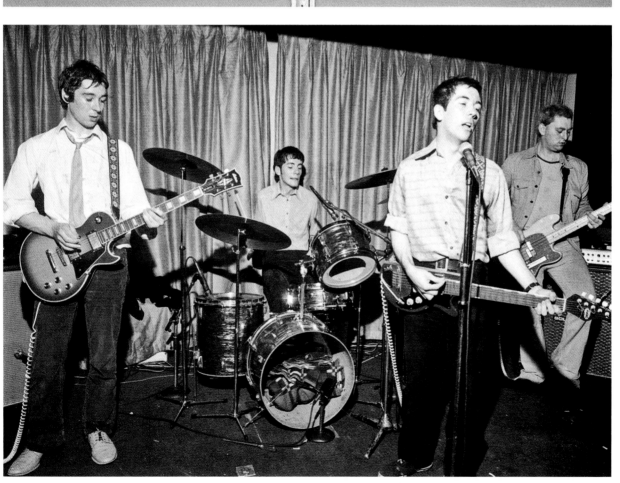

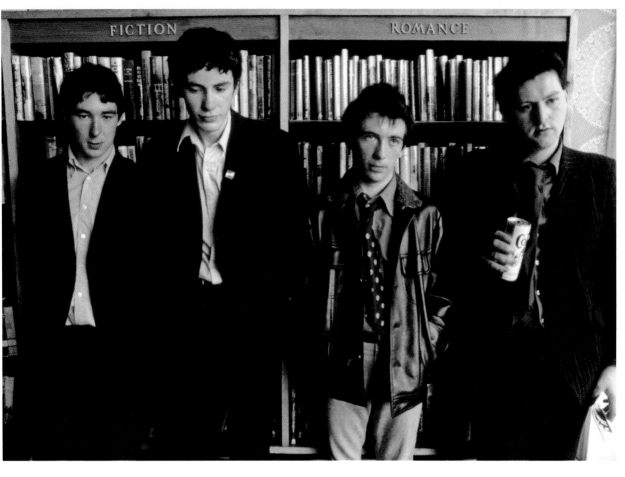

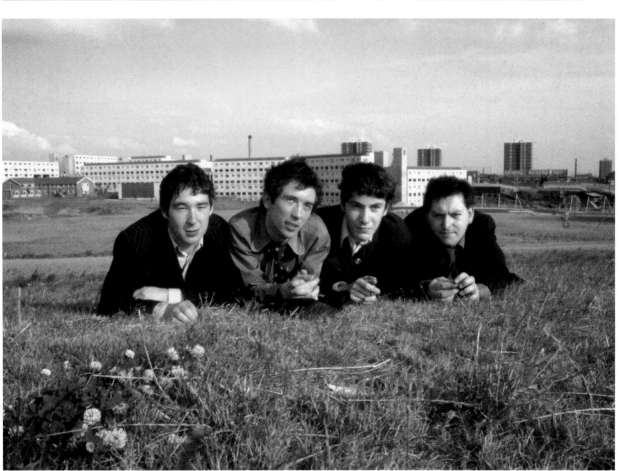
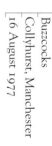

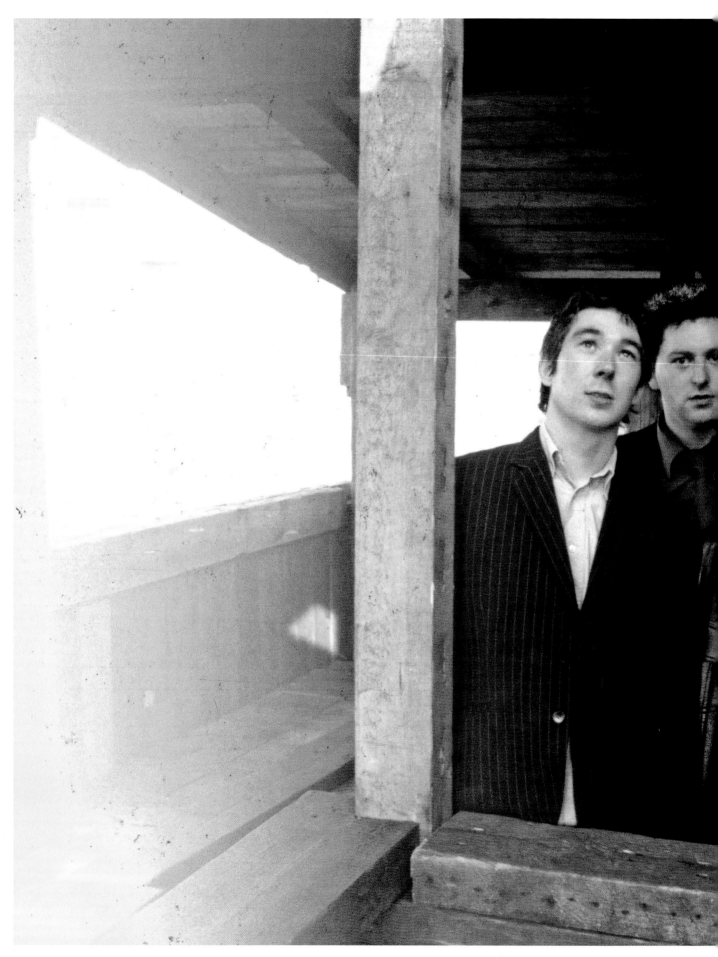

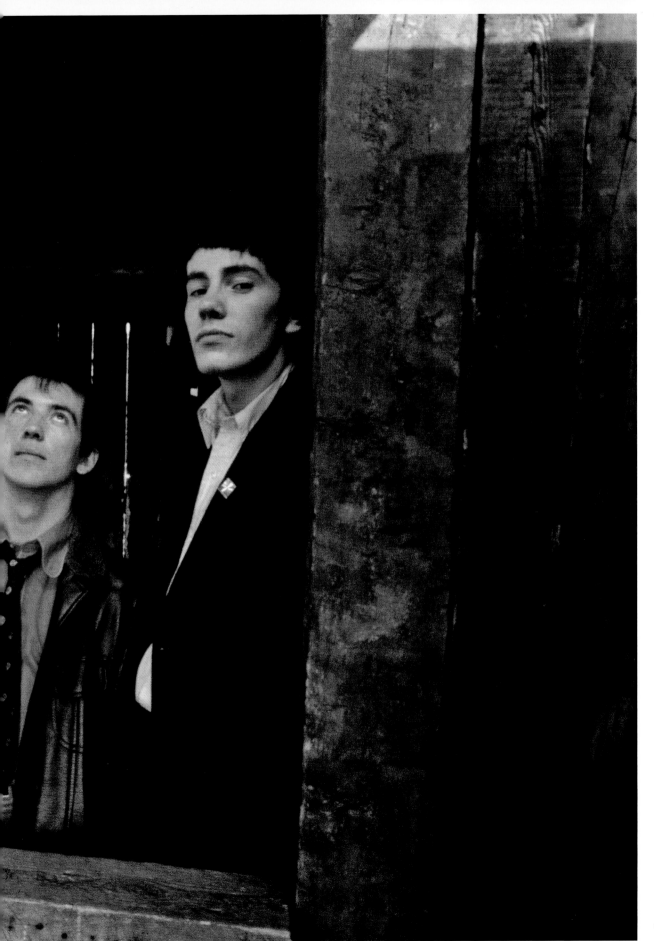

For Manchester is the place where people do things . . . 'Don't talk about what you are going to do, do it.' That is the Manchester habit. And in the past through the manifestation of this quality the word Manchester became a synonym for energy and freedom and the right to do and to think without shackles.

Judge Parry

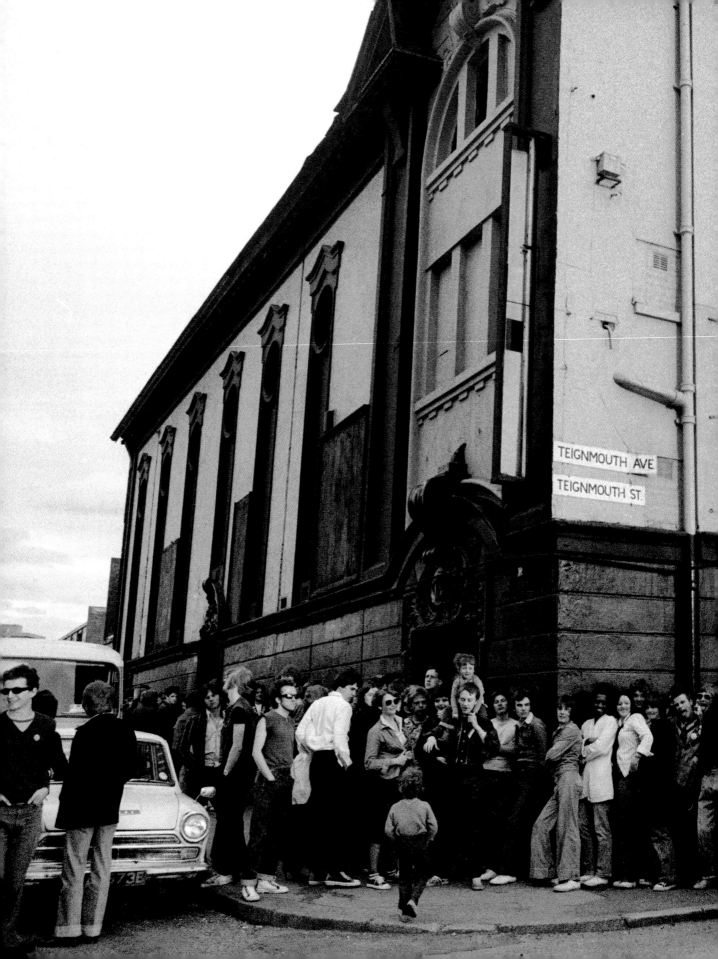

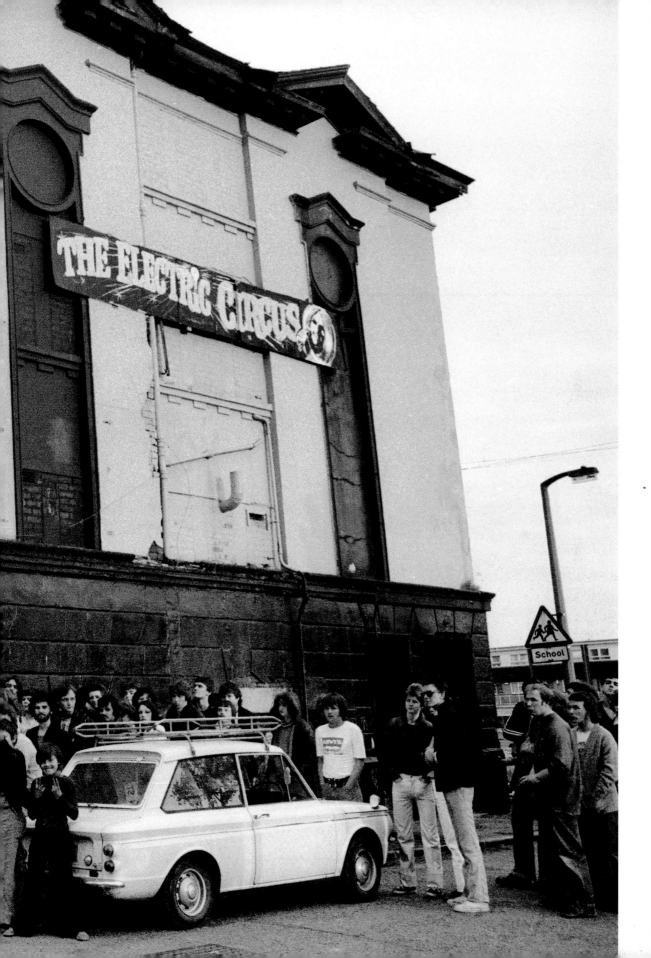

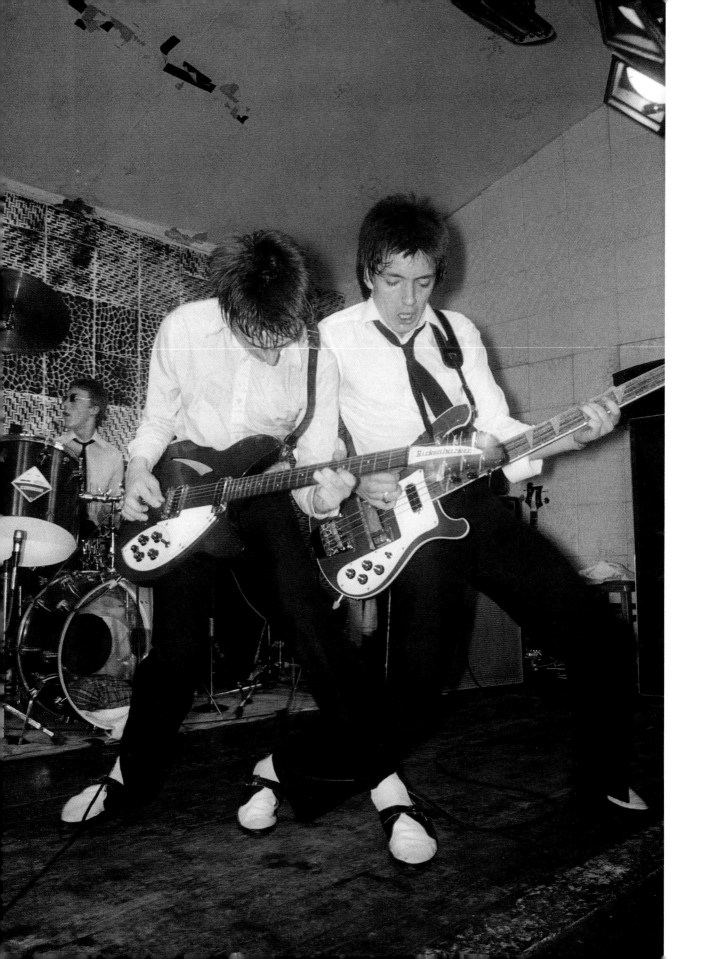

The Clash
Electric Circus, Collyhurst, Manchester
May 1977

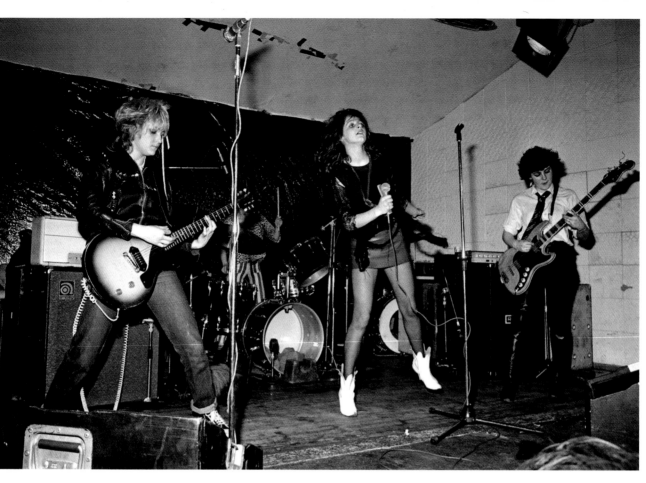

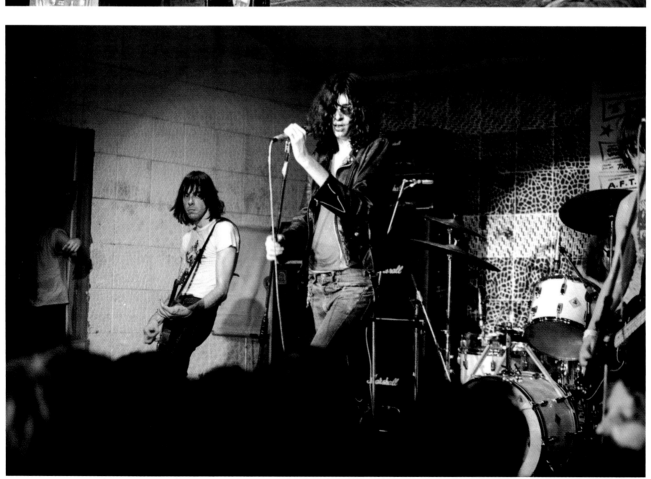

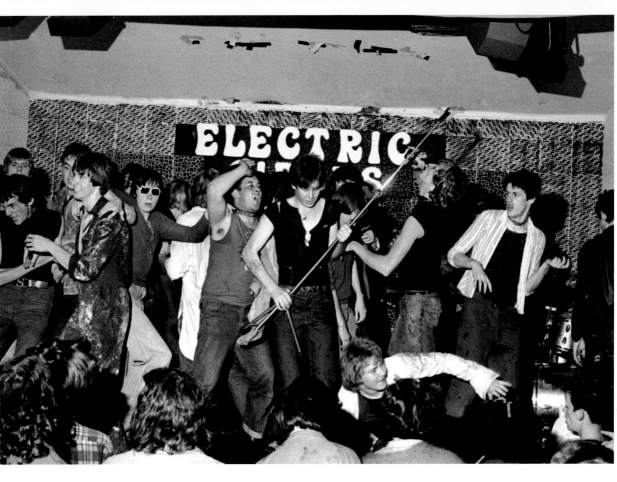

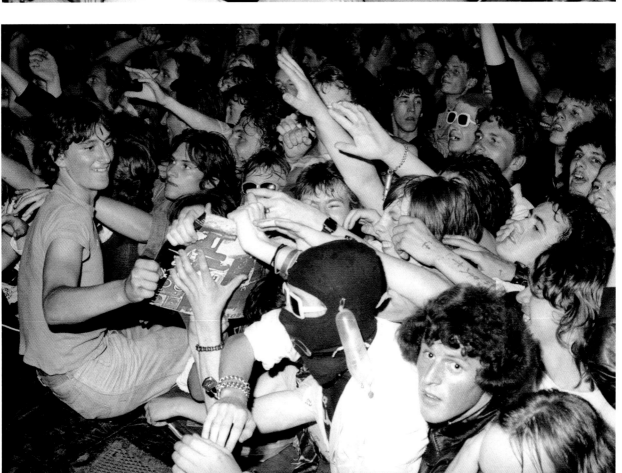

Live at the Roxy gig
Elizabethan Hall, Belle Vue, Manchester
9 July 1977

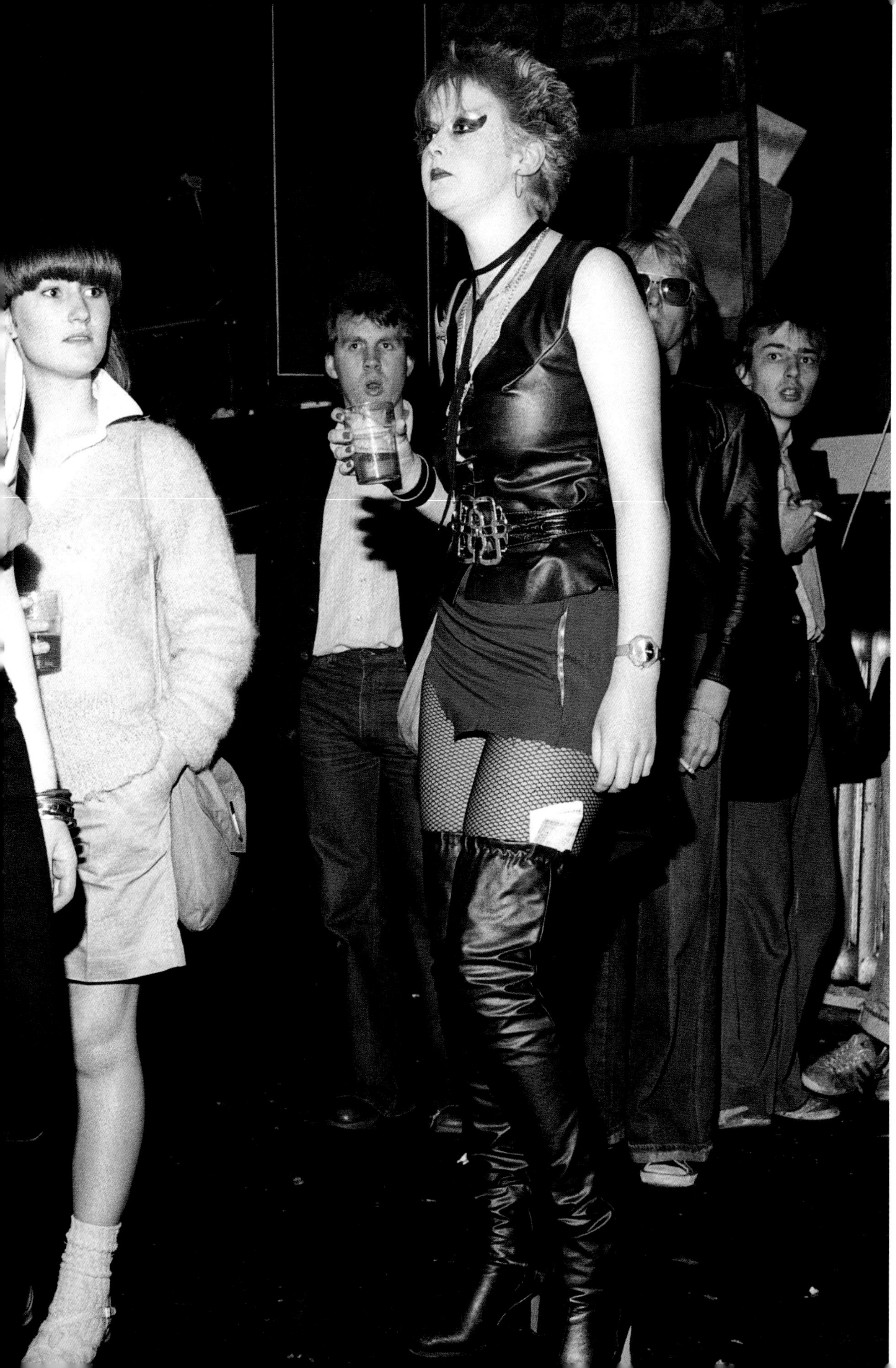

Denise
Electric Circus, Collyhurst, Manchester
June 1977

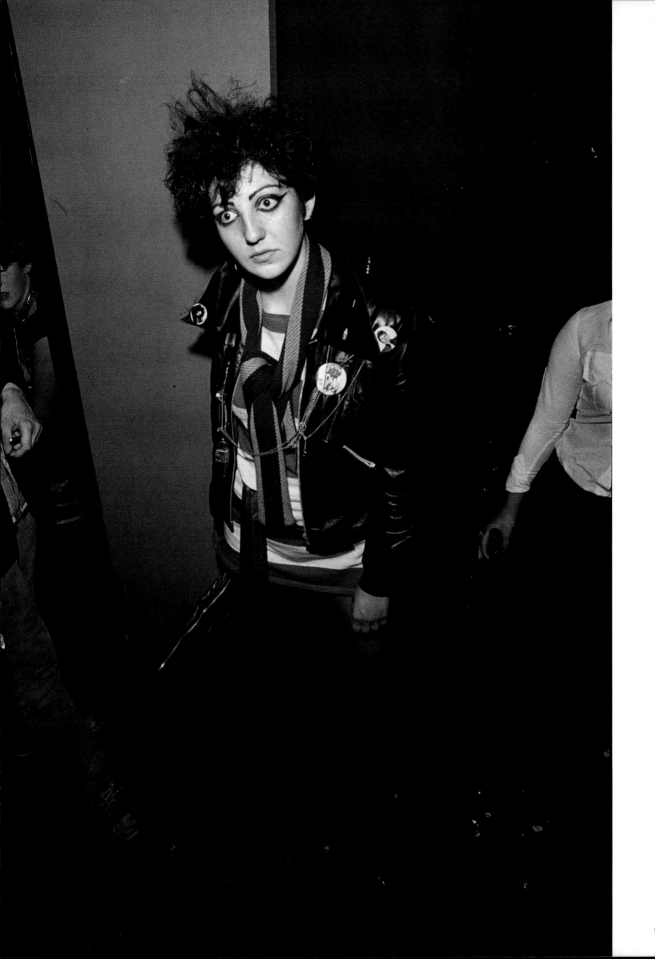

Manchester . . . the only place in England which escapes our characteristic vice of snobbery.

A. J. P. Taylor

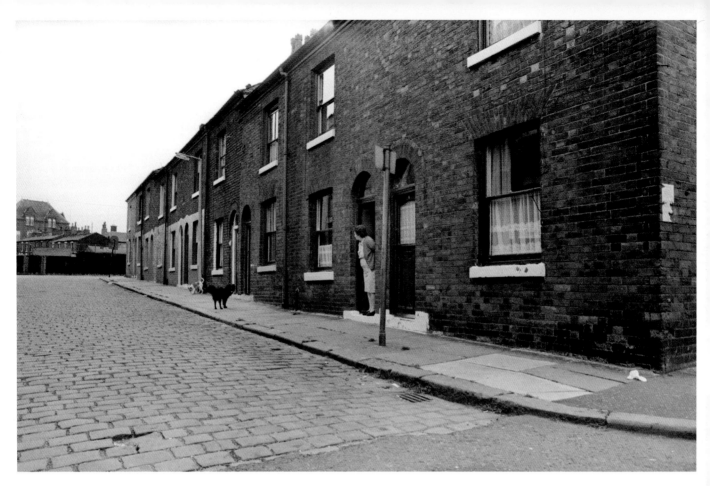

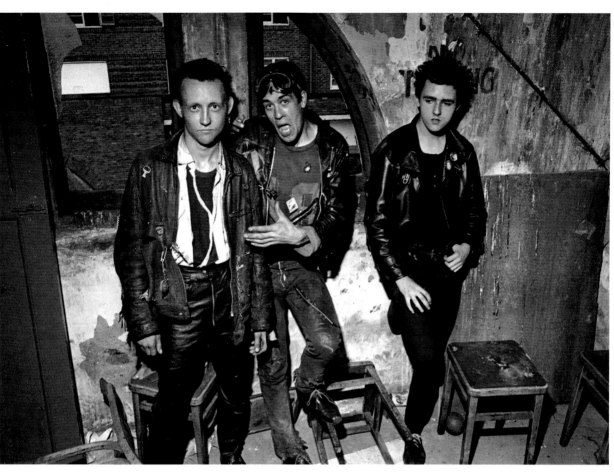

The Worst
Electric Circus, Collyhurst, Manchester
17 July 1977

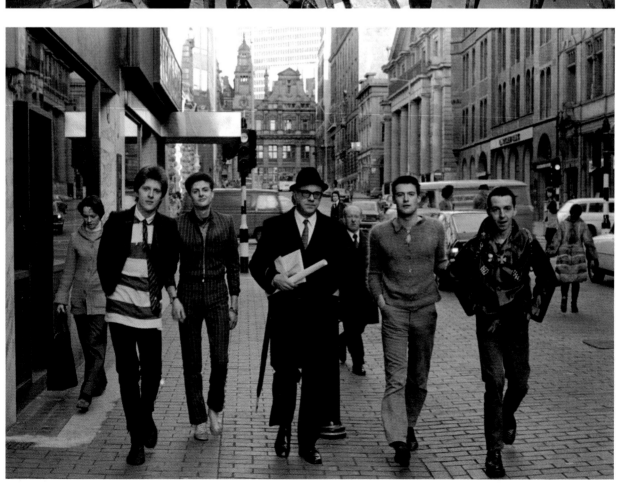

The Drones
King Street, Manchester
March 1977

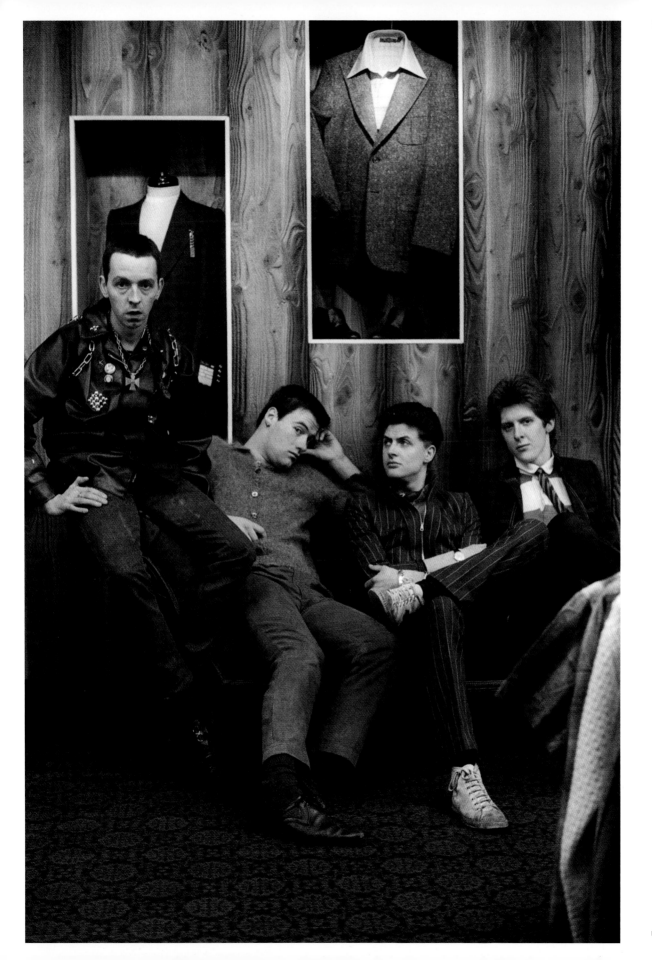

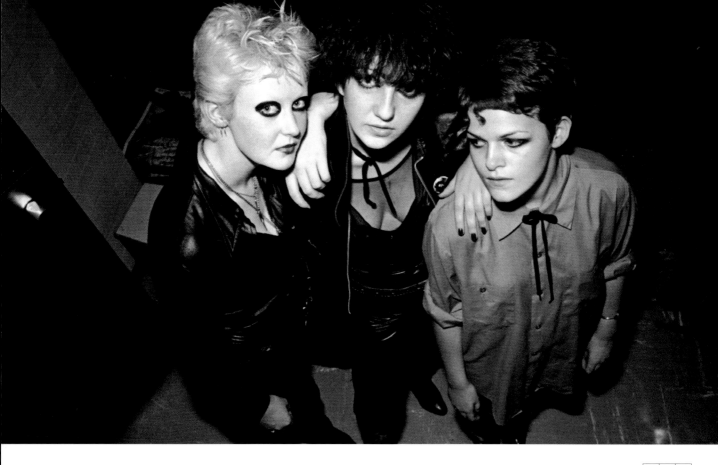

Denise, Joan, Jody
Middleton
26 August 1977

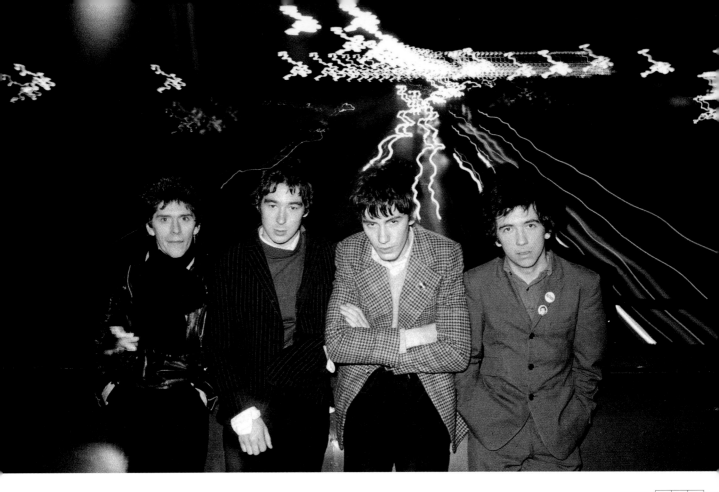

Buzzcocks
Toddington service station bridge, M1
23 November 1977

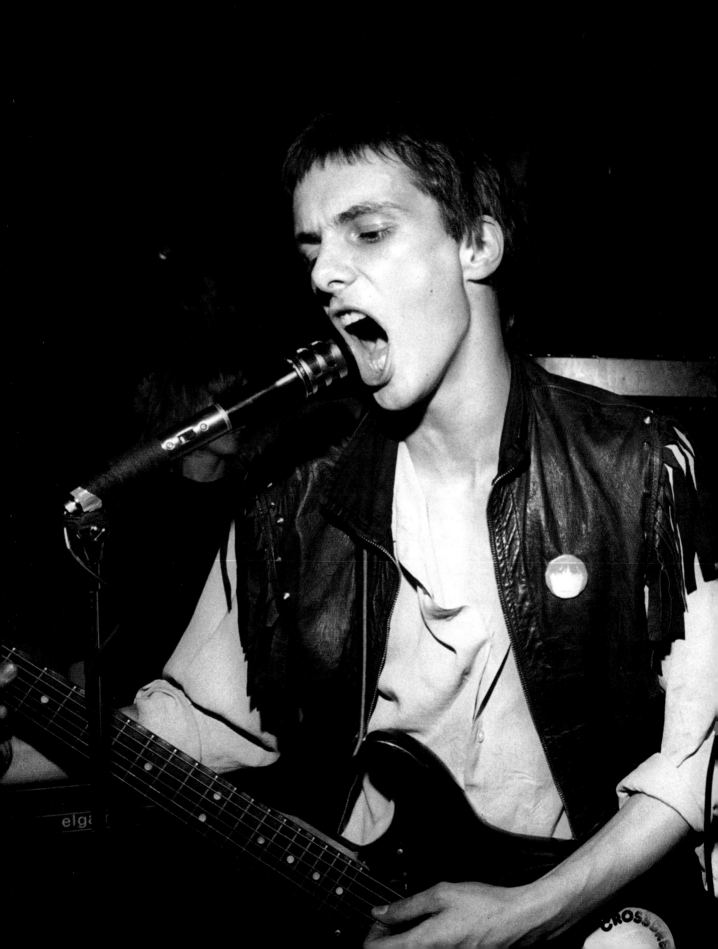

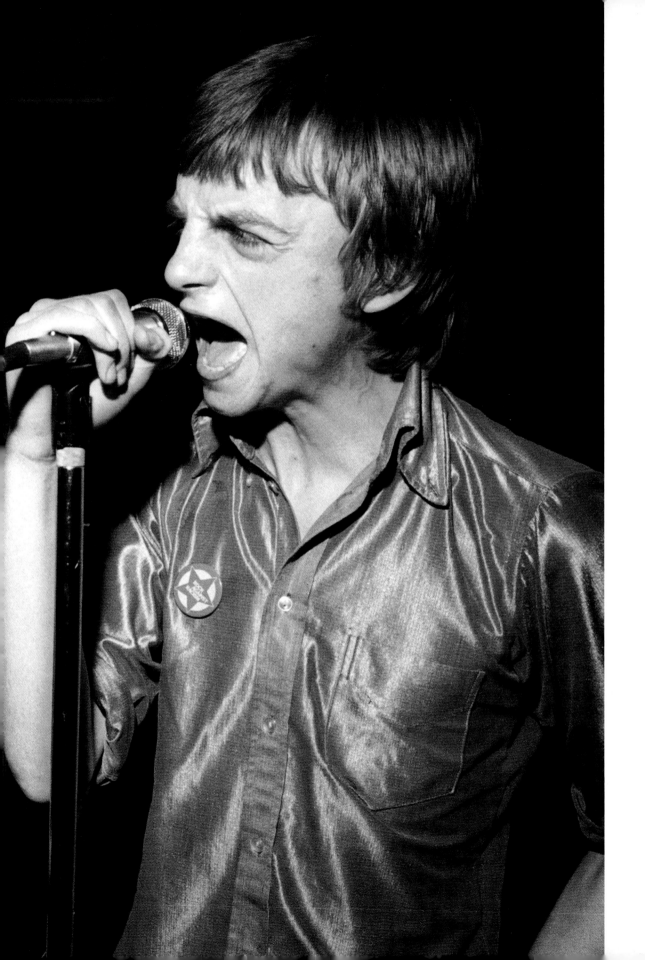

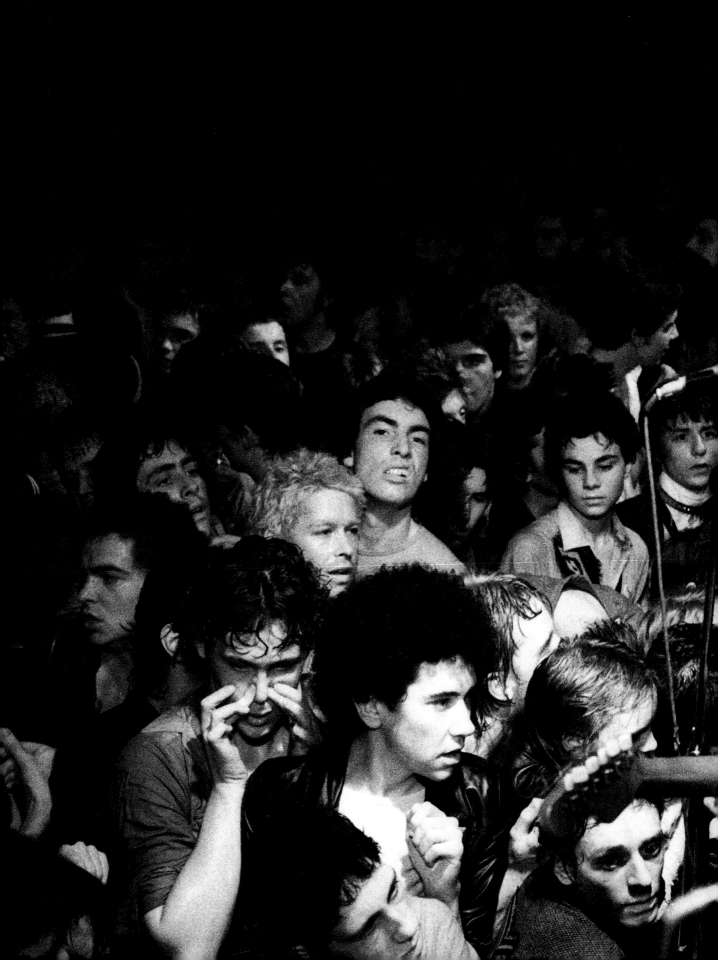

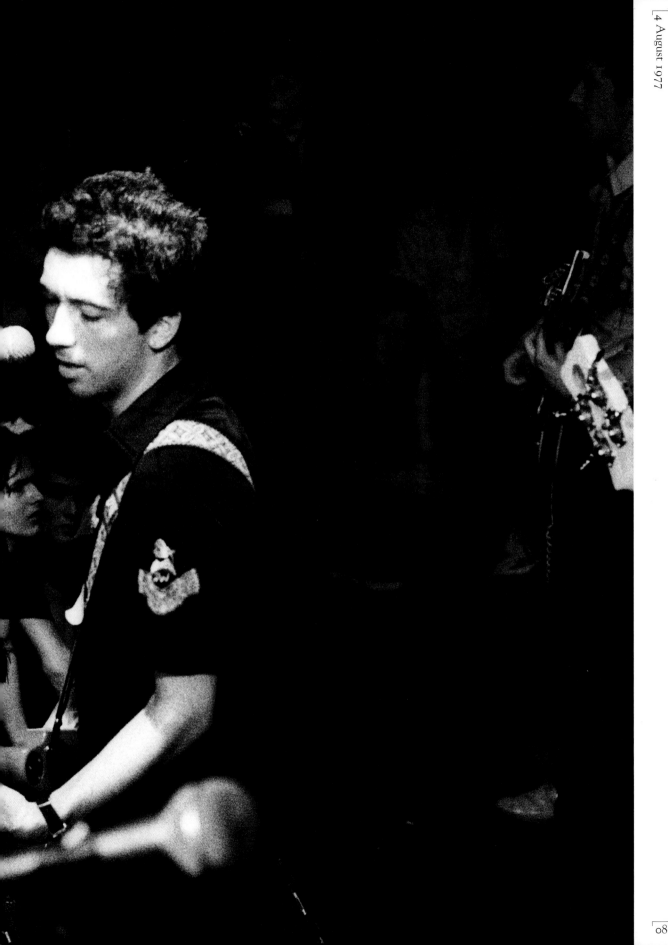

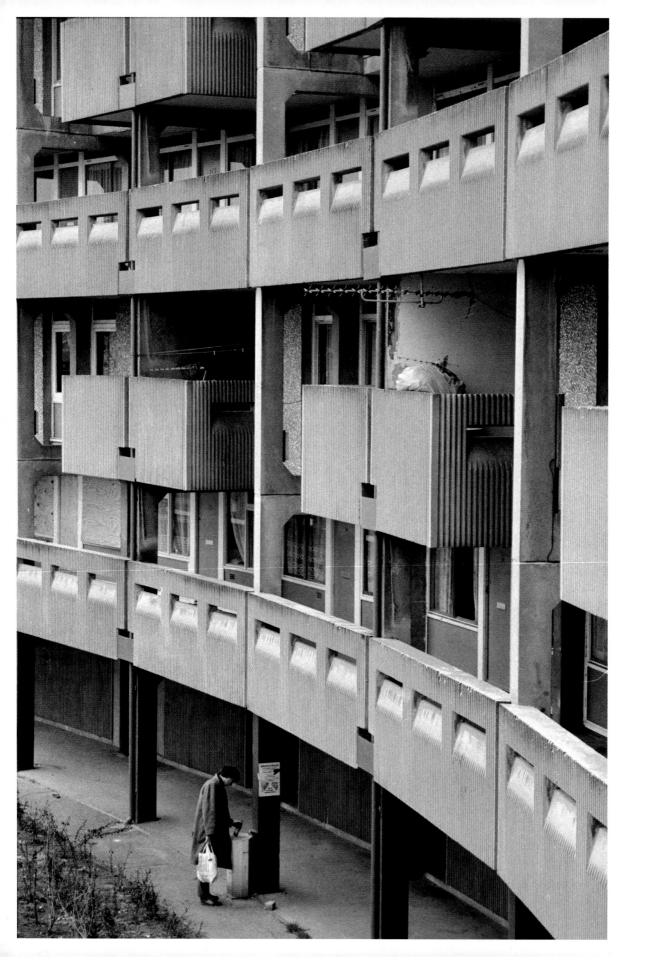

The Age of Ruins is past. Have you seen Manchester? Manchester is as great a human exploit as Athens.

Benjamin Disraeli

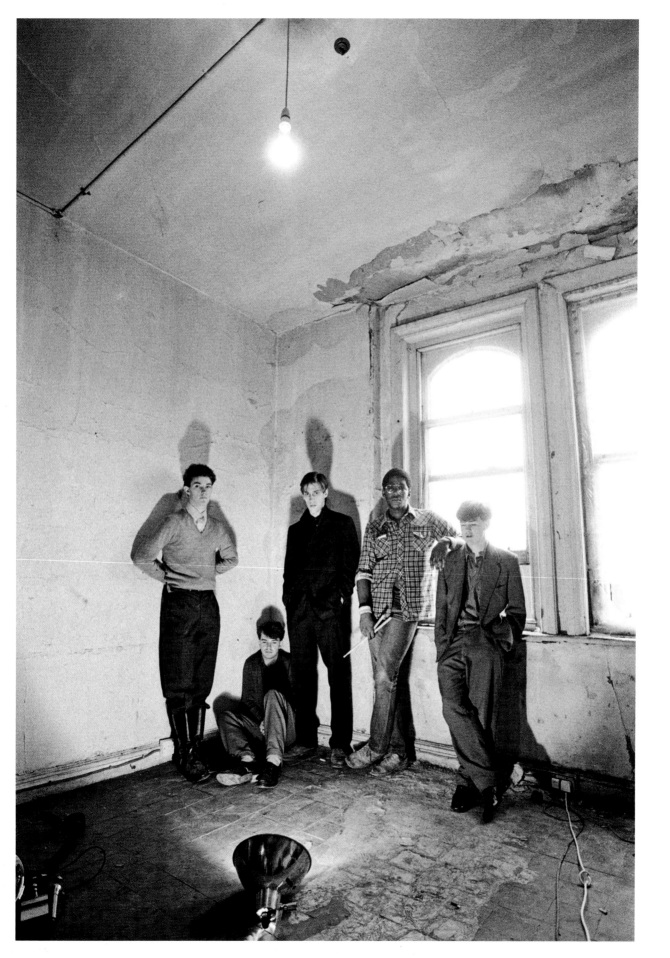

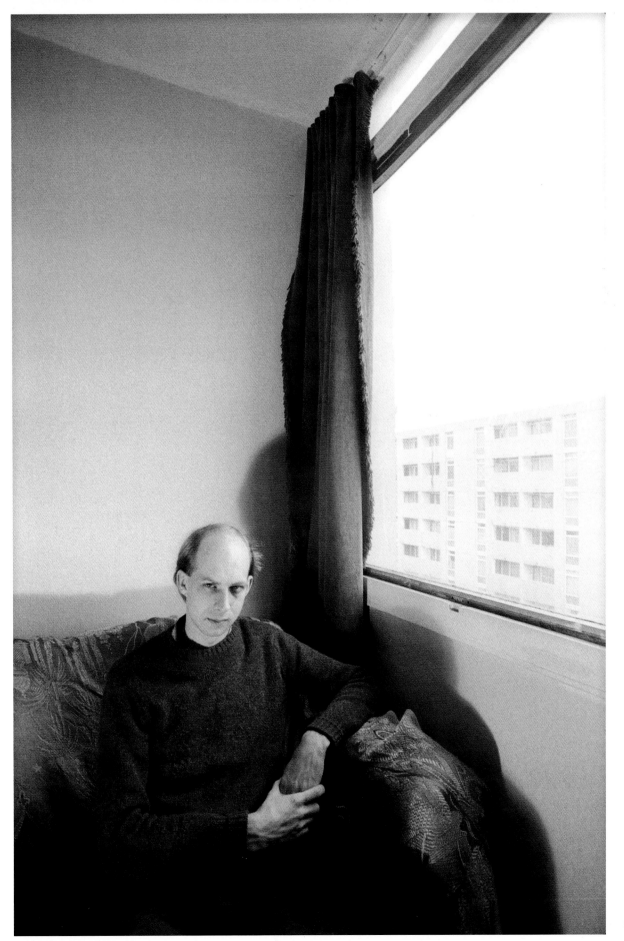

Steve Solomar, DJ, Electric Circus / singer, Spherical Objects
Hulme, Manchester
2 December 1979

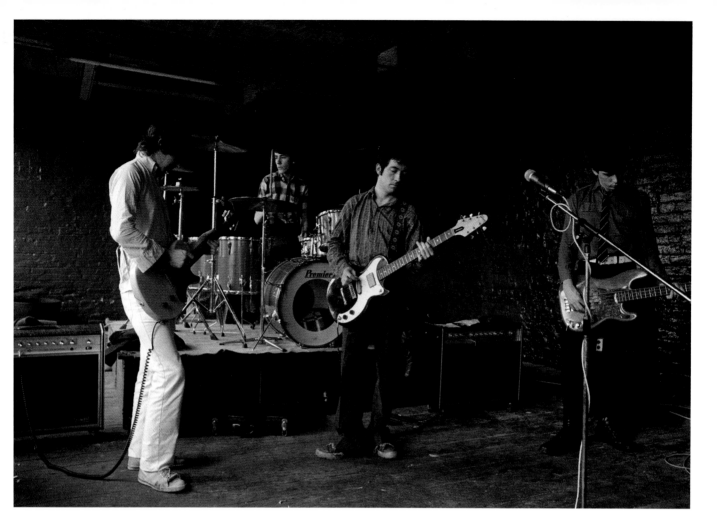

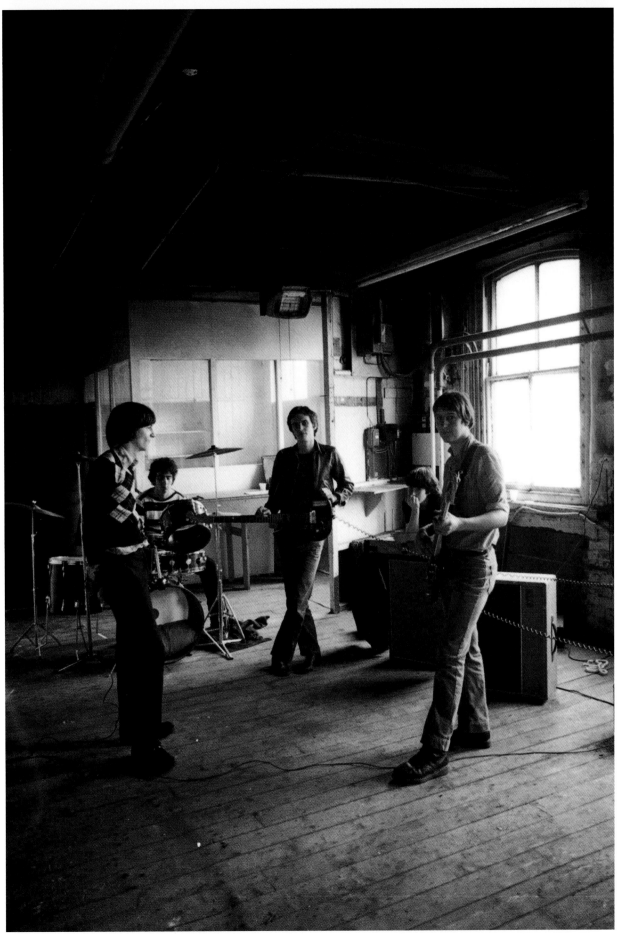

But the most
horrible spot . . .
lies . . . immediately
south west of
Oxford Road and
is known as Little
Ireland. The race
that lives in these
ruinous cottages,
behind broken
windows, mended

with oilskin, sprung doors, and rotten door-posts, or in dark, wet cellars, in measureless filth and stench ... must surely have reached the lowest stage of humanity.

Friedrich Engels

Ian Curtis, Joy Division
Art and Furniture, Chapel Walks, Manchester
6 January 1979

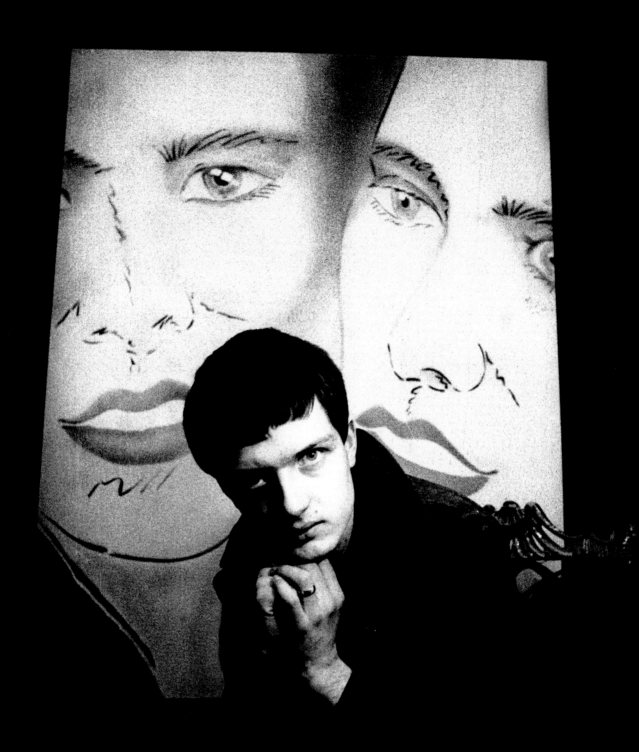

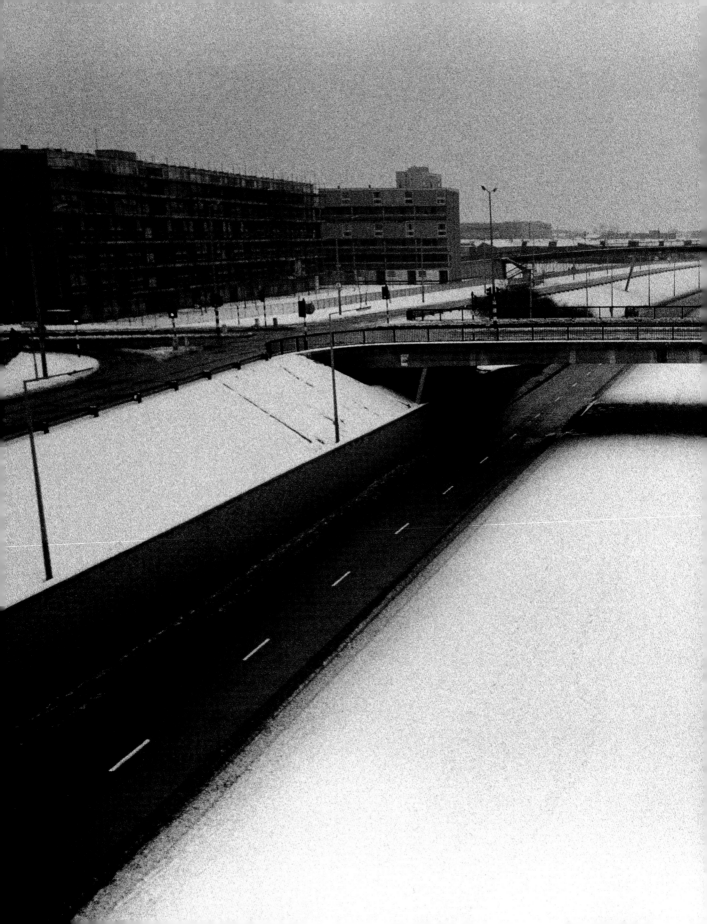

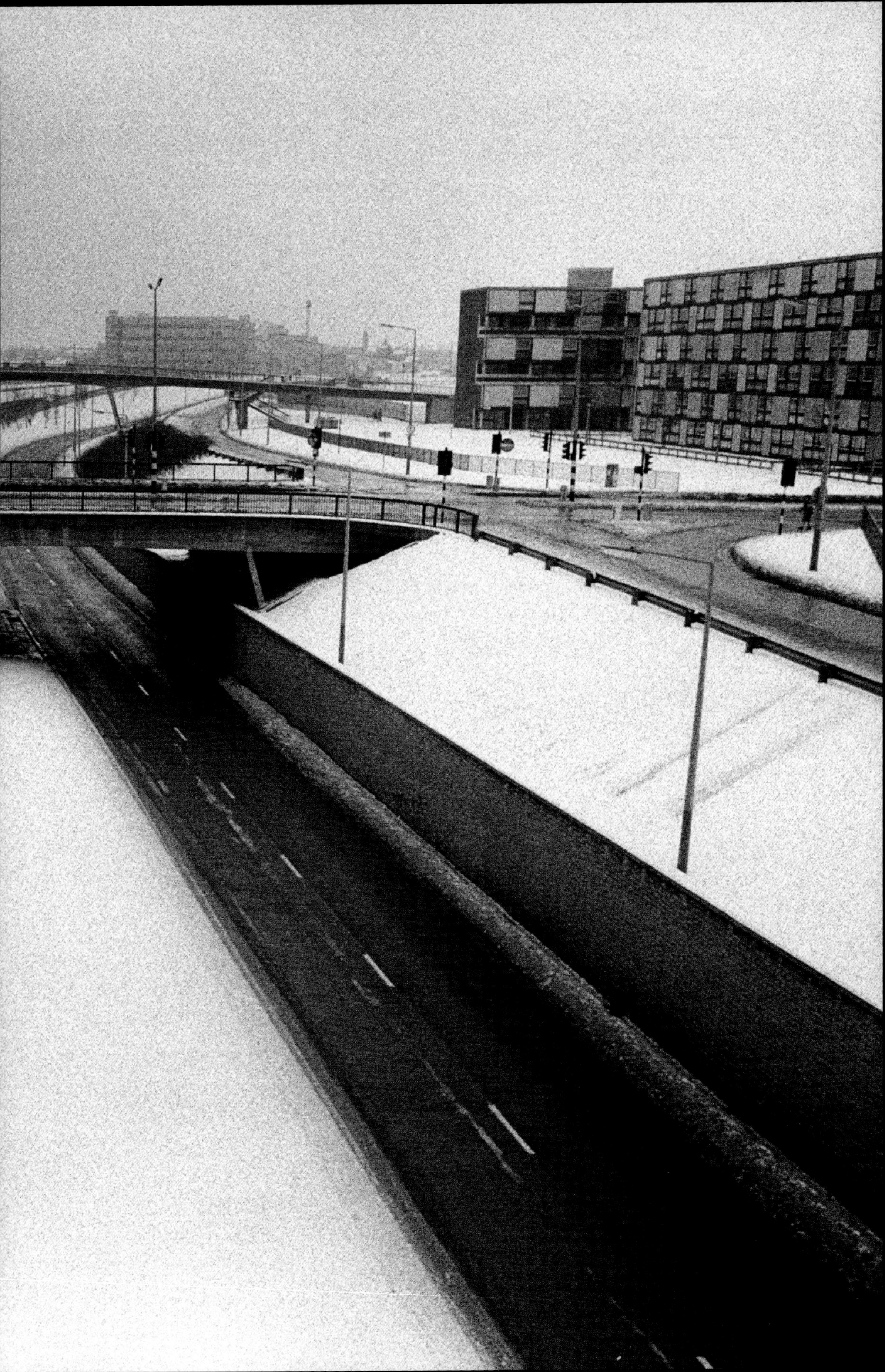

Princess Parkway
Hulme, Manchester
6 January 1979

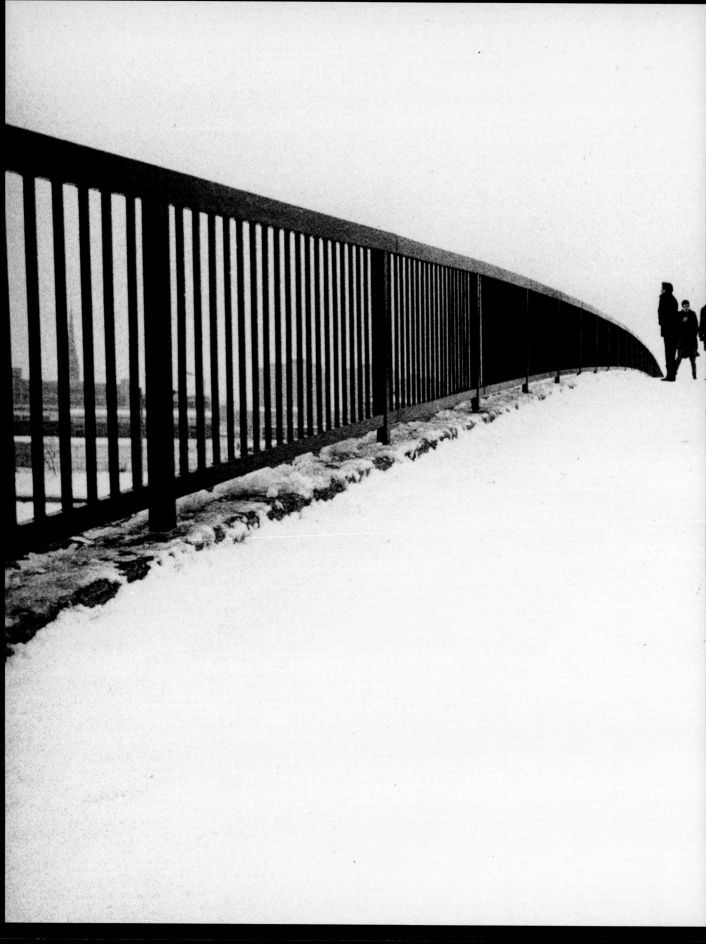

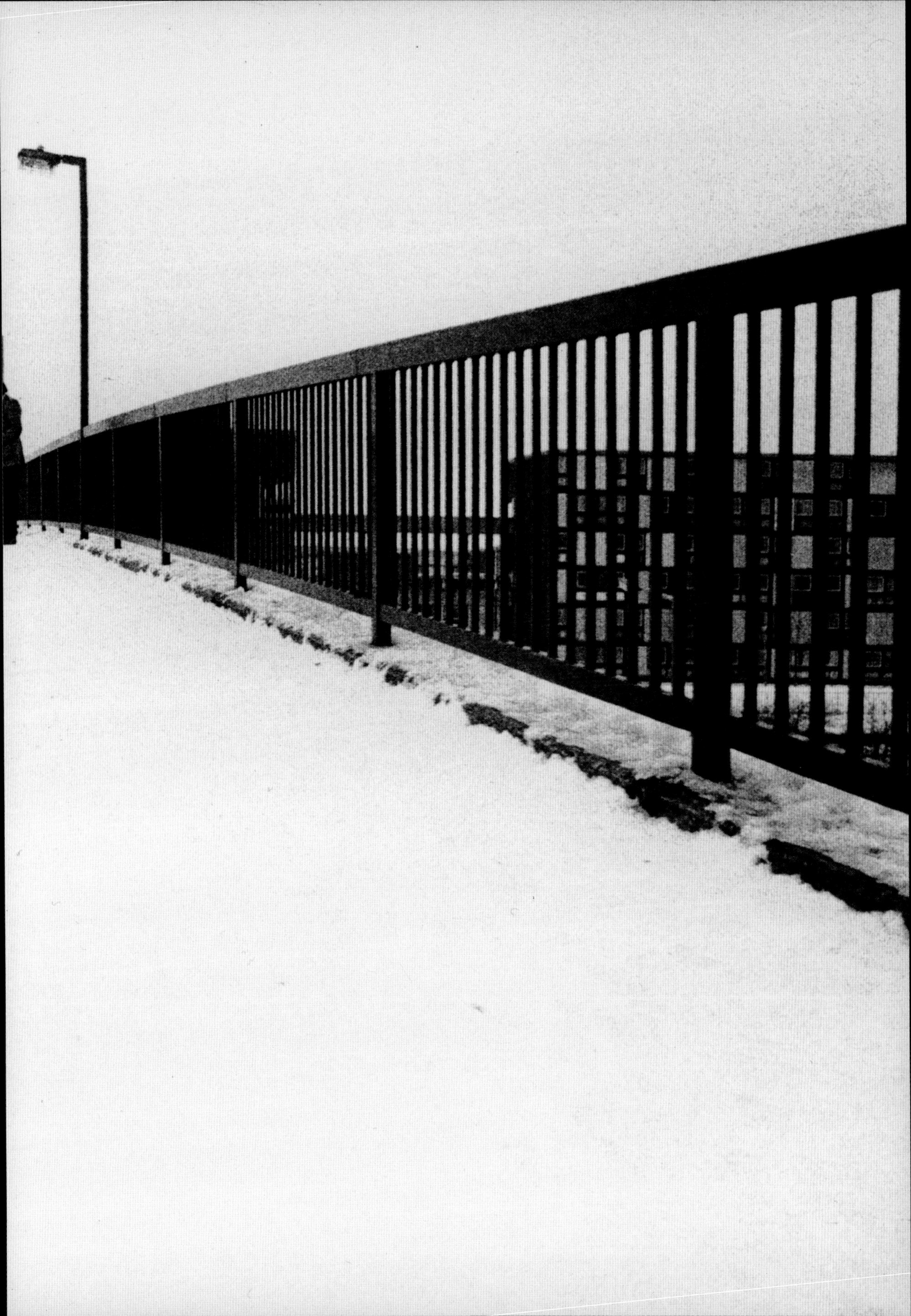

Joy Division
Princess Parkway, Hulme, Manchester
6 January 1979

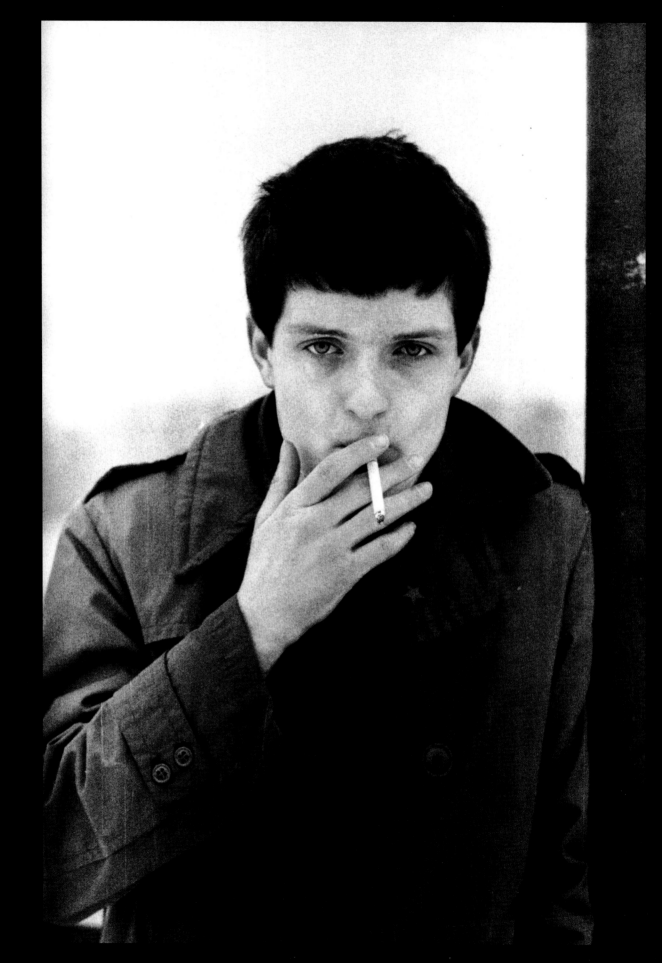

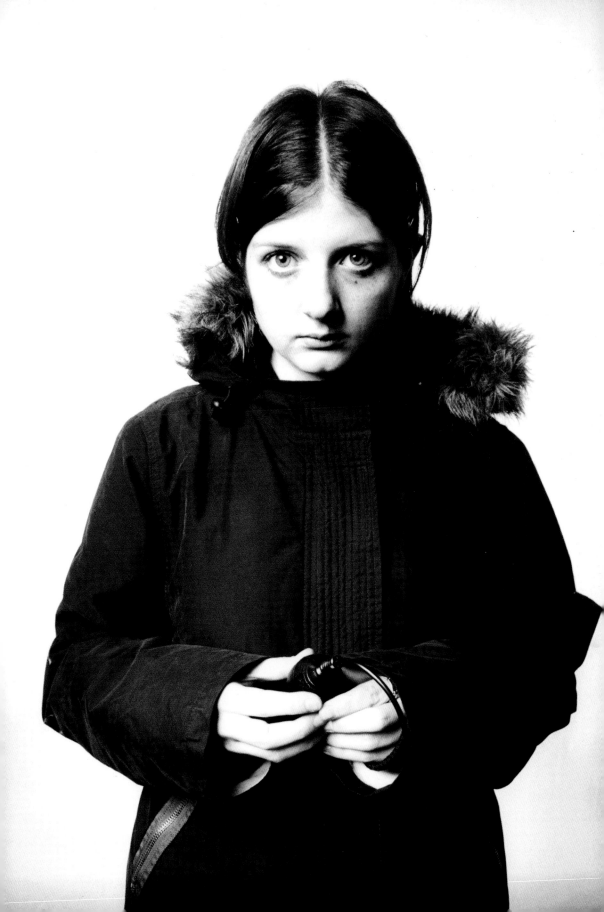

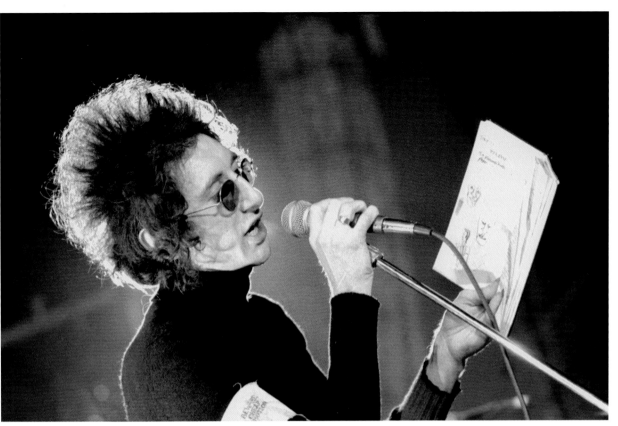

John Cooper Clarke
Elizabethan Hall, Belle Vue, Manchester
14 November 1977

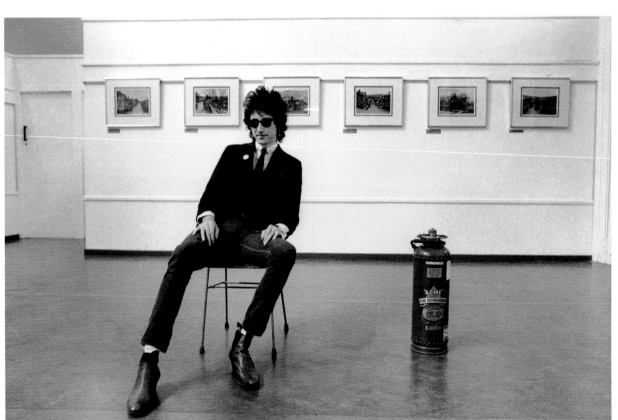

John Cooper Clarke
Salford City Art Gallery
August 1978

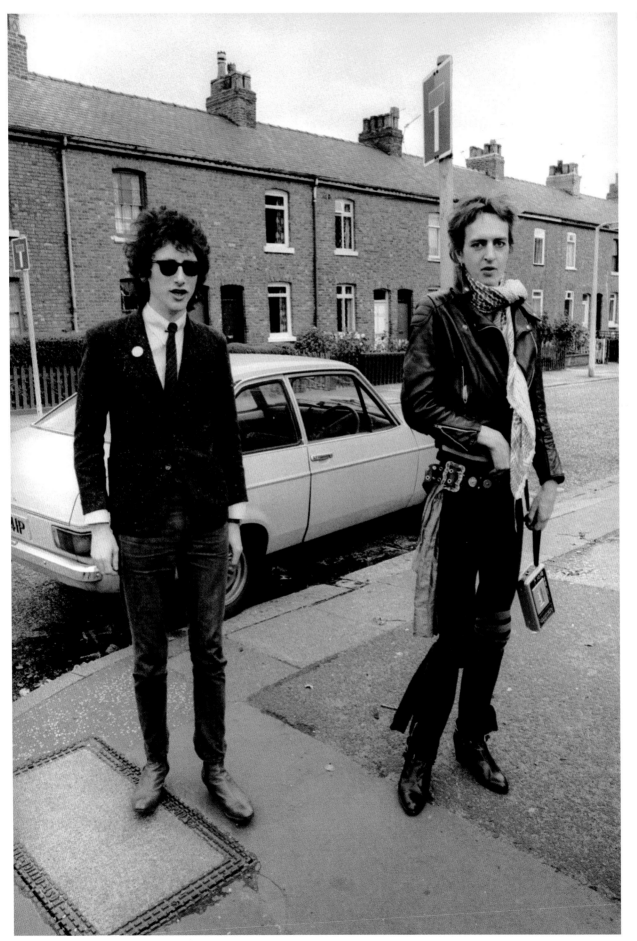

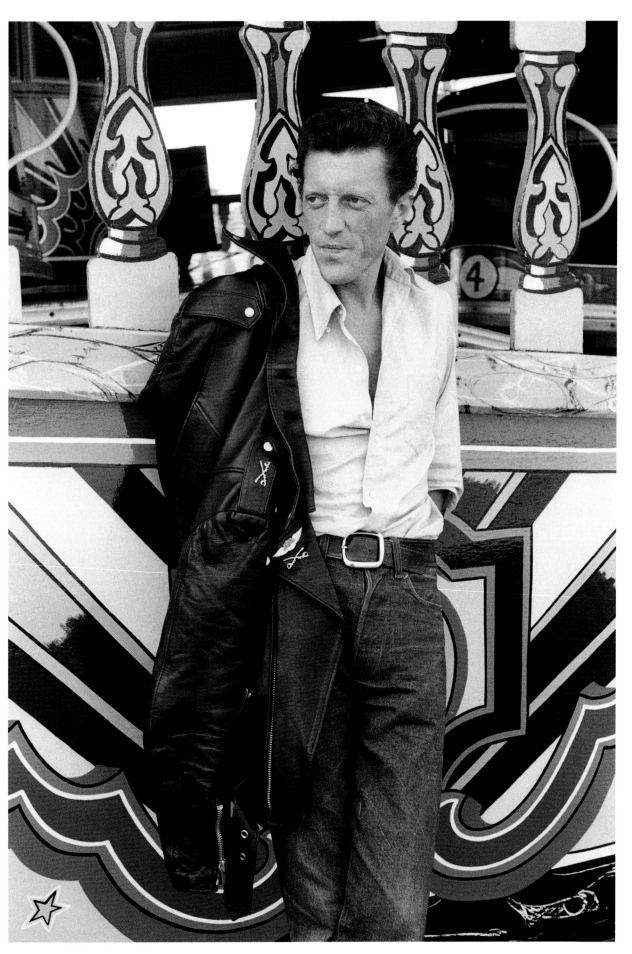

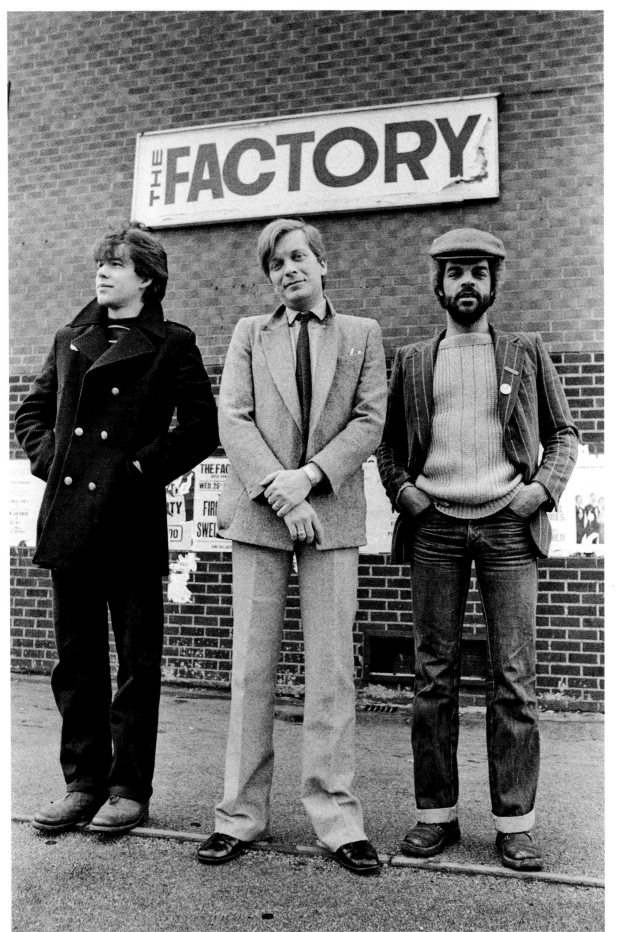

Peter Saville, Tony Wilson, Alan Erasmus
Outside The Factory / Russell Club, Hulme, Manchester
April 1979

(Next page)
The Factory / Russell Club, Hulme, Manchester
22 August, 1979

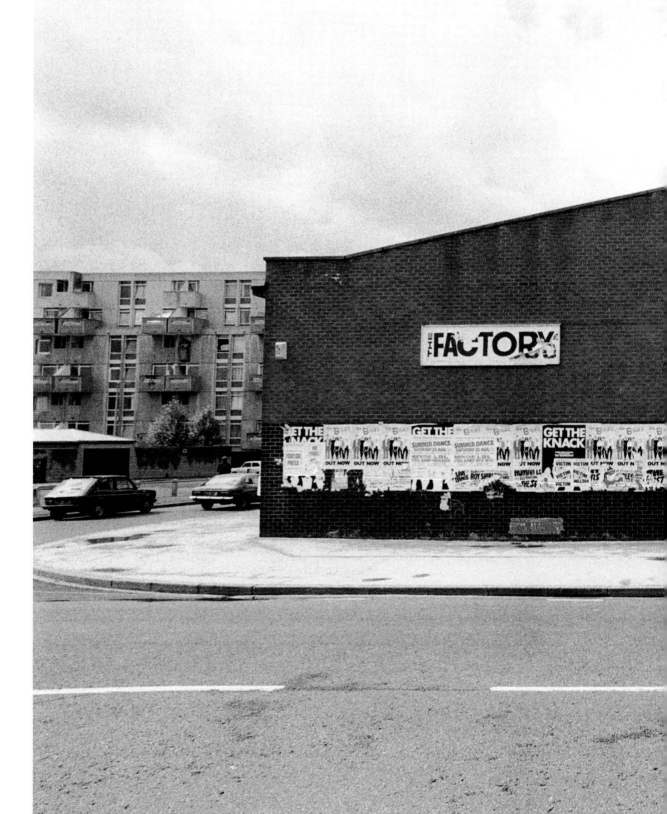

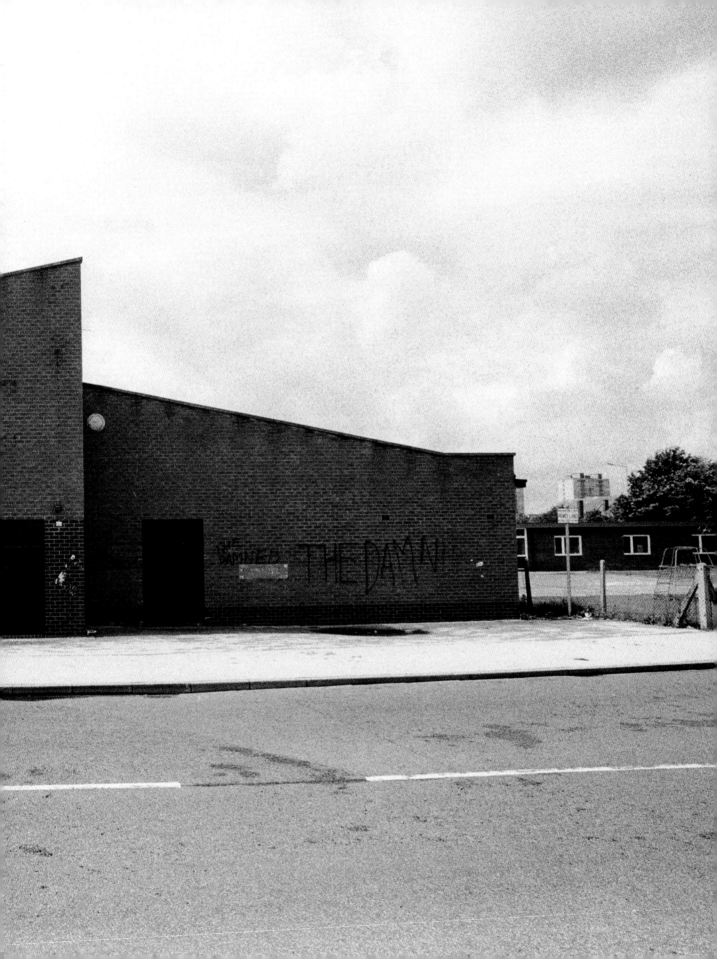

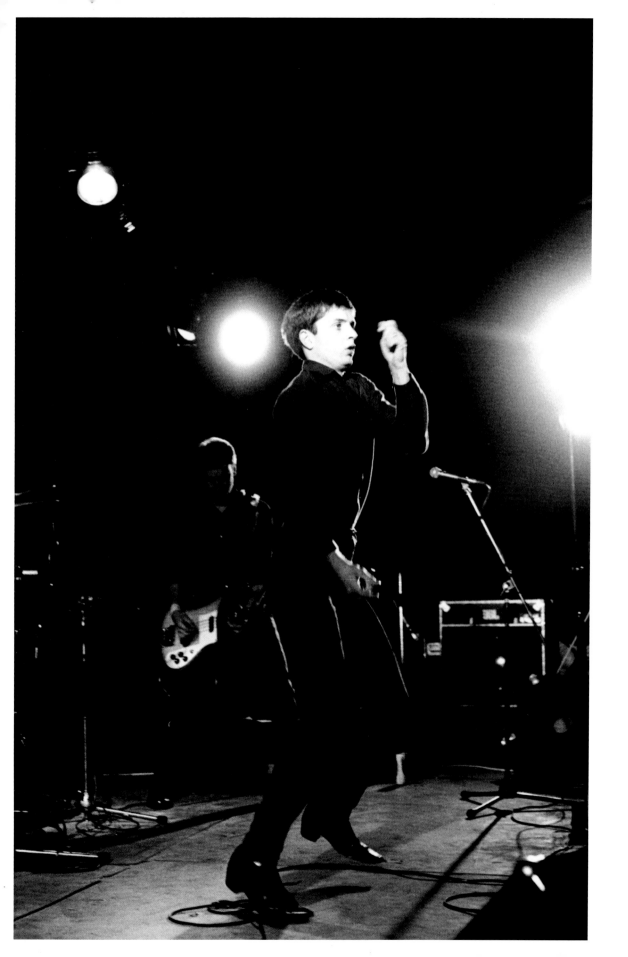

Ian Curtis and Peter Hook, Joy Division
Zoo Meets Factory Halfway, Leigh Open-Air Pop Festival
22 August 1979

Ian Curtis, Joy Division
Futurama, Queen's Hall, Leeds
8 September 1979

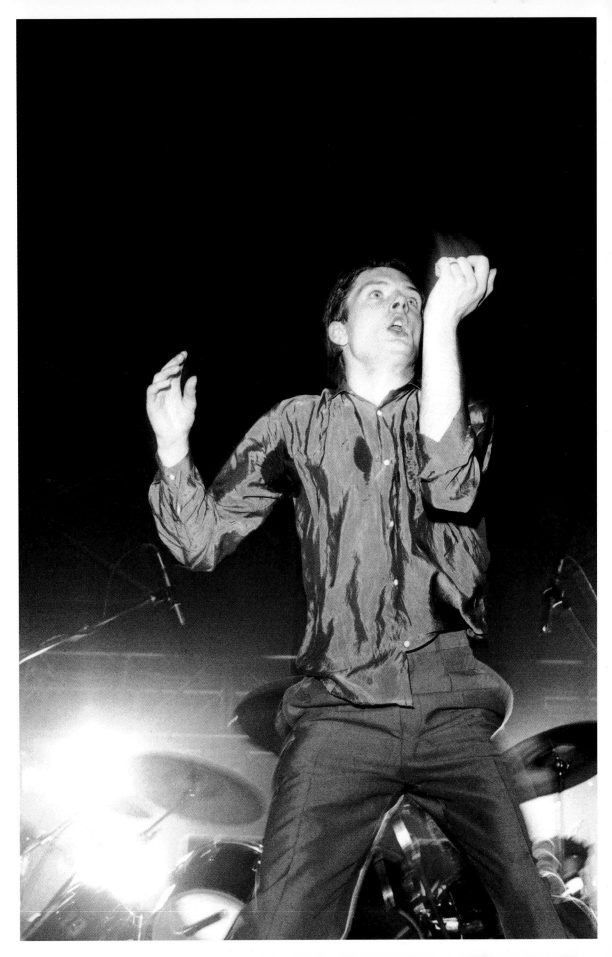

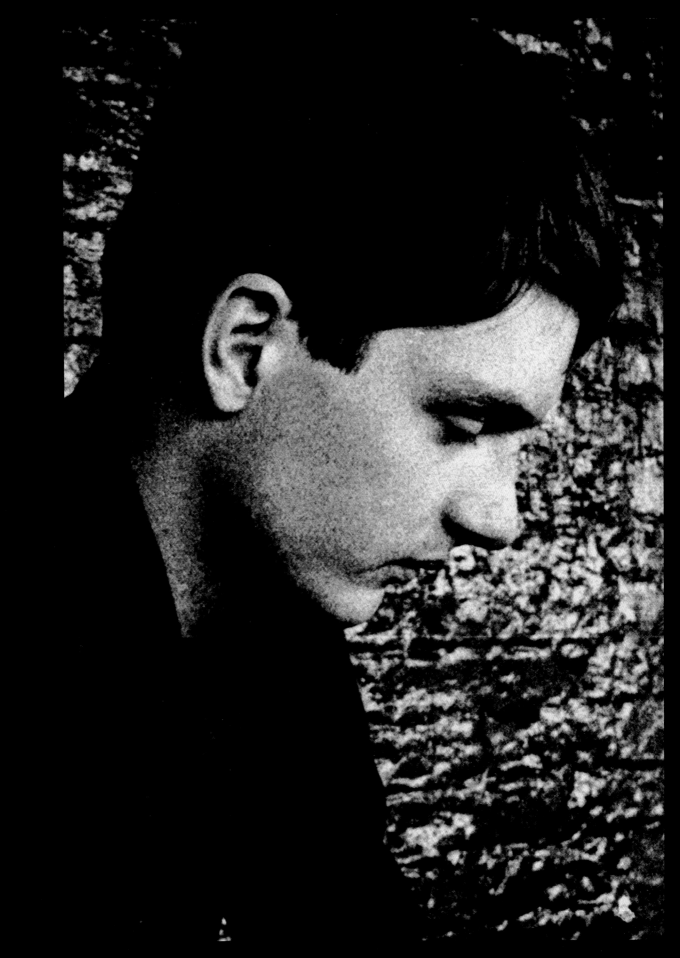

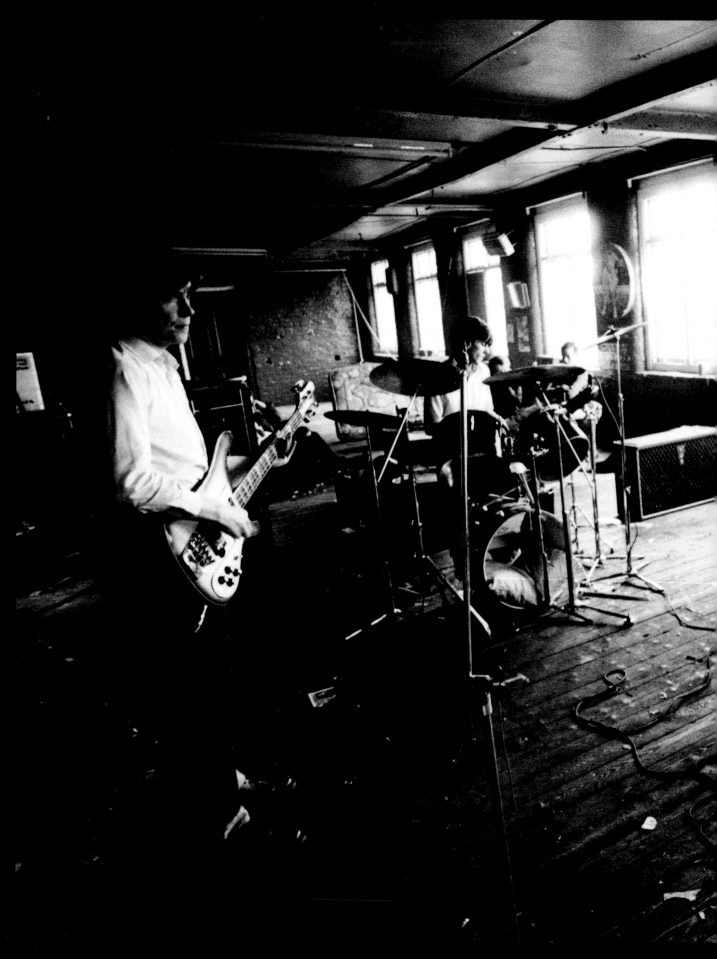

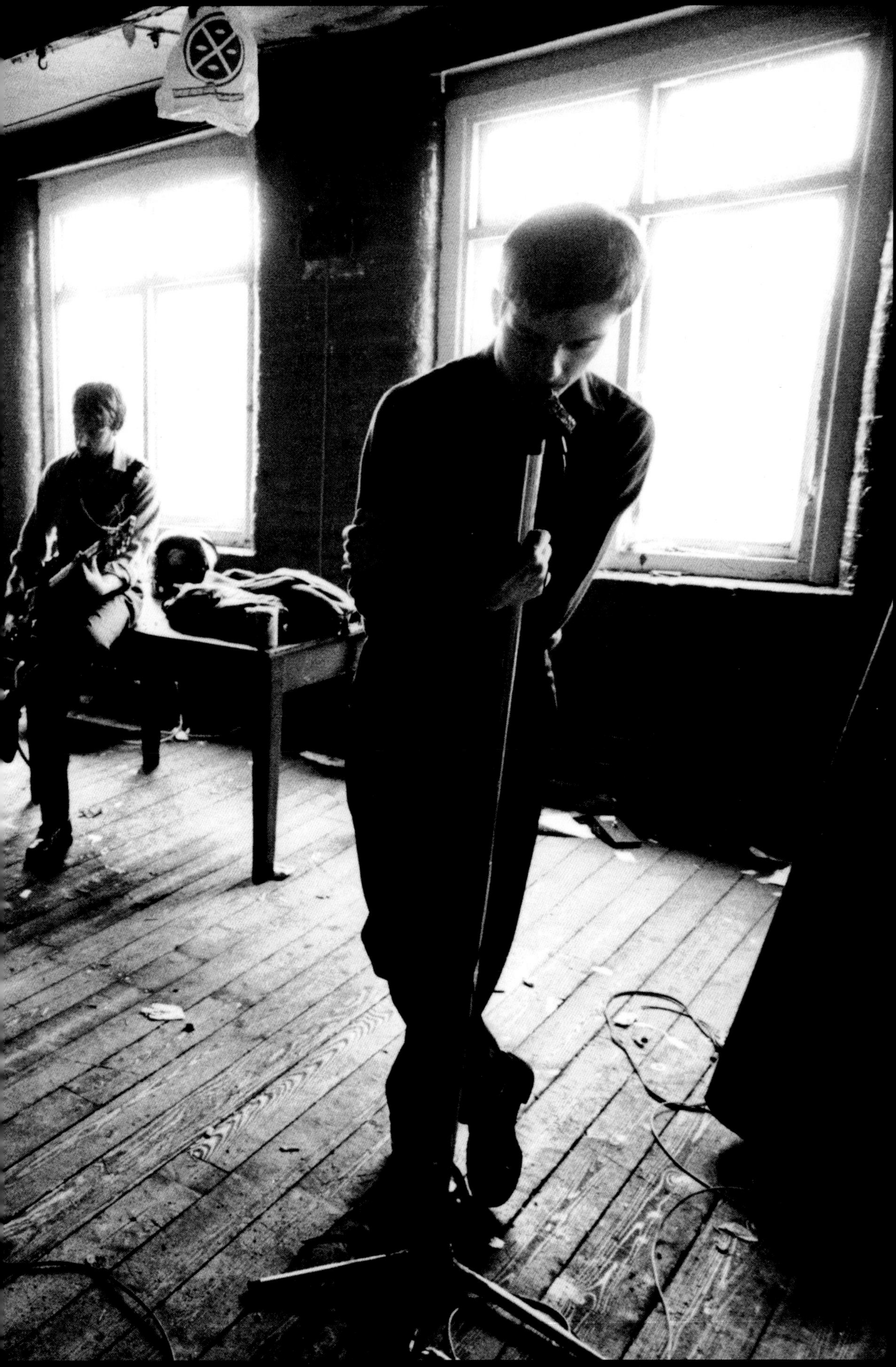

Joy Division
TJ Davidson's rehearsal rooms, Manchester
19 August 1979

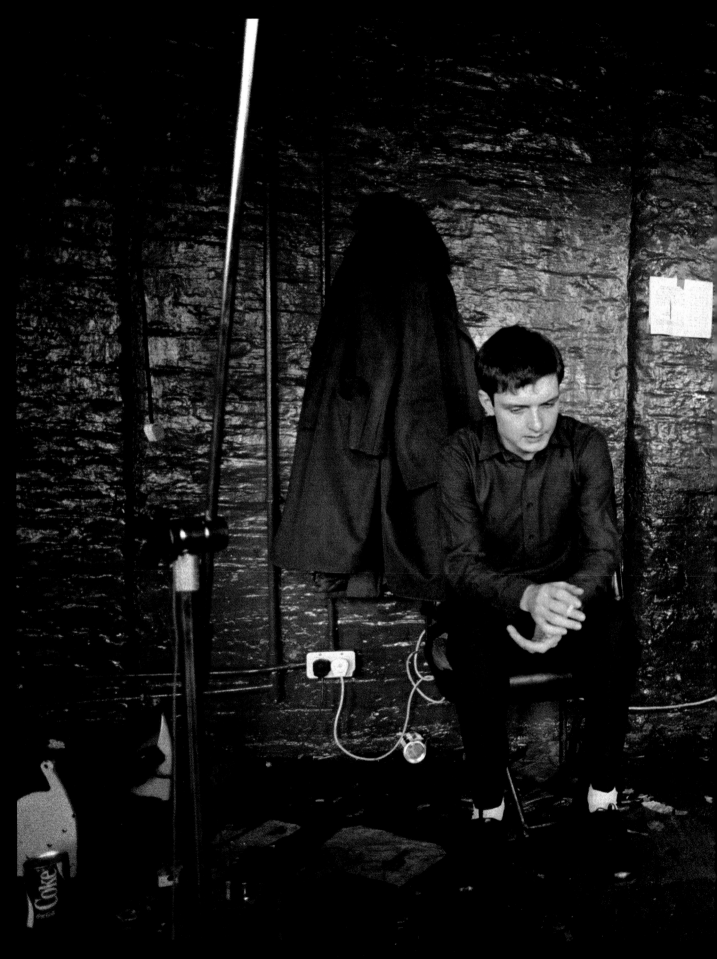

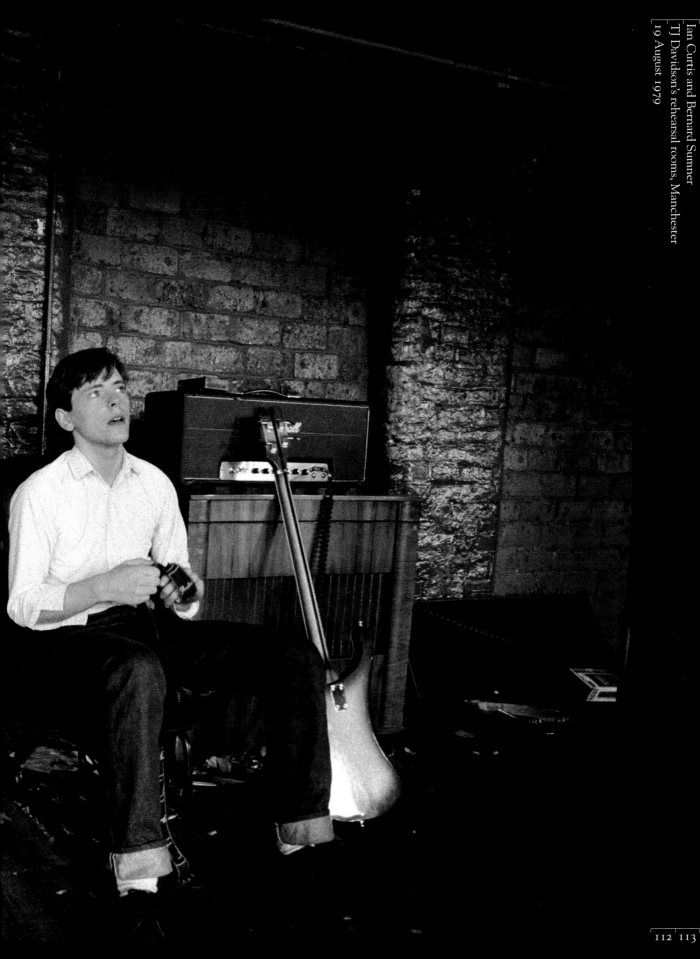

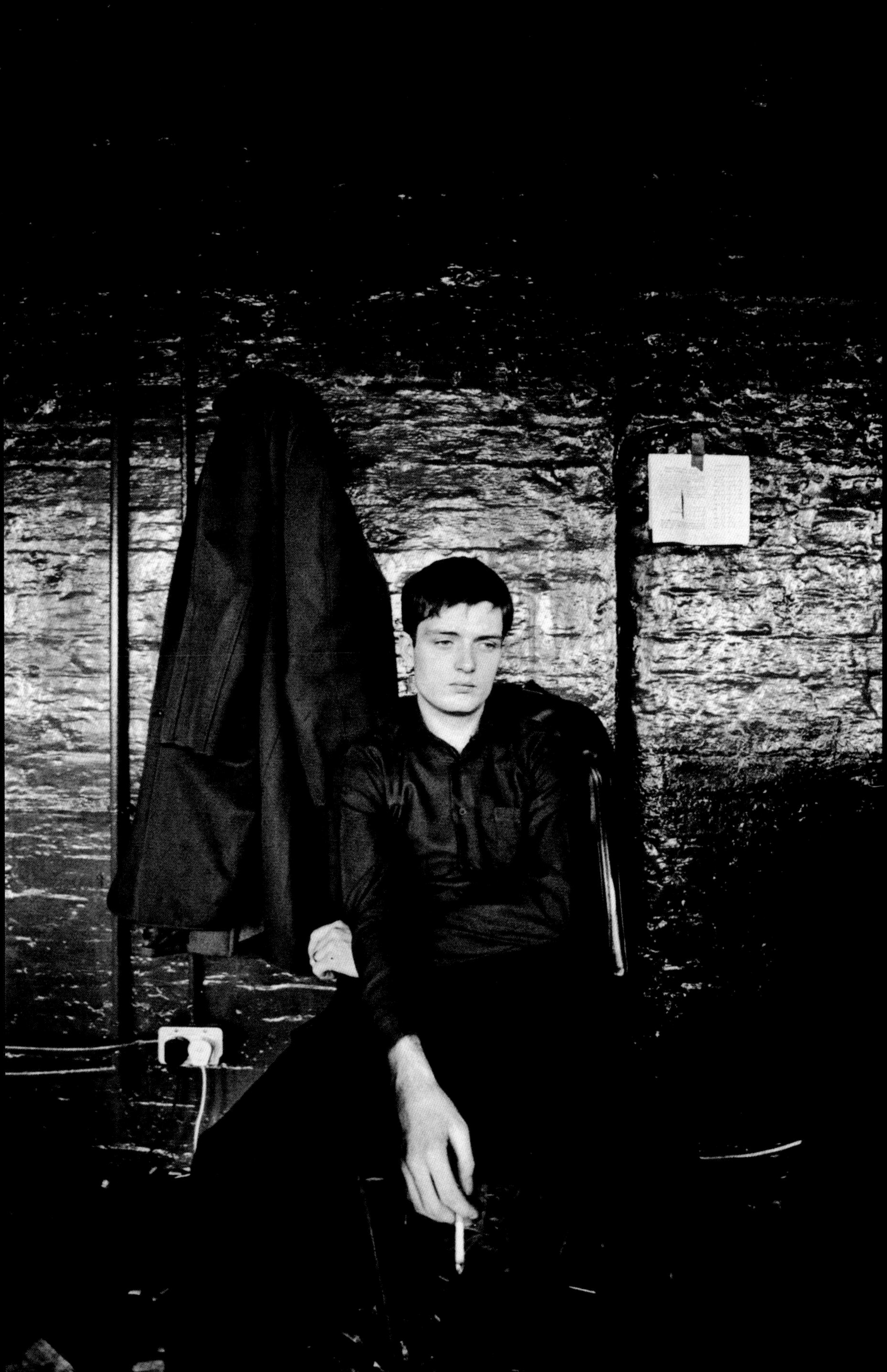

Ian Curtis
TJ Davidson's rehearsal rooms, Manchester
19 August 1979

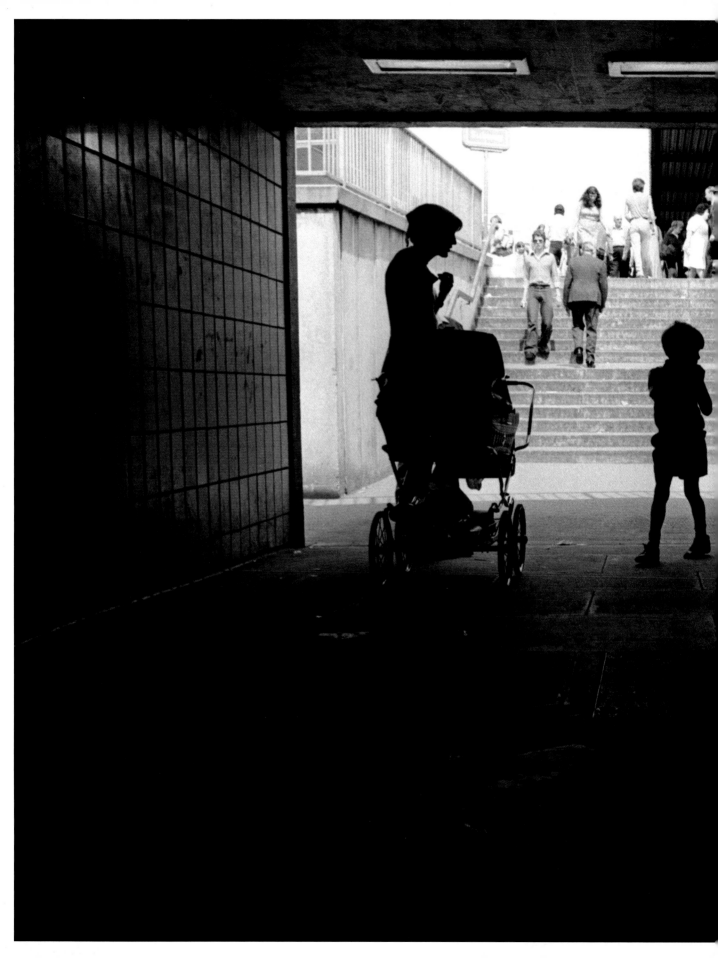

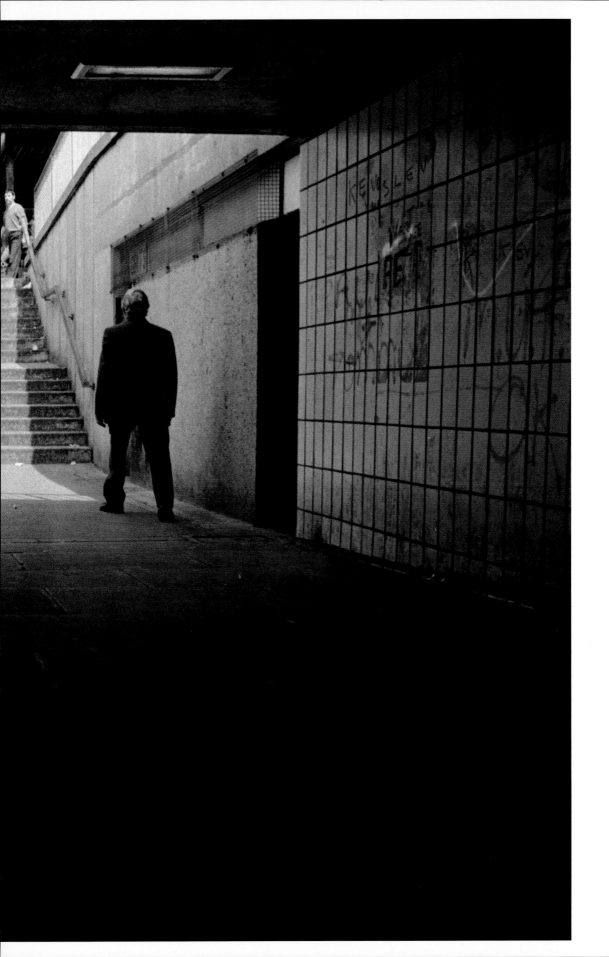

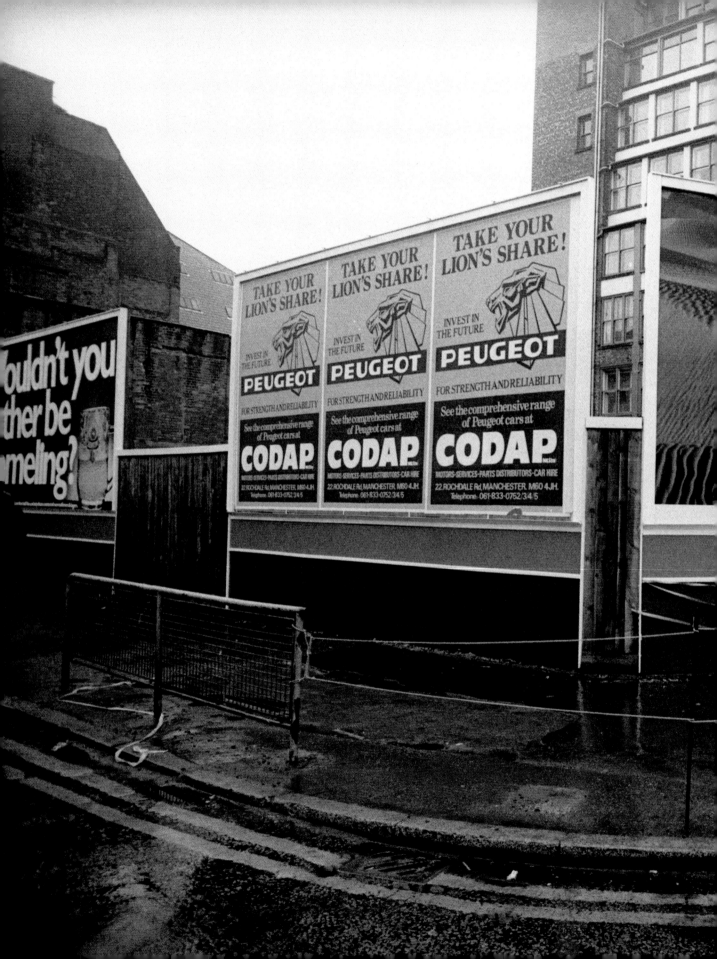

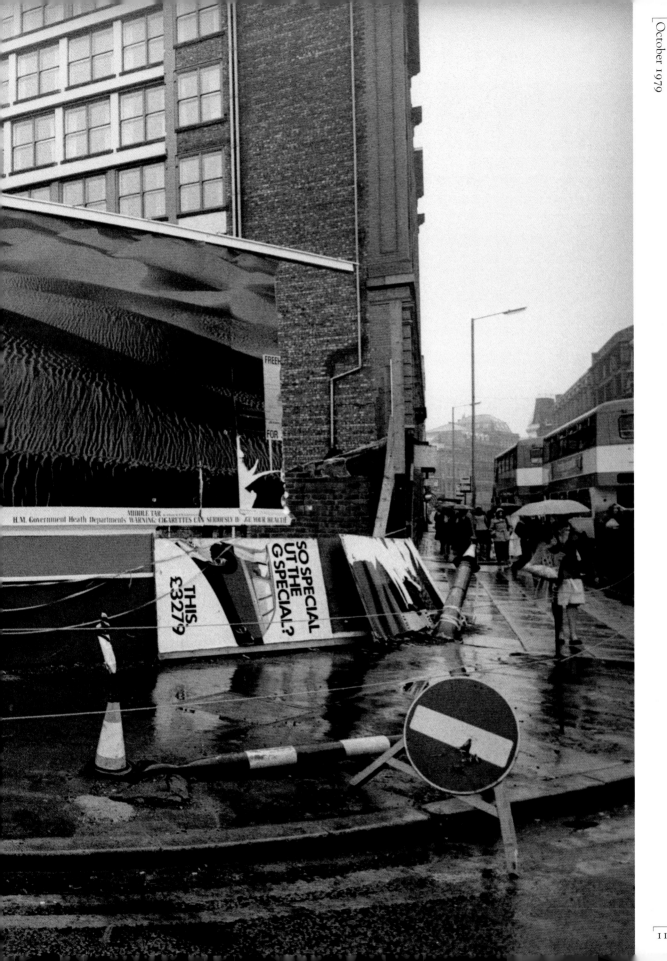

The Fall
Central Station car park, Windmill Street, Manchester
August 1978

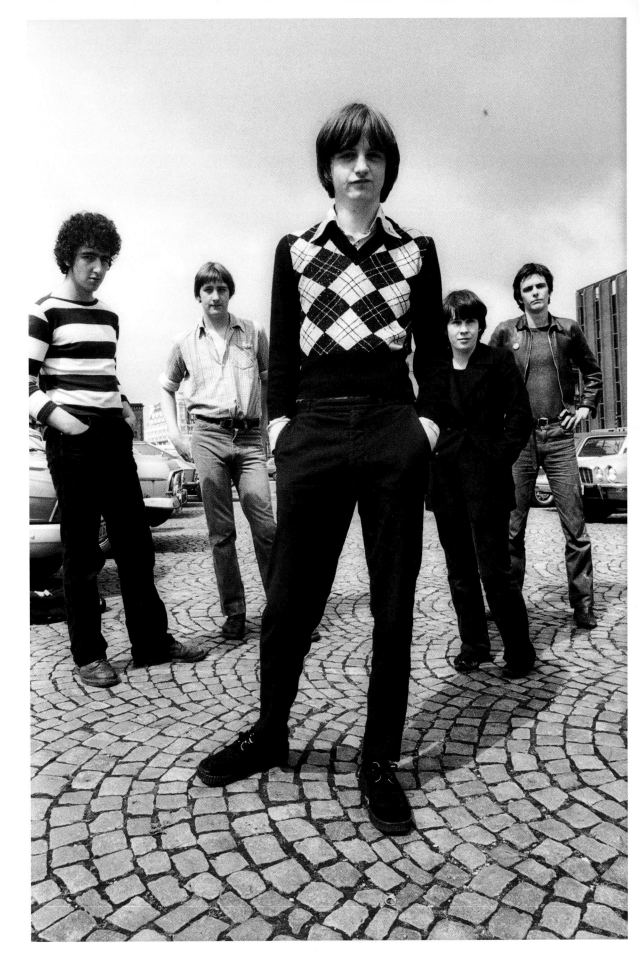

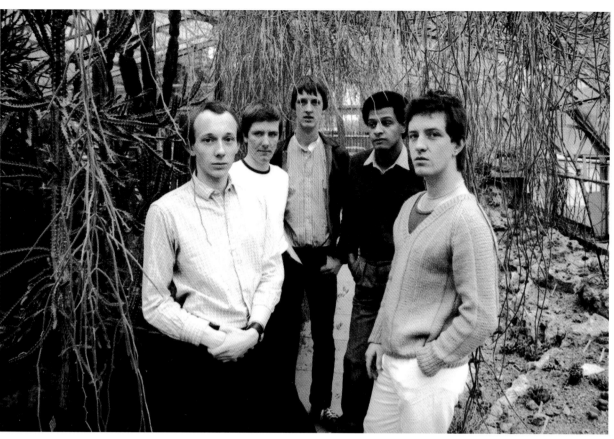

Magazine
Alexandra Park, Moss Side, Manchester
22 September 1977

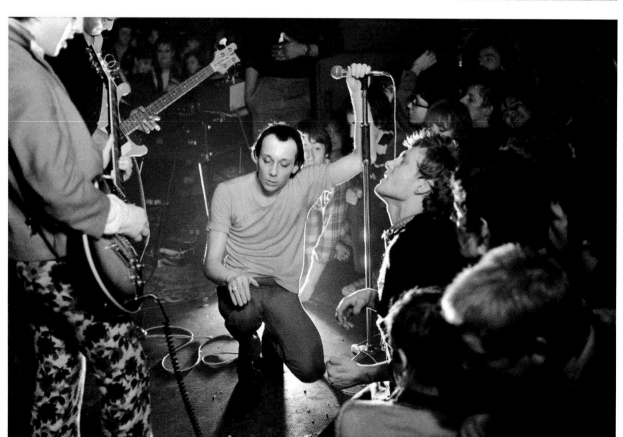

Magazine
Rafters, Manchester
26 January 1978

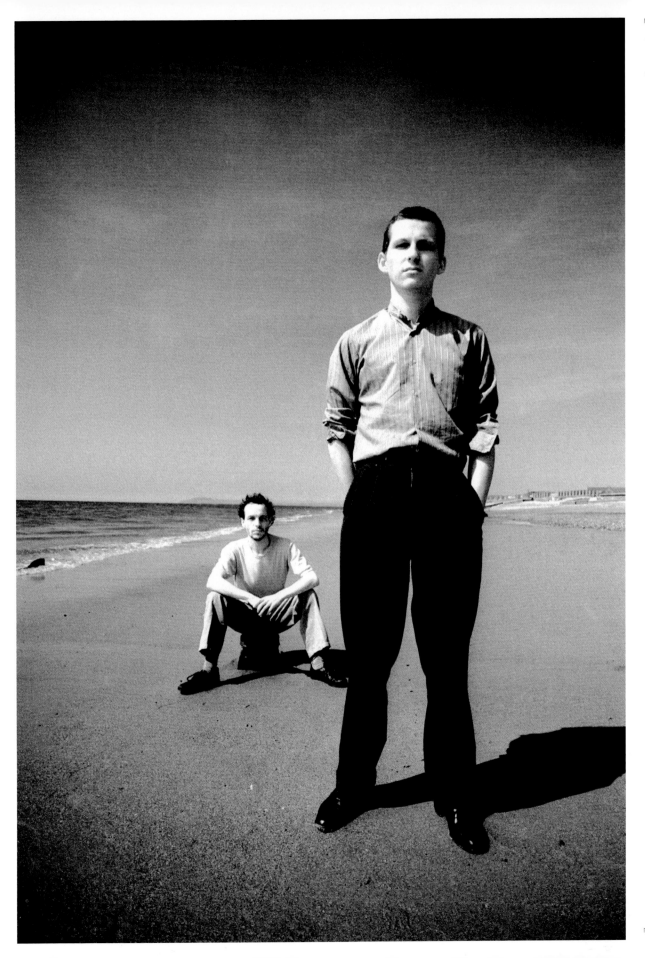

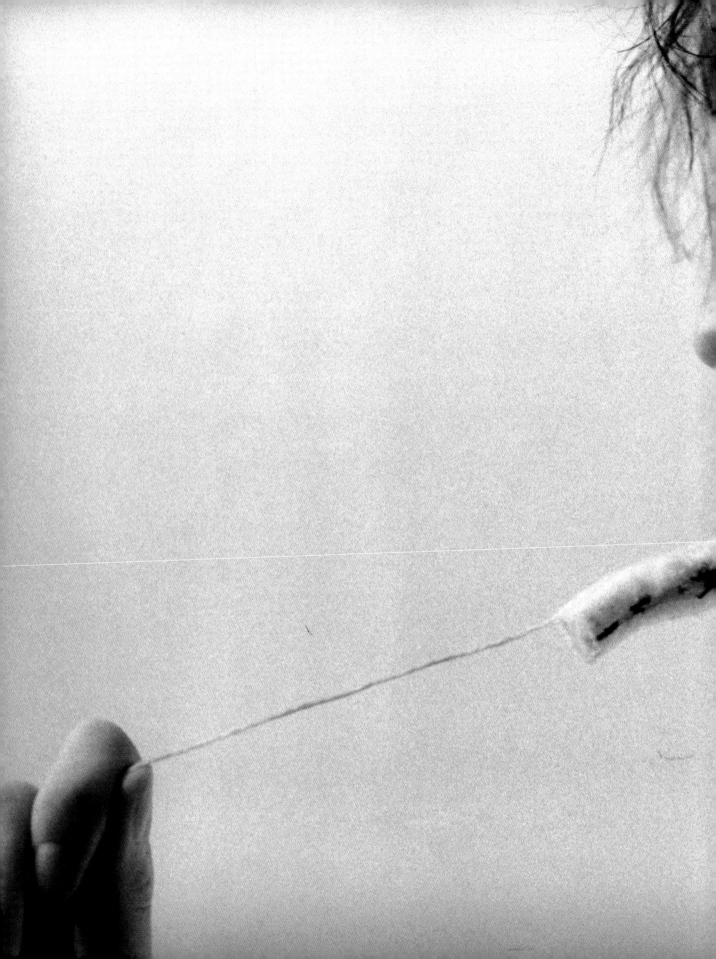

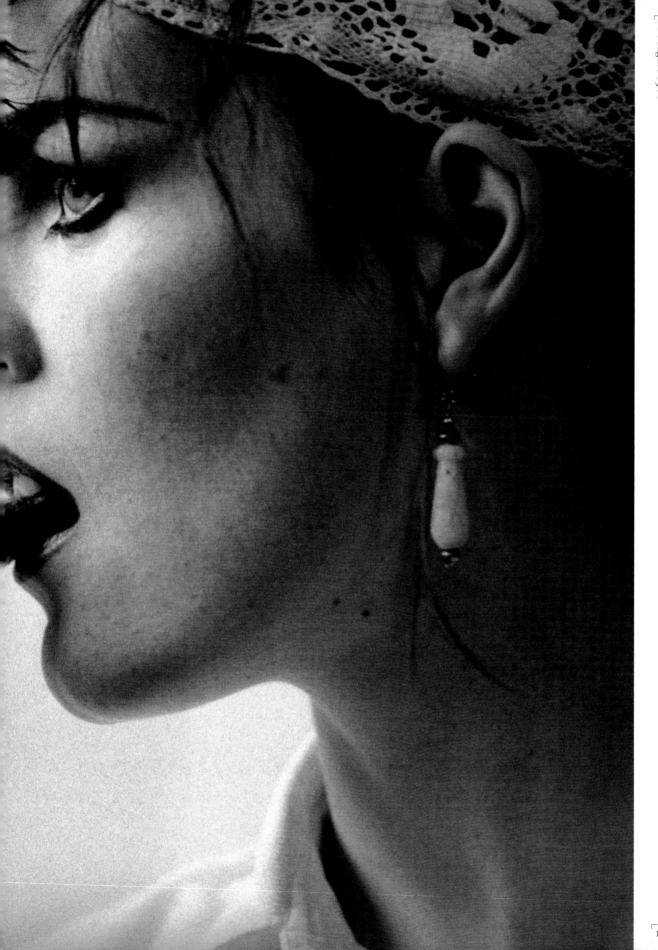

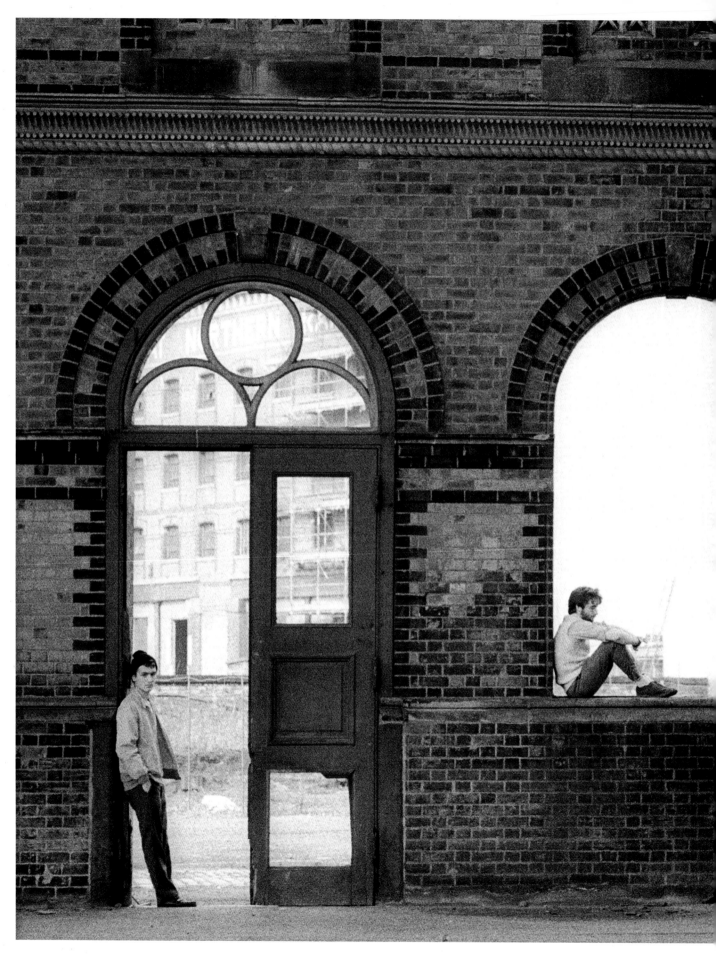

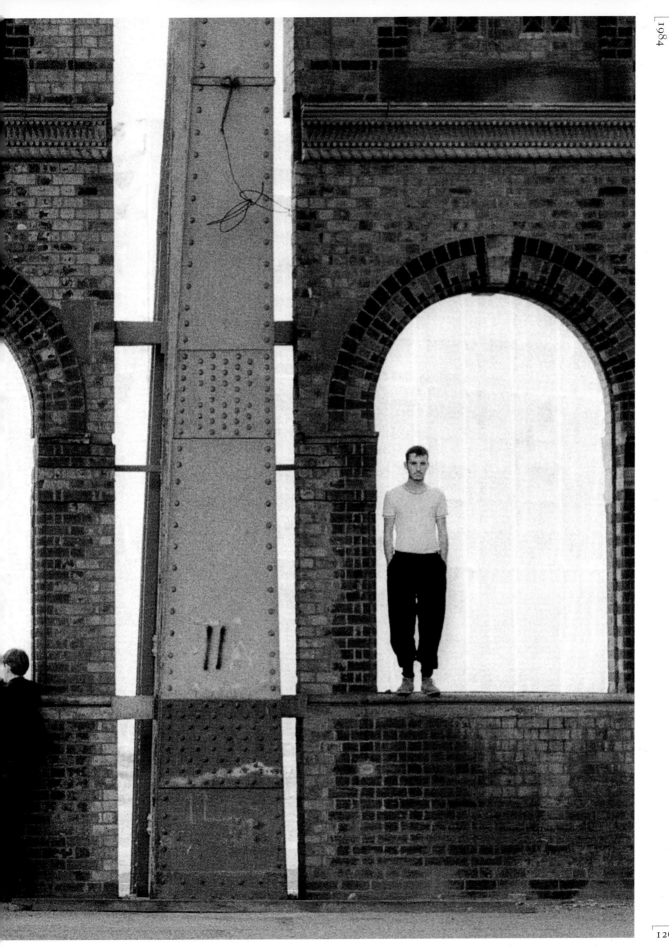

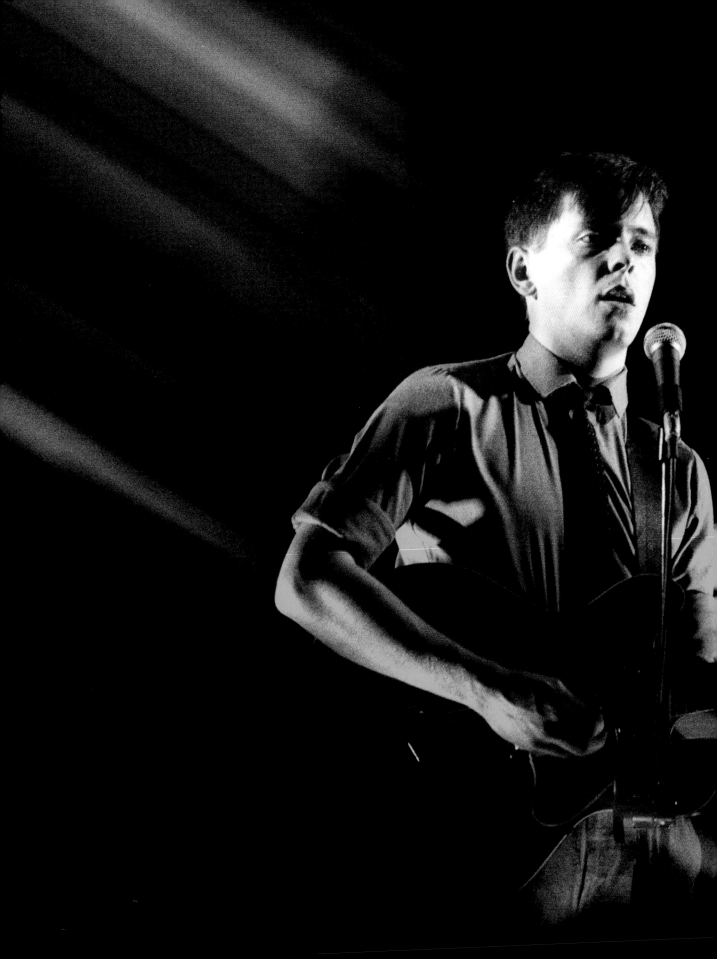

Bernard Sumner, New Order
C.O.MAN.C.H.E. Student Union, Manchester
6 February 1981

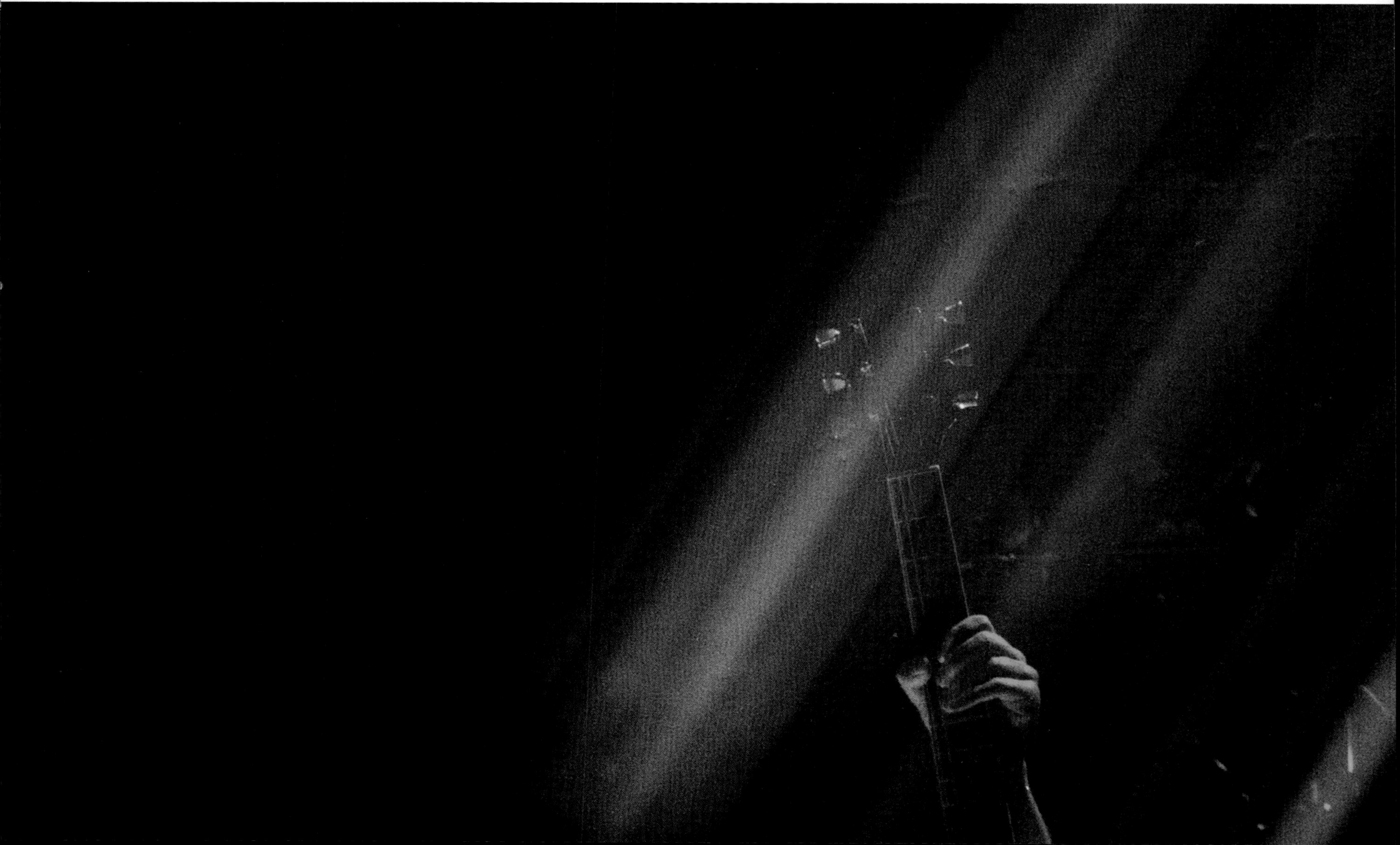

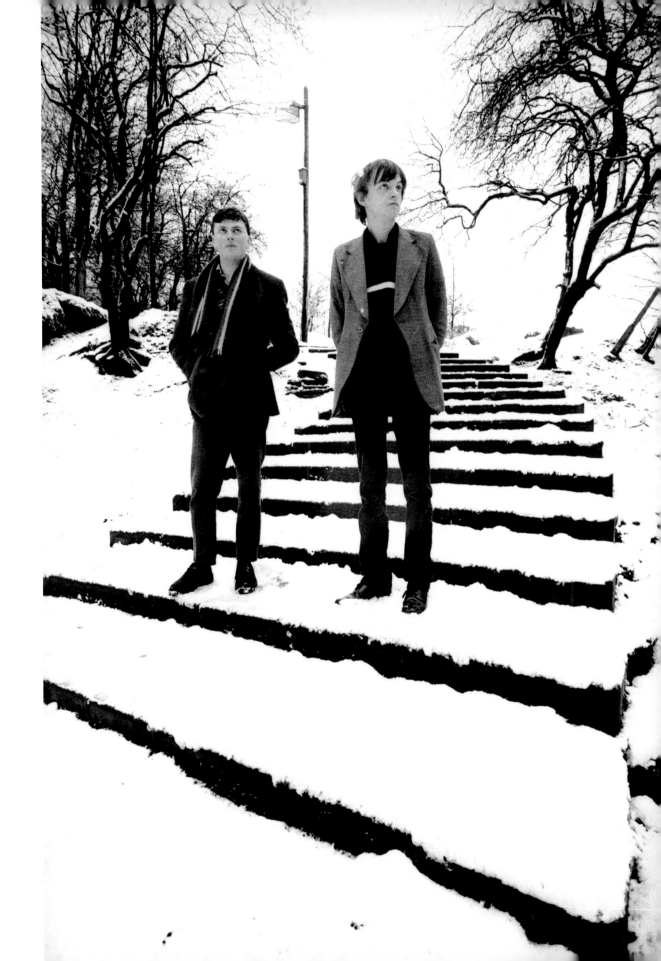

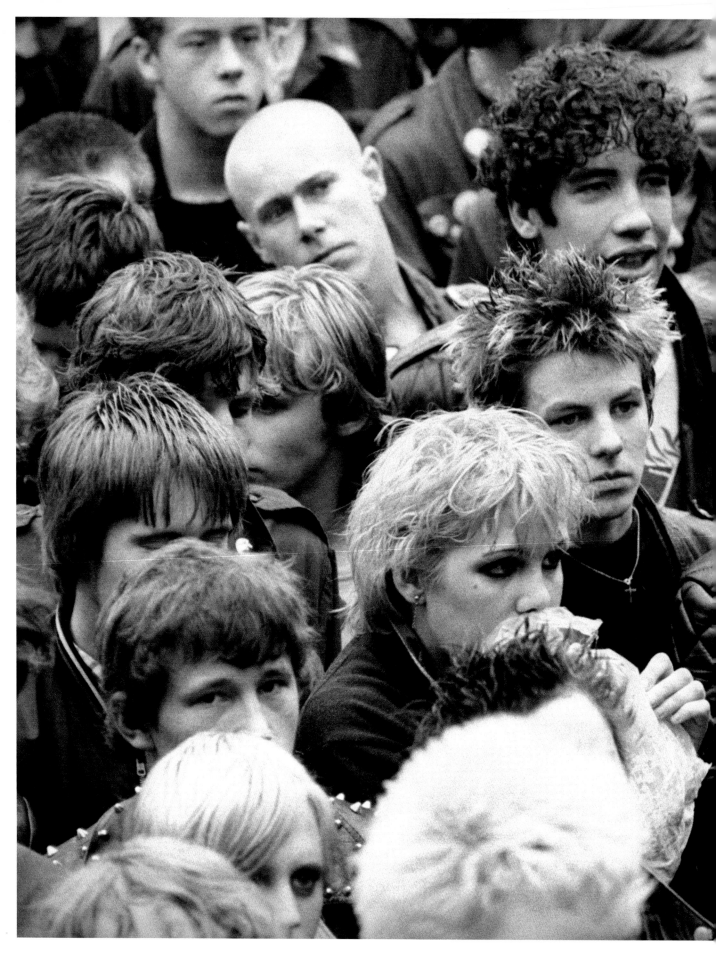

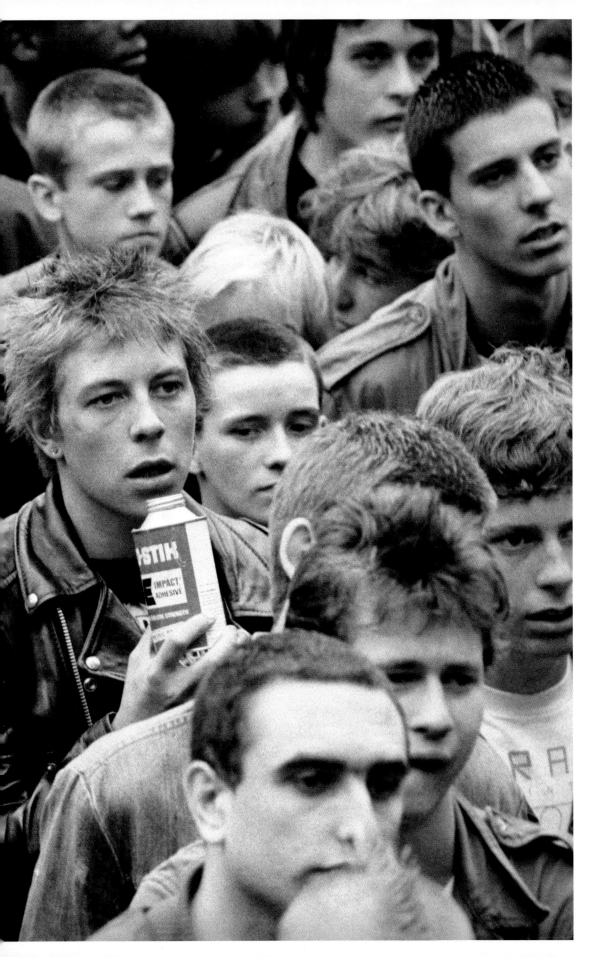

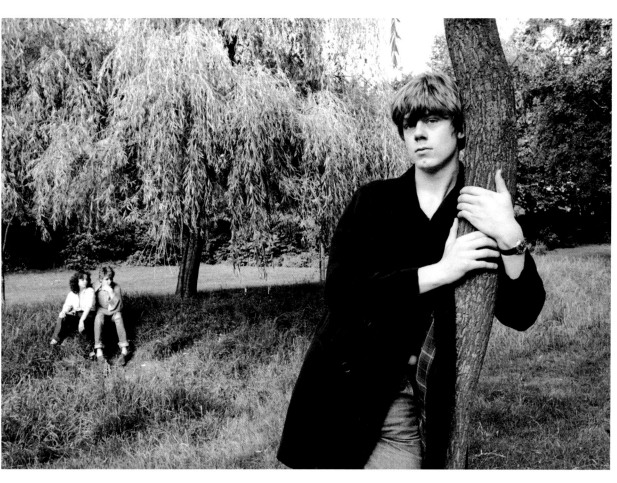

Jilted John
Didsbury, Manchester
19 July 1978

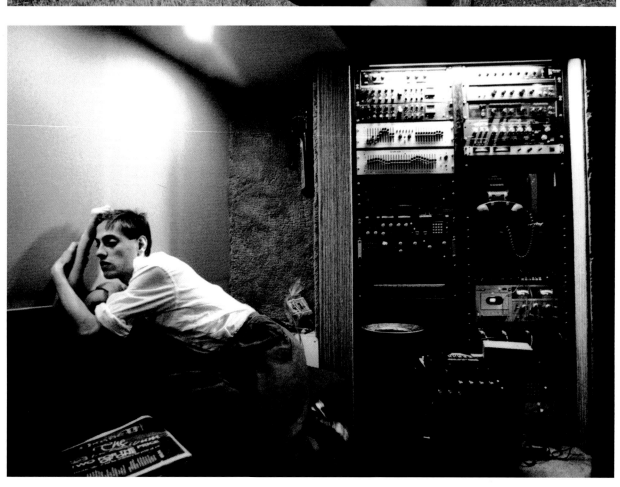

Jez Kerr, A Certain Ratio
Strawberry Studios, Stockport
20 November 1980

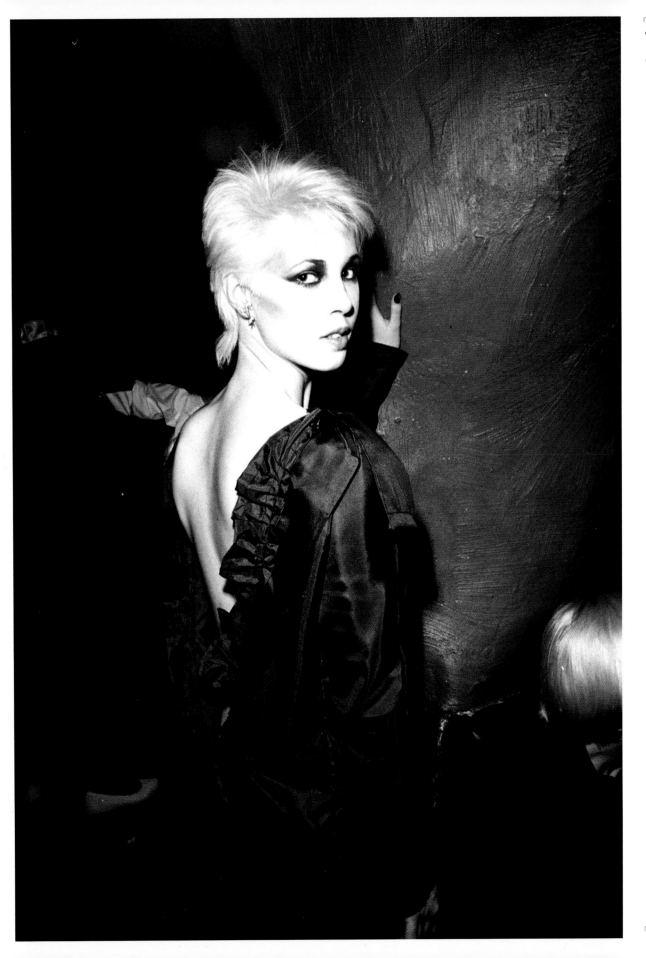

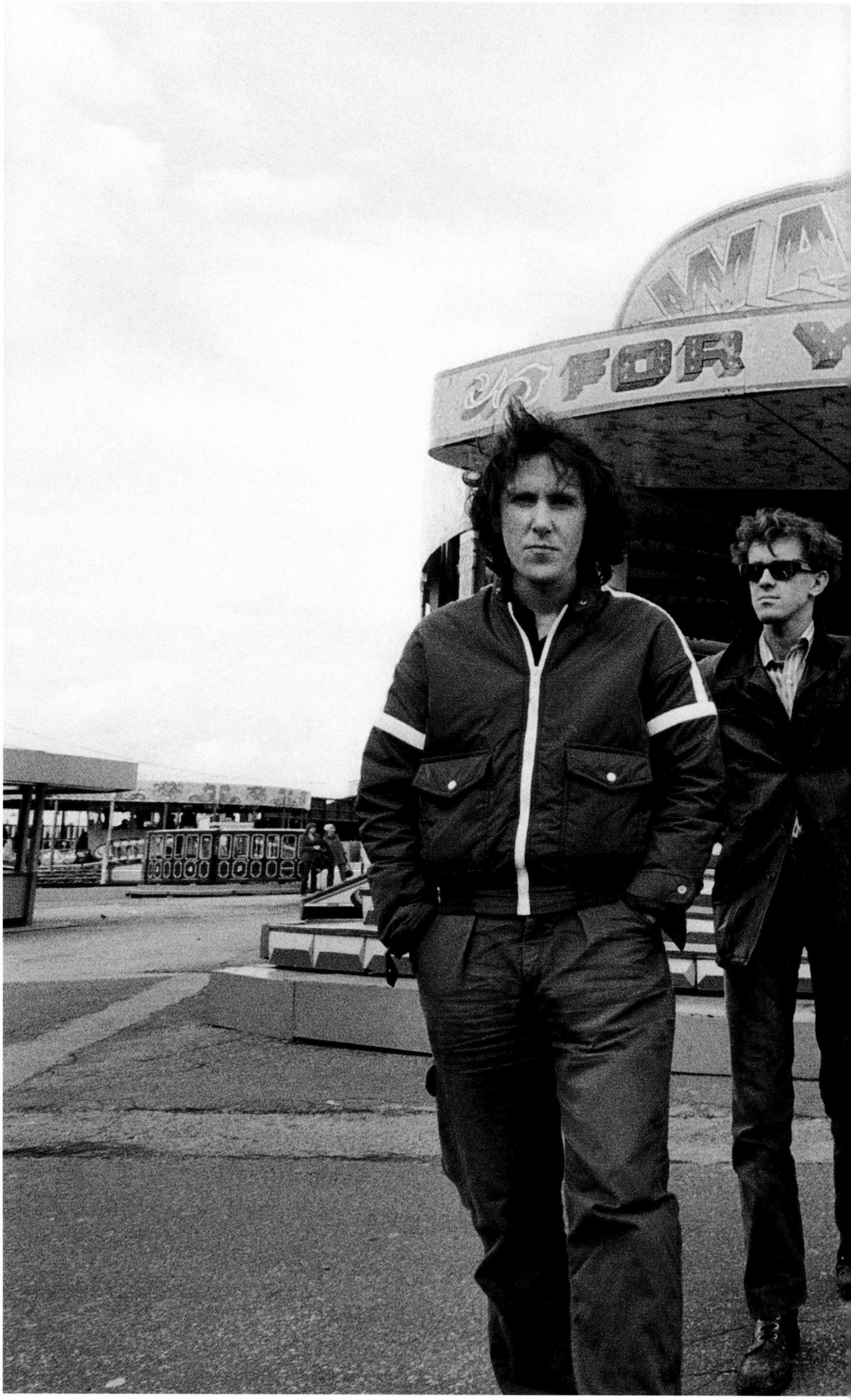

The Distractions
Belle Vue, Manchester
22 August 1979

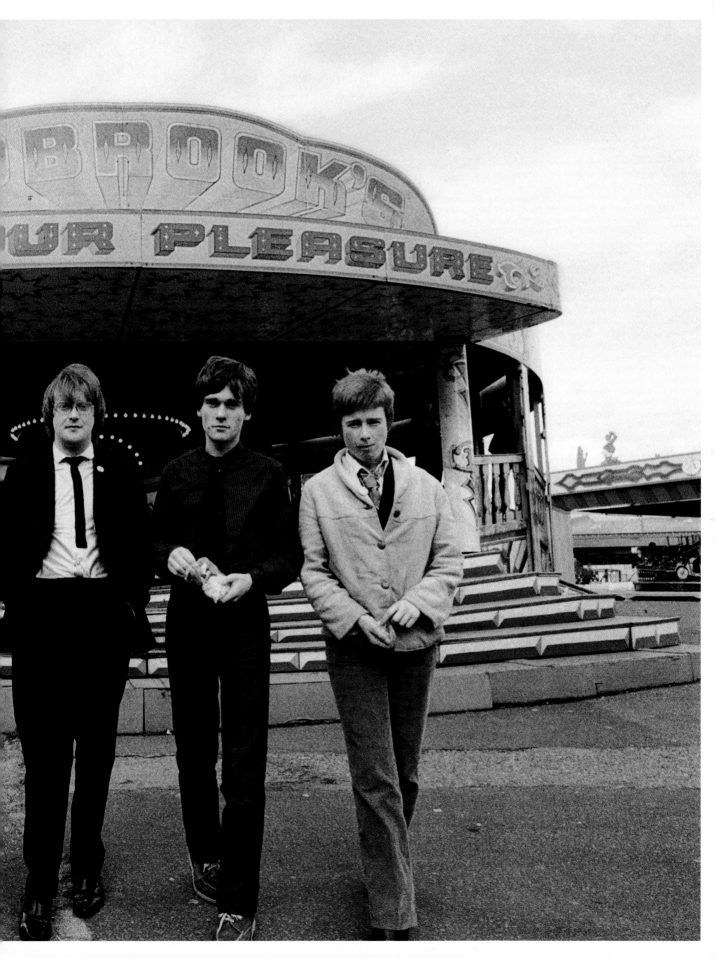

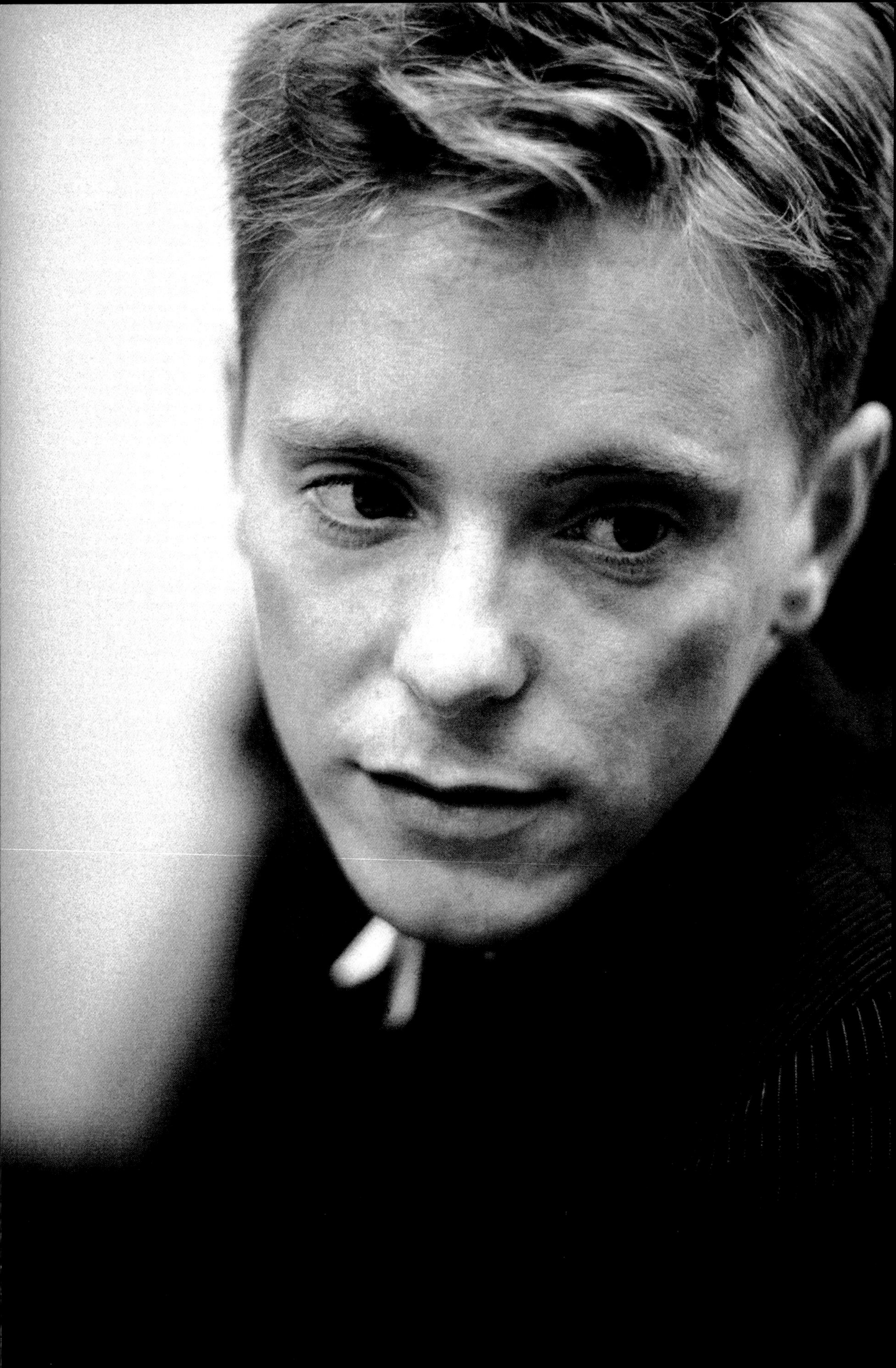

Bernard Sumner, New Order
Haçienda dressing room
21 May 1983

Peter Hook, New Order
Heaton Park, Manchester
7 June 1983

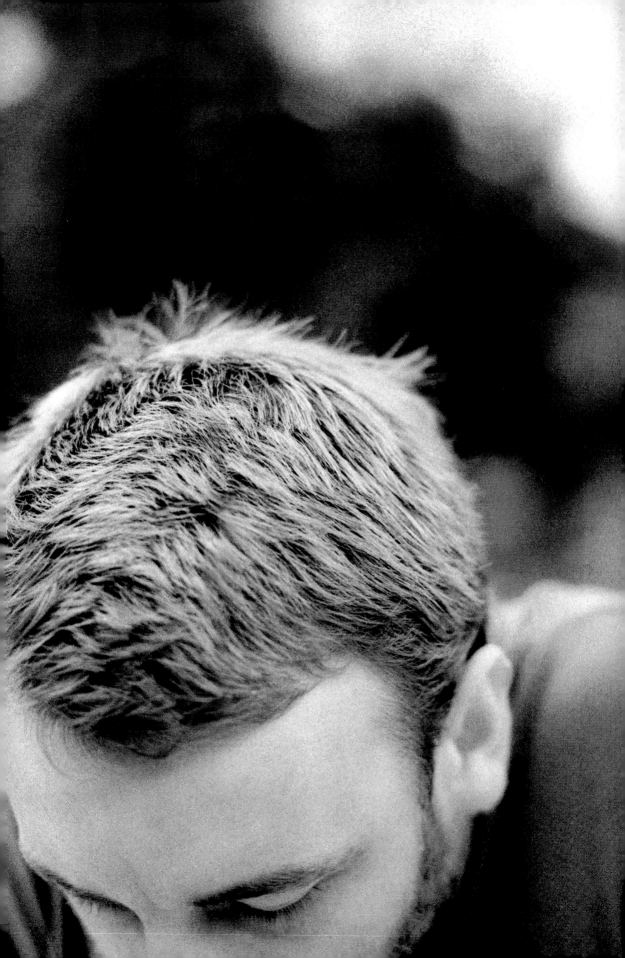

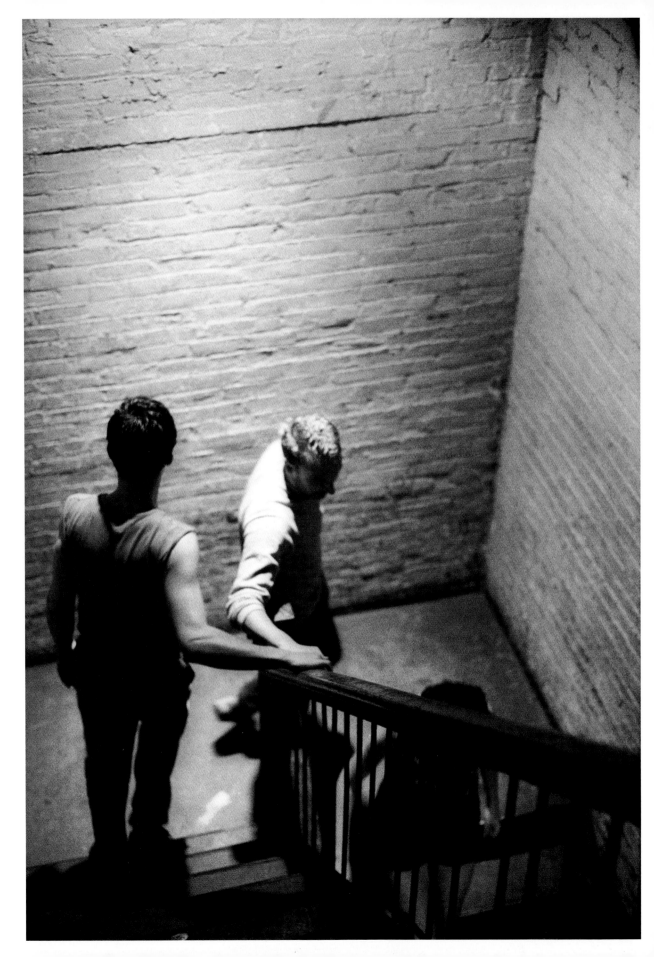

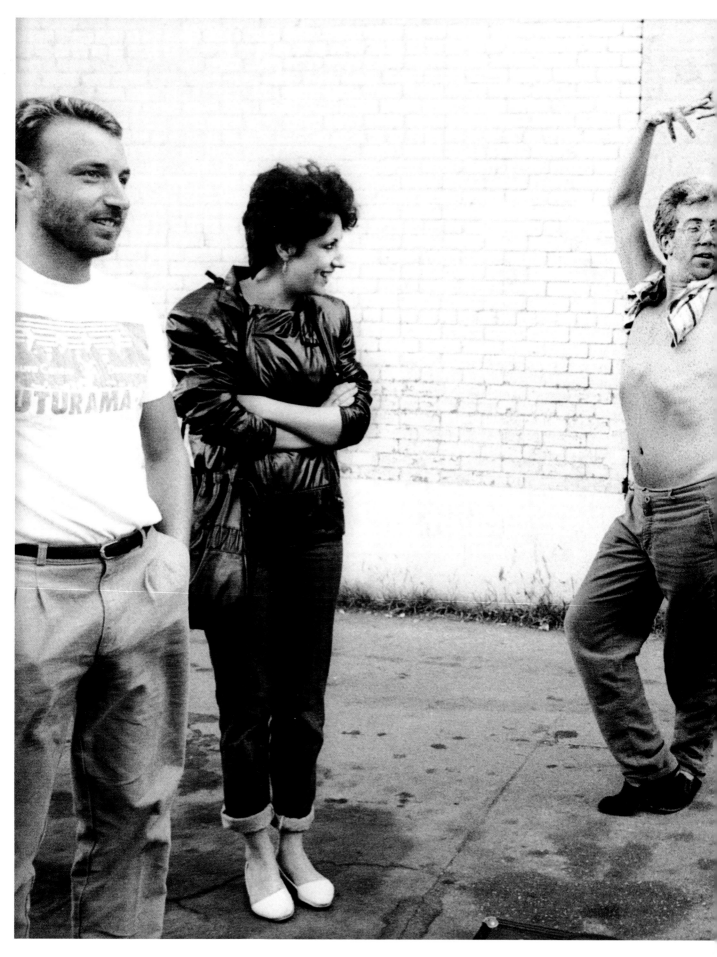

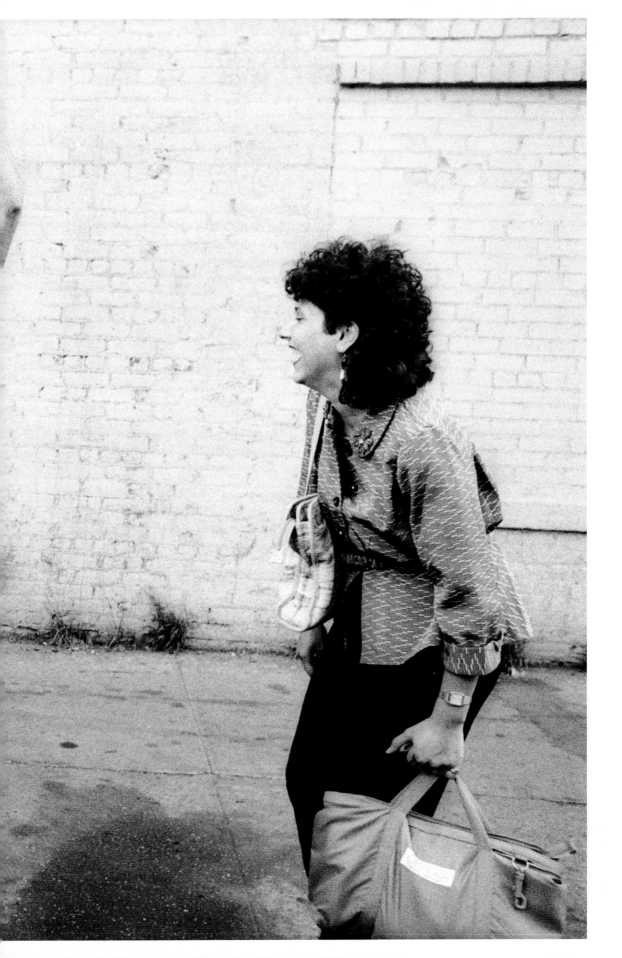

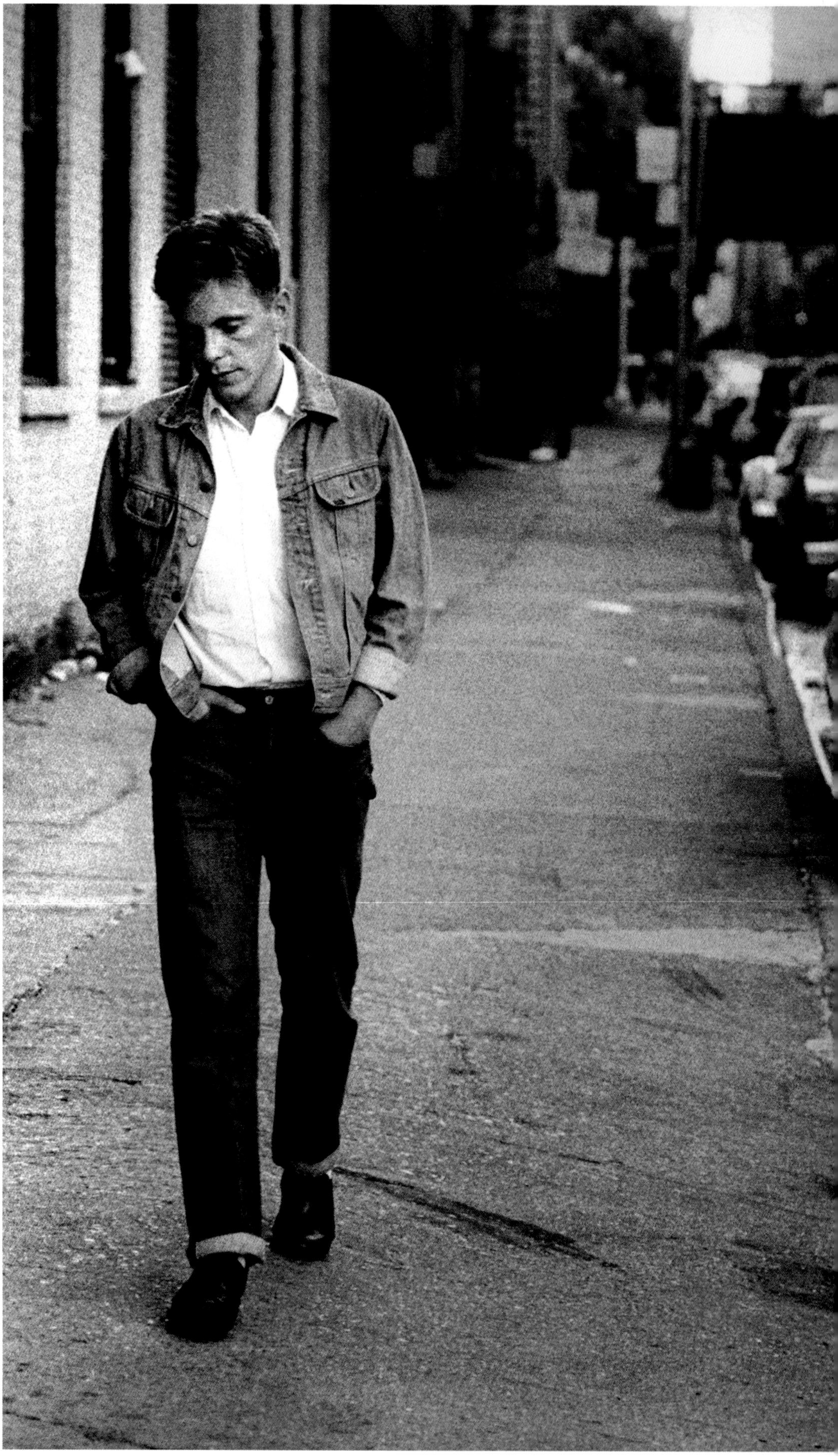

Bernard Sumner
6 a.m., New York City
July 1983

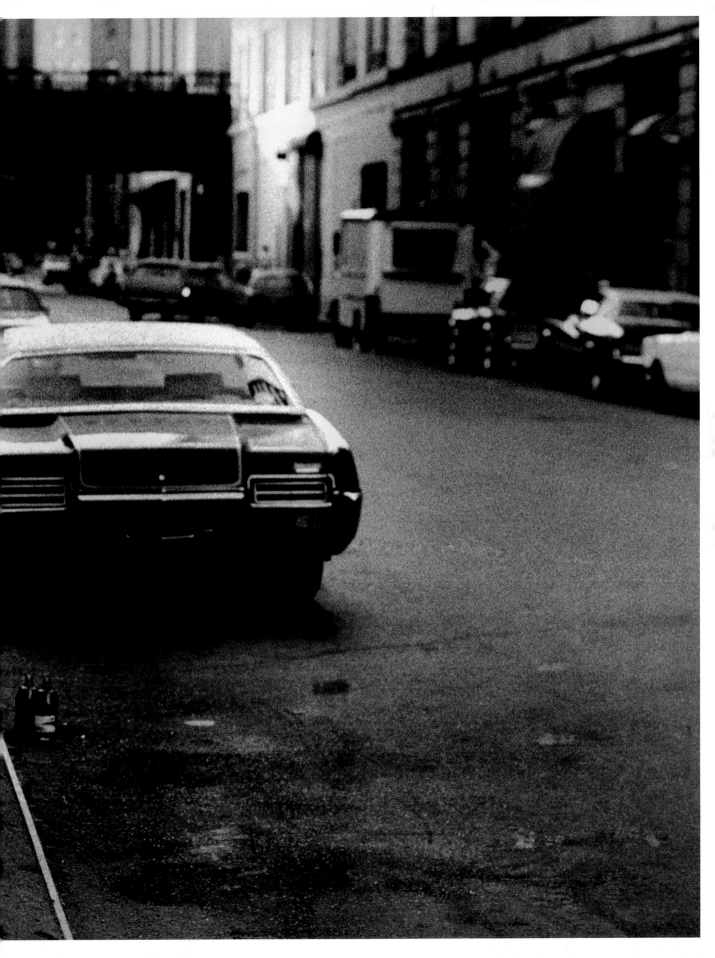

My relationship with Morrissey was very intense and we were kind of let loose really – to be as highly strung as we liked. That probably would have contributed to the lifespan of the band being only five years. That helped the burnout. Our wick was burnt down very quickly – it was blue hot. Looking at it philosophically, that's what made us what we were – there was an intensity in the music and the way we did things. It was very dramatic, quite manic but living that is quite difficult when you're young and managing it – which was my job. The actual minute-by-minute overseeing of what I regarded as my band was quite a high-maintenance job.

My parents were record obsessives, still are to this day. They brought all their records over with them from Ireland, mostly American music, The Everly Brothers were very big, American country music, The Hollies, some Beatles. It was the pop music of the day and my mother was absolutely obsessive about charts. She did her own charts up until my late teens. When I was five or six they were in their early twenties and going out to a lot of the Irish clubs to see Irish show bands, a couple of them visited our house.

When there were weddings and christenings these bands would play in the rooms above pubs in Ardwick just outside the city centre, like the Carousel and the Belle Vue. I was brought up with an avid appreciation of growing up in Manchester. There were two lots of mindsets around me when I was a kid. One was the Irish who were always wanting to go home, moaning about it. My parents were very anti that. Their appreciation of Irish culture, music and iconography was balanced with an appreciation of everything that Manchester was gonna bring us really.

I played with the family at parties in the house – all the kids were encouraged to do so. I remember toying with the harmonica 'cos my dad played and was really good on it, but I was always utterly obsessed with the guitar, everybody knew that guitar was my thing.

Each year at Christmas I'd get a guitar in a little triangle box under the tree and it would get bigger every year. Finally I got one that I could strum some chords on and I promptly customised it: I put beer-bottle caps on it to make it look like an electric. I was copying what I saw on television. Late sixties/early seventies – you took whatever music you got where you could find it even if that was the Royal Variety Performance or *Sunday Night at the London Palladium*.

Until I was eleven we lived in Ardwick about six streets away from the Apollo. Then we all got relocated. The whole Irish ghetto got spread around and we moved to Wythenshawe.

That was an absolute turning point in my life. Even though it's got a reputation for being edgy it was a bohemian atmosphere compared to the one in Ardwick. I moved to a neighbourhood where there were loads of guitar players who really took themselves seriously, a lot of older guys.

Before I met those guys I'd go to West Wythenshawe youth club – letting off a load of steam, showing off, copying each other's clothes and chasing after girls to a soundtrack of the charts and a jukebox that had a lot of retro singles – the Stones, 'Albatross', Fleetwood Mac, 'Layla', 'Jumping Jack Flash', 'Rebel Rebel' and 'Jean Genie'. The DJ would play whatever was in the charts – Roxy, Bowie and T. Rex. He also played 'Do the Bus Stop' by the Fatback Band, 'Galaxy' by War and Northern Soul stuff secretly hoping it would turn into the Wigan Casino – it was a pretty comprehensive education.

We managed to blag the school hall next door to the church to practise but we had to repay the favour by turning up on the occasional Mass with our acoustic guitars. That was pretty funny 'cos we just turned it into a bit of a laugh really. Me, Andy Rourke and Kevin Kennedy, who ended up on *Coronation Street* – Wythenshawe was a real hotbed of would-be rock stars.

I didn't have too many problems with older guys asking me to be in their bands, which was the first indication for me that I was any good. Guitar-playing came naturally and was such a passion I never had to be encouraged to practise or learn or play along with records, which was what I did all the time. It was never that much of an effort or a stretch for me to do it so I was a little cavalier about it, casual even. I've been accused of being that way now.

Billy Duffy and I were mates, still are. I first met him because he was the best friend of this guy Rob Allman. Rob has since died unfortunately. He was a very creative guy. He was always trying out different directions and ways of writing, very accomplished.

Billy was one of the first punks I knew and he sold me my first amp. I don't remember it being at a particularly discounted price – knowing Billy – but he made up for it by throwing his pink button-down shirt in the bag – I always thanked him for that.

Billy was really unusual in that older guys normally don't have the time of day for the younger ones. I used to hang around with him and find out what he was reading about in the music papers – he turned me on to buying NME and Melody Maker. He hit me up as to where to get the best clothes and I'd hear about his exploits. Billy was able to get into some clubs before me.

I considered it a little lame that I had to go to school every day so most of the time I didn't bother and I just hung out with those guys. Me and Billy and Rob would go into town and hang out where anybody who was anybody hung out – Virgin Records. We would hang around there trying to get in a decent band. There wasn't a great reserve of front men. The only real front man I knew at that time was Wayne Barrett, who was the singer in Slaughter and the Dogs.

WARRINGTON TECHNICAL COLLEGE
STUDENTS' UNION

PRESENT

THÉ HEARTBREAKERS
The Buzzcocks
SLAUGHTER & THE DOGS
D. J. — Bob Hayes

at the PARR HALL, PALMYRA SQ., WARRINGTON
FRIDAY, 13th MAY, 1977   8·00 p.m. to 2·00 a.m.
Late bar   Late Transport
TICKETS: STUDENTS £1.00   OTHERS £1.25

Slaughter were godheads in south Manchester. Wayne used to go to my school before he got kicked out and every day he'd get on the bus with different colour hair and he had the whole Ziggy thing down – the right haircut, no eyebrows and wearing a girl's blouse. He was a right United tough nut as well. Football fans in Manchester were into Bowie whereas in London there was a bit of a Clockwork Orange vibe going on.

In the North it was more a Ziggy thing and that was super-incongruous because there was a strong undercurrent of violence – these guys didn't mess about. They had bright red hair and no eyebrows and a really mincy manner but they'd kick the shit out of you if you had the wrong colours on. I got in a few scrapes but because I was one of the smallest I came off better than most.

You'd meet up in Piccadilly Gardens on Saturday afternoon and you'd have scarves round your waist or up your arms and that was echoed in some of the bands that were on television on Top of the Pops that week.

Street culture was separate from the mainstream. Now pop culture's been completely corrupted by the corporate world but up until ten or fifteen years ago it was illicit and charged with drugs, sex and violence.

The first show I saw was Rod Stewart at Belle Vue. I met Britt Ekland. She was near the mixing desk and I was with an older guy and he said, 'There's Britt Ekland,' and I just went up to her and said, in a very squeaky voice, 'Are you enjoying the concert?' Or maybe she said that to me. From then on I always assumed I was going to meet movie stars at gigs. It was downhill from there, ha ha.

Gigs smelt of patchouli before punk. My memories were the people who I would meet outside who were not paying to get in and were sneaking in and were working-class. Once you got inside it was a lot of middle-class guys and students, great coats. The gigs were all pretty serious affairs before punk. I saw Slaughter a few times. That was different because they were local boys but I saw bands like Be Bop Deluxe and a load of really dreadful bands – Barclay James Harvest, just whoever was in the music papers.

I saw Rory Gallagher a lot. He always played a lot and he was great. Manchester was always a big town for him. I got into him because I was looking for something of me own, without my mates. Discovering he was Irish was a bonus! You're always looking for something to discover yourself and I kept seeing him in record racks in jeans and a T-shirt with a battered old guitar and I thought his name was really exotic. He looked very street because a lot of the bands were still wearing make-up or feather boas and just looked like they were depressed. Rory looked like a rock 'n' roller. Another band who were favourite of lads were Thin Lizzy. Lizzy rocked but they were pretty glamorous because they had hits and they were on *Top of the Pops*. It wasn't dour student time. You would actually see girls at their gigs.

In '74–'75 Keith Richards just seemed to be the coolest man on two feet – or the coolest man on his back. What he did was everything that I was interested in. Being the guitar player, the powerhouse of a really good band with great riffs – just perfection really. I learned so much about the ethics of being a guitar player and a founder member of a band from Keith Richards. No showboating, be understated, learn your craft, live it, back up the singer, be a songwriter, front the band, be cool. Right there was the manifesto.

Now you can't move in Waterstone's for five different volumes of the fuckin' Maximo Park biography but in those days there was Chris Salewicz writing a book about Mick Jagger, David Dalton would do a book about the Stones . . . they were rare but they showed you a doorway.

Now I look back I never considered whether it was within my reach or not. Without getting too new-agey about it just the journey was 'it' anyway. I didn't really consider that the destination was unobtainable because I kind of considered that what I was doing was the real thing in my own mind – I had a pretty fertile imagination.

Rehearsing with my band wasn't as frustrating an experience as it could have been because the actual playing and doing it was heaven to me. I was in bands with Andy, lots of different names and different incarnations. We started off playing Thin Lizzy stuff, which was 'Don't Believe a Word', and then we ended up doing a couple of songs by The Cars.

The first punk gig I went to was Slaughter and the Dogs at the Wythenshawe Forum and first on the bill were the Nosebleeds who at that point were called Wild Ram.

I'd seen guys wearing Slaughter T-shirts in town and they looked different, they were fuckin' scary, man. A couple of them were reputed to be rent boys and probably were. They were all speed freaks so they were pretty unpredictable. They looked amazing – nothing like the kind of surly Mohicans, leather-jacket abominations that most people pass off as punk nowadays.

They were wearing proper Levi's that had been taken in to drainpipes, V-neck sweaters, Fred Perry shirts, flick fringes with little studs for earrings. Very sharp and unadorned. There wasn't a whole load of stuff hanging off them. They were very stripped down and pretty lean, mean speed freaks.

I just thought that's the way to go. It felt modern and it felt now and something that I could pull off. I was still looking like Keith Richards on *Black and Blue*. Probably had a scarf round me waist and a fringe in my eyes and an earring. It wasn't like I had a long corkscrew perm or a ponytail. It wasn't much of a stretch really but I definitely had to get me jeans taken in.

I didn't think I had the conviction to be a front man but I wanted to form my own perfect Manchester four-piece. So I always had it in mind to find the right front man.

When I got to about sixteen I was quite fretful. I got disillusioned with people I was playing with, aside from Andy, who I knew was a Grade-A musician. I met Angie in 1979 which was a major event for me because the thing that takes up most boys' lives is hormones and the search for a girl was taken care of for me. I had a girl I wanted to be with and I was lucky she wanted to be with a musician.

During that period of fretting I just bonded with *Raw Power* pretty much exclusively and that forged my direction as a guitar player and a writer. It kept me in good stead when I came to write *The Queen Is Dead*. The whole atmosphere on *Queen Is Dead* in my lateral-thinking mind, certainly a few tracks, was forged from listening to *Raw Power* in my winter of discontent.

I'd heard about Morrissey through Billy Duffy and Mick Rossi and the Slaughter and the Dogs guys. Slaughter and Buzzcocks and that period set off absolute fireworks. I am down on record a lot for being anti-punk but that's because I wanted to forge something out of my own generation. If I look through my singles collection I've got pretty much every UK and US seven-inch record that came out by anybody in plimsolls. Tuff Darts or Wayne County or The Adverts or The Saints – not all super-credible either.

It was a very fertile time and it's often said by a lot of musicians that they saw punk bands and they thought, 'I can do it too.' That was a very useful thing for me because I saw bands putting records out and not necessarily having hits. Records that I knew weren't that much more proficient or better than me and my mates. Without a doubt had there been no punk there would have been no Smiths.

People knew Morrissey because he wrote letters to the music press. How it went down was, Phil Fletcher, an avid Dolls fan, was in Virgin on Saturday morning and he saw someone hovering around the New York Dolls section – which was only two records. Phil asked him was he Morrissey, the guy who wrote letters to the music press? They struck up a conversation and Phil went back to south Manchester and Morrissey went to Stretford and Phil introduced Billy to Morrissey and connected him to the south Manchester scene.

I met Morrissey at Patti Smith's gig on her Easter tour at the Apollo. I was only fourteen, it was before I met Angie. There was utter non-interest, disinterest, on Morrissey's part and a reserved curiosity on my part because he didn't look exactly as I'd pictured him. I knew he was the only guy around that really took himself seriously. He regarded himself as a front man. That was very impressive but I kind of forgot about him for a couple of years, so it wasn't like I was walking around from that moment hatching any master plan.

That meeting was kind of forgettable but anything would have been in the light of Patti Smith's performance that night. It was a real life-changing moment for me. I actually saw with my own eyes the embodiment of rock 'n' roll up close first-hand from an American – that was very important to me. Most of the bands I'd seen at that time were UK and it was . . . the only word for it was transcendent. It was like a doorway to a different agenda – otherworldly. It was beyond your normal sensory experience, really, you didn't know whether she was on drugs but, wherever she was at, you wanted to be there.

Two years later I'd moved out of my parents' house. I always had Saturday jobs in clothes shops but I started working full-time in a new clothes shop, X Clothes, and helped set that

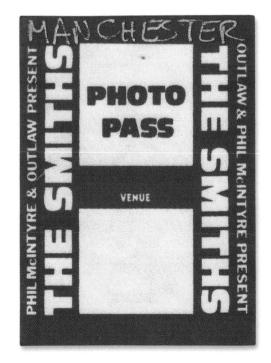

shop up. That became a very hip place. Next door to that shop was Crazy Face Clothes, which was slightly more mainstream but hipper in its own way because it played really great music and you could smoke in there. My boss was a wanker so I'd be nipping next door to hang out and smoke cigs and listen to John Lee Hooker and whatever was on rotation there. The girls who worked in there were sick of hearing it and they would rather have been listening to fuckin' Donna Summer, but they told me the boss made them play John Lee Hooker. The *Vee Jay* compilation had just come out on Charly.

One day I bound in there and the owner Joe Moss was there. I just went up and introduced myself. He was talking about Smokey Robinson and he told me he had a guitar and he had it for the one reason alone – to be able to play 'My Girl'. So I said, 'I'll teach you.' I went across town to where his factory and his offices were and that started a daily habit – a daily ritual just going over there every day. I started to work there and moved into the house. It's been one of the most important relationships of my life – Joe still manages me now.

Each day I'd go in with a new concept, kicking stuff around with Joe about the Brill Building and Phil Spector and The Drifters. I was getting very into that sixties New York Broadway situation, the girl groups 'cos I never really ever lost my thread from being a Patti Smith fan. Me and Morrissey were getting a lot of our influences from the same people – the Dolls used to do girl groups so we got into the girl groups.

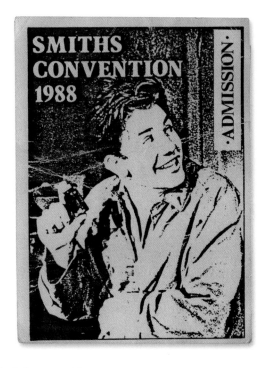

When I was eighteen I looked like it was 1962. I was really into the way Stu Sutcliffe looked in Hamburg. That was my kind of thing – the beatnik thing. If you look at the really very early Smiths photos with the flowers and I've got the Ray-Bans on and the quiff, that's what I'm doing. I'm actually doing Stuart Sutcliffe. Then when I got the bowl haircut that was Stuart Sutcliffe also.

I sought everything from the sixties. I was into the pre-Beatles thing, combing me hair down wasn't wanting to be The Byrds. I was following Stu Sutcliffe. I thought I was the only person on the earth certainly who was looking that way and listening to The Shirelles. I was super-specific about what world I'd created.

I was living at Joe's house with his family and he played a video of the Lieber and Stoller *South Bank Show*. I was watching it and midway through it he said, 'Check this bit out,' because I was talking about my frustrations with finding a singer and a partner and I'd heard about Morrissey. Every few days I'd say maybe I should track that guy Morrissey down.

Jerry Lieber got Mike Stoller's address and went round and said, 'Let's form a writing partnership,' completely out of the blue. Joe didn't tell me to do that – he let me draw my own conclusions and in that moment I had the lightning flash of inspiration – the eureka moment as it were.

The next day I went back to Wythenshawe and made a couple of calls to try and find Phil Fletcher – I was on a mission so I fronted him up and got Morrissey's address. A couple of days later we got on a bus and Phil showed me where he lived and I knocked on the door and told Morrissey what I wanted to do – on the doorstep. Then he let me in.

I obviously convinced him very quickly that I meant business, it wasn't very hard because I DID mean business. It wasn't like I had to do a sales pitch. I was gonna do it. It's become quite a well-known story now but we went to his room and he invited me to put a record on. I started looking through his singles collection, which actually wasn't that vast but it was impeccable, and he had 'Paper Boy' by The Marvelettes, which I couldn't believe. You have to understand how incredible it was for me to meet one other person on the planet who I was about to become a partner of who had records that impressed me because I was SO specific. I was a connoisseur because I had all Joe Moss's singles. I had pretty much every Little Richard speciality single. To see all these perfectly kept laid-out Motown singles was really impressive – he passed the audition straight away. I went to play it and I played the B-side – I can't remember what it is on that label – I played the B-side to be a smart arse. It was supernatural, cosmic because so much was at stake for me and my path in life and how life could unfold.

It was the same for him. You have two really big stories because the two of us were two big personalities. He gave me some lyrics – straight away. He had a whole stack of lyrics. I took 'em away and started kicking 'em around but I felt when I left that we were on. He'd arranged to call me the next day and I remember thinking – if he calls we're definitely on and if he doesn't I'll forget it. He called me on the dot the next day. I was really impressed. We arranged to meet each other a few days later to go through some tunes and I think 'Hand That Rocks the Cradle' was one of them. It was only really when we actually got together nose to nose that I married the music with the words really. That happened every few days for what seemed like a long time.

I always had some sort of chord progression and riffs that I was working on 'cos I was a guitar player. I still do. If I click with the right partner I just pull 'em out the bag.

It was a really interesting world that opened to me. I was aware of Shelagh Delaney and I'd spent most of my teenage life trying to erase any trace of that kind of aesthetic from my memory. I was the one that grew up the longest in that environment out of all The Smiths. That was my background. That two-up two-down in the city centre was what I was trying to get away from.

We didn't have a phone till I was eleven. We didn't have a car till I was fourteen, we didn't have an inside toilet till I was eleven. The idea of putting Albert Finney outside a factory or wherever on my record cover was not something I was thinking about.

Literary influences and literary aspirations, that was what he brought with him. When you get involved with somebody so closely it's a sea of unknown influences or baggage or experience. I'm very proud that he brought that very defined aesthetic. I had the musical aesthetic and he had all those other things. One absolutely complemented the other.

I was on one about Factory. I had a friendship with Mike Pickering – in fact that day Mike Pickering and Tony Wilson were given the plans by Ben Kelly for the Haçienda they brought them in the shop and laid them out on the counter to show me – that's how excited they were about it.

Tony Wilson had asked me to be the guitar player in Section 25 and I knew Jez from A Certain Ratio. My best friend at the time, Andrew Berry, who I lived with, was a very significant early DJ at the Haçienda. So I had plenty of Factory connections and because of that I wanted my own band to have autonomy.

Morrissey knew Tony Wilson better than I did and I remember him going round to Tony Wilson's to play him our stuff to get his opinion, to get a buzz going. Tony in his wisdom decided to remember that as our pitching for a deal that he turned down. Whatever . . . but I was very much into not being on Factory simply because it was so obvious. We would have just become another generic Manchester band. We would have had to work for a year and a half just to carve out our own autonomy. Because Factory had such a strong aesthetic and style you immediately would have become a Factory band and I was keen that we didn't do that.

I got into the habit of writing songs in batches of three right from the start. That held us in good stead because we were such a prolific singles band. The form was that we'd write a very good B-side because it was a cool and great thing to do and we remembered Roxy Music, Sparks and people like that always had interesting B-sides.

We decided to take it a step further with twelve-inch releases and write a third strong track. A couple of years before I'd really liked the Gun Club's version of 'Run through the Jungle', which was a cover of a Creedence Clearwater track. I wanted to do something that didn't have many chord changes and that was my weird inspirational association . . . dirgey and swampy and druggy. I wrote this sprawling kind of groove track and then we laid down 'How Soon Is Now?'. I did what I always did, which was sort the bass out and then break out the guitar.

I'd wanted to do something with a strong tremolo guitar part for years. When I was a kid I was fixated by the groove on Hamilton Bohannon's 'Disco Stomp' and Bo Diddley, 'Mona' and all that.

The intensity came from being slightly in an altered state about 3.30 in the morning.

I was very young to be in the biggest British band or whatever we were but at the same time if there was ever an eighteen-year-old that was ready for it – it was me. I'd devoted all my waking hours to doing it.

Making sure all the characters were happy. Making sure we were all going in the right direction, making sure that I had some ideas, making sure that we weren't being ripped off, whatever was said about us in the music press wasn't gonna wind us up, that my partner was happy with the bass player, my partner was happy with himself, that the drummer wasn't fretting. I was looking out for Andy's drug thing but it was worth it – the records have got an amazing bass player that is part of the language of the band.

The first absolutely symbolic gig was the third Haçienda gig, which was the same night as we appeared on *TOTP*. We had to get the train back from appearing live on *TOTP* on Thursday night, which everybody had seen – it was some kind of marker for indie music, I guess.

At the train station in Manchester we were picked up by Rob Gretton and Mike Pickering in his car. We couldn't get into the Haçienda because there was two thousand people outside and two thousand people inside. That was the night we felt we'd done it, getting into the hallowed halls of *TOTP* with our flowers and blouses and Rickenbackers. It was a fucking victory for everyone of our age group, like a new day after punk rock.

Sometimes I puzzled over lyrics for what seemed like minutes, ha ha ha. There were great codes to unblock, you'd drive yourself crazy just trying to work some stuff out. We were our biggest fans, no one could have loved us as much as we loved us. We were absolutely fucking sincere.

Even before I was in that band I was famously nocturnal. When I left the shop and stopped working I was just able to become terminally nocturnal – for a while it kind of suited me and suited the band.

I never had an entourage of lots of guys and girls being loud and popping champagne and hitting clubs. We were very indoorsy, sitting around ghetto blasters listening to tapes of Velvet Underground bootlegs and The Beatles' *White Album* – even when we were on the road we were like that.

The rock 'n' roll lifestyle that I did partake in was always just with a select group of three or four people – my guitar tech, Andy Rourke and a couple of people like Andrew Berry. We'd just stay up watching videos and listening to tunes and getting stoned and not eating very much.

A lot of early activity happened at my flat in Earl's Court. There was quite a few songs written there – 'How Soon Is Now?', 'Please Please Please' . . . A lot of the *Meat Is Murder* album was written there. Then we recorded it in Liverpool to get the northern vibe on it. After that period Angie and I bought the house in Bowdon where nearly all of *The Queen Is Dead* was written.

Where I was living tended to be the band HQ, which was nearly always great – except when we'd been on tour in America. You'd all get on a coach from Heathrow airport in the middle of the night back to my house and the crew would end up staying there. Wear sunglasses indoors at all times, own a hundred guitars, have a number one album, own a fast car, crash a fast car, drink lots of brandy on the road and be rock 'n' roll. That was my to-do list – it was just no more serious or sinister or dramatic than that really. Even though it was unhealthy and then eventually debilitating and made me ill, drinking a bottle of brandy after each show was actually probably a good way of escaping from what was going on after the shows.

There was always some drama – people being fired or people in fear of being fired or worries about how we were going to get to the next venue because quite often we didn't have a tour manager in America. Often crews bitch and I would be the person that everybody came to to do their offloading.

In spite of all that it was all done with a lot of love. We all really were very very close. It was intense and difficult. I did it because that was my role aside from playing the guitar and being the main musical writer. That was the role that made up the band

and that was my role in it, just maintaining it really.

Morrissey was gonna come a cropper with the wrong person and Frank Owen at *Melody Maker* was looking to make a name for himself. Those two elements were the reason for that big storm over 'Panic'. Morrissey stuck his tongue out a little bit too far, not for the first or last time. I was just not gonna stand by and let the whole band be tainted with some slur and I think I was right in standing up for the band. I was very quick to point out all our influences to the contrary. Morrissey was being glib to the wrong person.

On a musical level I felt going into the last record that we were about to run dry. I obviously didn't want to turn The Smiths into a rave band nor did I expect to take The Smiths into the direction that I pursued directly afterwards with Electronic.

I was a very young man who was always looking out to be turned on by what was going on in pop culture – and to be challenged and look for surprises. I felt that the musical style that we found ourselves the centre of was becoming generic and a little bit corny. The C86 cassette had come out which now enjoys a certain kind of respectability but everywhere I looked it seemed like there was piss-poor imitations of The Primitives or some really naff band. The white English rock scene in the UK had become a poor reflection of Postcard in 1982, really lightweight, and we were being lumped in with that.

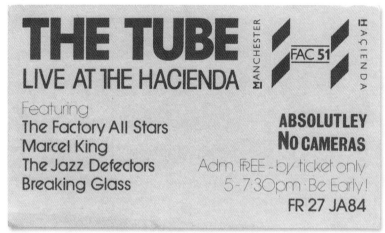

Morrissey and I probably needed a break from each other. It was put to me a while before the split that we should have a holiday. By that time we'd officially recorded four albums but we'd done seven albums' worth of material. I wanted to go away for two weeks but there's no point bleating about it now. Also there was business stuff that was completely unacceptable to me. Just after the last album I was told that once again the acting manager that had not been brought in by me [laughs] was gonna have to be fired – by me! That was unacceptable. To this day I've never found anybody who can give me an argument against The Smiths not having a manager. We were one of the biggest bands in the world and the biggest rock band in the UK and the twenty-three-year-old guitar player was being told that he was gonna have to manage it again – like he did in the early days. I just refused to do it.

There was a cultural revolution round the corner and that was a revolution in technology, a revolution in music, a revolution in fashion, a revolution in drugs, a brand-new non-retro thing and it was happening right in my home town. It would have been insanity for me to draw the curtains, close the door and continue watching old re-runs of *Saturday Night and Sunday Morning* every day. Who would want to do that at twenty-three? The musical movement that happened from Manchester and parts of America in '88 onwards was very very healthy and great music came out of it.

The problem with that particular movement was that it went on way too long and was too tied up with hedonism which eventually becomes the death of creativity anyway. The flip side was walking down Portland Street in Manchester on Saturday morning and seeing almost everybody around your own age living a similar lifestyle to you and listening to the same kind of music, not dissimilar to the original Mod scene. It was pretty fantastic and you couldn't wait to go out again the next night. There was this shared, communal, tribal experience and I wouldn't have missed it for the world. It was just fantastic.

I heard that Bernard wanted to contact me to write some songs with him and I was in San Francisco when New Order were playing so I went to see them. Our paths had crossed many many times before – I first worked with Bernard in 1982 or '83 on a record he was producing for Mike Pickering on Factory. I knew he was a good guy off stage and I was very admiring of his approach as a musician. I regarded him as the best electronic musician that the UK had produced.

Back home he would come round to my studio every week and we'd start to kick ideas around. Before we knew it we'd got a ton of ideas together and had this idea of performing a sort of non-group, a kind of sanctuary for the experiences that we'd had in both our Mancunian big bands. We rather naively expected to put music out on Factory Records as white-label releases. We honestly didn't expect the kind of fuss that happened about us getting together.

I saw it as a way of moving forward. It was very exciting and very appropriate to be able to have a non-group group. It was the time when people like S'Express and Technotronic – those kind of pop groups – were born out of musicians in the studio. I saw us as following the tradition of Brian Eno and David Byrne and Kraftwerk was a very important touchstone for Bernard.

It was about getting away from the paradigm of a four-piece rock group. Suddenly the world opens up where you're allowed to be a musician and collaborate with other people – it was heaven-sent for me.

There's a thing about second cities that I recognise in the relationship that Melbourne has to Sydney and that Seattle has to Los Angeles and that Manchester has to London. You have this creative freedom, you can enjoy all the benefits of a large city with a decent economy but it isn't a media centre. You're releasing your music to be judged by a fairly discerning community. If I put a record out I know I'm gonna bump into Damon Gough or Jimi Goodwin from Doves or, back in the day, members of The Fall or New Order or the Mondays. Ian Brown or whoever. They don't have to be famous. You know that there are people around that are gonna judge you and you respect their opinion. There's a there with all those cities I mentioned – people who choose to live there as adults kind of do it resolutely.

I moved back to Manchester as my main base after a brief stint in Los Angeles in 1988 because Manchester just coincidentally happened to have a musical buzz. It was not because of my roots or my family – I have an escapist gene in me anyway. It was just purely because that's where everything was happening and I didn't really have any reason to move.

Having said that, I've had a fifteen-month spell living in Portland recently – everybody bumps into each other and everybody knows each other and it is very much like Manchester in the early nineties. That is, basically a town full of guys living off their girlfriends.

Manchester's been great and I just figure it's a pretty good place to bring up kids as any. It has its moments – it's far from idyllic but I'm very lucky. The environment, the life I have in my house and my studio could be anywhere really. When I shut the gates people tend to not see me for weeks at a time.

I've never really been free of Ian and I don't want to be. I'm quite happy that my life is in tandem with Ian's memory and his iconic status and he surrounds me all the time. Whenever I DJ I play Joy Division songs, whenever I sit in my office pictures of Ian and Joy Division paraphernalia surround me. He isn't here physically but he is very very much in my life metaphysically.

Manchester was a very industrial city and at the end of the seventies there was the decline of the coal mines and the beginning of the Thatcher era. So it was a bit of a grim place. I don't think Manchester was very special at all. It was like Leeds, Newcastle, Hull, they were all the bloody same. If I knew what made Manchester become a musical centre I'd be a fuckin' millionaire! I've no idea. My only thought is that we all united to kick Liverpool's arse.

I got involved with music when I saw the Sex Pistols. Before that I had no interest in it. I used to go to concerts – Led Zeppelin, Deep Purple, Wishbone Ash – but I never really had an interest in making music. Everybody seemed to be a virtuoso on their instrument and it all seemed clanny and quite remote. With punk you felt you could grab hold of it whereas you didn't feel like you could grab hold of Led Zeppelin.

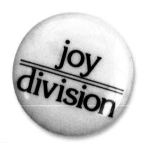

I used to read the weekly music press, devour it – *Sounds*, *Melody Maker*, *NME* – wait outside the newsagent for them to come in. I read about the Sex Pistols when I was on holiday in Torquay in 1976. I bought the magazine where they'd a fight. I thought, fuckin' hell this looks like a wild bunch – you don't see Led Zeppelin or Deep Purple brawling. I always read the *Manchester Evening News* from cover to cover – I still do. Don't know why – it must be one of my addictions. I was reading the *Evening News* when I came back from holiday and I spotted a little tiny advert for the Sex Pistols, 50p, Lesser Free Trade Hall, in the 'What's On' section. I phoned up Barney and Terry Mason, who was our friend at the time, and took them down. I'd known Barney since I was eleven, that's forty years! You get less than that for murder.

With punk you just felt you could be a part of it. The music sounded fuckin' dreadful but I think that added to it. I listened to a bootleg of the Sex Pistols concert years later. They actually played really well – it's the sound that was shit. So, ironically, the sound guy inspired me to form a band. How weird is that?

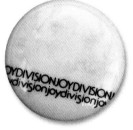

We met Ian at a later Pistols concert, when they played on the *Anarchy* tour at the Electric Circus. We didn't want a charismatic front man. It was simply that Ian was interested. He was Mr Available. We auditioned a few lead singers and they were a bunch of fucking idiots. We couldn't actually join up with Ian right away 'cos he had a group. Eventually his guitarist and drummer left and he found himself free.

What became Joy Division developed quite slowly over a period of about eighteen months. We were playing gigs to nobody then playing the same material to thousands six months later.

The thing about us is that we never really replicated anything. We very much did our own thing right from the start. Even now I find it very difficult – probably part of being tone-deaf – to play other people's music. As a self-taught musician I think if someone teaches you to do things in a certain way it's not a good idea.

We were outsiders because other bands were middle-class art-student types. There was a period where we felt ostracised by Buzzcocks and Howard Devoto. I don't think they considered us to be arty enough. But we fucking showed them, didn't we?

We met Rob Gretton when he was DJing at the Rafters on the Stiff Chiswick night. Kevin Cummins was a drummer in a group with Paul Morley called the Negatives. They were fucking shit and they elbowed us down the bill until I chased Kevin out. I said I was gonna rip his fucking head off 'cos he was a cunt. They were just fucking around and we were serious. The Negatives were Paul Morley's statement that anybody could be in a band and didn't have to be good, which is true at the start but not if you want longevity.

We'd been going at it a long time so we didn't find their efforts very funny AT ALL. What did amuse me was no matter what they said about not being able to play and being anarchic they didn't wanna fuckin' go on last. They weren't that anarchic.

It was the same night that Ian told Tony Wilson to fuck off – it's in *24 Hour Party People*. Rob bumped into Bernard in town later and said, 'I'd like to manage you.' Barney forgot to tell us. Rob was very working-class as well. It was only when we got involved with Factory that we became exposed to dope-smoking liberals talking bollocks.

Bernard always says, and it's quite astute of him, your first album took twenty years to write and they expect you to write another one in a year. Subconsciously I suppose we were affected by our surroundings. I didn't form a band to move to LA like Billy Duffy. I formed a band to stay in Manchester. Maybe there was a subconscious desire to get out of Manchester but it certainly wasn't a conscious desire.

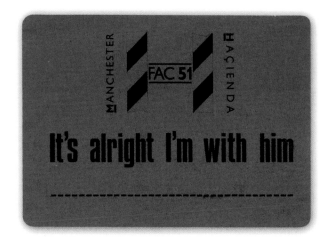

The Stiff Chiswick night was the first night Ian played drunk. He went wild because we'd been so wound up by the Negatives and everybody else. We ended up going on stage at half past two in the morning. Ian was drunk and fuckin' mad. That was the first time I actually saw him kick off – we thought, yay, fucking great – trash the gaff.

You knew people as well as you could in that situation. Ian was a good mate. We were in it together. The falling-out stage hadn't arrived, petty arguments were just beginning and there was his illness, worrying about him, looking after him. He'd been in the band about six or eight months before we knew he was ill.

It was a completely different world then, people didn't talk about their feelings. Ian wasn't very open with us and I'm sure we weren't open with him. You spent time together and you sympathised but I think men were men in them days. If I knew then what I knew now he wouldn't be fucking dead. I would have fucking sat with him, stopped him.

But I didn't have the nous to stop it – didn't have the education, didn't have the experience. If I looked at someone now who was acting like Ian I'd say this guy is going for a fall. He needs looking after. All of us round Ian just let him carry on.

After his first fit I had the dubious honour of looking after him and holding his tongue rather a lot.

What always used to send him off were the fuckers flashing the lights. That was how our whole lighting theme came about for Joy Division and New Order – slow washes so it didn't send Ian into a fit. Changing the lighting too fast always triggered his epilepsy.

He fought against his illness. The doctors said to him, 'You need to be quiet, you need to not drink and you need to lead a very stable life,' and he just went, 'Fuck that – I'm going back to the group.'

We were living for today, we weren't thinking about the future. New Order and Joy Division have always been shit about looking after the future. We made mistake after mistake and gave all our money away over the years. If Ian was all right when you put him to bed and he was OK when he woke up in the morning then that was the only thing you thought about.

Those early gigs were fantastic – the joy and the hardship of playing to one person in Huddersfield in 1977 really far outweighs the buzz you get from playing to ten or fifteen thousand in Wembley. I know we could play Wembley Arena any time now – it might not be full but at least it would be quite full. It just doesn't have the same excitement as someone giving you your second concert.

I never heard Ian's lyrics till we went into the studio with Martin Hannett to do *Unknown Pleasures*. I'd never heard them because the equipment we were using was so fucking bad. I'd never heard Barney play guitar till we went into the studio to do *Unknown Pleasures* either.

Bernard and I were very young and very obvious which is why we didn't like *Unknown Pleasures*. We wanted it to sound like it did in the rehearsal room – upfront and rocky. Martin Hannett gave it depth. I don't mind it now that I'm older and able to appreciate things like that.

Martin was impossible to work with, an absolute fuckin' pain in the arse. The more he got into drugs, the more difficult he became. Bernard and I just watched what he did, then, soon as we felt we could do it without him, we got rid of him.

I don't think I had the experience or the depth to look into Ian's lyrics. Maybe the thing was in some ways you were guarding yourself because it was so shocking.

When he died I was lucky I was in a group – being together carried us through. If it had been my best friend or something I'd have been on my own. Outside the framework of the group I might not have been able to handle it, but because we were all together it was 'Ian's gone, we must carry on.'

We sort of stepped out of the public eye; Rob quite rightly stopped us doing anything. We just went off to grieve.

I think once the grief subsides there's a certain attitude with suicide where you think they've left you up shit creek without a paddle. In that way you could say we carried on to show Ian that we didn't need him, but we didn't really do that.

We didn't know whether we were going to be able to pull it off. We didn't run out and get another singer; we tried to find a way to do it that was self-contained. I suppose that was quite unnerving but it did take your mind off Ian's demise.

The thing is we didn't know anything else. We'd had a fantastic time for two years. We'd found our niche in life, we'd found what we wanted to do, we were enjoying it and even though Ian died all of us got the strength from being together. We didn't know how we were gonna carry on or what we were gonna do – we just did it.

It took us rather a long time to figure out a way of moving forward musically because we always relied on Ian to tell us what was good and bad.

The title for 'Everything's Gone Green' I got from a book. It was just an experiment with the electronic equipment Bernard and Steve were very into using. I'm a bit of an old stick-in-the-mud and would have preferred to rock out for ever but Steve and Bernard really embraced the technological side so I couldn't resist it. 'Everything's Gone Green' and 'Temptation' were the first products of this new equipment that they had.

When we were in the studio I used to read a lot, to keep meself sane before I discovered drink and drugs. Anything I thought would be interesting for a title, I'd write it down. *Power, Corruption and Lies* I got from a review on the back of *1984*. '*1984* is a wonderful tale of power, corruption and lies.' It was just like that – you got titles from the books you were reading, write them on the wall and try and use them later.

'Faith' was out of a book about the Catholic religion but Bernard and I were the only two Protestants at Factory. Everybody else in Factory was Catholic. Tony Wilson always used to go on about Catholic guilt and we'd go, 'Fuckin' hell, Tony – we're Protestants, you plank.'

Tony didn't have that much effect on us musically. He enabled us to put it out and filled everyone around us with this arsey bullshit that made us seem more intelligent, intellectually deeper than we actually were! He was middle-class, university-educated, and he was a world apart. He always used to describe us as 'those dreadful oiks'. Where Bernard and I grew up you fight anything like that – you don't pretend to be what you're not. We never fell for that.

I do think we'd have made a football song like 'World in Motion' with Ian – he had a wicked sense of humour. His widow Debbie's revelations have been fucking fantastic – like Ian Curtis riding the back of a pig with a pink fluorescent fur jacket on. It goes against the dour image – fucking hilarious.

I never considered New Order to be that different from Joy Division. I think a lot of the music harks back to Joy Division and I see a very strong thread going through it. My golden age with New Order was when we used to write everything together. I felt that when Bernard started writing his own lyrics and vocal lines on *Technique* it changed – the power shifted.

Before that we split the songwriting with Rob – because we were young and foolish. But he was very much part of the process. He didn't write the music but he did tell us what was shit and what was good and what to change – not that we took any notice. The feeling was we were all in it all together right from the word go.

As soon as you start arguing about song credits you're guaranteed to fall apart.

This argument absolutely reaches its peak with Morrissey. Morrissey and Marr said they wrote The Smiths' songs whereas listening to them and talking to Andy Rourke and Mike Joyce, they contributed. Even the judge said that. You also have the same problem in The Stone Roses – Ian Brown and the guitarist. They said that Mani and Reni didn't write the songs. Listening to Reni and Mani's interplay I find that an absolutely fucking preposterous suggestion – but it stands. The publishing for Stone Roses songs is 'Squire and Brown'. If I was Mani I would have chopped both their fuckin' heads off. Andy Rourke should have killed Morrissey ages ago and fuckin' laid Johnny Marr out.

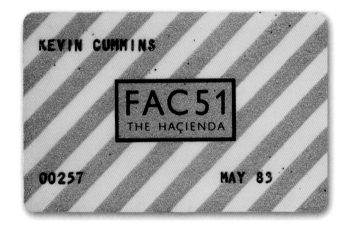

I never saw a drug till I was twenty-eight. I didn't start taking drugs till I was thirty-four. But I made up for it then. The reason I started doing drugs was because I was sick of sitting there with a load of people talking absolute shite. Peer pressure. Unfortunately once I started doing it I couldn't stop.

We didn't have any money thanks to the Haçienda or think of anything in a commercial sense. When Barney sat in that hotel room in LA and said he wanted to go off and do Electronic, he didn't do it thinking 'I've made enough money in New Order, I can afford to do this now.' It was a purely emotional decision.

Johnny Marr asked me to work with him first, which was the big argument I had with Bernard and Johnny Marr. We did a gig in San Francisco and Johnny Marr turned up with his wife, maybe he was off his head. When he started working with Barney I said, 'That's really weird 'cos Johnny Marr asked me to work with him and I didn't take him up on the offer.' It was annoying. I felt fuckin' betrayed by Bernard but once I got rid of him I realised how much more enjoyable life could be.

I knew The Stone Roses' manager really well and he asked me if I'd produce them. He insisted on paying me even though I was very surprised. We agreed a sum of £400 and he actually gave me a thousand. Then he phoned me up and said, 'I'm talking to the record company here and you've not discussed points.' I said, 'I don't want any points.' I thought, 'It's the band's record – let 'em have it.'

He was going, 'No, no, you should have points.' I didn't even know what fucking points were. He put me down for two points and I made a fortune from those two tracks. I didn't even expect it because all the bands we produced at Factory we did for nothing. Not one of us got paid for any group that we ever did, just did it for love. We made some really good records. Even now when I listen to a lot of the records we made – like Section 25 Bernard did, Stockholm I did, great records, really good songs, interesting music – we never got paid for any of it.

Joy Division could have been as big as U2. New Order are as big as U2 in many ways – not financially, but I think you find that people who know music respect New Order's music more than they respect U2's music.

There have been a lot of frustrations in the life of New Order and Joy Division –

Factory going bust with all our money, the Haçienda taking the rest of it. My accountant says to me, 'It will never truly bother you until you do not earn money. When you do not earn money you will look back on those happenings and go mad. As long as you can earn money and still get creatively and financially satisfied by working,' he said, 'it won't be a problem.' He's quite a philosopher, our accountant.

I'm not as fucking rich as Bono but I do very well. I work hard. I deserve what I get so I'm quite happy at the moment.

I don't regret being involved in the Haçienda, I had millions of good times there. But it was like sending the village idiot out with the whole government budget for the year. What's he gonna do? He's only gonna come back with six magic beans, isn't he? He's not gonna come back with a revolutionary economic concept, is he? When you look at what happened you start thinking, 'Fucking hell – what a chance we missed. If it had been run well we'd be as rich as Bono.'

I'm very lucky – even though I live in Manchester I get to travel all round the world. When I come home all I want to do is chill out and relax and enjoy what Manchester has – that's a constant source of annoyance to my wife and children 'cos they want to go off somewhere. I'm spoilt. I've always been allowed to travel AND have a very exciting and interesting place as my base. Manchester never ceases to be good on a musical level. It's always very revolutionary. There's always something going on. It's a very important place for music now in England, in the world.

The important thing to me now is the compliment people give – a song like 'Love

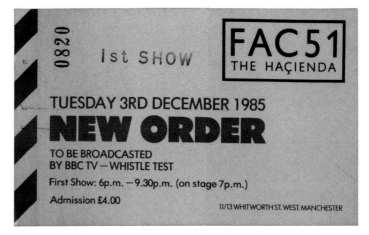

Will Tear Us Apart' has lasted so long. It's fucking amazing to think we spent three hours writing that in 1977 and thirty years later it's still fucking really popular. It's unbelievable; I'm absolutely fucking delighted. I saw Sofia Coppola use it in *Marie Antoinette*. I thought the result was absolutely beautiful. The way she used 'Ceremony' too. It made the song better!

I don't know fucking hell this again let's see my dad or my grandad both worked for themselves it occurred to me a couple of years ago I'd never thought about it before that I'm not a foreman I'm more like a football manager really I always thought I was going to turn out to be a bit more of a loner y'know but that's not the case at all I was pretty late in getting into music believe it or not it wasn't until I was about fourteen that I started to split into music and it sort of accelerated dead quick then I had a group by the time I was eighteen nineteen it went quite weird I wasn't like well when I was in primary school music was girls' stuff we were more into sport really I can't really say what got me into it I think it might have been just that I was able to buy a single and my dad getting a record player and things like that it was *Paranoid* by Black Sabbath which well that says a lot don't it this was when it first came out of course and I just bought it because of the name really I was getting into books then too 'paranoid' was like a newish word and I thought Black Sabbath what's that about something to do with witchcraft or something I was reading a lot of horror books at the time like you do when you're fourteen hur hur hurgh it wasn't something I thought I could do not particularly I remember seeing a picture of Black Sabbath and they were drinking beer in a garden and hahahahahaha I thought that would be all right for a job hahahahahahahaha I can always remember thinking that I didn't take it seriously at all I never really thought about it to be honest I wanted to leave school as soon as possible well I thought I wanted to get out and get my own flat y'know that was my main idea get out of the house really it just looked like a nice way of life y'know what I mean because eh y'know when I was at school you still got caned for having long hair and everything y'know I mean that was the environment I was in y'know in the grammar school we were like the obligatory ship-in kids three or four from the ah Salford area that was a whole new world it was all right I used to get picked on for ah for the way I talked y'know I don't think the other three lasted it the five years but ah it never bothered me I don't have a hang-up about it y'know it was great I got left alone and I had some good mates y'know what I mean they used to leave me alone it's very strange being a Smith you could always get away with it y'know there's about forty in the whole year hahahahaha it's quite good there never was a problem with that definitely not no because they got all the ports here y'know you have Salford well I used to work on them they called them Salford Docks y'know you'd see all sorts of people y'know you'd just get shipments from Ghana and Africa and there used to be Africans on the dock in the pubs and obviously it seemed a bit more of a problem in the south really London always had a problem Liverpool was always good like that too y'know the only shows we used to do moving on for about a couple of years yeah a good two years two and a half years the only group that'd put us on top billing is Liverpool I mean place that would put us on we'd never get a full gig in Manchester or anywhere really but Liverpool was on the ball with us pretty much from when we started for a couple of years I remember that we were still sort of supporting all sorts of crap in Manchester but then London was the second the Marquee I remember that but seeing as this book is about Manchester but we kept apart from everyone y'know the scene there because what I could see coming was there's always been a Manchester scene y'know even before new wave or anything or punk or anything there was always Manchester pop groups y'know and I didn't see a lot of them being that much different y'know hahahurgh especially the new-wave Mancunian groups y'know I never liked them at all really there was always something more interesting in Liverpool or London y'know the group was started you got to remember the group was started when I was writing a lot of prose at work at lunchtime and that on a typewriter and ah y'know where we've a couple of me mates were into Patti Smith and the Ramones and the things like that y'know and so that's what we used to do we used to get together about twice a week and we'd read poetry out or read something out daft as y'know whatever and just play electric guitar with it y'know it was sort of hahahahahurghhurgh was like sort of a beatnik sort of thing we never thought of having a drummer or a bass player or anything y'know what I mean so anyway one of my mates turned to the bass and then it got on and I was getting into ah German music and stuff at the time so and sort of had a vague idea of getting it in with words but as I say it wasn't that serious y'know it was about a year a couple of years after the Pistols came and all that when we started taking it very seriously I was quite lucky really well not lucky but that was the time when the docks were really being wound down and I basically got laid off part of the reason being that I was always being late for work y'know what I mean but I enjoyed my job y'know the docks was a vanishing world I get lost now in Salford me y'know what I mean and that was about it I thought this sounds pretty good and then we got into the Musicians' Collective and got a drummer y'know hahahahehehehurgh and we just did it you know outsiders yeah that's right the Collective was as well but we weren't going to get a show anywhere else it was pretty rigid in Manchester there was only the Electric Circus at the south end of town it wasn't that though it was fairly selective it was pure punk rock y'know so when we used to play there we used to get bottled to shit you know and because of that we did the schools youth clubs and working men's clubs which you know you could develop then because hahahahaha they weren't listening to you half the time sort of separate from a lot of things y'know and then we met the Buzzcocks and they financed the record and it all went from there really there was a rivalry very much with Slaughter and the Dogs they were glam rock weren't they hehehehurgh that was it they threw stuff at us but they did that to everyone it was quite tough on the dole but I wasn't on long can we pick this up later I got a few things and that Penguin book thing that's starting at one . . .

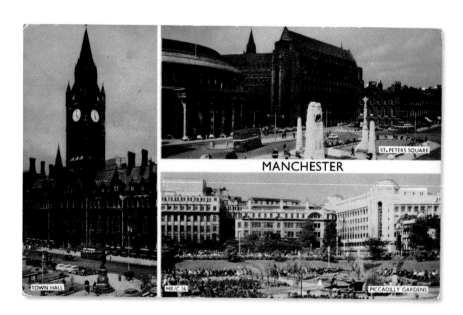

In those days
[pre-WW2] for
a Mancunian to
visit [London]
was an exercise
in condescension.
London was a
day behind
Manchester in the
arts, in commercial
cunning, in

economic philosophy . . . Manchester was generous and London was not.

Anthony Burgess

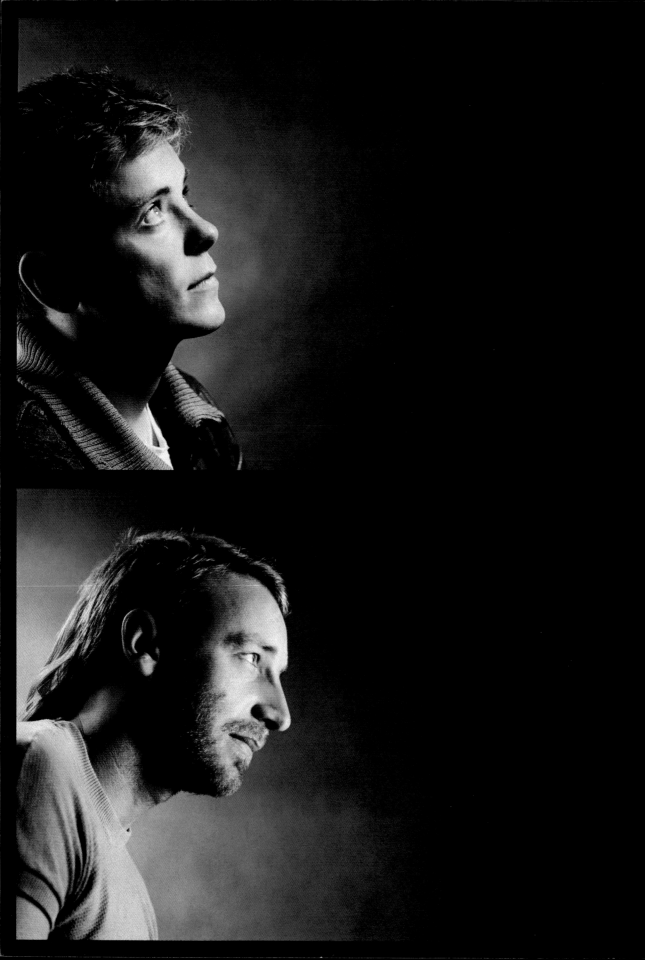

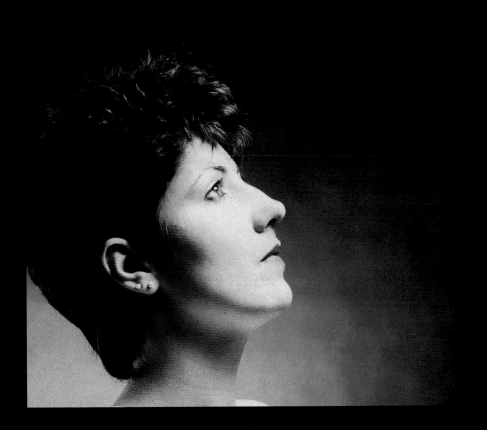

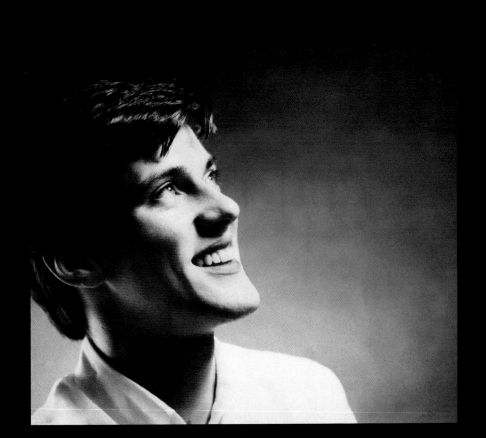

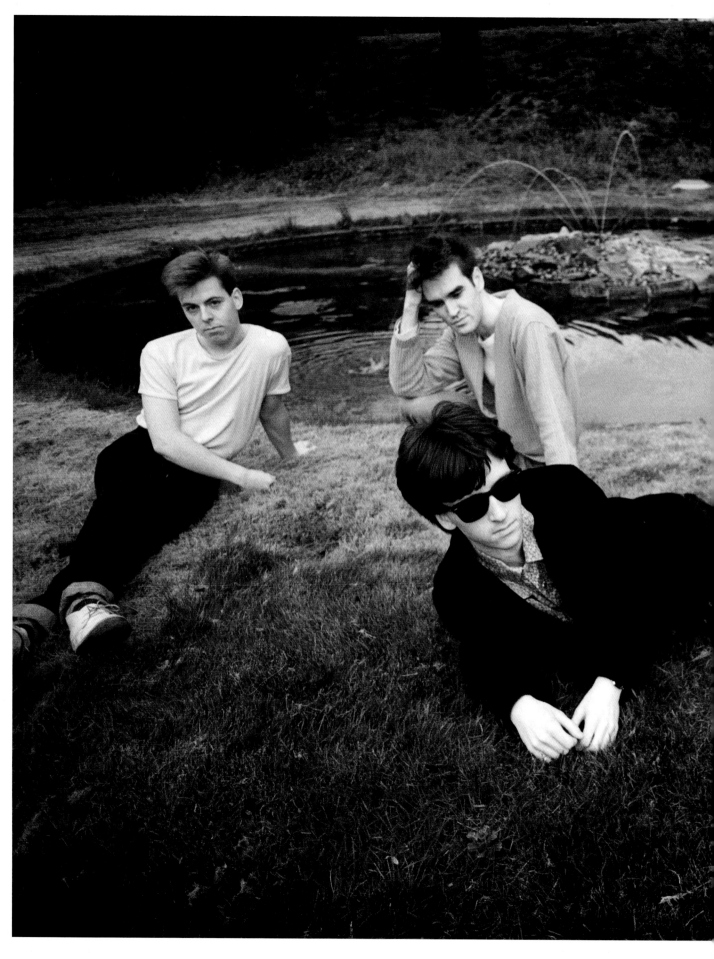

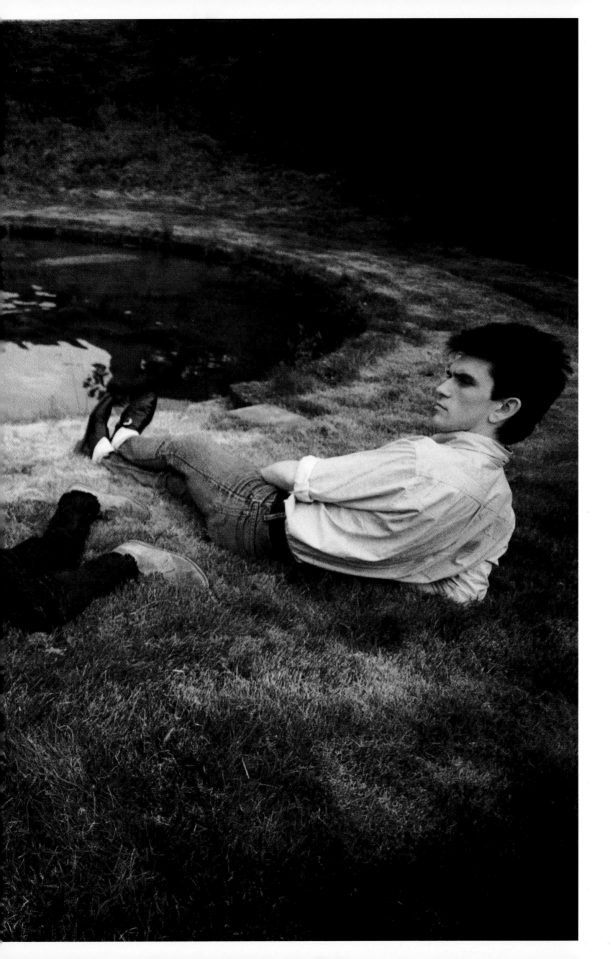

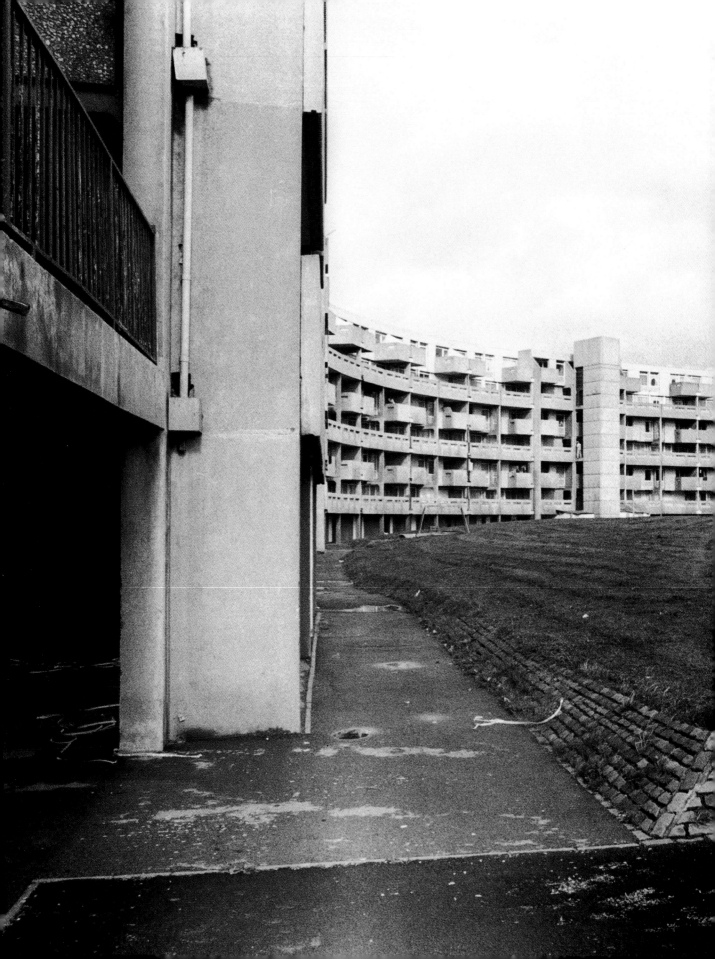

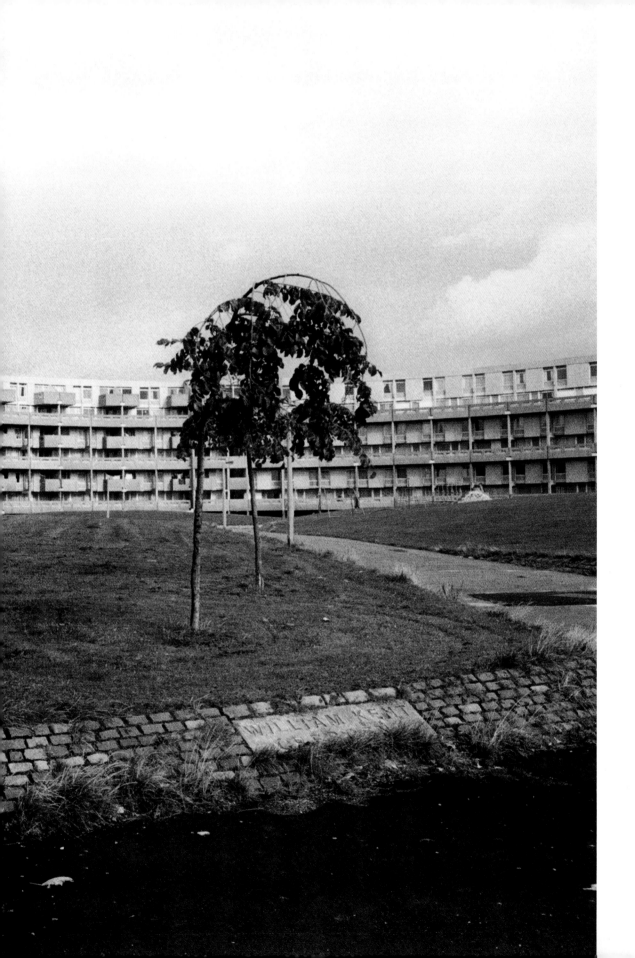

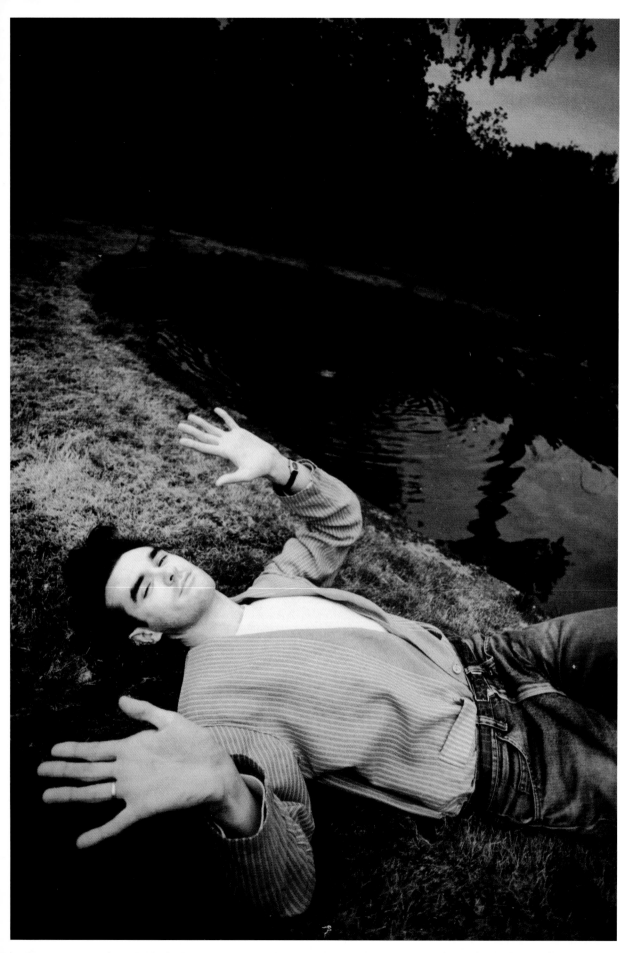

Morrissey, The Smiths
Dunham Massey, Greater Manchester
September 1983

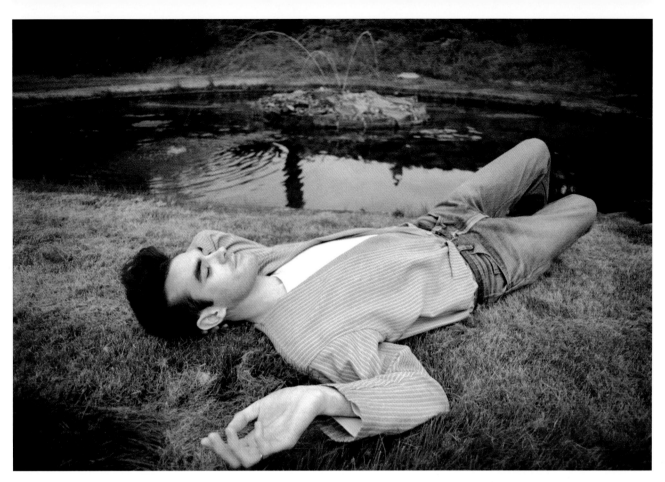

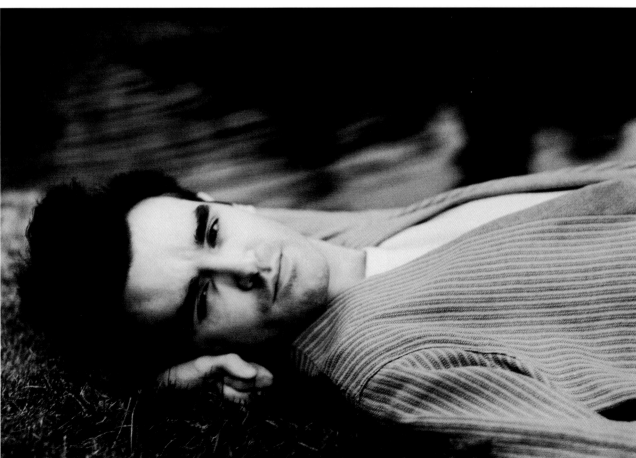

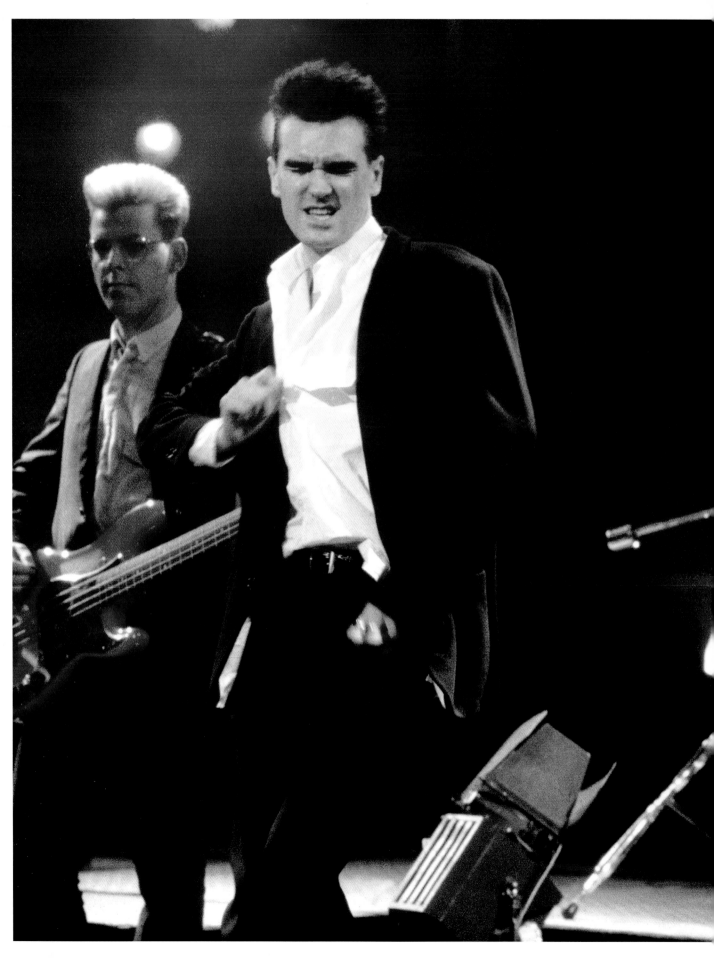

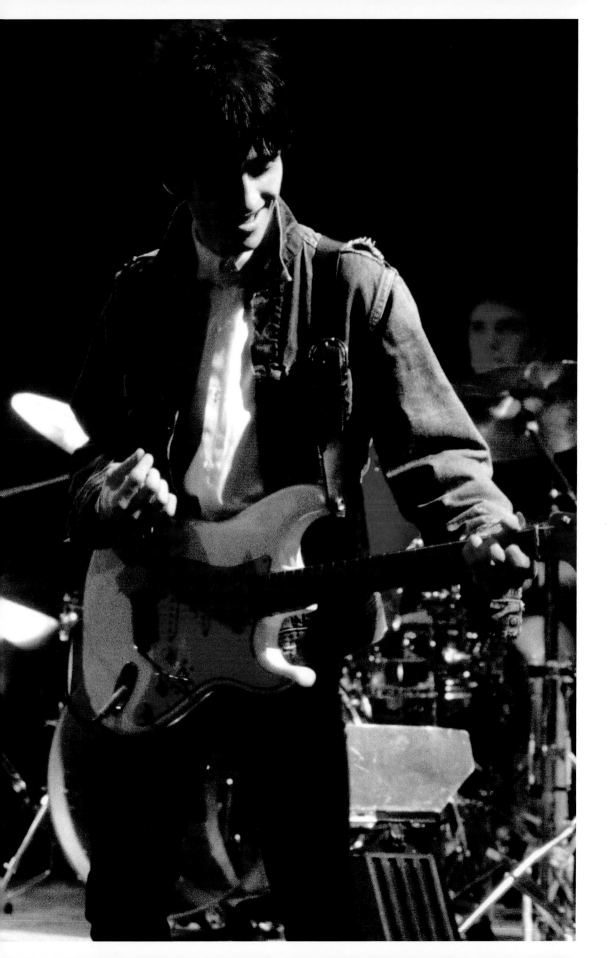

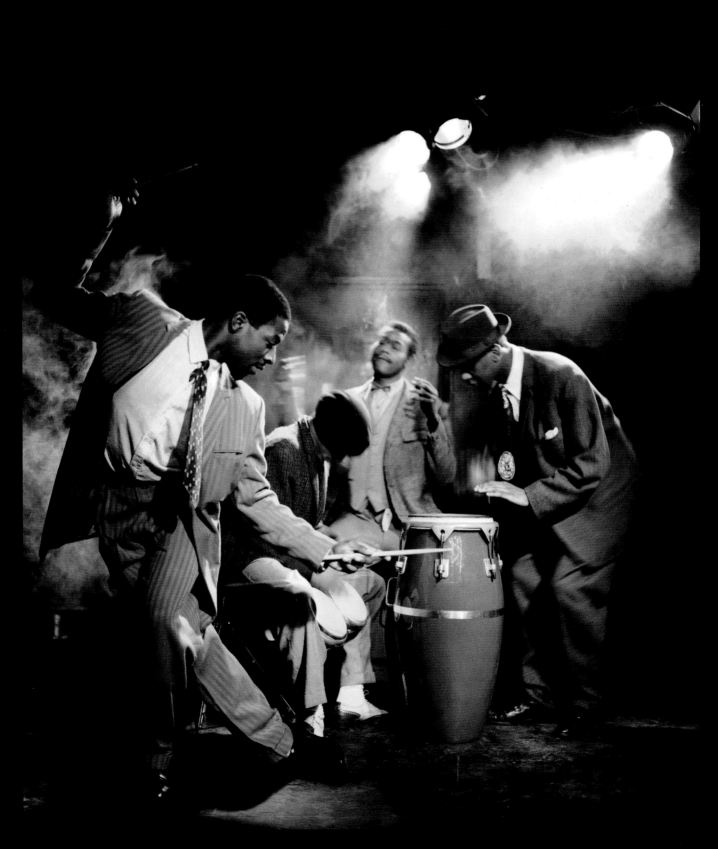

Andy Rourke, The Smiths
Blackpool
23 April 1985

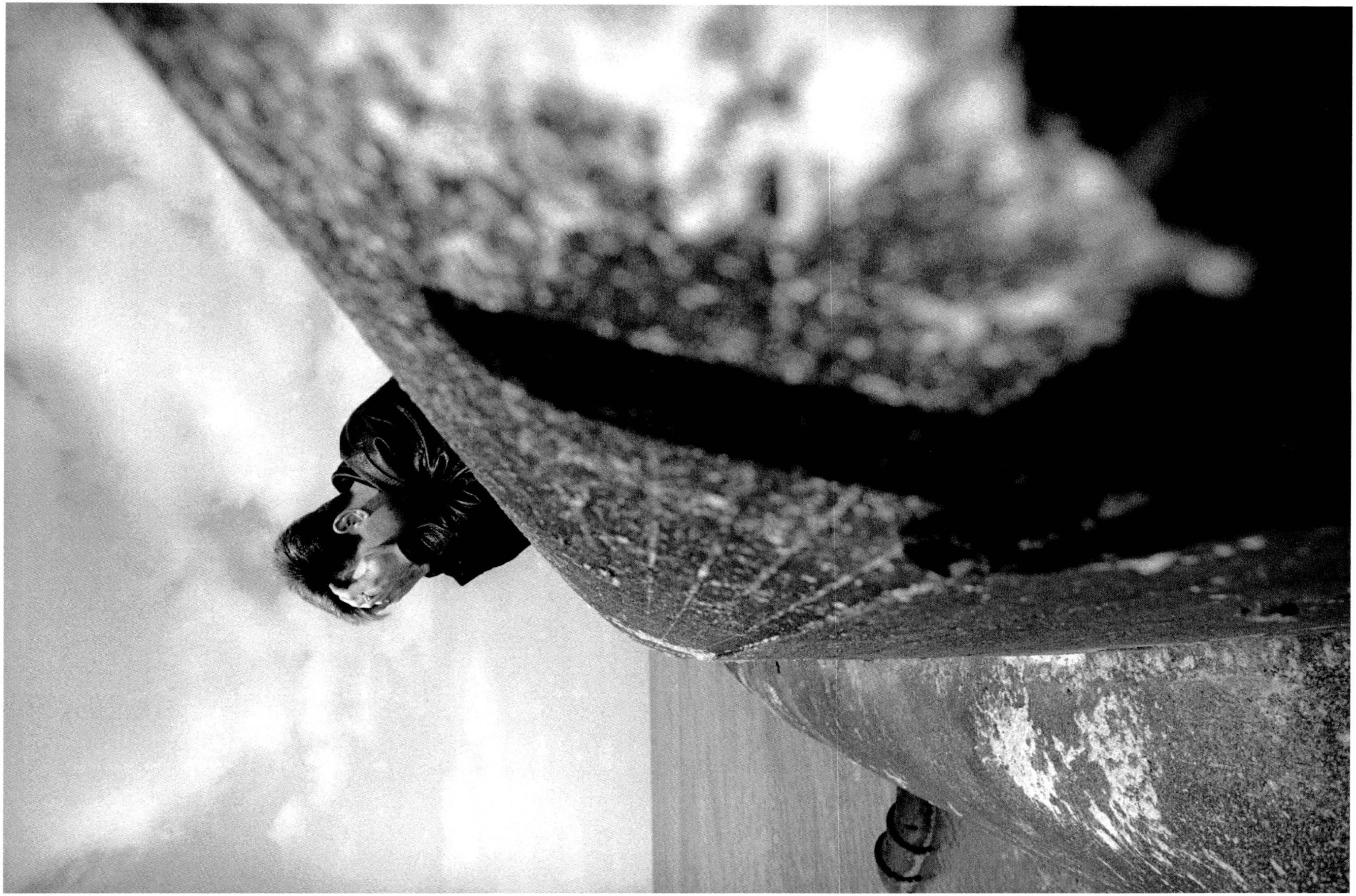

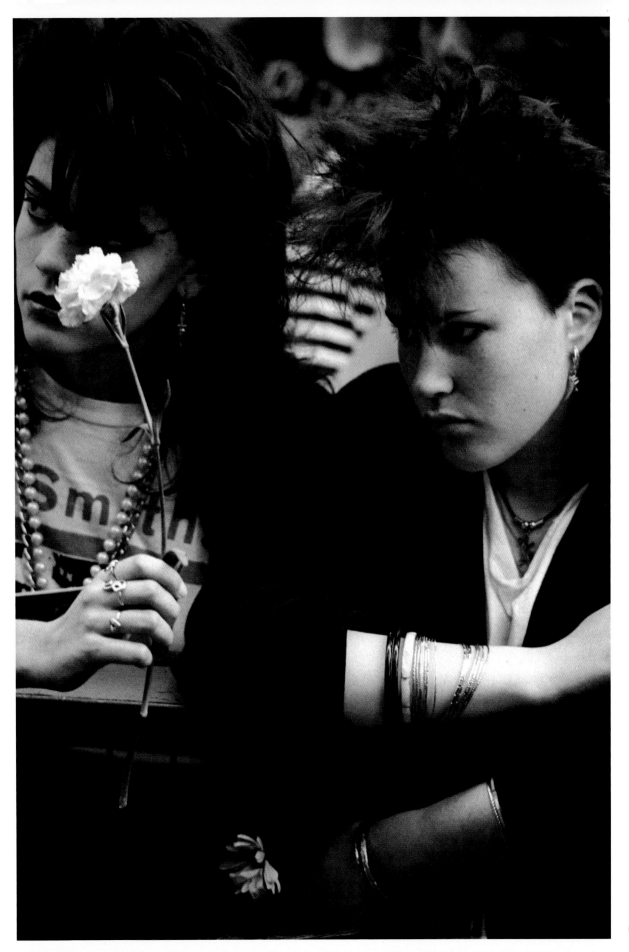

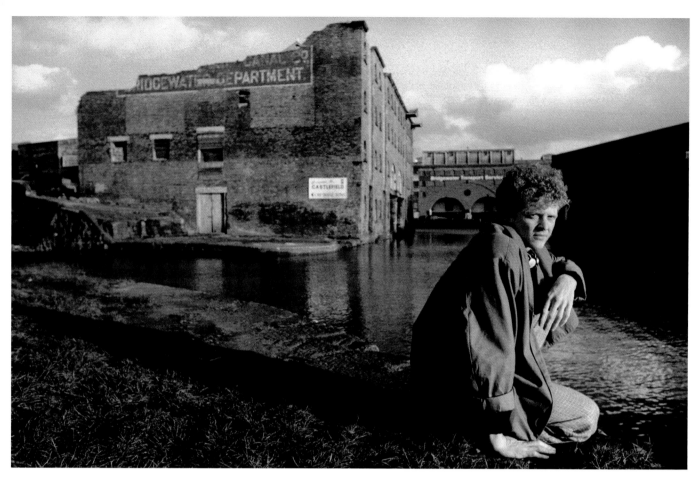

Mick Hucknall, Simply Red
Castlefield, Manchester
1 May 1985

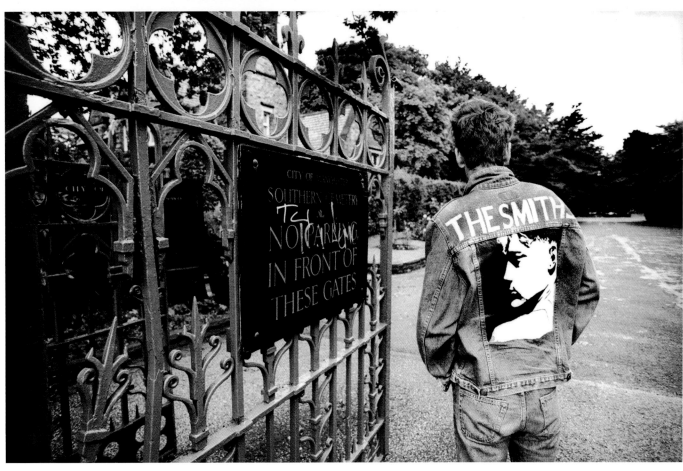

Smiths fan
Southern Cemetery Gates, Manchester
September 1988

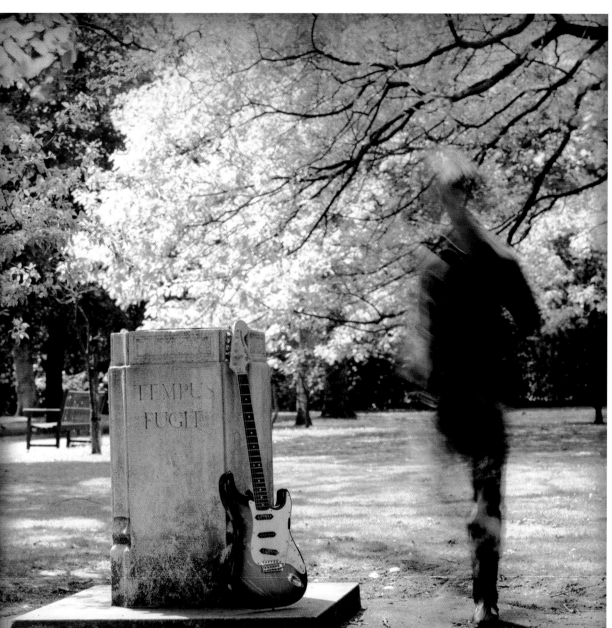

Vini Reilly, The Durutti Column
Marie Louise Gardens, Didsbury, Manchester
12 May 1986

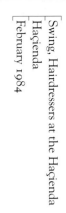

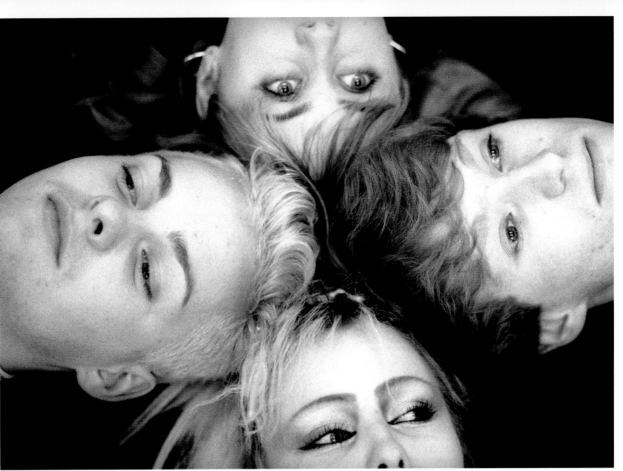

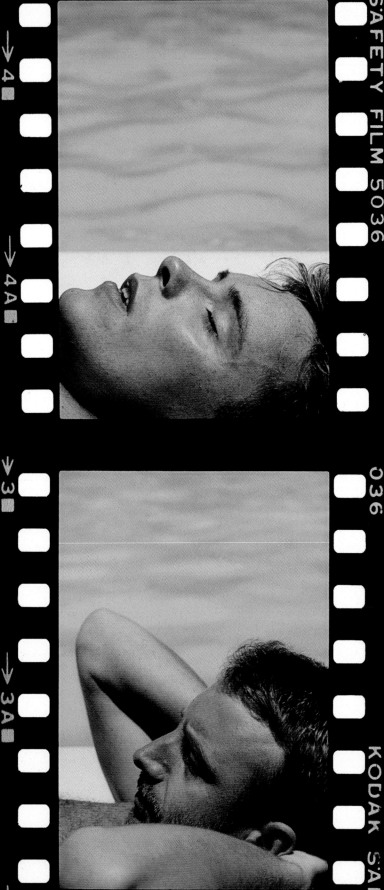

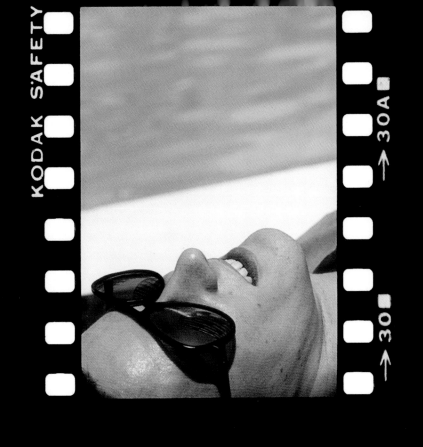

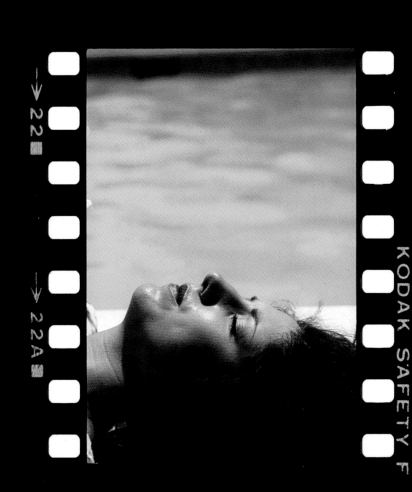

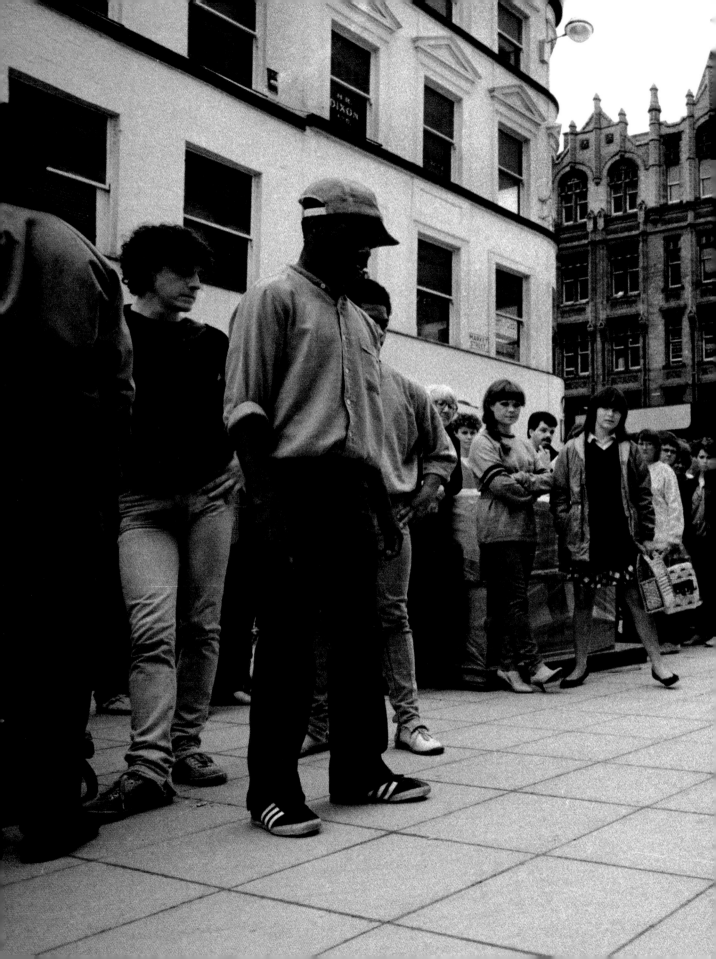

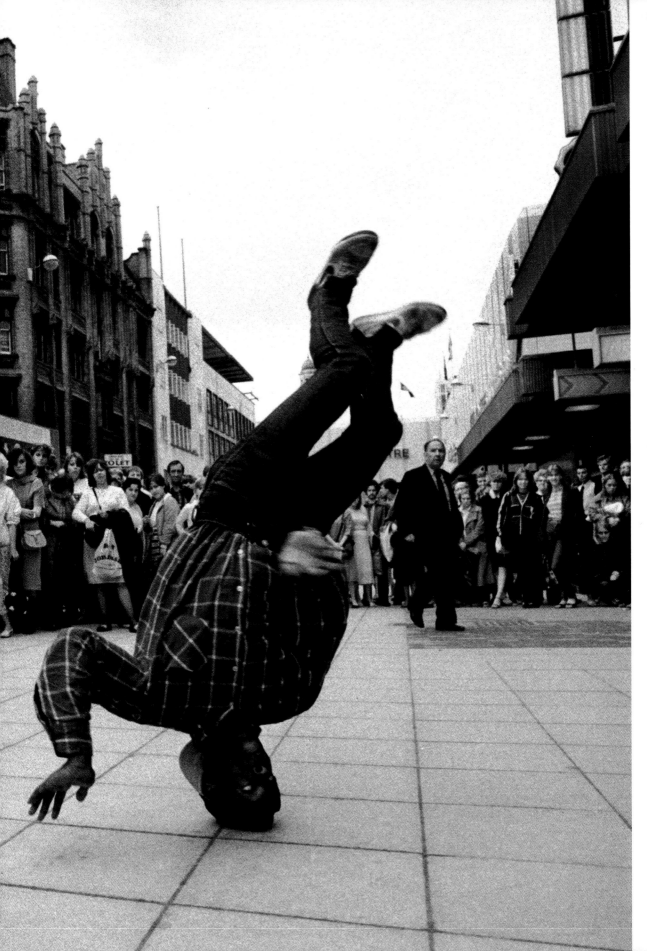

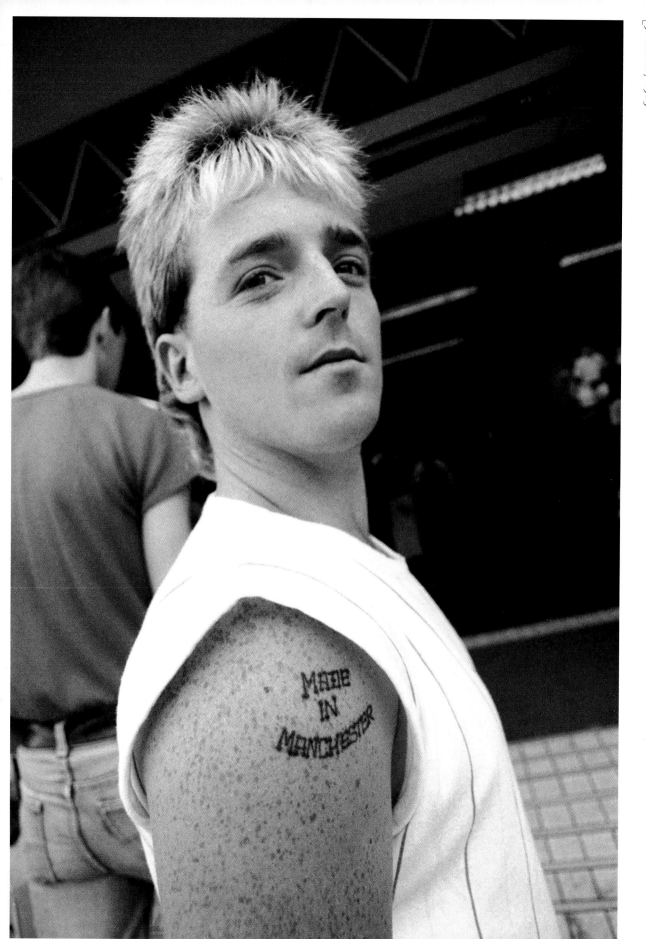

There is no such city as Manchester.

Howard Spring

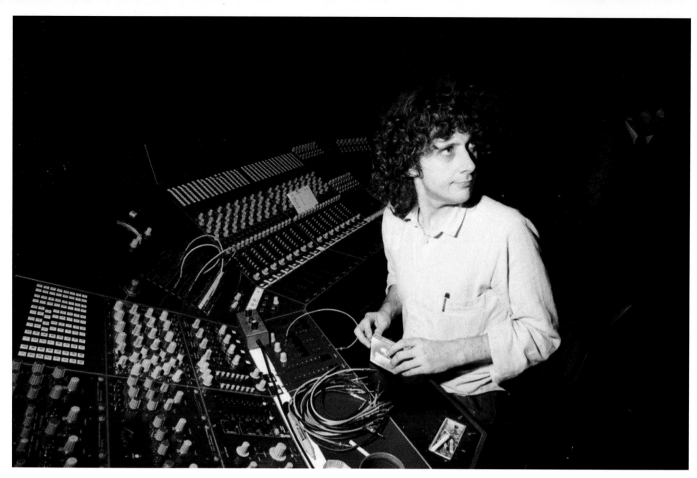

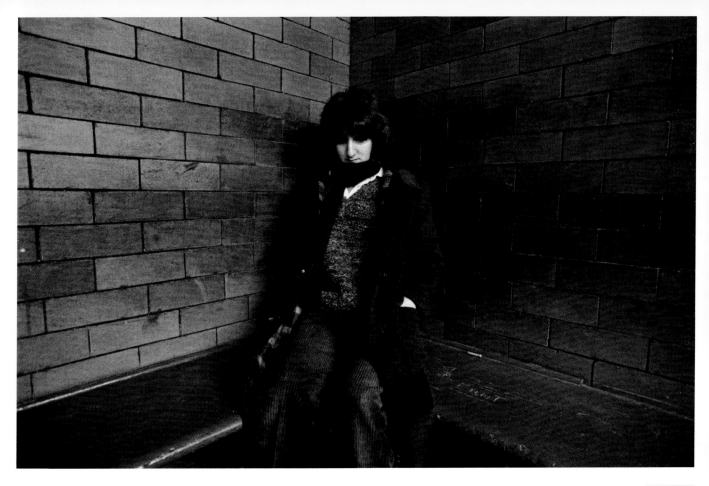

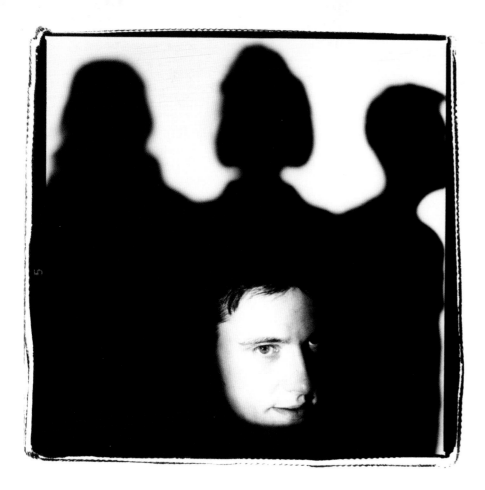

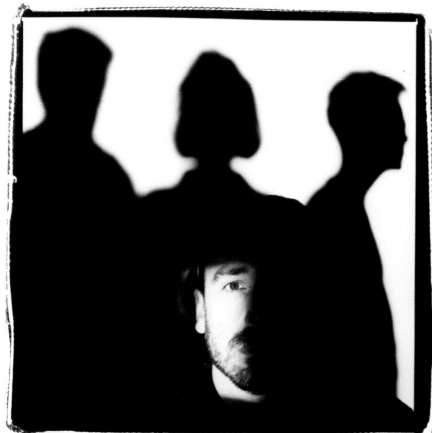

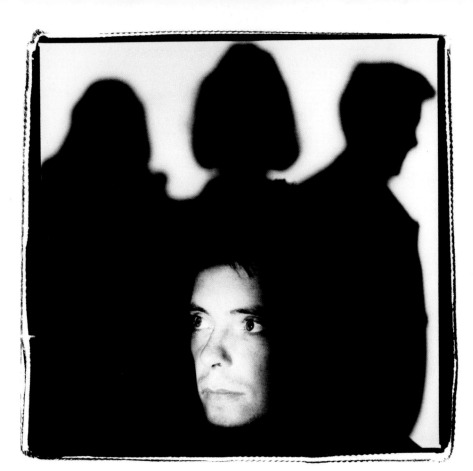

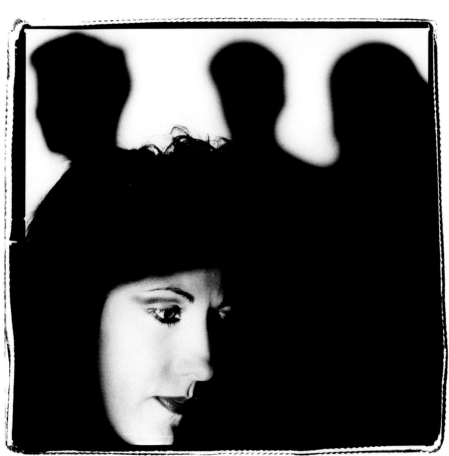

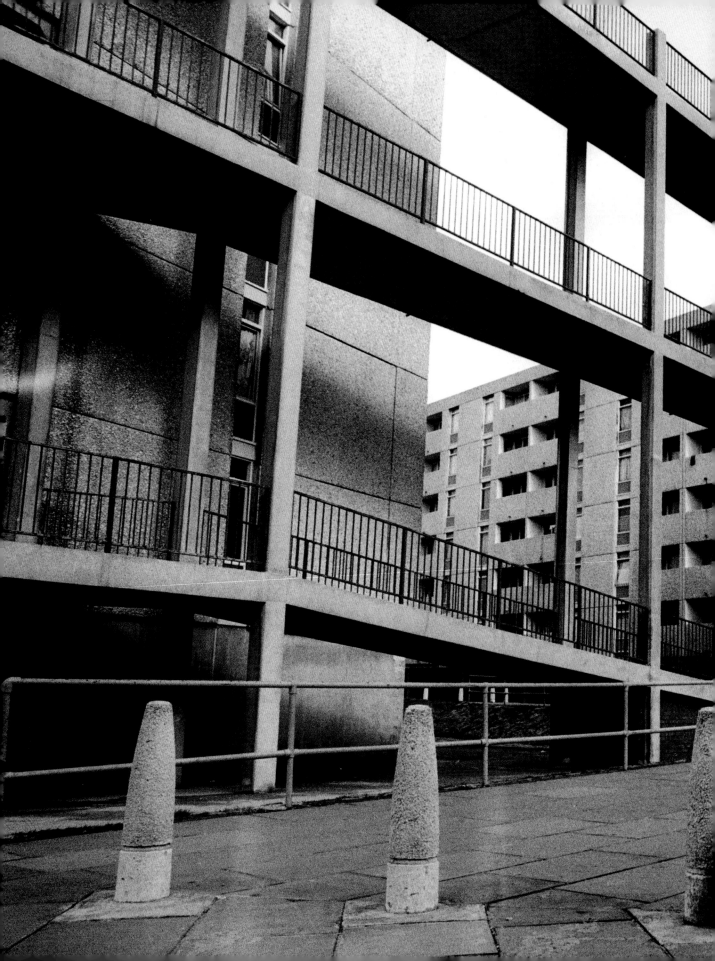

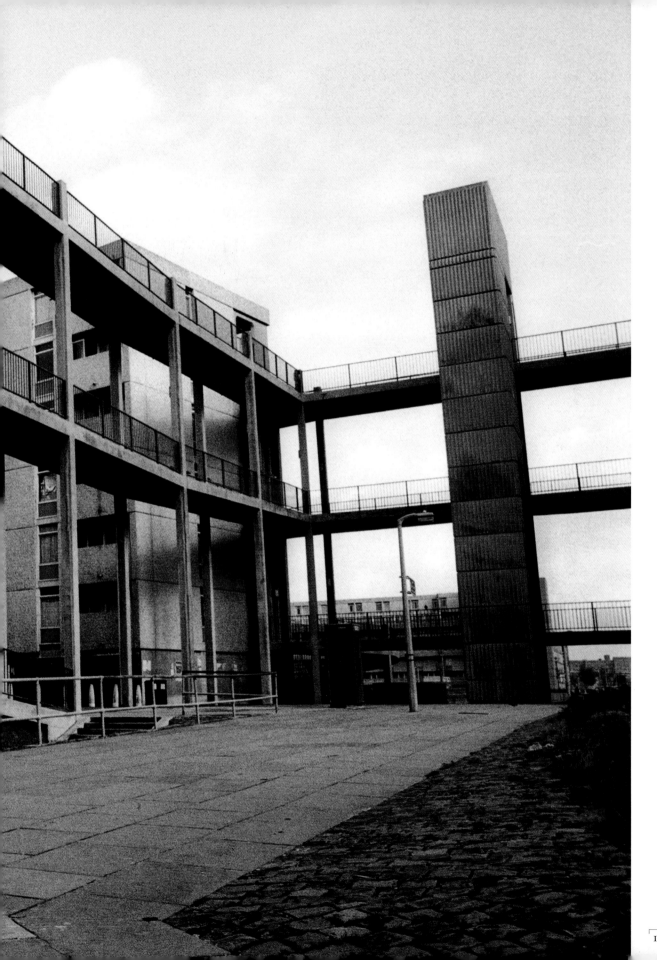

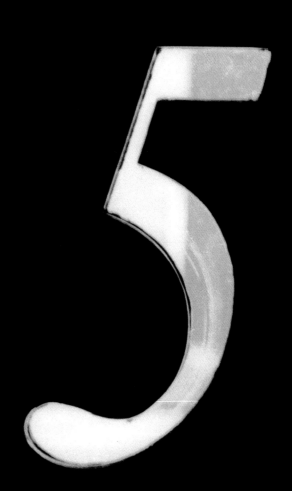

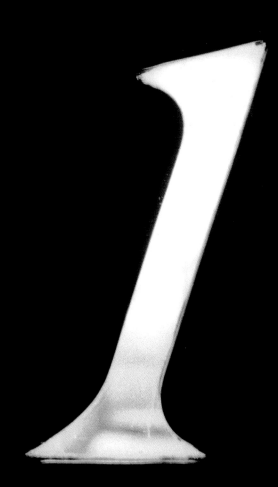

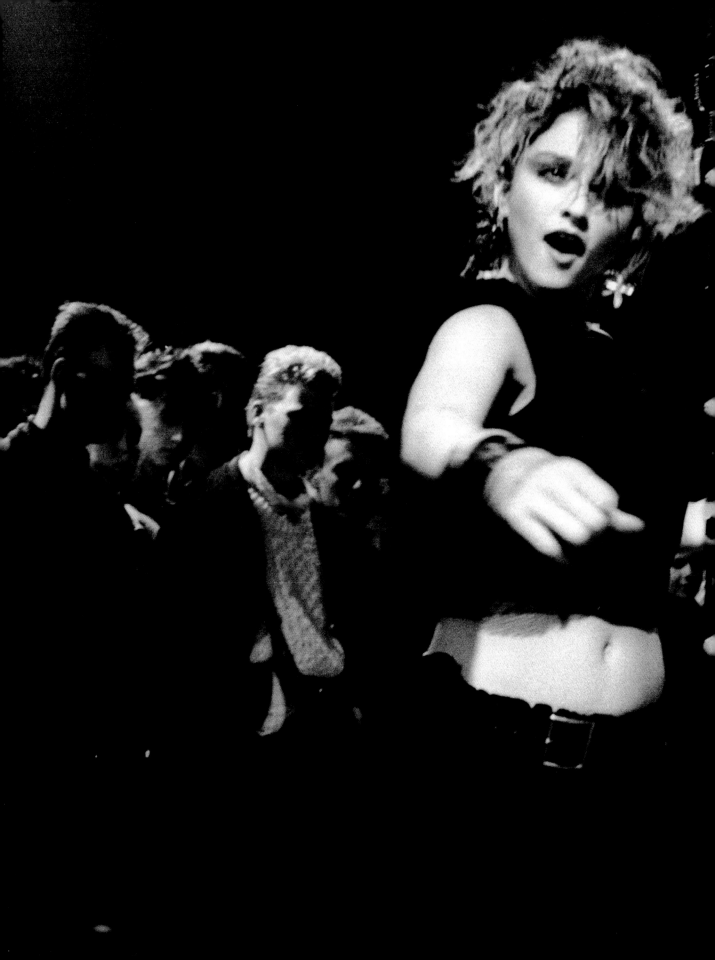

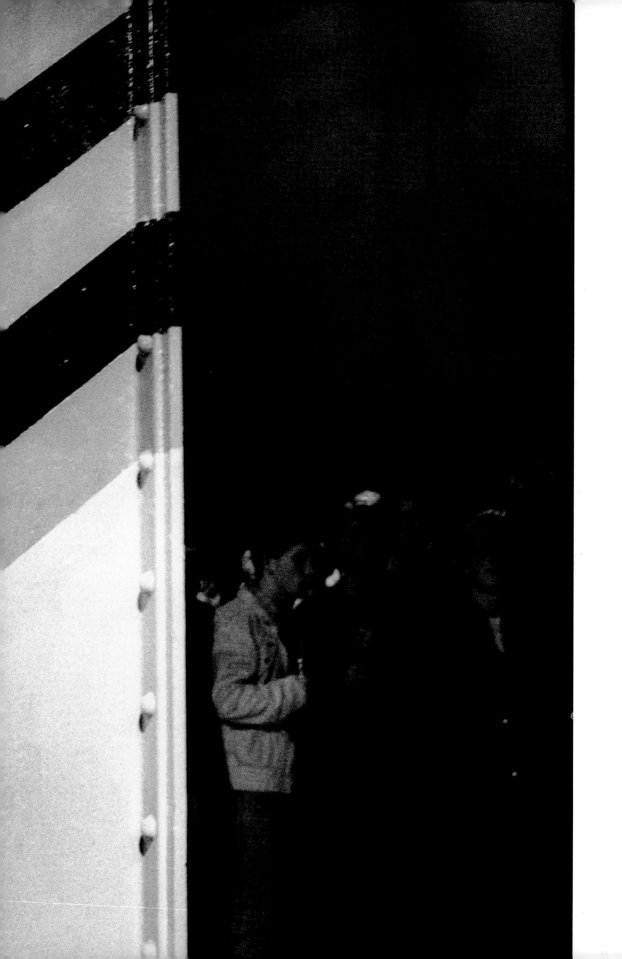

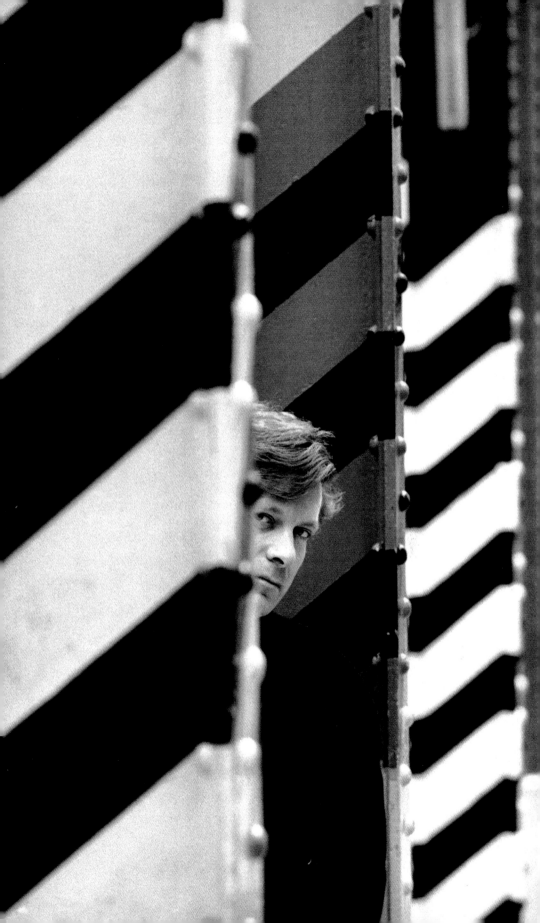

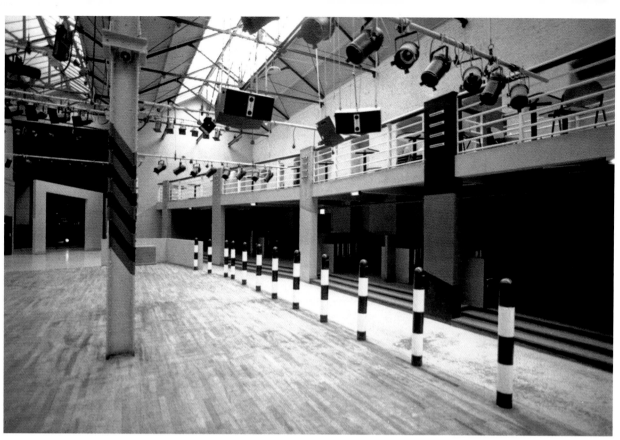

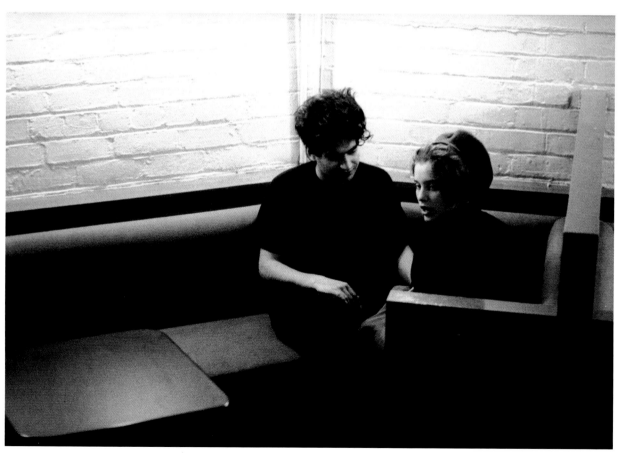

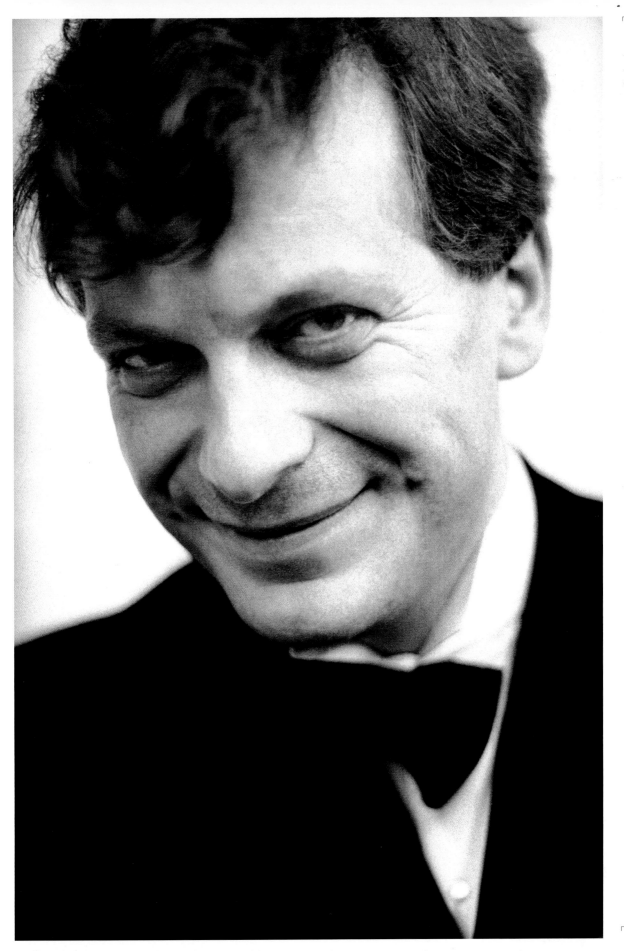

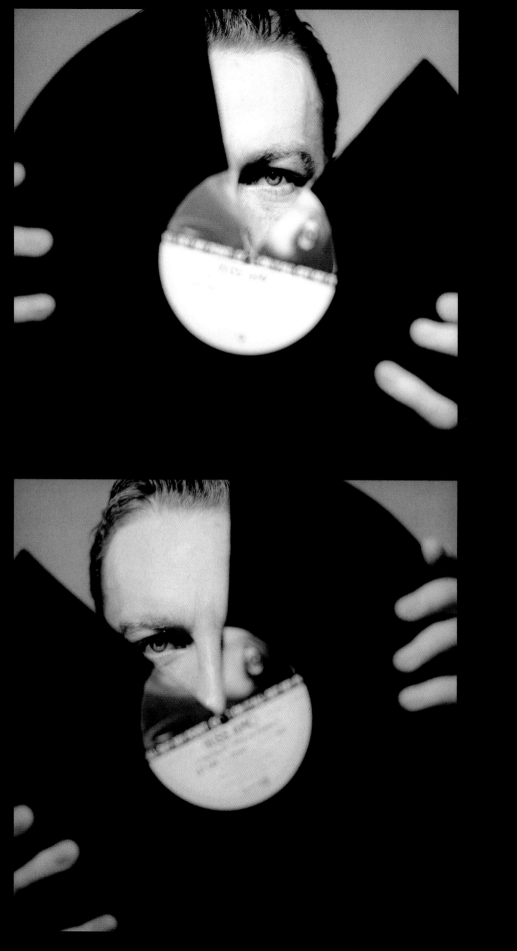

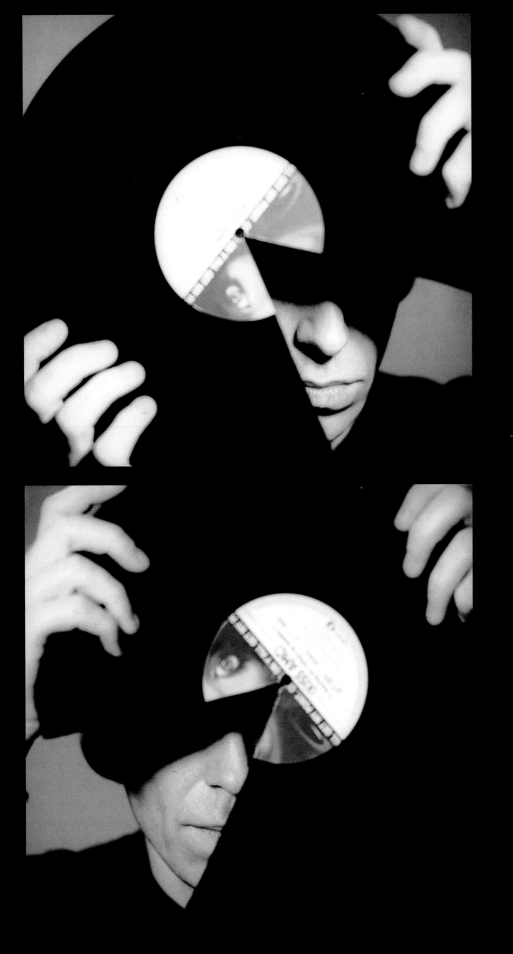

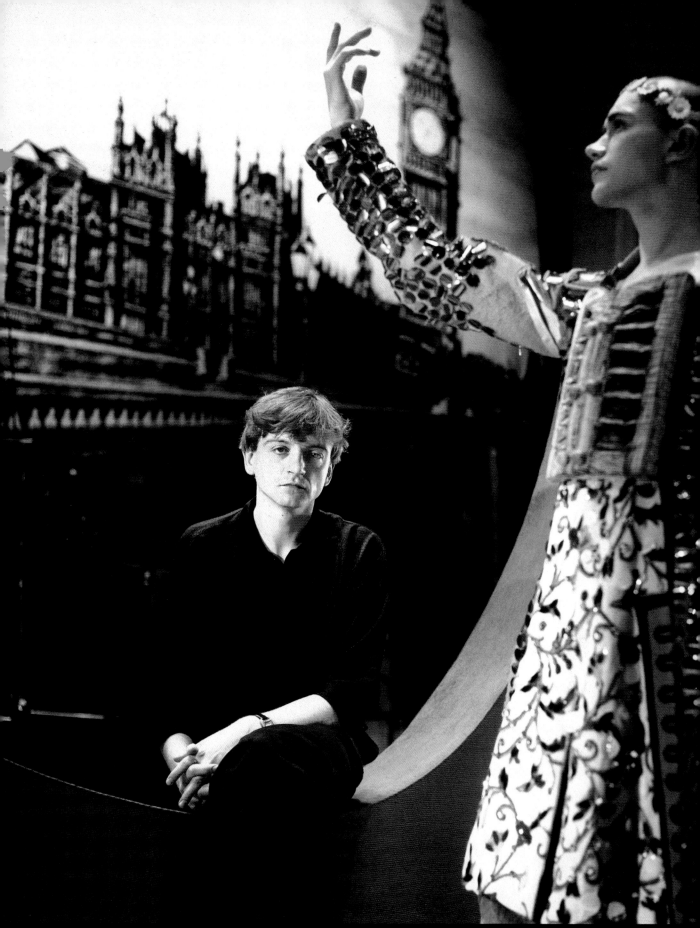

Mark E. Smith and Michael Clark
Set of *I am Curious, Orange*, King's Theatre, Edinburgh
August 1988

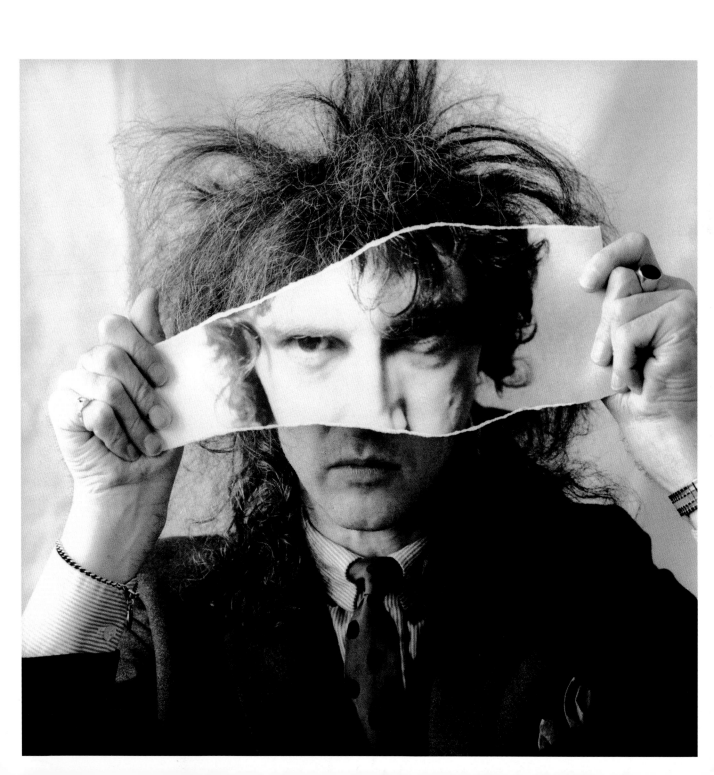

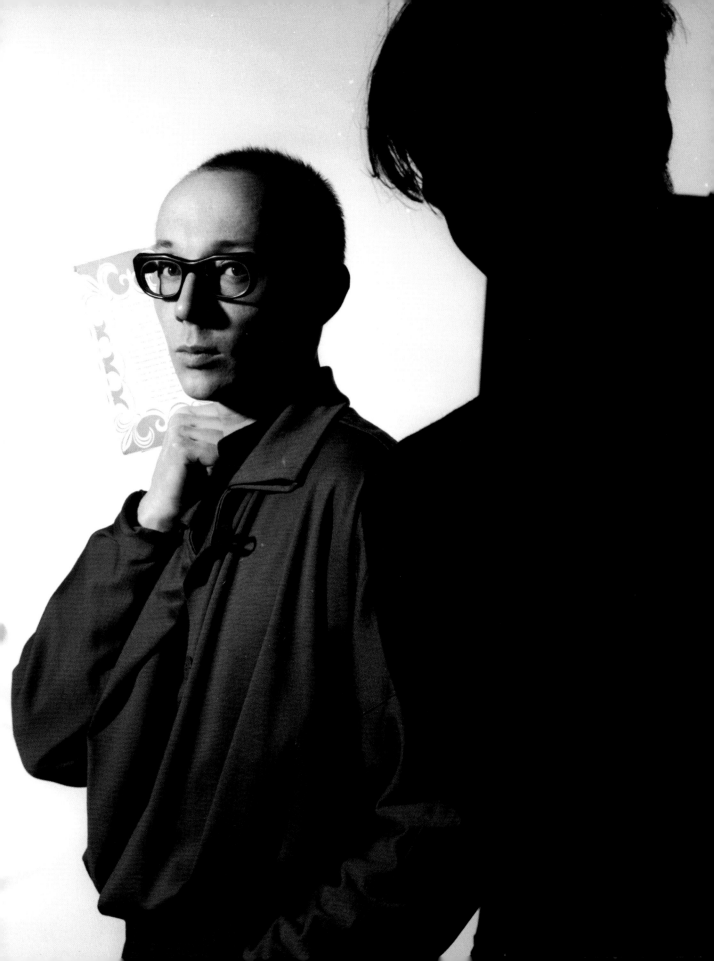

Howard Devoto, Luxuria
Studio, London
28 January 1988

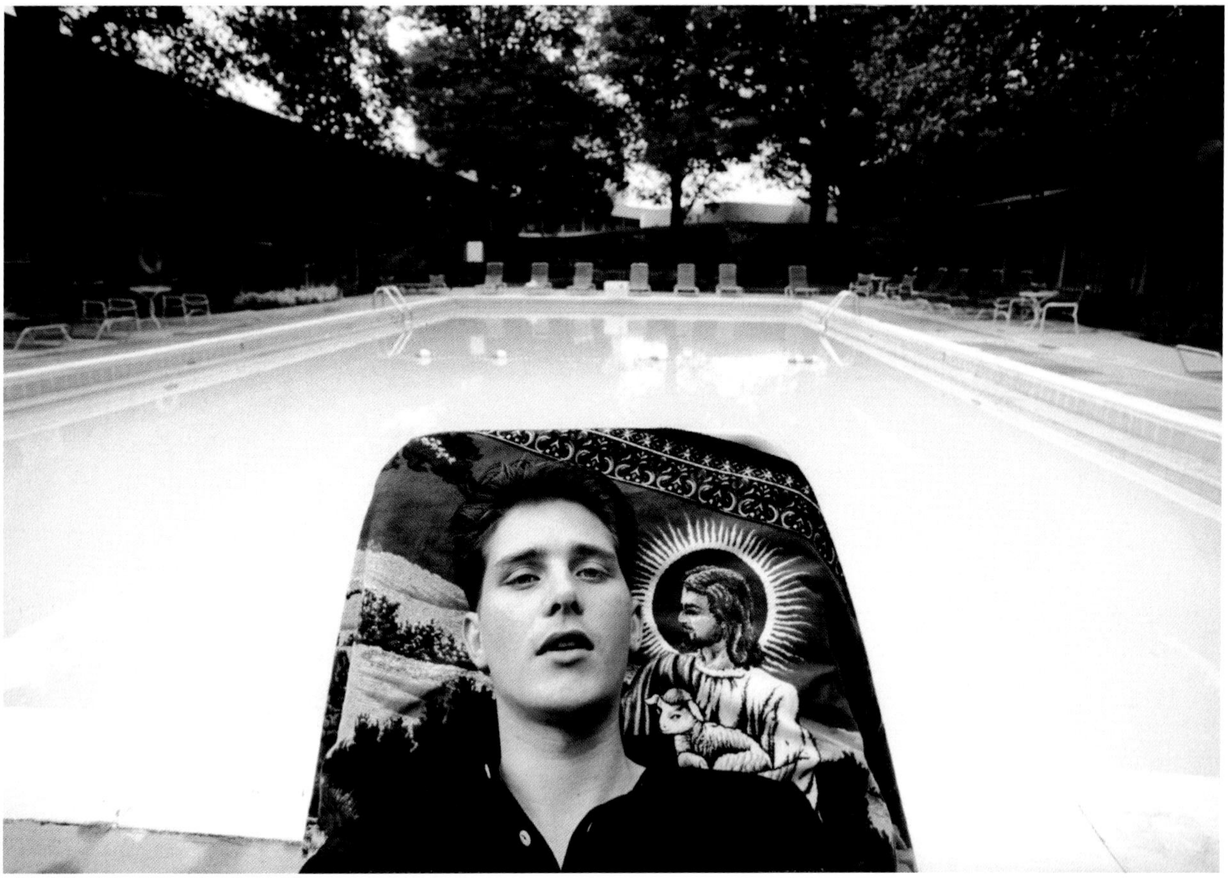

Gary Newby, The Railway Children
Atlanta, Georgia
4 July 1988

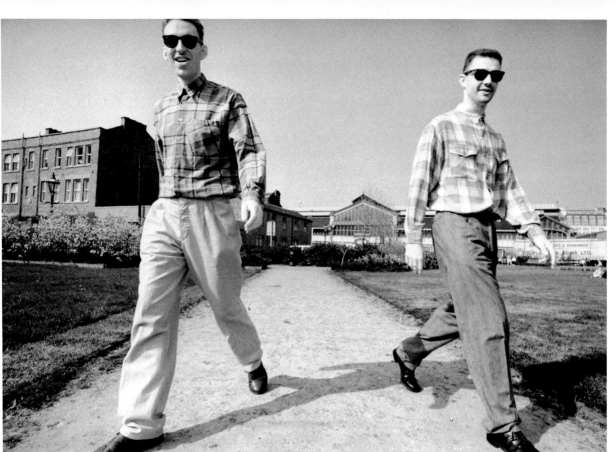

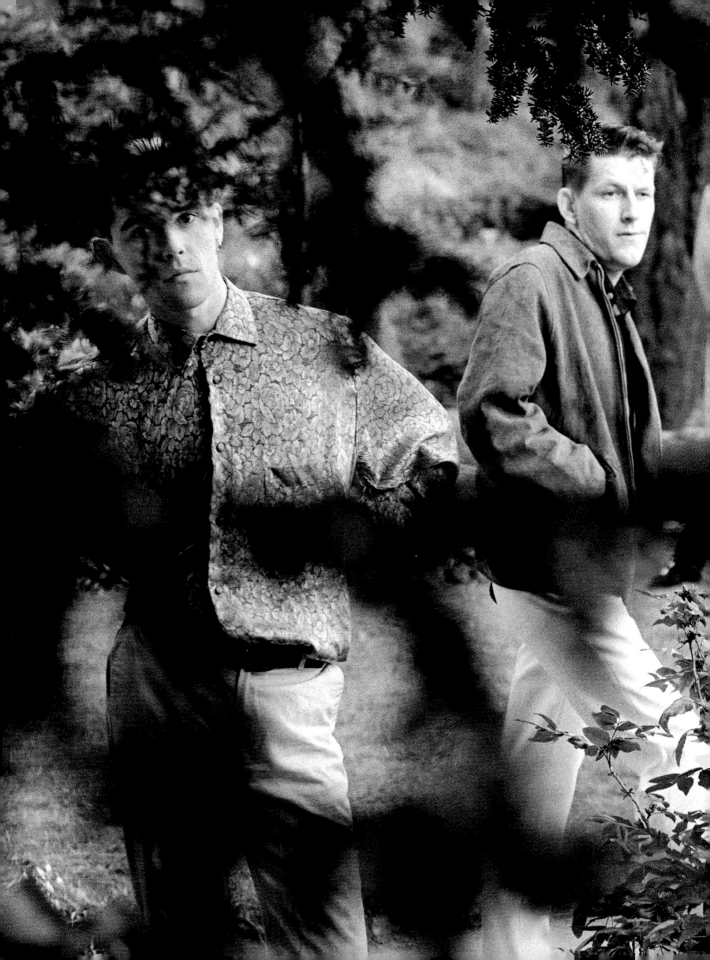

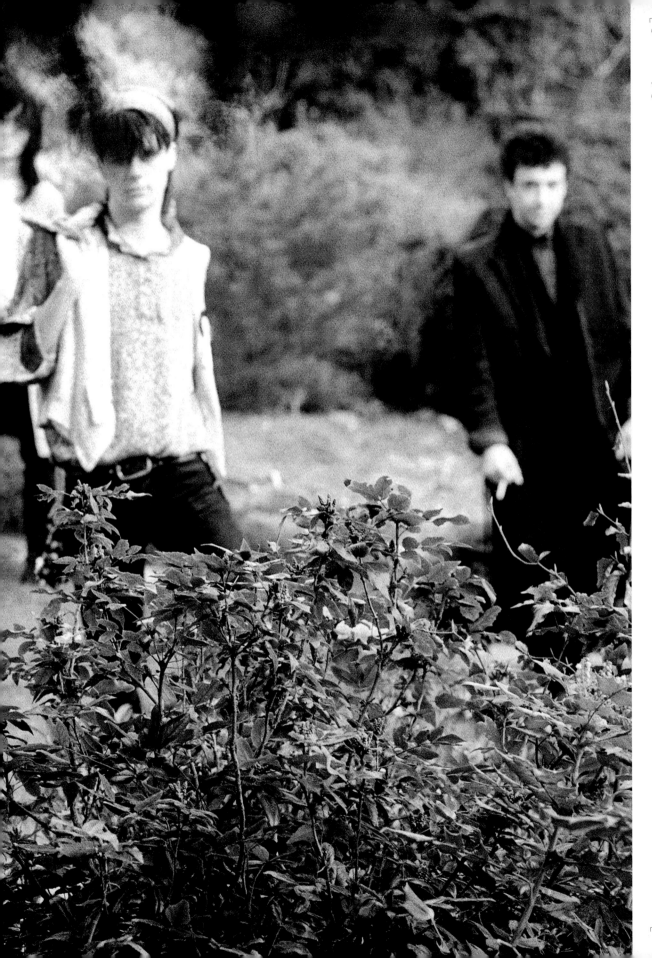

[Chapter Three – Stuart Maconie]

I can't remember the year, which in itself dates it pretty accurately I guess. 1990 probably: the height of the madness, the teeth of the blizzard, the monsoon season of serotonin storms and the full imperial pomp of the crowned heads of Madchester.

Tonight though the imperial court of Madchester has moved to Dublin, to an upstairs bar at the Point nightclub where the travelling court is in fulsome session. At the centre of it, looking every inch the demented, saturnine emperor in a full-length fur coat of what may be caribou pelt and resplendent in aviator shades, is Shaun William Ryder. Around him are the various jesters, fools, courtesans, showmen, hucksters and vagrants who comprise his retinue, scamps and scallies wearing fell-walking gear indoors and girls who would look underdressed for a Jacuzzi. Dragged along in the wake, swirled in the centrifuge of cool that surrounds the Mondays and the other Madchester royalty, are their musical peers, some curious, some amused, some jealous; tiny Bono and squat Van Morrison making appropriately small talk by the bar, Bobby Gillespie looking wraithlike in a darkened corner, someone who may be Kylie Minogue.

And why are Kevin and I here? What role do we play in all this gallimaufry? We, I suppose, are the scribes, the gossips, the mimics and caricaturists who will later relay these tales on village greens or by the drinking troughs in cobbled town squares to slack-jawed, toothless crowds. Or if you prefer, the readers of the *NME*, the music paper that Kevin and I work for, the paper that, with more than a little help from the two of us if I can be so bold, has become the house organ of Madchester, its parish pump, its marketplace, its court circular.

Because Kevin and I have been in at the beginning of all this, because we helped spread the word, fan the flames, whip up the hysteria, build the hype, as the green-eyed rival muckrakers who just don't get it daily accuse us of, we enjoy a strange and privileged position at court. We're two of the gang, two of the chosen few, insiders, or as near as we can be given that we are journalists. Later, things will change and the churls who have never got it will have their day and the Mondays will be vilified for the very things that the bourgeois hacks find so very titillating now: their laddishness, their fecklessness, the sulphurous whiff of menace and felony that clings to them. And then the romance will go sour and the bands will turn inwards and the music will dry up and the party will be over.

But in this bright chemical dawn, these early days of the new empire, the emperors know and we know that we will say nothing, write nothing and do nothing that will jeopardise this mutually beneficial state of affairs. And so they share their drugs and jokes and planes and secrets with us, and we will say, as the Mondays will later say . . . Yes Please! Knowing the codes and scratching the backs and nudging and winking, I get the good stories and Kevin gets the pictures.

A thought now occurs to me. Was Kevin there? Was it Dublin? Maybe it was Liverpool. Maybe it was Paul McCartney and not Bono. But I do know that I watch as Shaun Ryder moves towards the bar a little unsteadily, looking in his finery and shades like the First Lord of the Patagonian Admiralty in full dress uniform, the Emperor of Madchester. In his wake bobs a little flotilla of hangers-on and scenesters trying not to look impressed. I'm standing at the top of a spiral staircase to the right of the bar and I think he's seen me, though it's hard to tell what with the shades and that permanent look of drowsy malevolence. But, yes, here he comes, and the eyes in the room follow him towards me and as he arrives, he puts each hand into each pocket of his insane moose or elk or whatever it is coat and produces from each one a large balloon of Courvoisier. 'Brandy?' he offers in a voice of pure sandpaper.

I laugh and accept and we clink glasses. And then he sits on the rail of the spiral staircase, beckons me to follow, and we can go down and round and down and round and down and round into the delighted, shocked, upraised faces below . . .

Maybe Kevin wasn't there. That picture's not here, I see. And he'd have certainly got that one.

He'd have made me carry the camera bag and the lights and the spare film and batteries and then made me take them all back to the hotel. Afterwards, while he had a cocktail with the band.

But he'd have got the picture.

1986. I can remember this year. Seen from a misty vantage point in the foothills of the Pennines, it didn't look good. I come from Wigan, something that will greatly amuse Kevin Cummins when I get to meet him in a couple of years, and from my corner of Greater Manchester, the view is bleak.

A World Cup won by cheats.

England at war with itself under the permanent scowl of a monster and her acolytes; mad monks, Chingford skinheads, toads and liars and greasy secretary-shaggers.

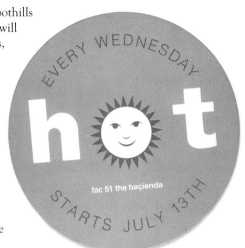

According to the leaflet that came through the door, we were all going to die of ignorance and a range of thrilling new diseases. Rampant privatisation meant that you couldn't even rely on a bus to get you out of town, though you could count on the cheap brown heroin coming up and down the West Coast main line to get you out of everything else. The Militant Tendency. The lingering aftermath of the miners' strike. Recession. YTS schemes. And in the middle of it all, the odd glimmer of defiance, like The Smiths and *The Queen Is Dead*.

Morrissey had a sheaf of great, darkly wonderful lines that year. But the best one didn't come from him, but from one of his heroines. It came from the pen of Victoria Wood, and was spoken by Suzie Blake, the glacial and scathing continuity announcer on *Victoria Wood on TV*. At the end of her news headlines, she shuffles her papers and fixes the camera with a steely stare.

'Finally, I'd like to apologise to viewers in the North.'

Pause.

'It must be awful for them.'

It wasn't great, to be honest.

I'm writing these words in a deluxe room at the Lowry Hotel in Manchester. If you watch the section in Michael Winterbottom's fabulous – in all senses – *24 Hour Party People*, there's a scene where Steve Coogan/Anthony H. Wilson is walking along the Rochdale canal doing a local news report. You can see the Lowry in the background, a glittering cliff of modernist chic reached by a curved white footbridge as elegant as it is practical. You can get a braised artichoke risotto and a rather good Rioja any time day or night and drink it on the balcony. The bed is the size of a tennis court and when you check in, the maid has left some Schubert on in the room.

Back in 1986 you could, if you were lucky, get some greasy fried chicken on Sackville Street and be lulled to sleep by the chorus of car alarms. Compared to Wigan, as Kevin would doubtless have told me, it was still Times Square, but the whole North was brooding under a pall. Though it pains me to admit it, the smug metropolitan clichés had a ring of truth; it was grim up north in 1986. A bad place and time to be old or sick or unemployed, or young and desperate.

In the sickly spring of 1986, I was working part-time in a college in Skelmersdale. There was no work there and so the whole town it seemed had gone back to college; laid-off car workers, single mums, scallies.

Technically, scally was a Scouse phenomenon. But it came to stand for a whole northwestern youth tribe. They liked football, 'draw', labels (Tacchini, Ellesse, Lois, Fila) and old-school music from their dads' and brothers' collections: Floyd, Krautrock, Sly and the Family Stone, anything druggy and not too commercial. With these albums and a little nefarious commercial activity, they filled the spaces in their day where there should have been apprenticeships and factory work. All that had gone, of course, swept off the map of the North with a sweep of the wicked witch of Whitehall's hands. The scallies weren't that arsed.

That spring, I heard a Peel session that sounded nothing like I'd ever heard before but seemed to frame the mood of the scally North in sound. The mid-eighties were something of a desert for music; multimillionaires like Clapton and Collins used *Miami Vice* cameos as promos for their expensive, useless beige in-car music. Meanwhile, the indie scene comprised groups of fey youths dabbling in shambling lovelorn whimsy. Apart from The Smiths and the occasional hip-hop or electro track, there was nothing to keep you listening to Peel except loyalty. He put it succinctly himself when he said, 'I don't even like the records I like.'

The Happy Mondays session of spring 1986 was different. The name may have made them sound like just another bunch of Oxfam-shop wets with girlfriend trouble but their music was, in its grimy way, revelatory. 'Kuff Dam' was a blurry, fucked-up thing bristling with prowling menace and buzzy energy. And the title was a bit of laddish reversed insult and badinage and a sly reference to Holland's stag-weekend capital. 'Freaky Dancing' was, in its own way, romantic. But it was the romance of the late-night bus stop, the pub car park, the crash of coins in the tray of the fruit machine, the late equaliser, the knee-trembler in the lift, the rain on the roof of the hot-wired car full of fierce herbal fug.

That Christmas they recorded an album called, messily, *Squirrel and G-Man Twenty Four Hour Party People Plastic Face Carnt Smile (White Out)*. I had the title track on a compilation tape alongside My Bloody Valentine and Pop Will Eat Itself and it got played a lot on my new Walkman, a device the size of a suitcase that helped shut out the world outside. They recorded the album with the legendary John Cale. He said later, 'When I worked with the Happy Mondays, I never really understood the process. It passed by in a jiffy, in a jiffy bag in fact. I'd stopped drinking and doing all sorts of other naughty things. I got a lot of flak for eating tangerines all the time.'

I loved that title track. I loved how it sounded like a Labour club band trying to play funk music on stolen instruments.

I loved that bellowed opening line: 'How old are you? Are you old enough? Should you be in here watching THAT?' It sounded both paternalistic and really frightening. Loved its queer but undisputed sense of rhythm. This bunch of chancers from Little Hulton have heard Can, I thought. And they had, as they'd later tell me. I didn't know it but they were lurking ahead in my story. As was Kevin Cummins.

I first saw the Mondays via Kevin's *NME* pictures. His first session with them was in 1986, the year of 'Freaky Dancing'. I remember being shocked. They didn't look like an indie band. They looked like the sort of people who stole the video and Calor gas heaters from Skem college every week. The singer could have walked straight out of *Martin Chuzzlewit* and could have been any age between twenty and eighty. He definitely didn't look like one of Tallulah Gosh.

Kevin later told me that when he first took those Mondays shots for *NME*, Tony Wilson of Factory Records, trying to impress his erratic charges with Kevin's pedigree, said, 'Kevin's

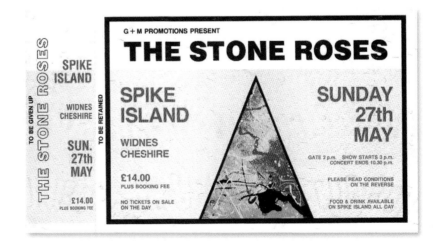

photographed the Sex Pistols and Ian Curtis.' Shaun replied, 'So what? They're fookin' dead!' He asked them what exactly they wanted, and they said: 'We want our picture taken with Rambo.'

I was rather more aware of Kevin's CV and portfolio. I had been devouring the music press since I was twelve (*Sounds* first, like a lot of kids, the *NME* being ever so slightly more cerebral, plus *Sounds* had posters). Kevin's was a name, like Pennie Smith and Annie Leibovitz, that you saw at the bottom of unimaginably exciting live snaps. Or, more usually in Kevin's case, some melancholic, evocative photo essay in stygian northern gloom. The pictures of Kevin's that I'd grown up with had been enigmatic and austere, glacial and shadowy. Joy Division on flyovers in snowy Hulme, Morrissey spread-eagled in a winter park. I'd guessed he was a fellow Lancastrian and I knew he 'did a lot of jobs' (as I'd later learn to say) with James Brown, the new firebrand at the *NME*. On an off chance one morning, with an hour to kill before teaching scallies about Auden and Marx, I wrote a review of Edwyn Collins, who I'd seen the previous night at the Manchester International. I sent it to the same James Brown and expected never to hear another thing about it.

James gave me a job at the *NME*. I'm still as surprised as you are. In those heady first few months, I got a lot of northwestern work: The Fall, James, my fellow Wiganers The Railway Children, a hairdresser called Andrew Berry who did Morrissey and Marr, was the subject of the former's 'Hairdresser on Fire' and would later invent the bowlhead Baldrick haircut that Shaun Ryder, Clint Boon and half of Madchester would sport.

I didn't work with Kevin for a while. But some nice things he said about me filtered back via James. He was glad to have a new northerner who could write a bit on the paper, even if, what with me coming from the benighted hill station of Wigan, he couldn't believe I could put two syllables together. I finally did meet the legendary Cummins at Victoria station, Manchester. He came to pick me up in his nice car. I was learning that photographers had nice clothes and cars and houses and credit cards whilst writers wore promotional Wonder Stuff T-shirts and lived in sub-student squalor and had overdrafts. He took the piss out of my haircut pretty much immediately. I think I ended up carrying his camera bag. We were off to meet the Happy Mondays.

For a while during that first year at the paper I'd known that something was stirring in Manchester, some rough beast slouching towards Deansgate waiting to be born, to paraphrase Yeats. Then one day the infamous 'face' Jeff Barrett, in his capacity as PR man, thrust a white-label copy of a cassette into my hand. Written in biro was the single word 'Bummed'. Jeff, in his corner-of-the-mouth, fidgety way that made even the most prosaic and quotidian of transactions – handing you a banana, say – seem like a massive drugs drop or microfilm exchange, muttered, 'New Mondays album. Fuckin' amazing.' I noticed that the first track was called 'Some Cunt from Preston'.

I played it on a train coming home from Euston. I can still remember the feeling of amazement and amusement. This was music that owed so little to the London music scene that it might as well have been Tuvaluan throat singing or Balinese gamelan. It was mad and funny and dirty and sneering, intimidating and at the same time anthemic in a weird terraces and dodgy nightclub way. The lyrics were a broken kaleidoscope of slang and speed babble and nursery rhymes and punchlines.

You better put your house up for sale, the Indians are coming . . .
Redneck, lorra lorra redneck in you . . .

You're rendering that scaffolding dangerous . . .

Henny penny, Cocky locky, Goosey loosey, Turkey lurkey . . .

Grass-eyed, Slash-eyed braindead fucker
Rips off himself and steals from his brother.

When he sang 'We're moving in with you', it was genuinely worrying.

Sometimes it sounded like psychedelic country-and-western music, sometimes like disco played by tramps. It was utterly self-possessed and yet clearly out of its tiny mind on drugs. It was wildly exciting. And it sounded strangely beautiful, with that cold, rainy urban glamour that Joy Division's music had. That was Martin Hannett, of course, making his last great record.

The next day I told James Brown we should put the Happy Mondays on the cover of the *NME*. He was keen, bless him, but some of the other staffers felt we should keep this august space of the paper reserved for Nick Cave and Einstürzende Neubauten and all the other hip London favourites. These Happy Mondays didn't just look like car thieves, they probably were car thieves. They were never going to sit easily alongside a retrospective of Taiwanese sci-fi at the ICA.

Thanks to James though, we got despatched to Manchester and I got to meet Kevin and go in his nice car and carry his camera bag, all the way to the Granada studios where the Mondays were recording a session for TV. Anthony Wilson was there, and Rob Gretton, New Order's manager, and Kevin sparred and piss-took with them all like the old mates they were. Legends all. I stood around a bit awkwardly; some cunt from near Preston.

I wandered out round the back of the building and immediately regretted it as I walked straight into a gang of ne'er-do-wells skulking by the bins. They seemed to be divvying up some drugs. They weren't unfriendly though and I shared a cigarette with them. During the course of this, it became apparent that these amiable scamps and toerags were, in fact, the Happy Mondays.

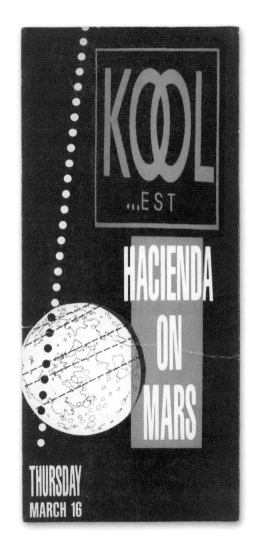

There were a couple of Dickensian brothers, Shaun and Paul, Fagins from Little Hulton with scowls and bumfluff, there was an amiable ex-postman who seemed to be called Cow, there was a drummer with ringlets who looked like a Turkish beach bum, there was a keyboard player called Knobhead who was gnomic in every sense of the word and whose role seem to act as a sponge for collective withering abuse, particularly from singer Shaun, who himself, in his padded coat and granny specs, was as far removed from the Robert Plant template of a rock front man as it was possible to be and could have been anything between seventeen and sixty.

Finally, there was a rangy wild-eyed court-jester figure who made random, surreal remarks, grinned dementedly and bobbed on the balls of his feet like a zoo chimp driven unhinged by captivity. I decided after a moment or two's almost anthropological observation that Bez had some kind of learning difficulty, was a cousin or some such, and was looked after by the band as an act of kindness. How sweet, I thought, as I watched him dancing to the music only he could hear and bumming fags. At this point, I couldn't have known that over the next year he would become more photographed than Jagger or McCartney or Robert Plant put together and would appear on the covers of magazines from Manchester to Milan to Manhattan. Many of these pictures would be taken by Kevin Cummins.

Eventually the band were corralled and medicated, and ushered back into the studio like unruly children, where they picked up instruments, with their air of the apes at the beginning of *2001: A Space Odyssey* getting to grips with their bone tools. Wilson, resplendent in a cream suit, introduced them thus: 'I work with them but this is not just nepotism, this is profound devotion to the cause, the cause of Happy Mondays. This song is called "Performance".'

I don't remember that, of course. My memory's not that good, particularly not of the Madchester years, which seem now to have been filmed under water by neon lighting. I've just found the actual clip from the programme, a late-night arts show hosted by Wilson and called *The Other Side of Midnight*, on the internet, where all our yesterdays are now preserved in jagged, buffering MPEG fragments. This may be the first time I've seen this since I watched it from the gallery with Cummins and Gretton and Wilson and producer Steve Locke eighteen years ago. Gratifyingly, I know I was right to lose my head the way I did. It is still extraordinary. Bez is a Salford shaman, locked into his private world, bent at the waist, dancing from the shoulders, head swimming from the leering funk all around him and the cocktail of chemicals in his bloodstream. Shaun Ryder seems to be his keeper, or a ringmaster, teasing and leading him with maracas and tambourine, like you'd amuse a puppy with a sock. They circle each other whilst Cow

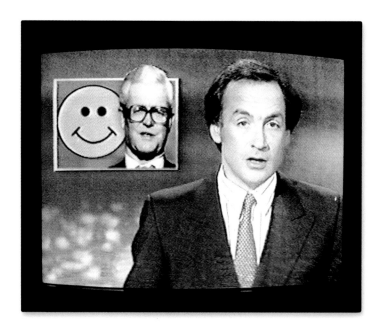

plays a scratchy northern version of Chic's stylised disco licks and Paul Ryder, dressed for a fishing trip or perhaps a warehouse burglary, plays a throbbing bassline straight from a classic Can album. I had forgotten just how great a band they were but here is the evidence. What you don't see here of course is the moment Rob Gretton turns gleefully to me and says, 'I've got two words to say about this. One of them's "Sex" . . . and the other one's "Pistols"!' Kevin and I laughed. It doesn't sound anything like the Sex Pistols. It's much better actually. But I knew what he meant.

We ended up drinking all day in the bar at Granada. Shaun Ryder demanded this in case 'any fit birds off Coronation Street come in'. As far as I recall, they didn't, but I could be wrong. Paul Ryder told me that he'd looked up all the complicated words in a recent live review I'd done of the band at the Irish Centre in Birmingham ('rebarbative' was one, I seem to recall) and he told me he agreed with most. Then he said something I couldn't instantly understand and brother Shaun turned on him with venom. 'What do you do that fucking shit for, eh? You're fucking stupid.' I had only the vaguest idea what was going on but was just being carried along by it all, a feeling that was to last throughout Madchester.

The course of the next year and a half was set, for me at least. The whole straggling, fragrant caravanserai they called Madchester would pull its wagons and pitch its aromatic campfires across British rock for a couple of years but it was that first heady eighteen months when all the great records were made, all the great nights were had, all the hits and myths created.

Wilson, this time in slate-grey Armani by the looks of things, also featured The Stone Roses on *The Other Side of Midnight*, introducing them thus:

> *A Manchester group whose rock 'n' roll stance I have seriously disliked for four or five or six years. Never had any time for the group, then four or five months ago . . . I heard a single from them, thought it was excellent . . . so 1989 begins with an admission of error on my part. I was wrong. Big apologies and here's the new one from The Stone Roses.*

The Stone Roses go on to play 'Waterfall' in what is another iconic performance on that bare white *Other Side of Midnight* studio floor. You probably know it. Ian Brown, looking about twelve, wears a yellow polo shirt and skips and bobs like a flyweight contender. There are soon-to-be-legendary licks and arpeggios, fringes and bobble hats and Mani in his black-and-white-striped top, playing bass in that distinctive style like a keen apprentice chimney sweep making exploratory thrusts with his brush. It is truly, truly great stuff. But Anthony H. Wilson had nothing to apologise for actually.

Because for the first three or four years of their existence, Wilson was right. The Stone Roses weren't that good. You can tell just by looking at their pre-'89 promotional pictures, all bandanas, scarves and frock coats. They look like a goth Waterboys, which is a scary prospect in anyone's book. The band themselves disowned their Martin Hannett-produced debut *So Young*, and its pushy belligerence has little in common with the woozy beatific guitar grooves to come. But something happened in 1989; Gary 'Mani' Mountfield joined, the drugs changed and so did the music coming in from the clubs of America, a gale of euphoric chemical bliss blowing through the shabby cobwebby squalor of British indie music in the late eighties.

My friends in the North, through the bush telegraph of rumour, hyperbole and rave reviews, told me that The Stone Roses were 'happening'. Forget the cravats and the goth leanings, they had washed that stuff right out of their hair. Get yourself up here to see them. I did and they made my head swim. They had the songs, they could play, they looked great and they had that indefinable, quintessential rightness, almost like a visible aura, that bands acquire when their time has come. It won't last. It never does. And that makes it all the more fabulous. All the more reason to capture it on camera. And in words. I sat in as live editor at *NME* for a week and used my new-found commissioning power to send Andrew Collins to the Haçienda to review The Stone Roses. He wrote that 'Stuart Maconie's fringe now makes sense . . . and I can tell my grandchildren that I saw The Stone Roses at the Haçienda.' It was yet more proof that the centre of pop's gravity had shifted yet again away from London or New York to Cottonopolis, soon to be rechristened Madchester.

What were the roots of Madchester? They were partly chemical, partly alchemical, partly industrial and heavily geographical. Wilson's characterisation of house as 'Obscure black homosexual music' may not have been accurate. But Anthony never let strict accuracy get in the way of his brilliant, scene-defining slogans, jousts and jibes. There was a real sense of kinship between the doomed industrial megalopolis of Henry Ford's Detroit and Chicago, tough passionate cities which used to thrum to the sound of engines, looms and lathes, and Manchester, formerly the aforesaid Cottonopolis, cradle of the Industrial Revolution, now a collection of smokestacks and empty factories on the Irwell.

House didn't just make landfall in Manchester. They were dancing to it in London at Shoom and at warehouse raves at the end of the 1980s. But it stayed merely an extension of London's peacocky, fashionista trendiness; in Manchester, it became a real subcultural force with its own values, drugs, language, music and clothes. The clothes were baggy, giant flares and long-sleeved T-shirts courtesy of Shami Ahmed and his Joe Bloggs label. The drugs were, by and large, ecstasy, dope, booze and a smattering of 'liveners'. Fringes were long, centre partings and bowlcuts were in. There was a new language to learn, one where good things were 'banging' and bad ones were 'snide'. There were grand hubristic slogans – 'On the Sixth Day God created Manchester', 'Cool as Fuck'. There were four hundred people on the guest list for the Happy Mondays gig at the GMEX centre in 1990. Kevin and I were two of them. There was a scene and KevMate was always on hand to take pictures of it.

I'm not sure when Kevin became KevMate. But I'd like to think I was instrumental in it. We'd done jobs together before the coming of the Roses and the Mondays. Jim Kerr in Frankfurt, the Pixies in Munich, Morrissey in Berlin. Most weeks you could find Kevin and me getting into an argument in some continental or US bar or hotel or restaurant. In this I was usually the unwitting, even hapless stooge, Steadman to his Hunter S. Thompson. KevMate would not fly United Airlines because of his Man City credentials, he wouldn't let his bags be scanned at airports in case precious film was ruined by the X-ray machine, though I was pretty sure they'd been 'film-safe' since about 1975. He tried to get my bar bill offset in an eastern European hotel on the grounds that lager counted as breakfast in Wigan. He once really insulted an Austrian barman not so much by accusing him of being rude but by assuming he was German. On these occasions, Kevin Cummins, sophisticated lensman who'd done exhibitions and everything, read Martin Amis and knew about wine and Jean Cocteau, would transmogrify into KevMate, International Manc, mission to sow discord. KevMate was always terrifically good if exhausting company.

What with the drugs and the parties and the flares, it felt like the sixties. And the shorthand cultural assessment was that the Mondays were the feral, demonic, unsavoury Stones to The Stone Roses' effortlessly brilliant, transcendent, beautiful Beatles. It wasn't really like that of course. But there was something in it. Just as he was in the process of 'iconising' the Mondays, KevMate was creating the indelible images that will forever be The Stone Roses: the whole band daubed and splashed in multicoloured hues of emulsion, a Jackson Pollock paint riot that said, 'We're clever, we're art and we're a bit mental.' These pictures of The Stone Roses in their pomp, in the first electric dawn of that debut album, are the polar opposite of the wintry monochrome of Kevin's famous Joy Division pictures. But the effect is the same, the creation of an image that mirrors the music beautifully and that the band will forever be identified with. At the end of '89, the readers of *NME* voted 'Made of Stone' their single of the year. I thought this was still a hangover from their stadium-rock days and so I fixed it so that 'She Bangs the Drums' – much more in keeping with the new Madchester ethos – topped the poll instead. We were making it up as we went along. It was fabulous.

With the Mondays – less pretty, less enigmatic, more malevolent – Kevin ostensibly had more to do but he still emblemised them for perpetuity. He shot the Factory building plastered in those brilliant, lurid disorientating Central Station Design posters of Shaun's face from the cover of *Bummed*. He later said of them, 'Although it's not a picture of the band, to me this captures the exuberance of that period. I know Factory owned the building, but it was such a bold gesture to cover it in Mondays posters.' He took the famous pictures of the band on the roof of a hotel in Sitges near Barcelona, in 1990. 'They had this sign on the roof spelling HOTEL in eight-foot letters. I was shooting Shaun and Bez under the letters HOT, but after half a roll of film I realised what the next letter of "Hotel" was.'

The Mondays and the Roses were the twin pillars of the scene – along with the great if anonymous dance tunes like A Guy Called Gerald's 'Voodoo Ray' or 'Rhythm Is Rhythm' by Strings of Life – but there were other photogenic youths to be immortalised. The Charlatans were mainly from Cheshire and the Black Country, but they had the moves and the tunes and the right air of druggy, captivating insouciance. Kevin seemed to think water their natural habitat and immortalised them up to their waists in a Swedish lake and then radiantly cute lead singer Tim Burgess out on the ice of a frozen pond in Warrington. Alongside The Charlatans, who were closer to the Brian Auger Trinity than Detroit House, the Inspiral Carpets were the most sixties of the crop. They were perhaps the first group since ELP where the keyboard player was the star. In this case, Clint

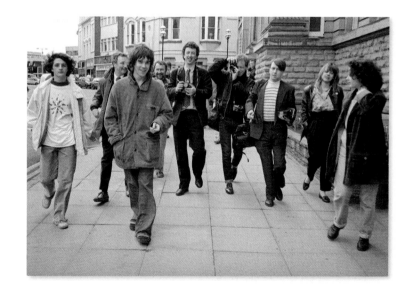

Boon, an organist, wit and bon vivant who was a sort of cross between Ray Manzarek and Roy 'Chubby' Brown.

All these bands made great records and great copy. By now I was practically living in Manchester and definitely living in their pockets, their tour buses and dressing rooms. Journalistically it probably lacked balance. But then rock writing has as much in common with real journalism as rock operas have with real operas. We drank their riders, we said they were banging, KevMate made them look great. But as well as the bona fide talent, Madchester had its fellow travellers too, make that fellow moochers, a parade of identikit saucer-eyed kids from the dead estates like Northside and the Paris Angels or a bad, self-aggrandising rapper who made a hilarious appearance on some worthy arts show explaining his new lexicon: 'I say things like Nish and Clish and banging. Nish? Well, that doesn't mean anything. And Clish. That doesn't mean anything either . . .'

Such was Madchester's allure and cultural clout that, oh sweet irony, London had a Madchester band. They were called Flowered Up and they were rubbish. KevMate's pictures were the best thing about them.

It couldn't last of course. The Stone Roses played some epochal gigs and then vanished, became creatures of myth like unicorns for an age, mired in legal hassles, excess and creative torpor. By 1991, the wing of the *NME* that had never been keen on this provincial pantomime seized on a few ill-chosen remarks by Shaun Ryder and turned on them with fury. Left-wing hacks found to their dismay that the real working classes often have attitudes that wouldn't sit easily in *Time Out* or the *Guardian*. Kevin took the pictures for an *NME* cover in 1991 that featured Shaun grim-faced and straitjacketed.

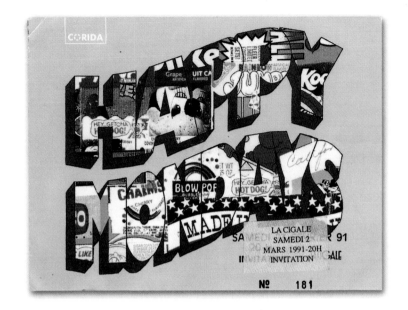

This was a very difficult picture to do. All the middle-class journalists at the *NME* suddenly decided that they couldn't cope with working-class lads like the Mondays, so had turned against them. It was a simple idea – to show Shaun in a straitjacket, to represent how he felt tied up by the press.

Like the first Summer of Love, this one ended in violence. Meredith Hunter was knifed to death by a Hell's Angel at the Altamont Speedway, the bitter irony being that those woefully naive Home Counties boys the Rolling Stones had actually employed the Hell's Angels as crowd control. In the same way, organised gangs infiltrated the door and the security teams of the Haçienda, temple of Madchester, and guns became the latest must-have accessory. Some nights even New Order, the people who owned the club, couldn't get in, waved away with menace. It all ended in the sporadic crack of gunfire and a really bad Happy Mondays record called *Yes Please!*. The world said, 'No, thank you,' and everyone had to listen to Nirvana until Britpop came along.

If you want to know what Madchester was really like, you have a few options. You could watch Michael Winterbottom's wonderful *24 Hour Party People*, one of the only rock movies to have given any flavour of the scene it purports to record, by being as funny and odd and amorphous as the city itself. There's a bit in it which I am convinced is supposed to be me and KevMate in the back of the Mondays' tour bus at the height of the madness. It doesn't really look much like either of us. But an eager cub reporter is trying to make notes whilst looking cool and his mate is lounging around cracking jokes with some girls so I assume it's us.

Or, best of all, you could listen to the banging tunes whilst casting an eye, a moist one in my case, over KevMate's pictures of those heady years. The Haçienda in its dark booming cathedral of excess glory, the Mondays on the lam and the lash in sunny Spain, The Stone Roses as art happening. Then spare a thought for me, somewhere out of shot, holding a reflector or some camera bags, trying to placate some irate Austrian barman, wondering what I did with my notebook and all my traveller's cheques.

I did the words. In a way, KevMate did the music.

I would like to live in Manchester. The transition between Manchester and death would be unnoticeable.

Mark Twain

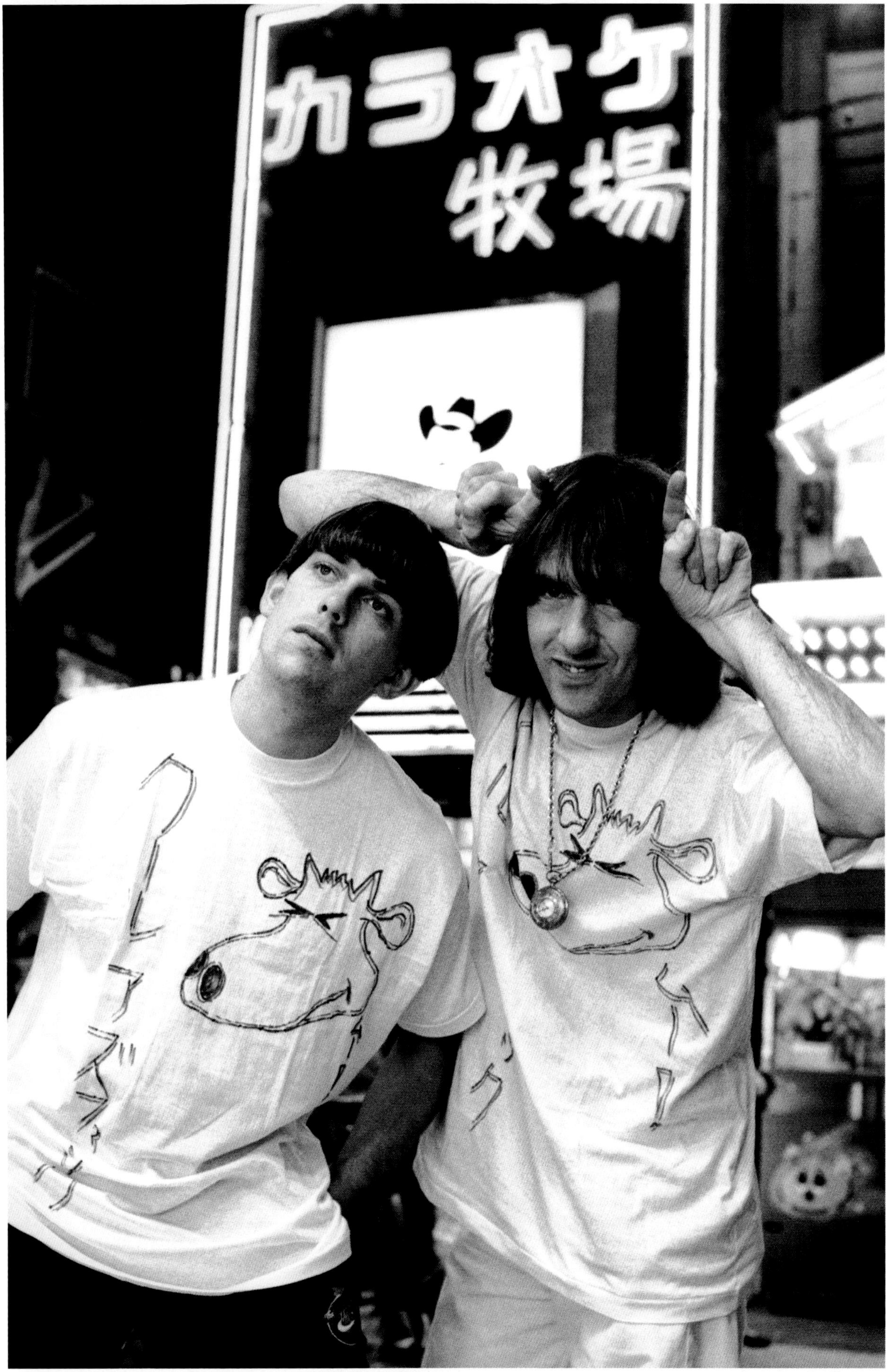

Tom Hingley and Clint Boon, Inspiral Carpets
Tokyo
October 1990

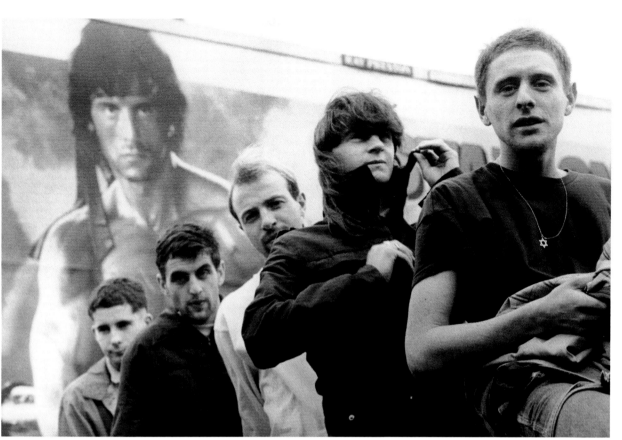

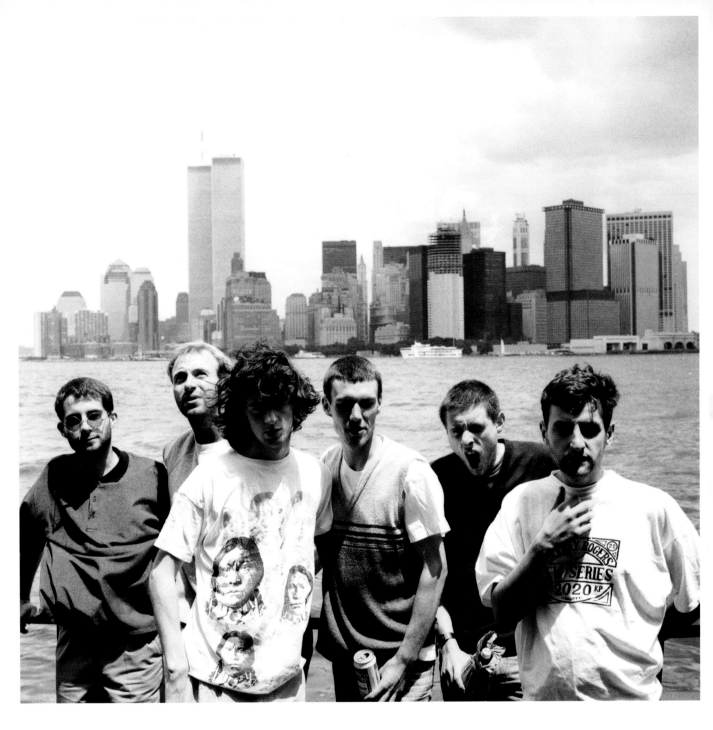

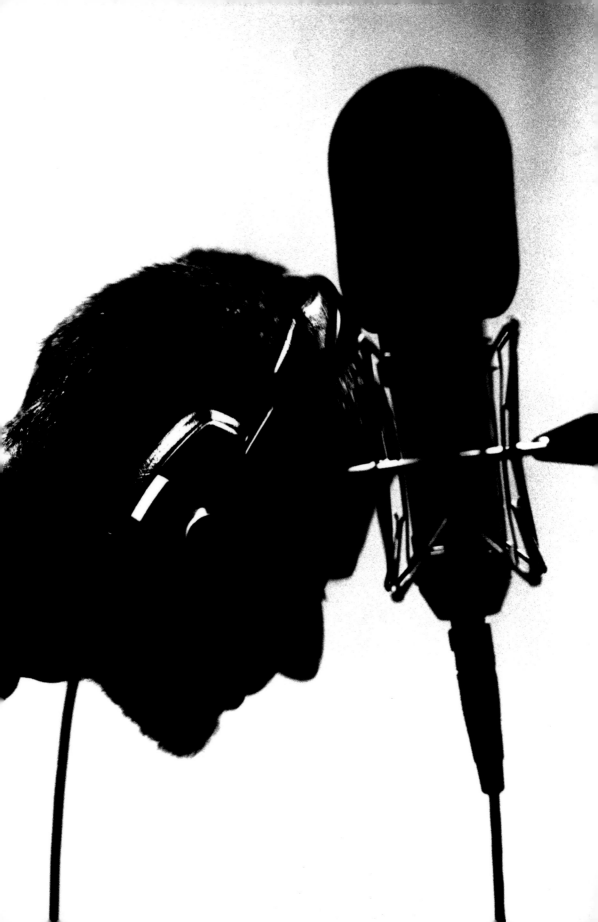

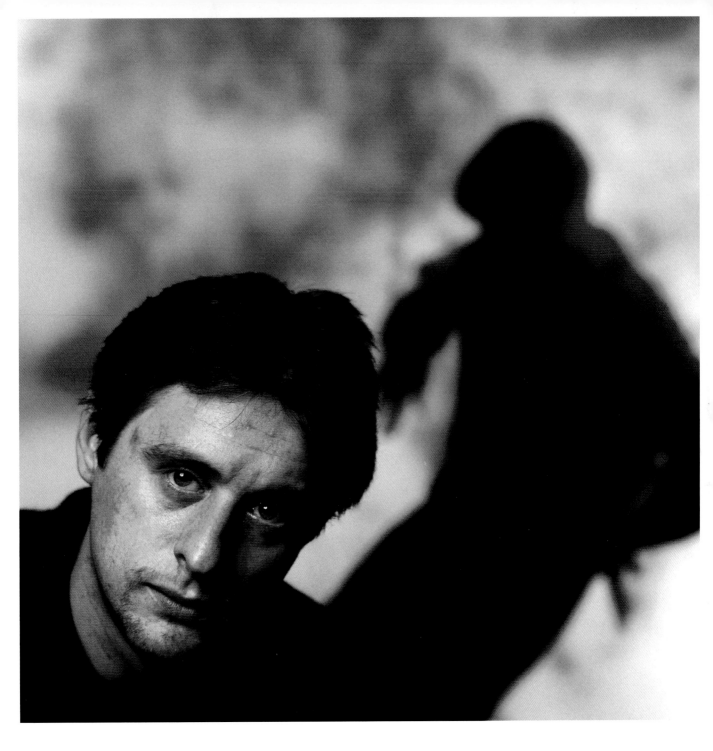

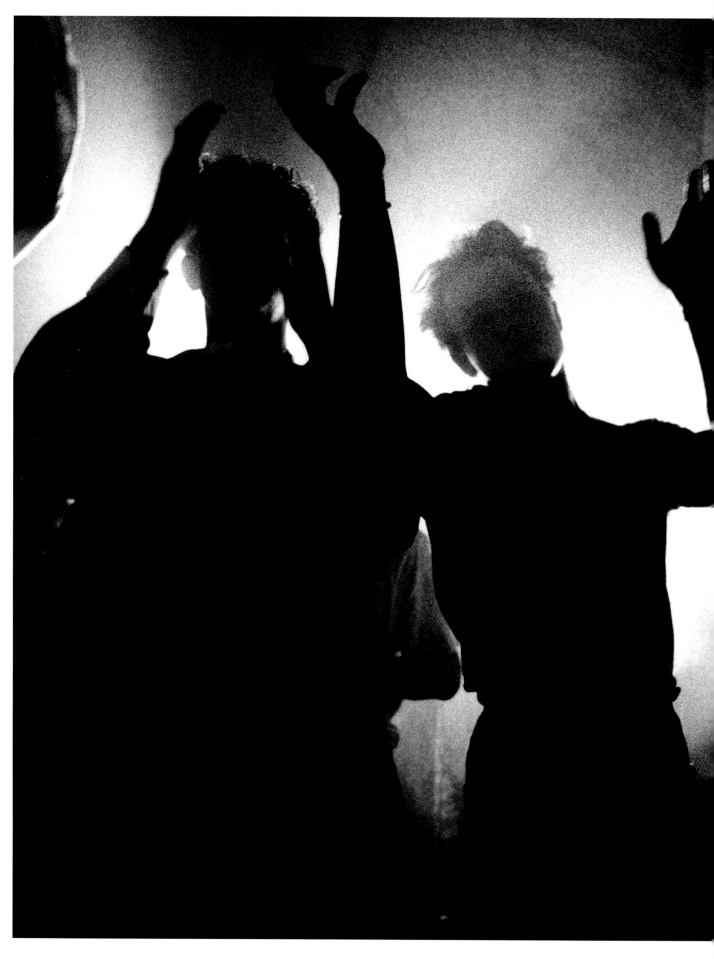

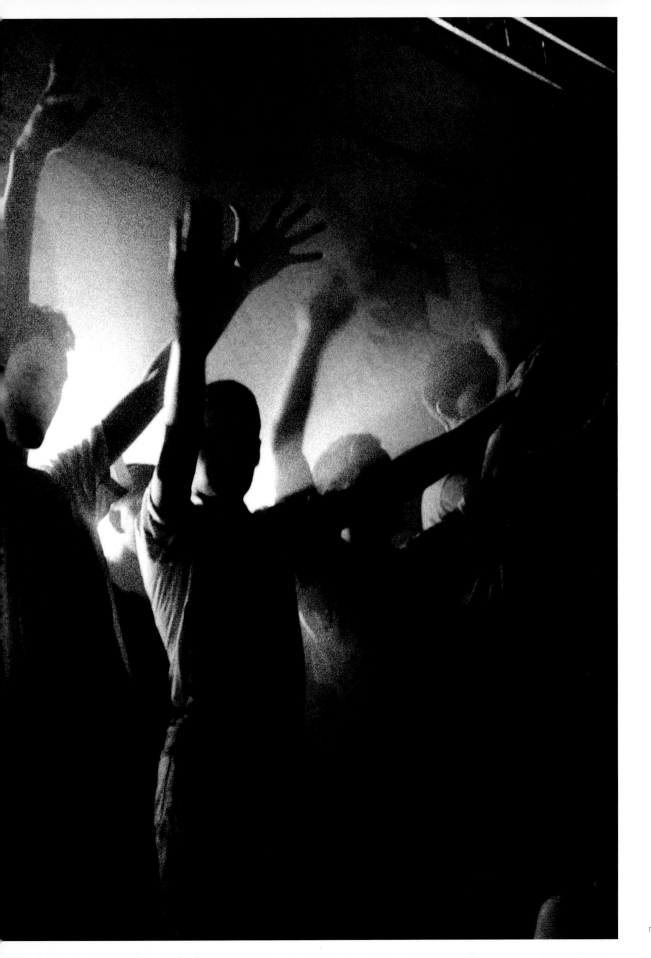

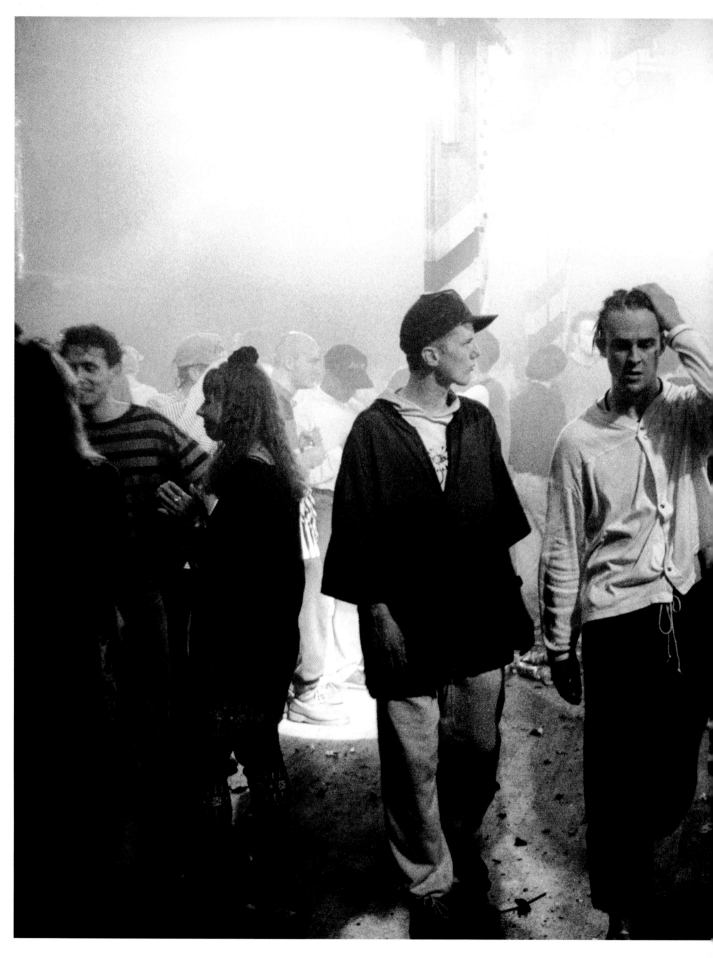

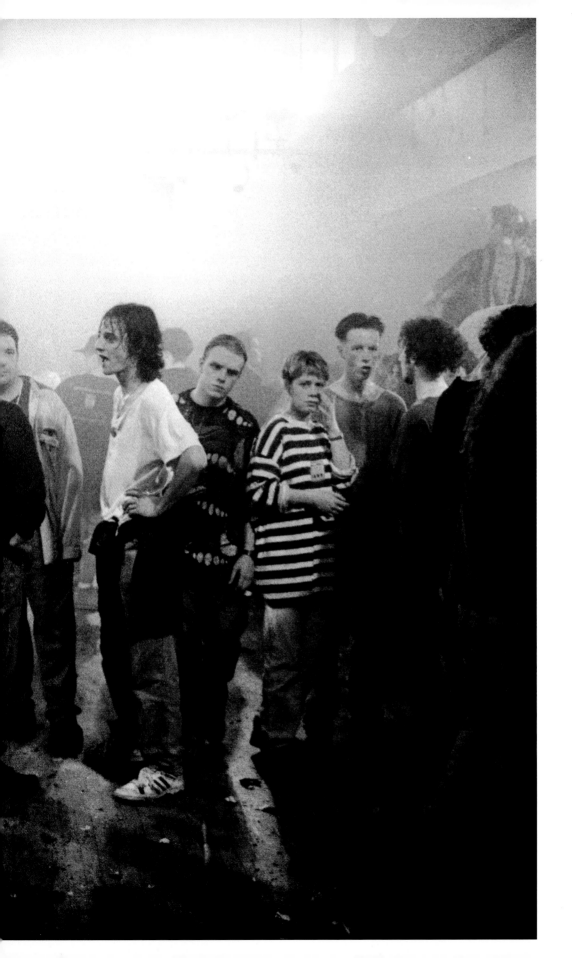

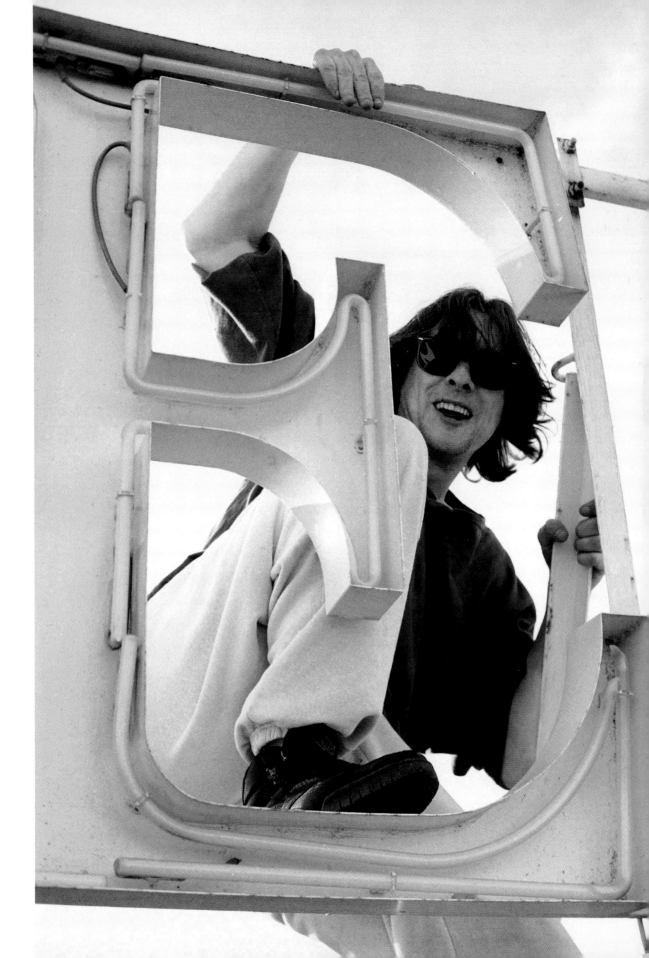

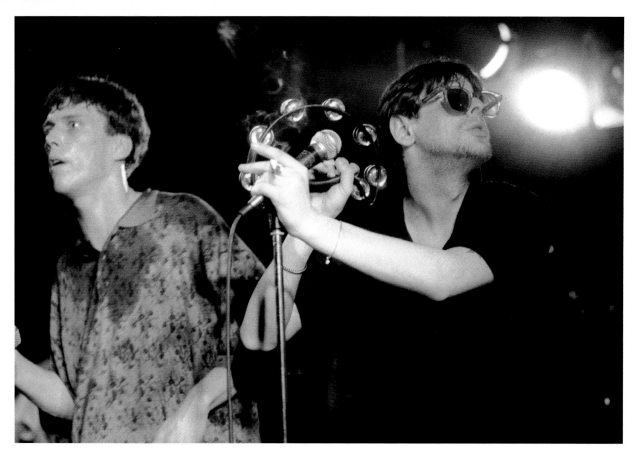

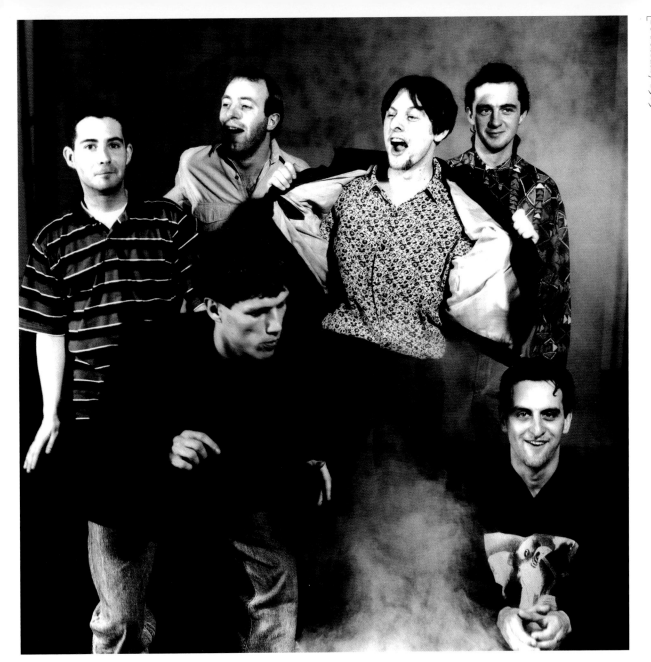

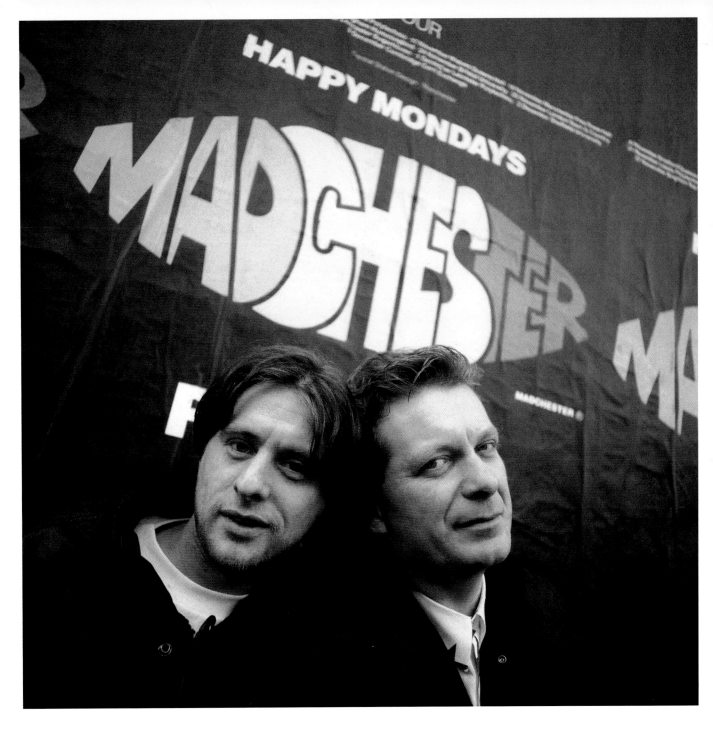

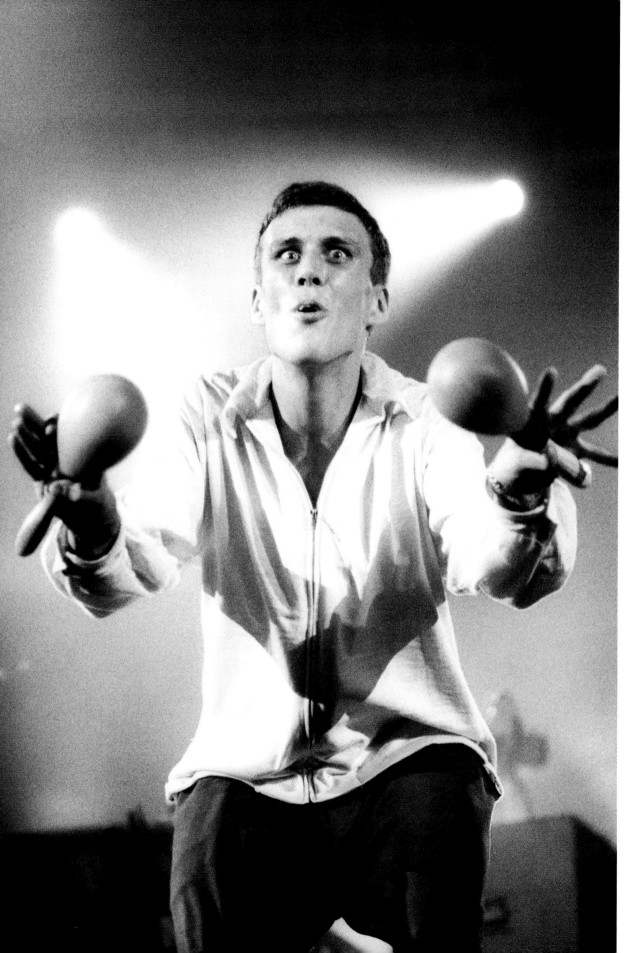

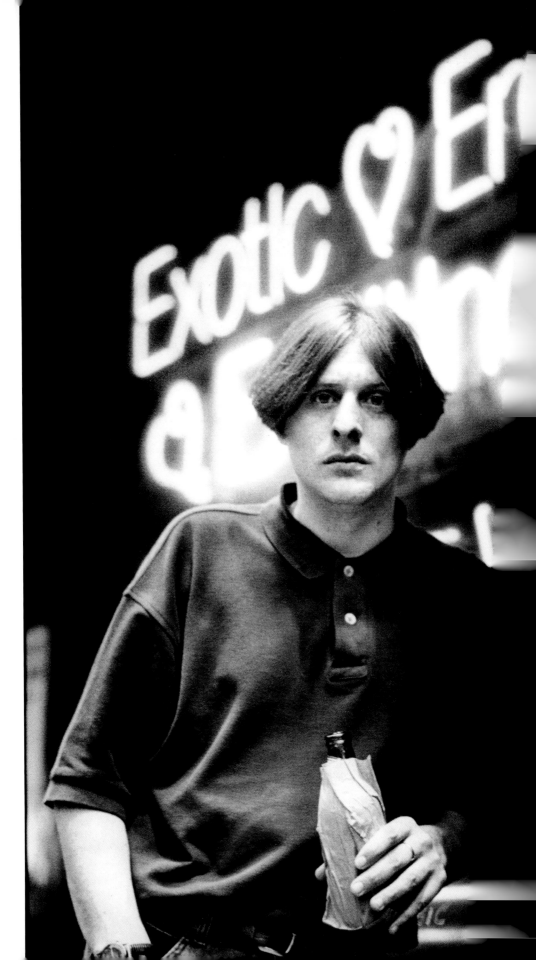

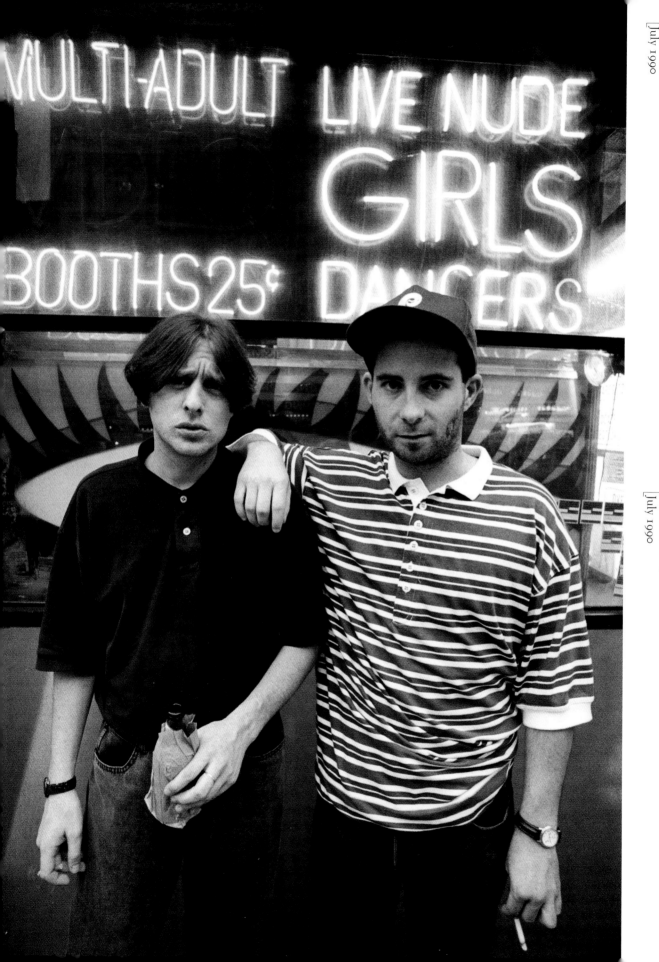

Shaun Ryder and Paul Davis, Happy Mondays
42nd Street, New York City
July 1990

Bez and Paul Ryder, Happy Mondays
New York City
July 1990

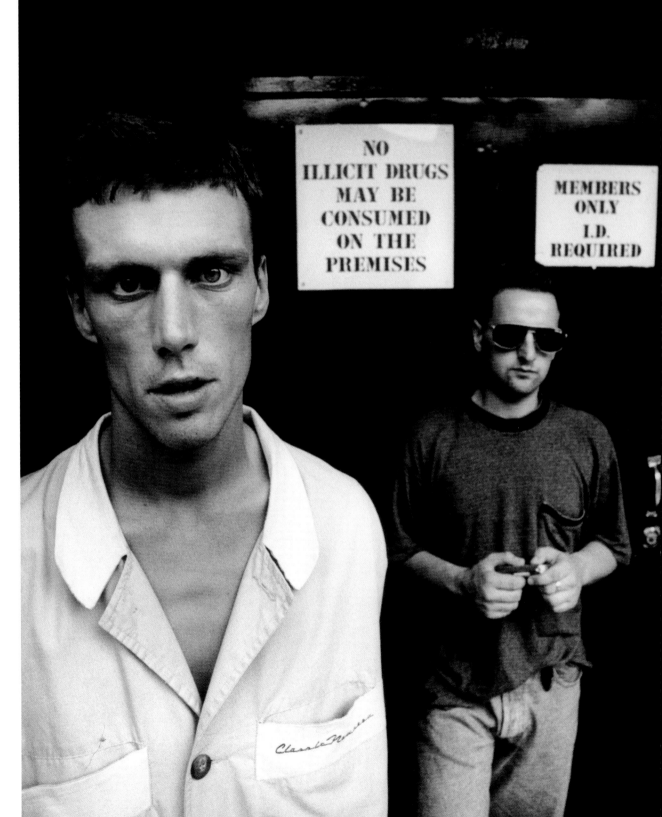

When entering ... Manchester, a stranger, over-whelmed by the new and interesting spectacle presented to him, scarcely dares look this giant full in the face.

J. G. Kohl

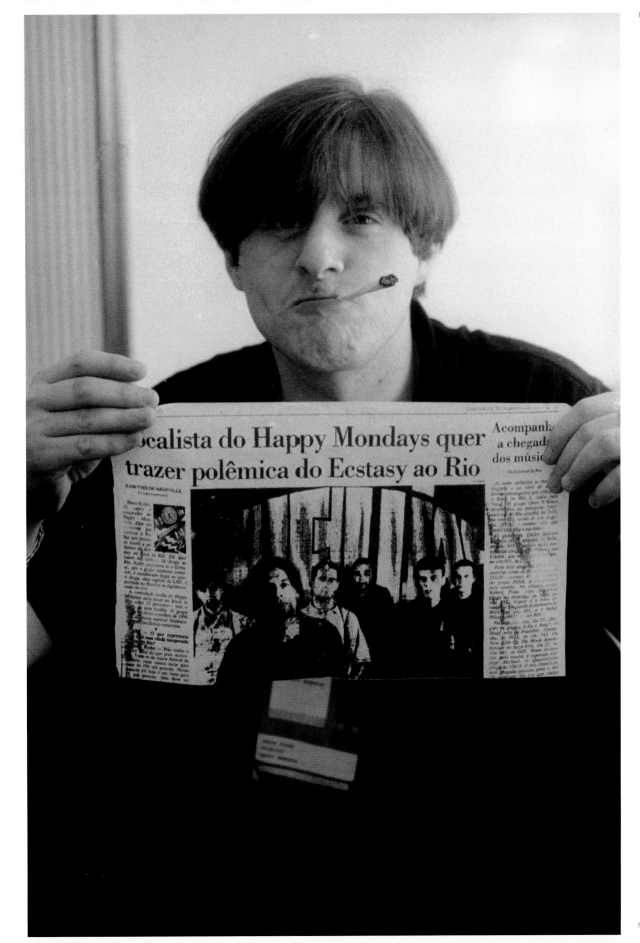

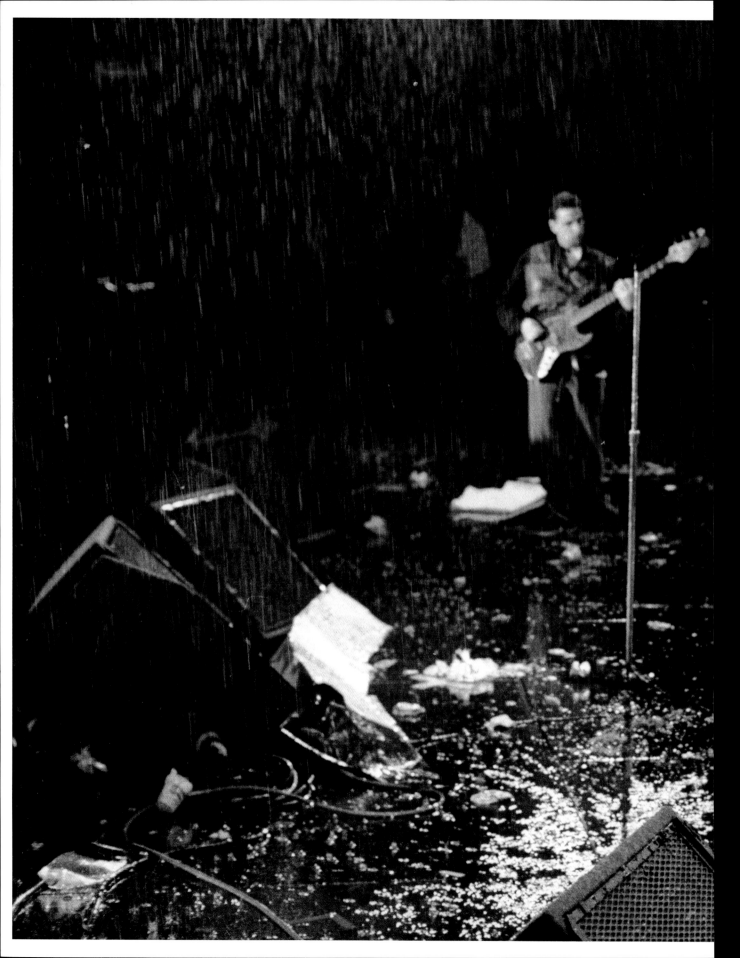

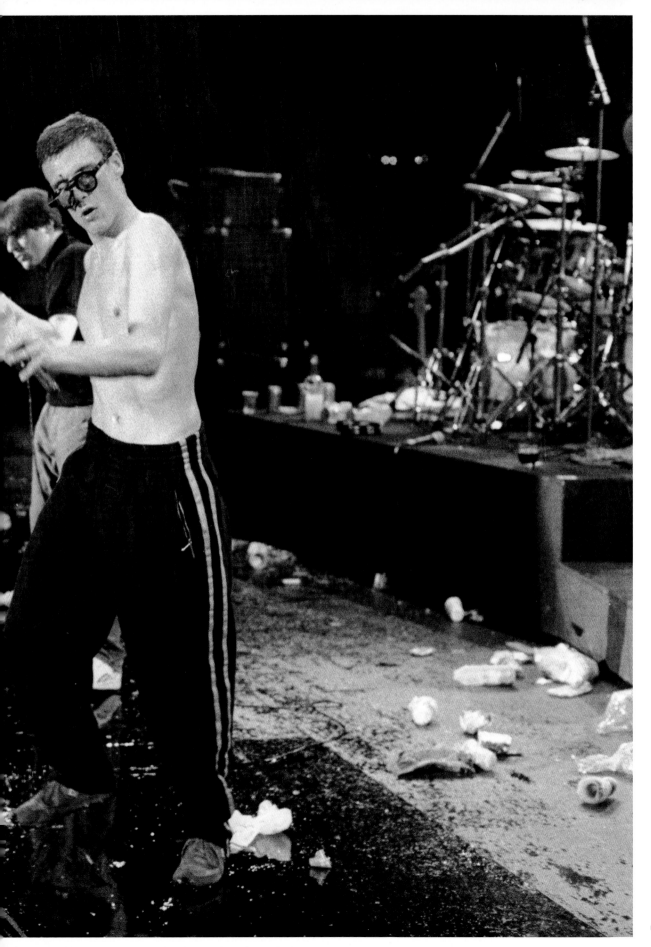

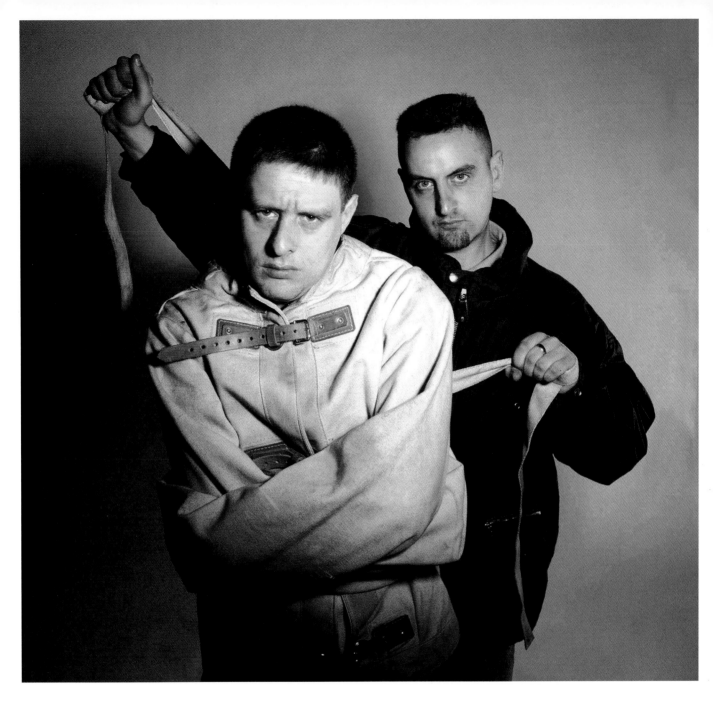

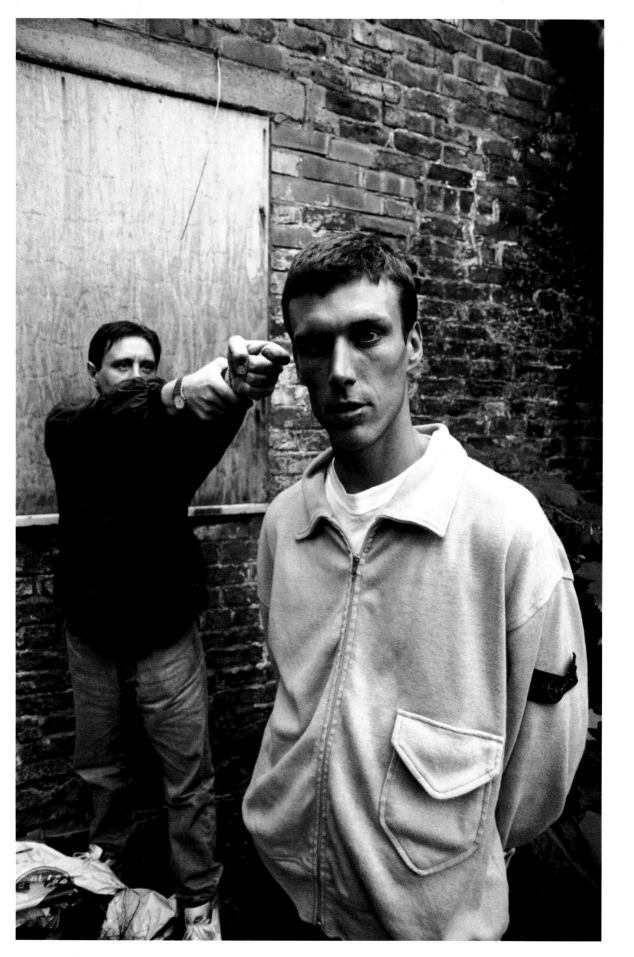

Shaun Ryder
Studio, London
20 February 1989

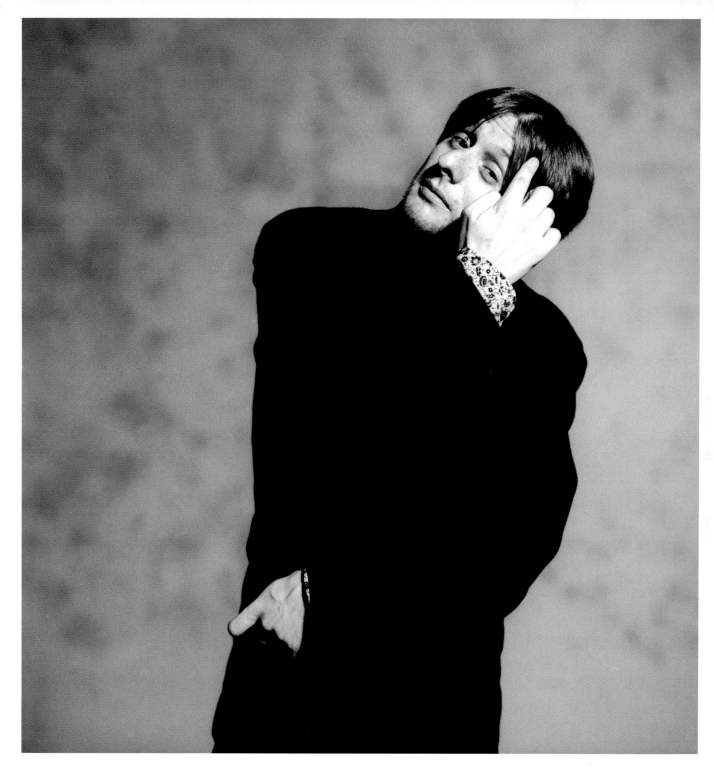

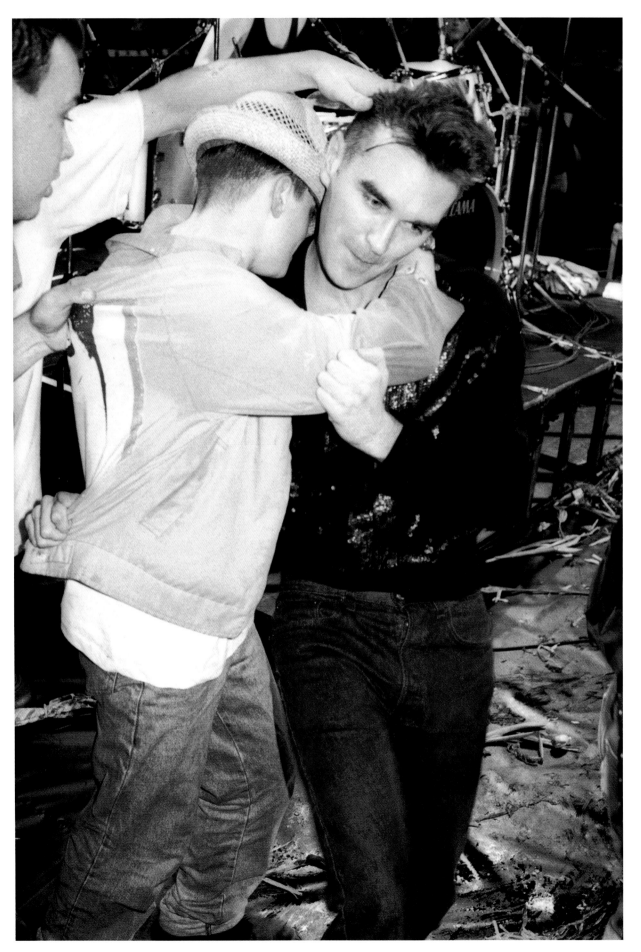

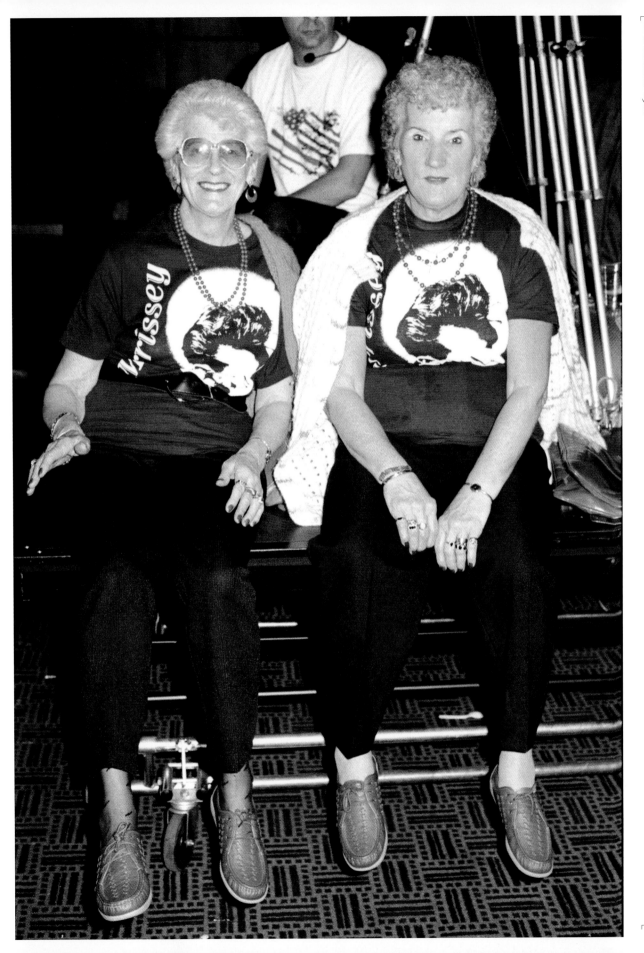

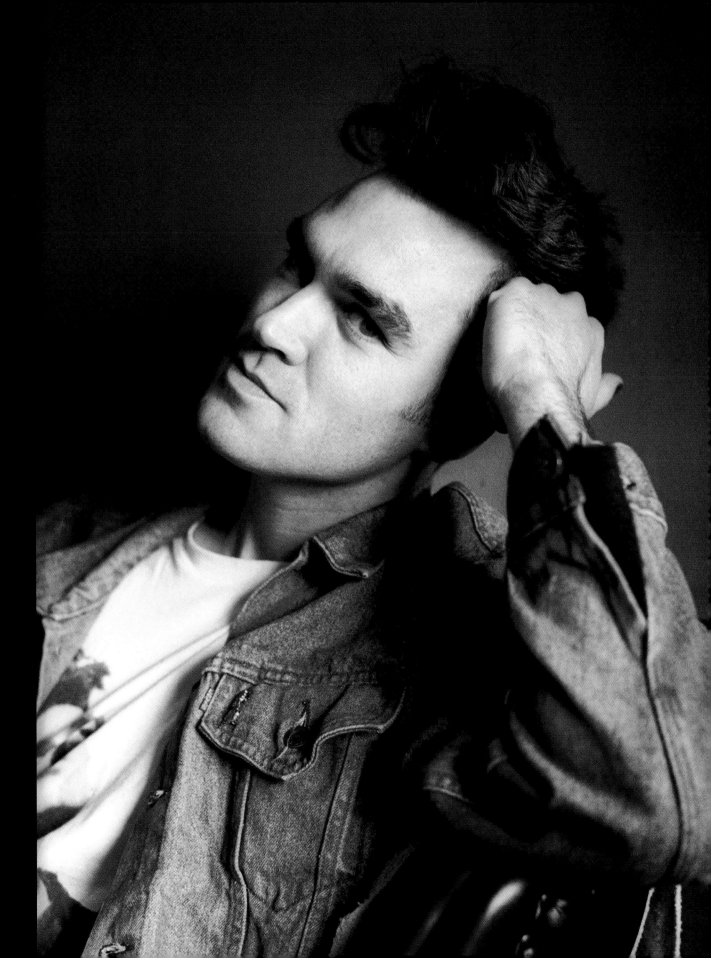

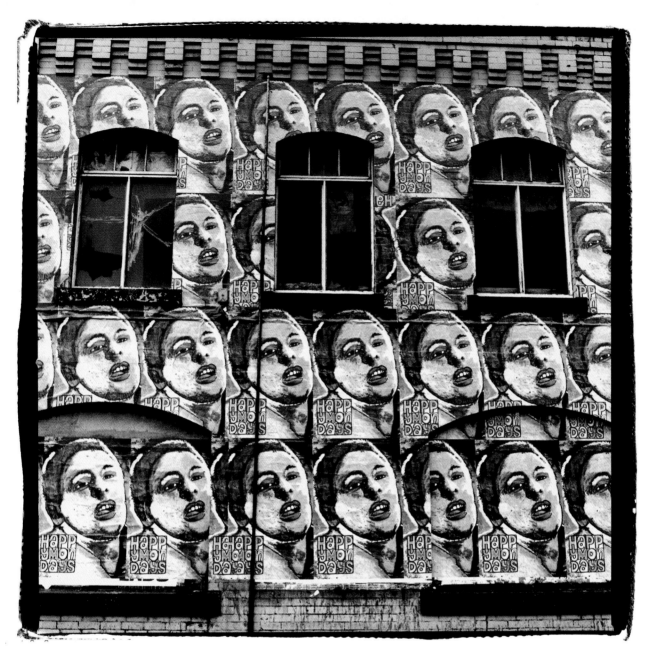

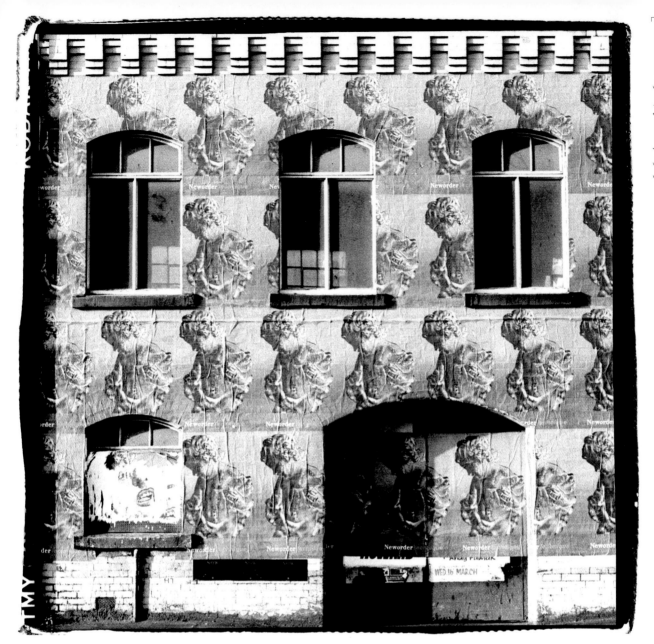

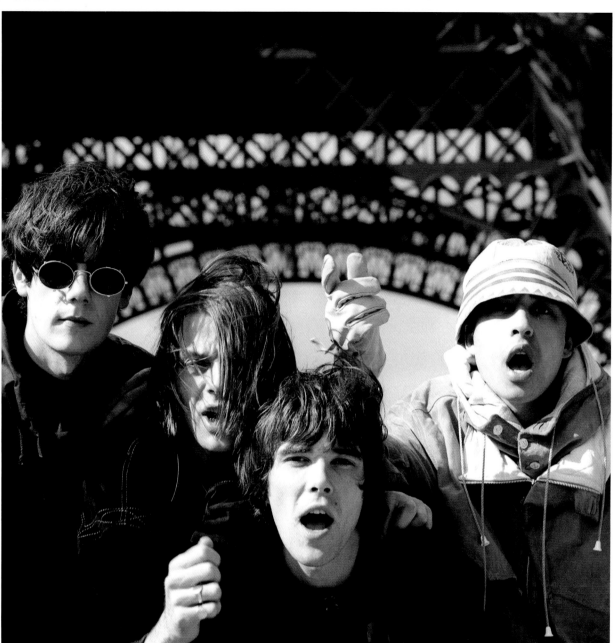

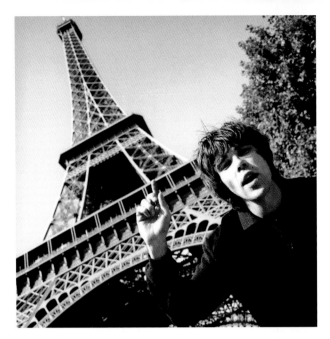
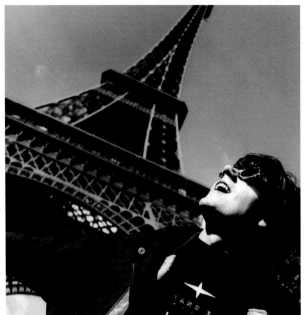
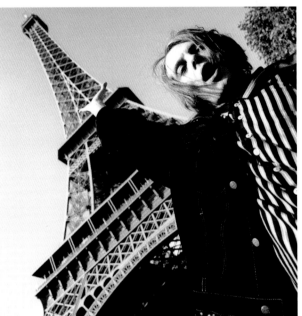
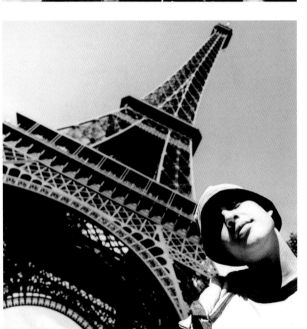

Reni's hat
Studio, Manchester
5 November 1989

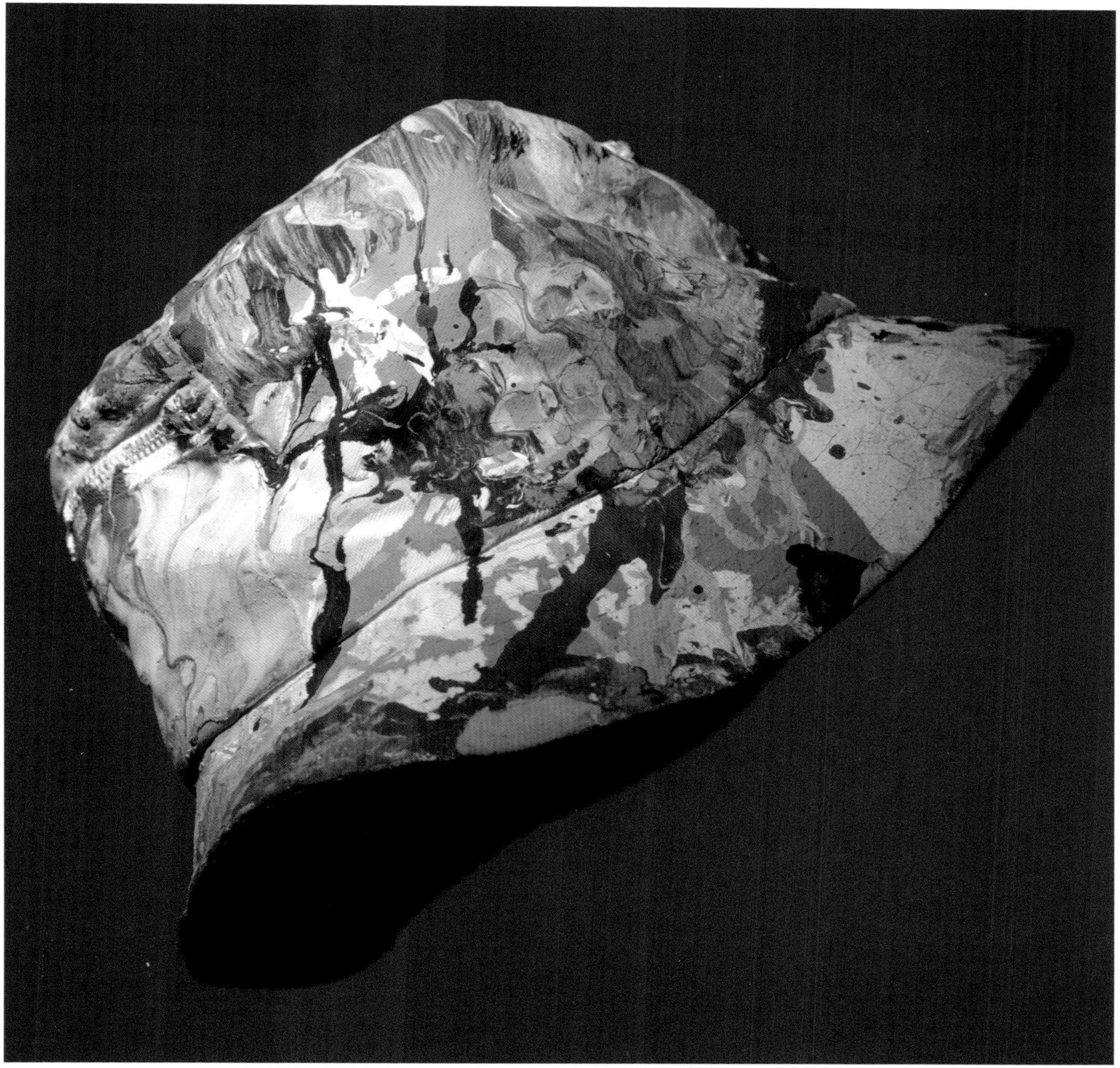

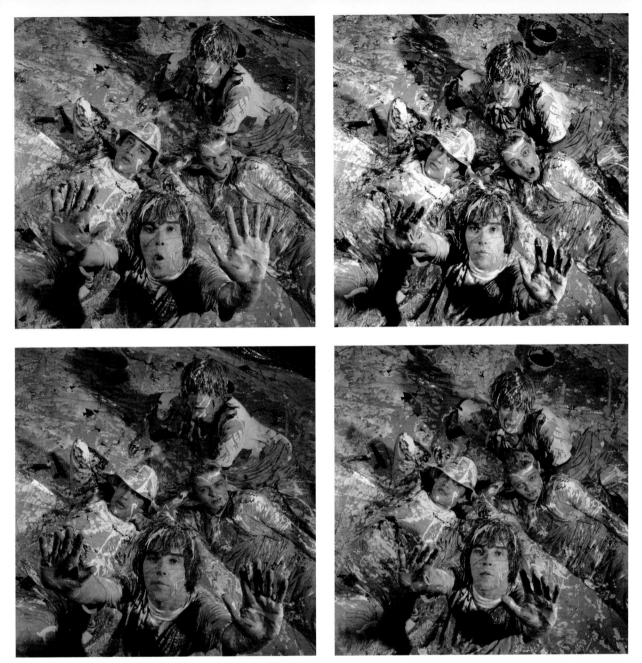

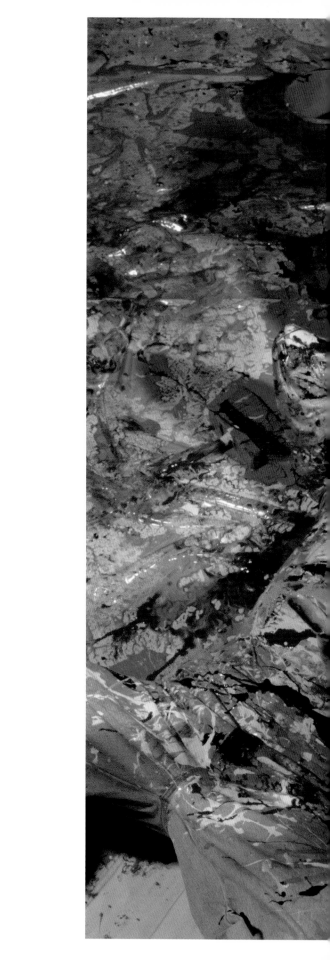

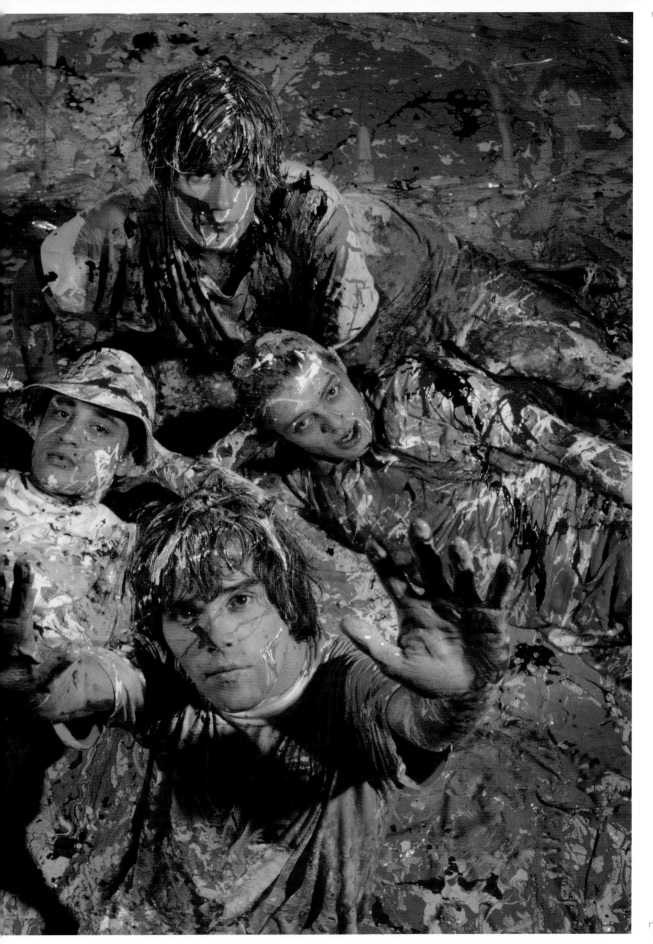

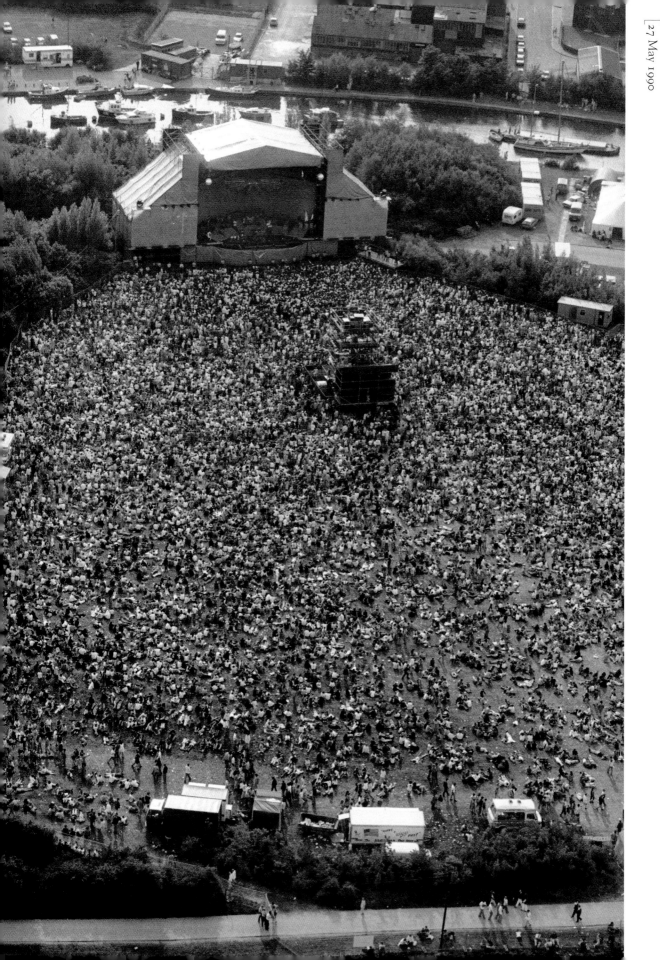

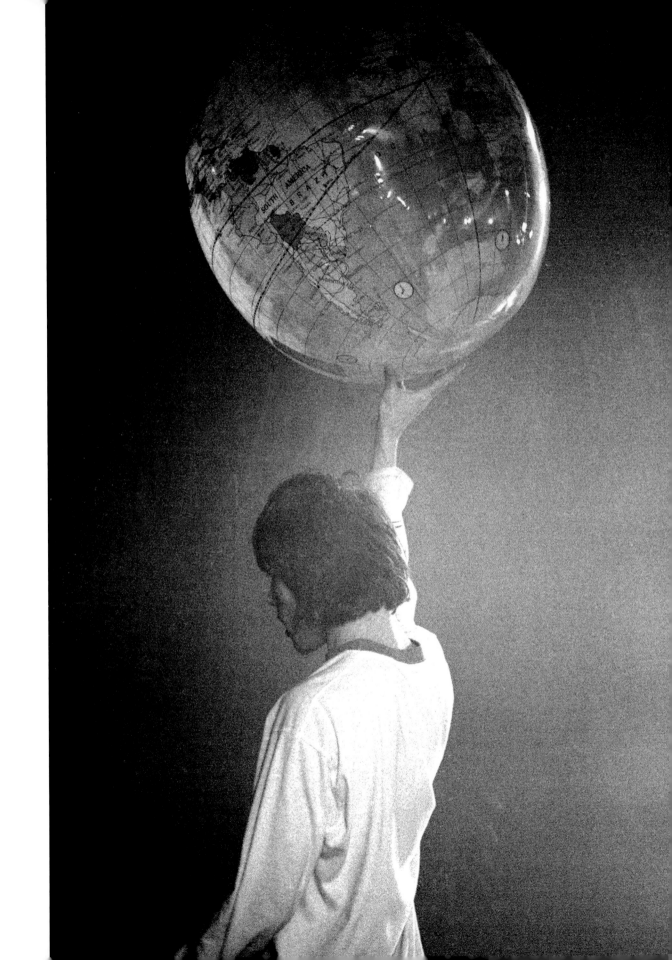

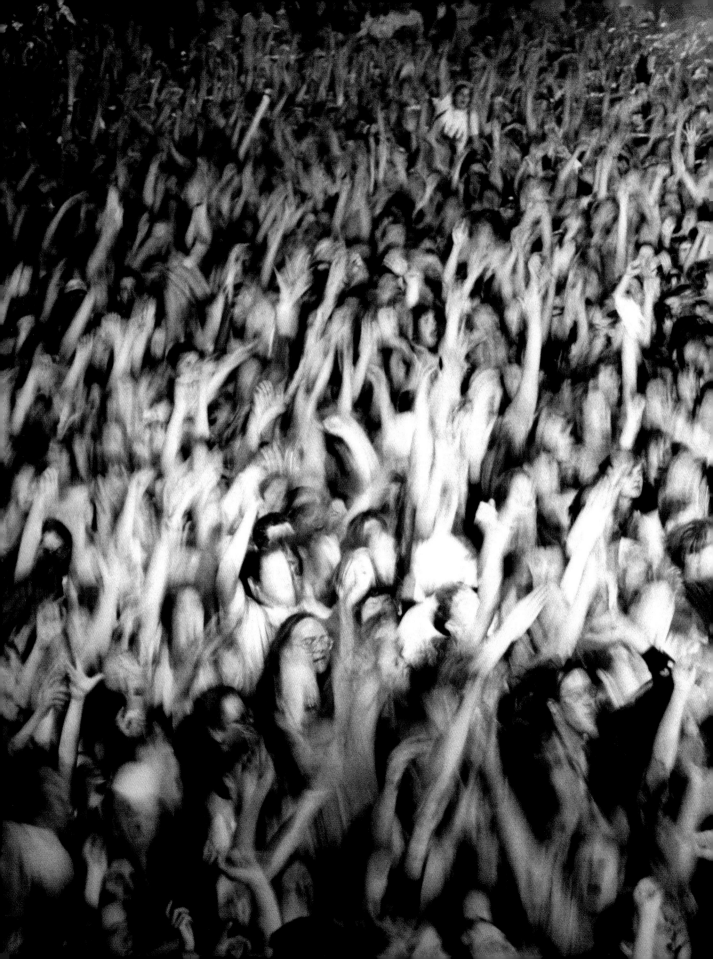

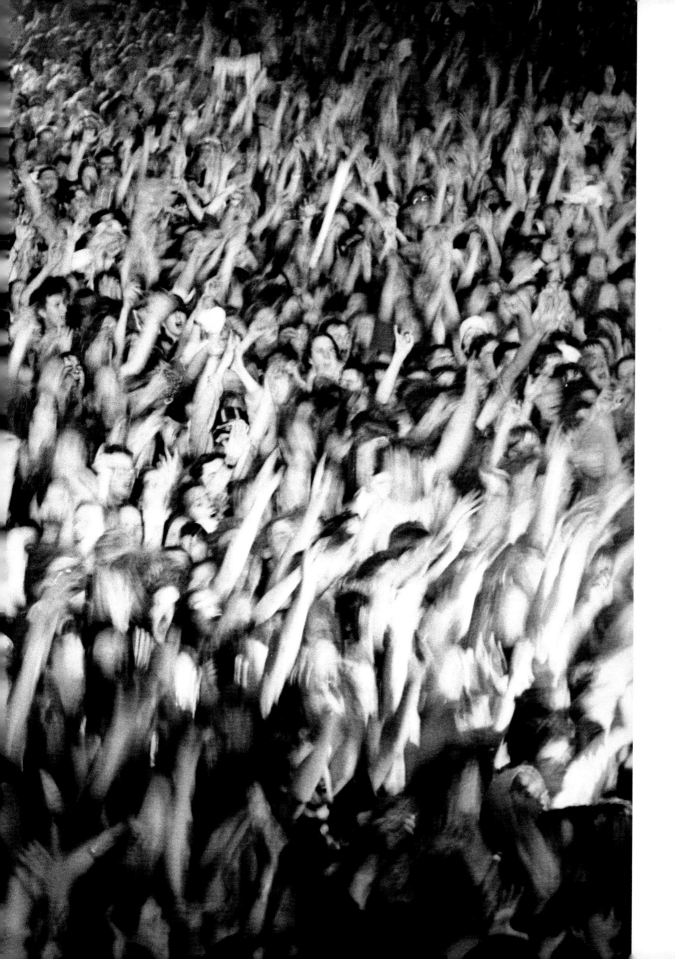

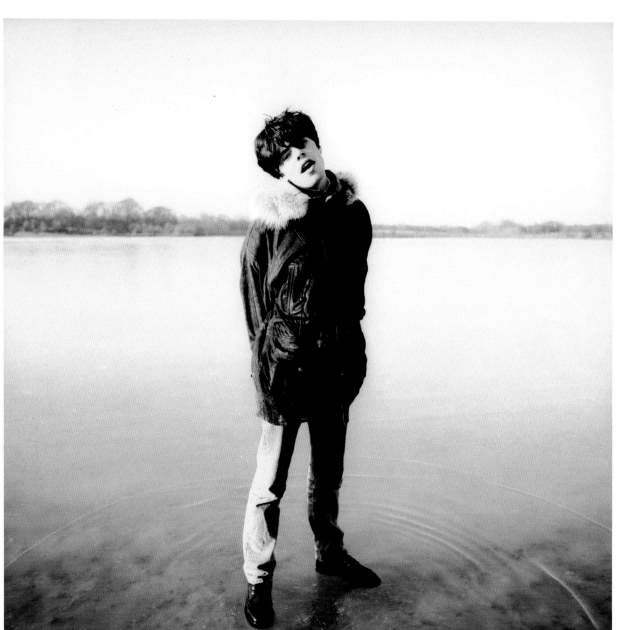

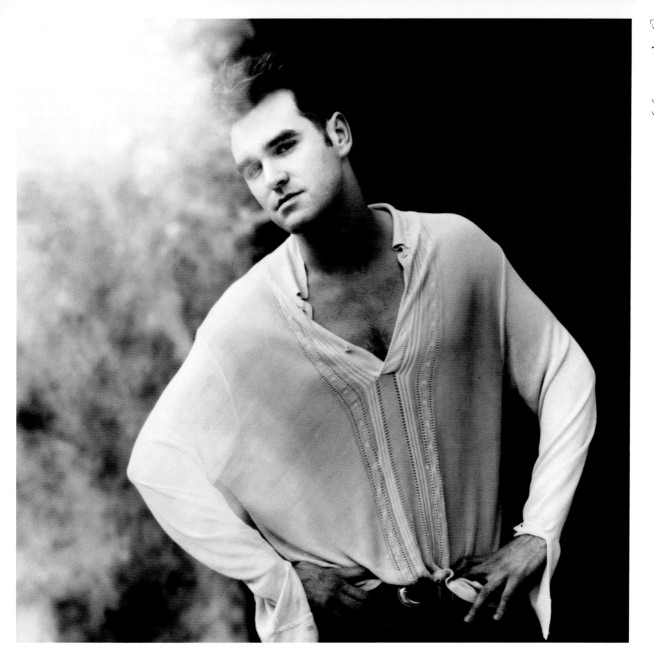

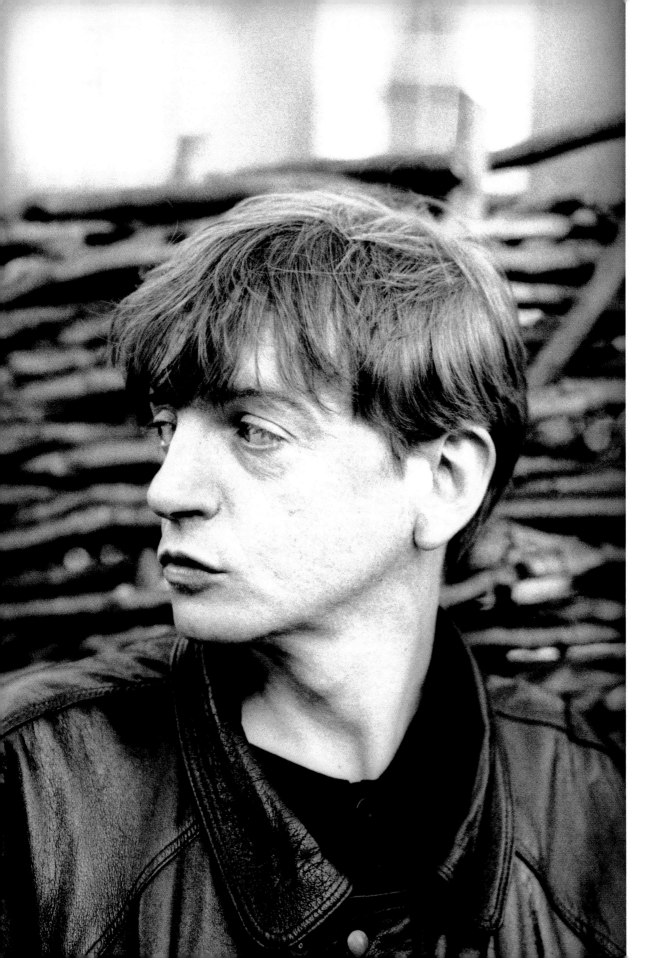

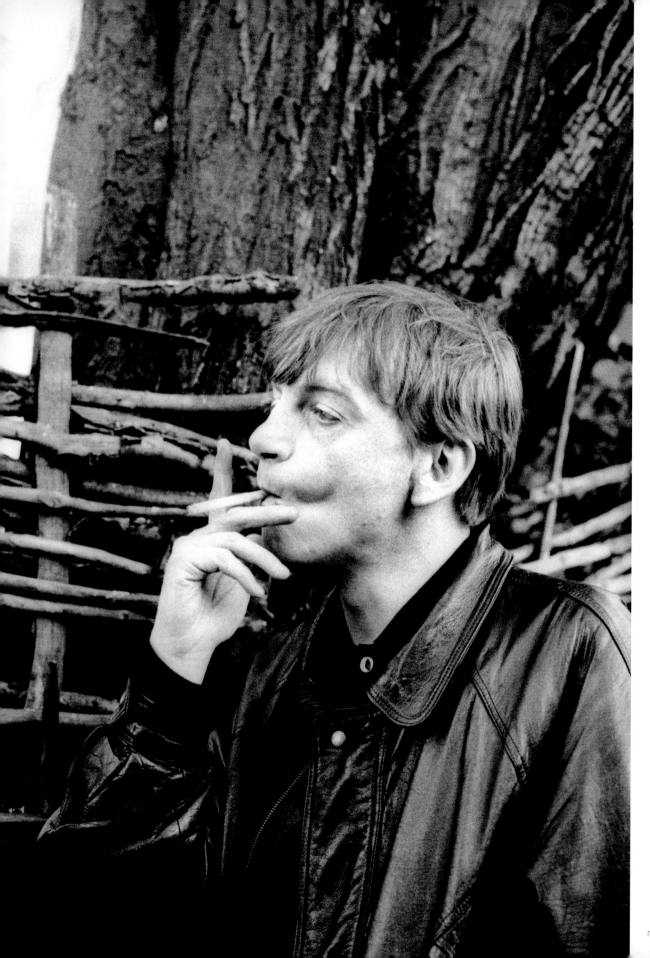

Mark E. Smith, The Fall
Bayswater, London
10 March 1993

If I should be so blessed as to revisit again my own country, but more especially Manchester, all that I could hope or desire would be presented before in one view.

J.G. Kohl

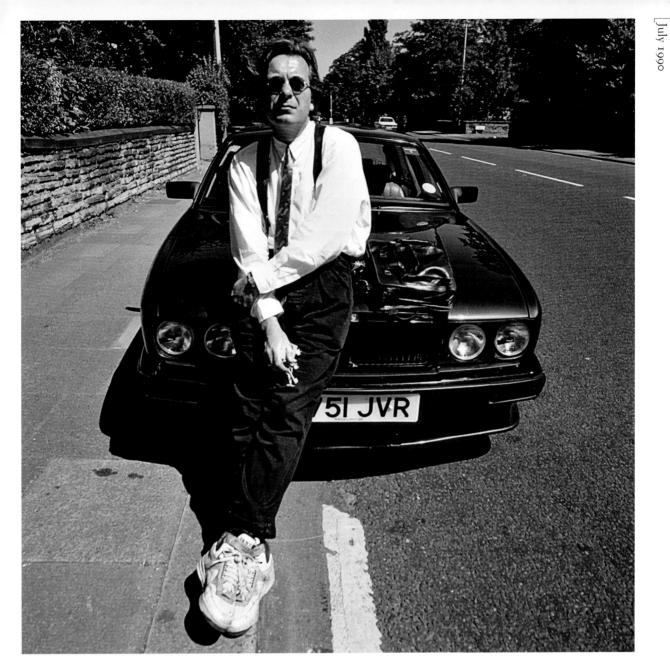

Morrissey
Rochdale Canal, Manchester
5 September 1989

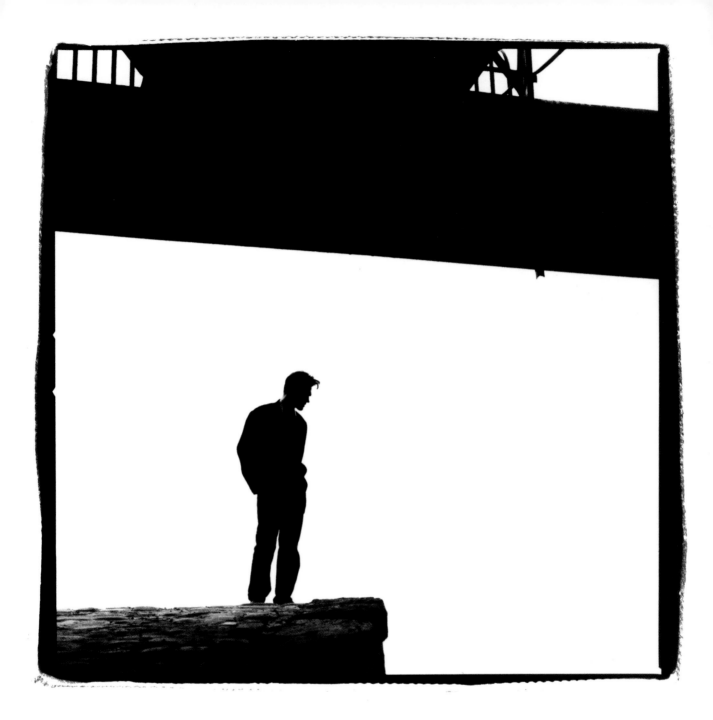

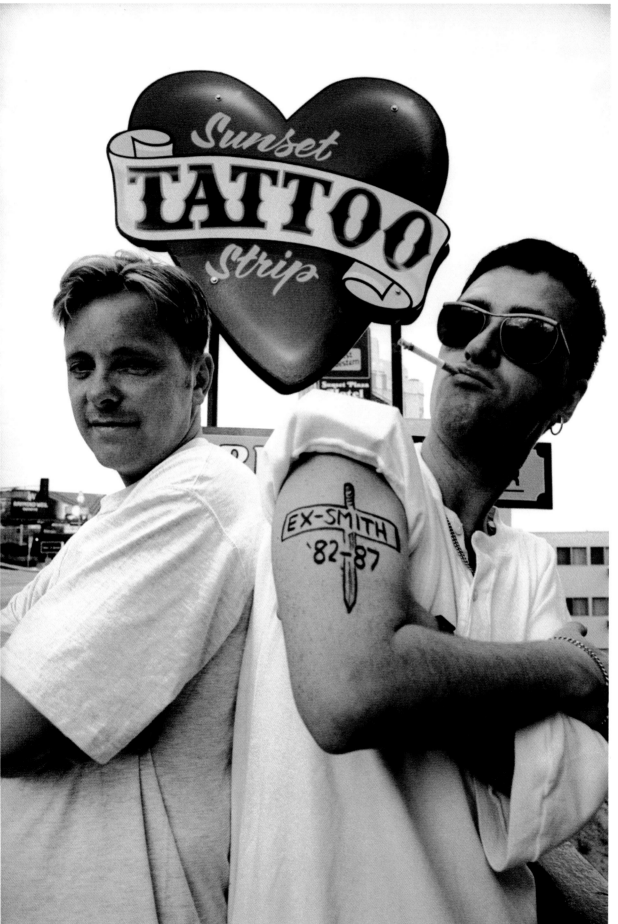

Bernard Sumner and Johnny Marr, Electronic
Sunset Boulevard, LA
August 1990

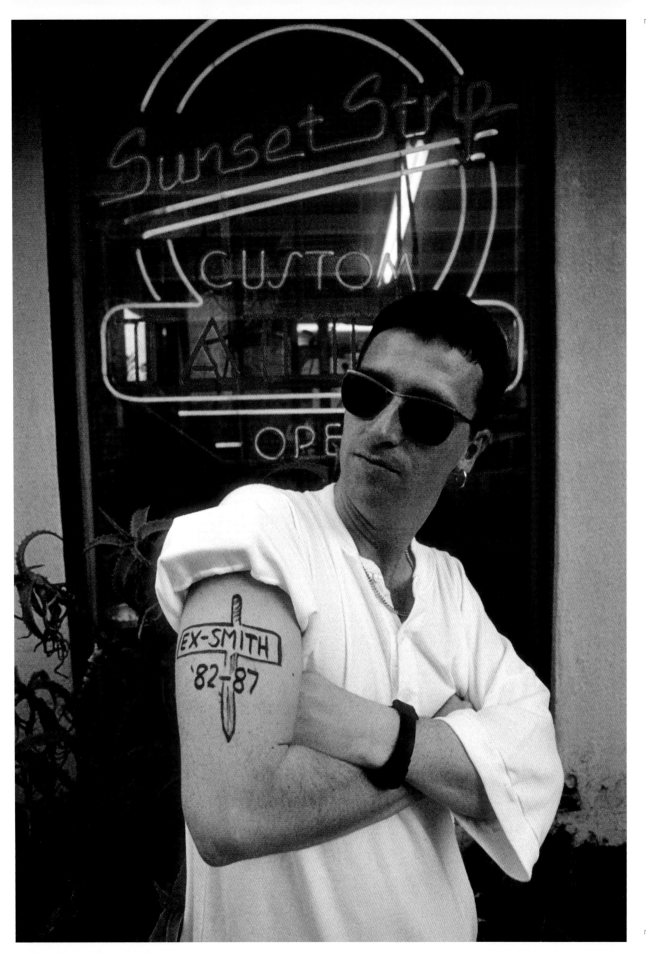

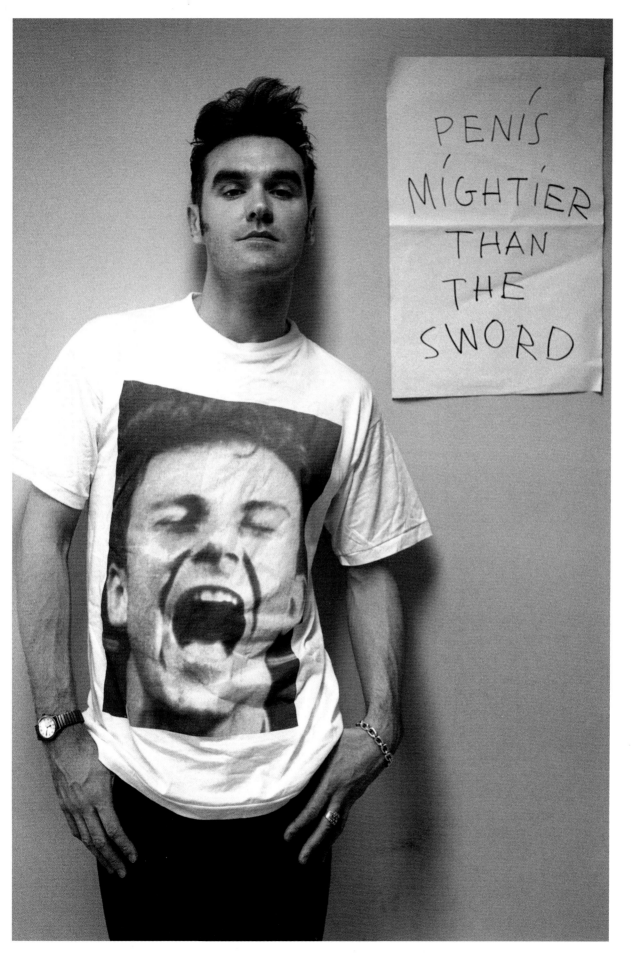

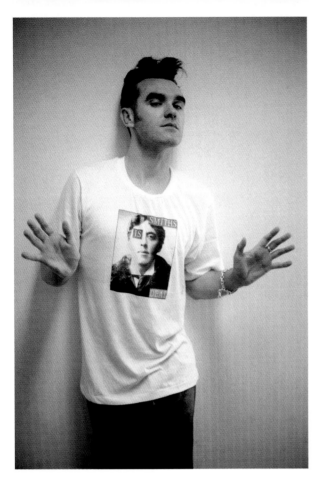
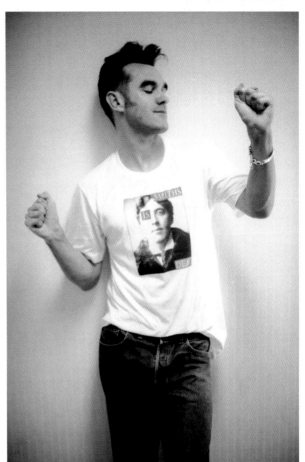
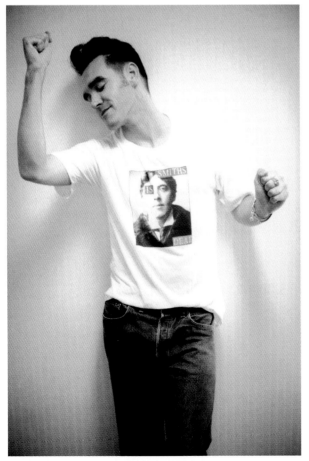
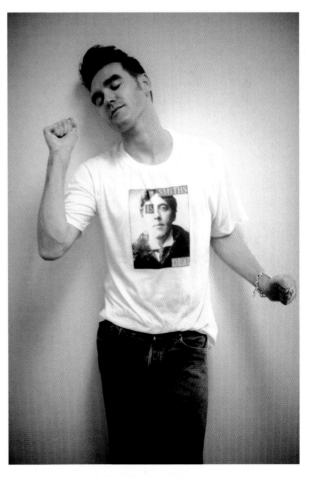

When I reached Manchester, it was raining heavily.

Beryl Bainbridge

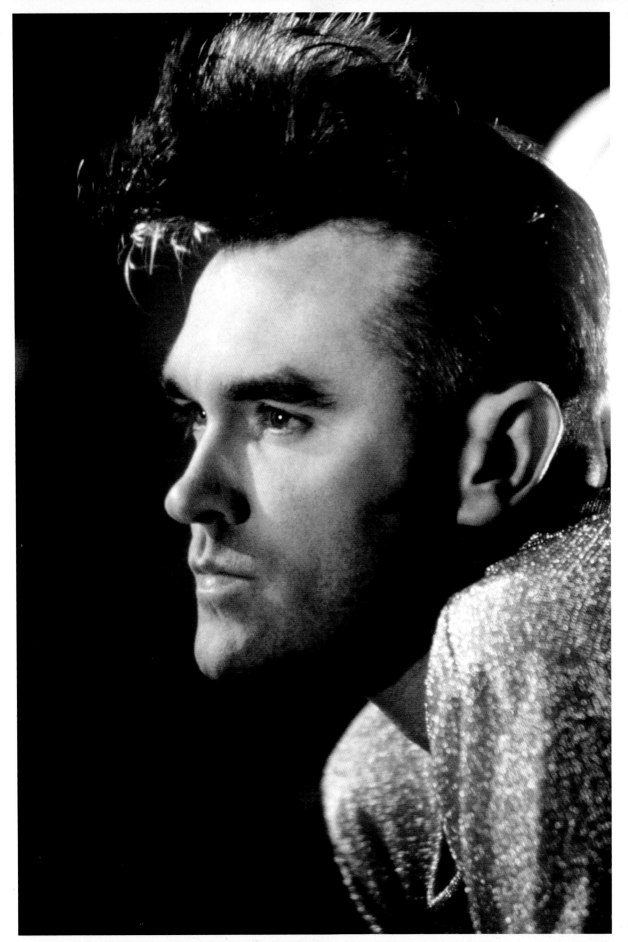

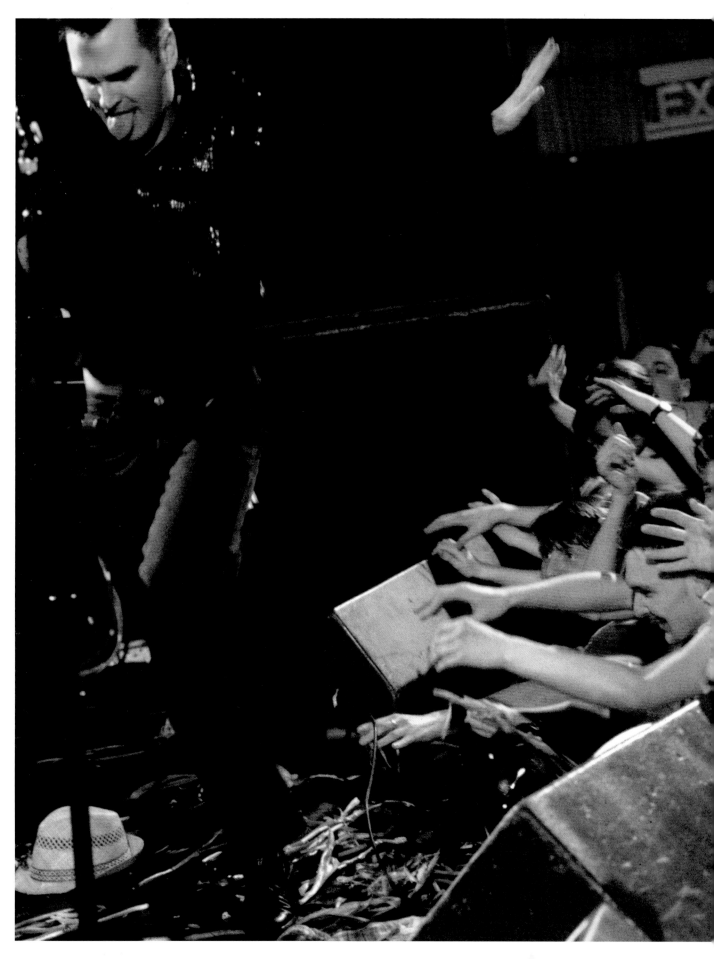

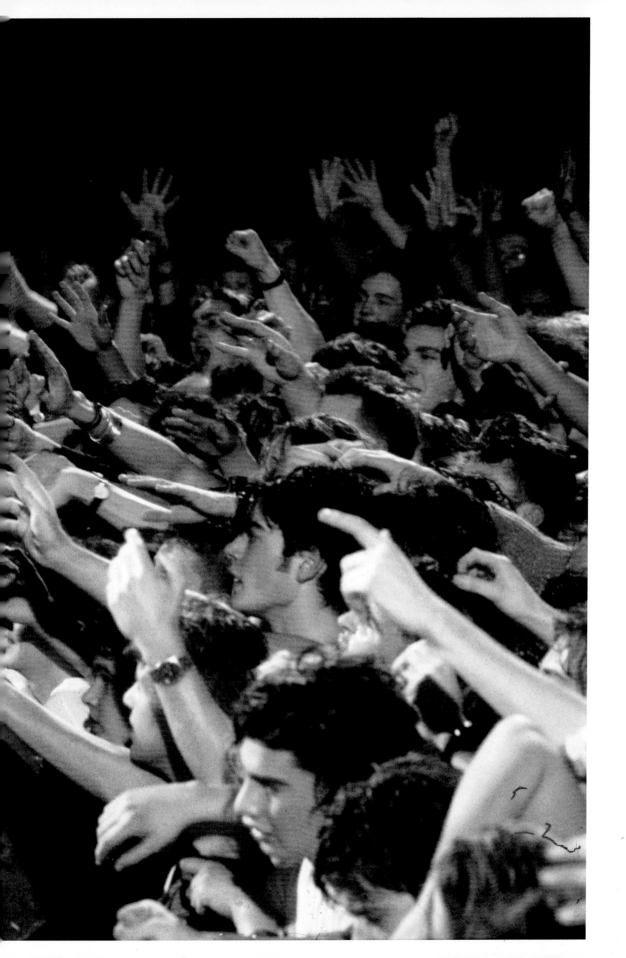

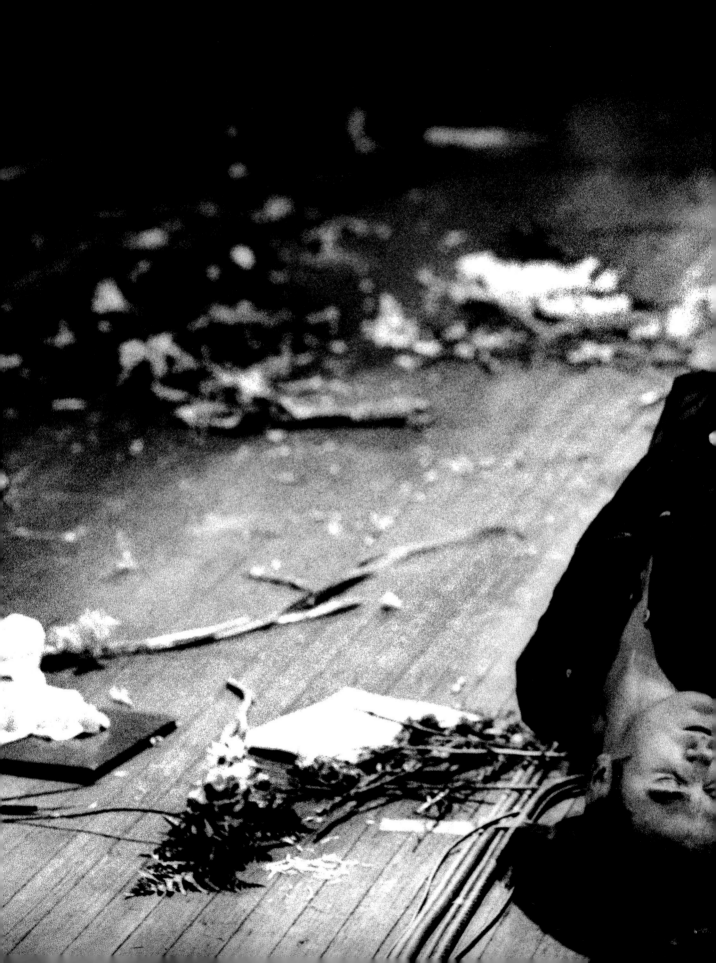

Morrissey
Jones Beach, Long Island, New York
July 1991

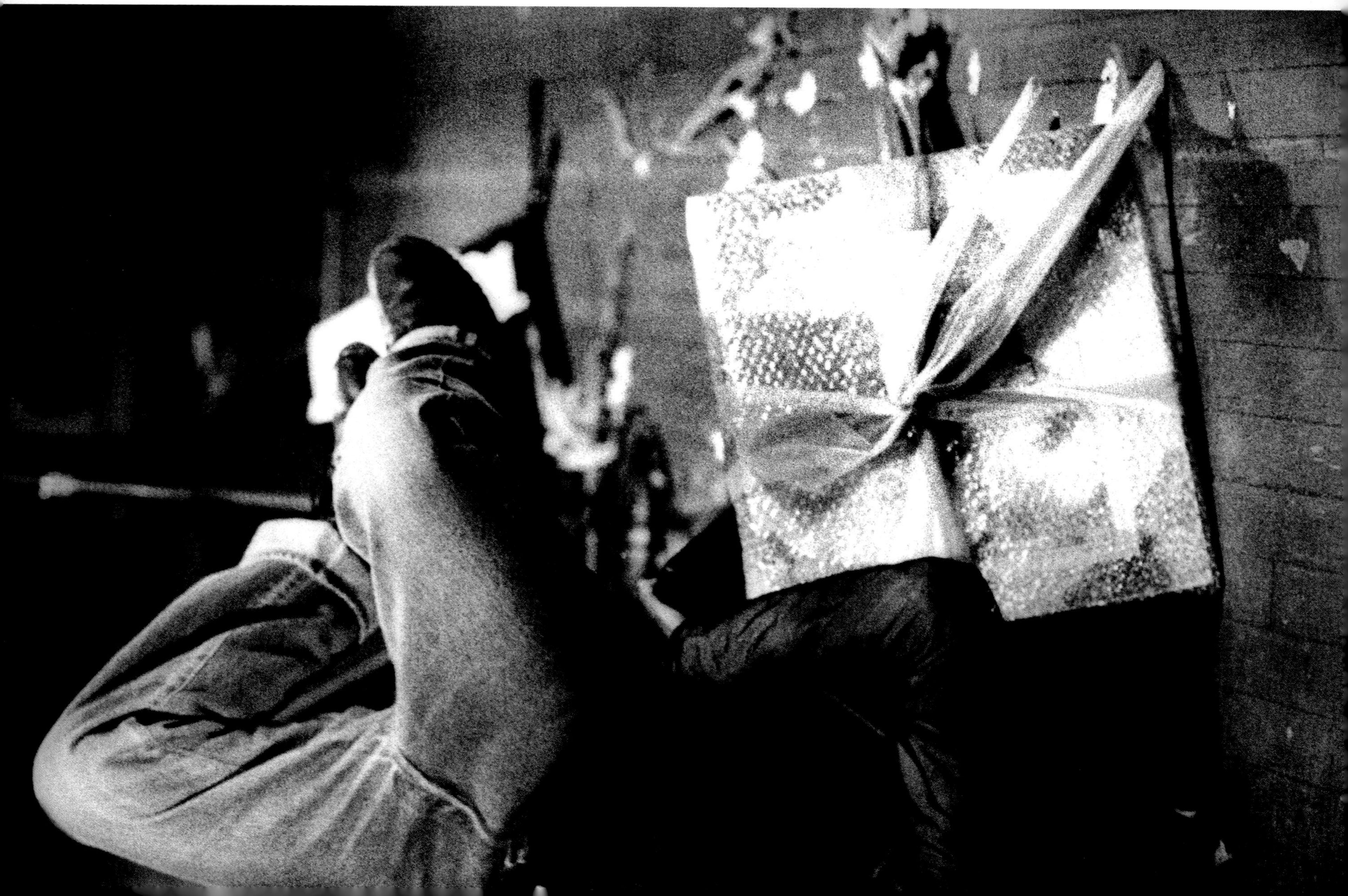

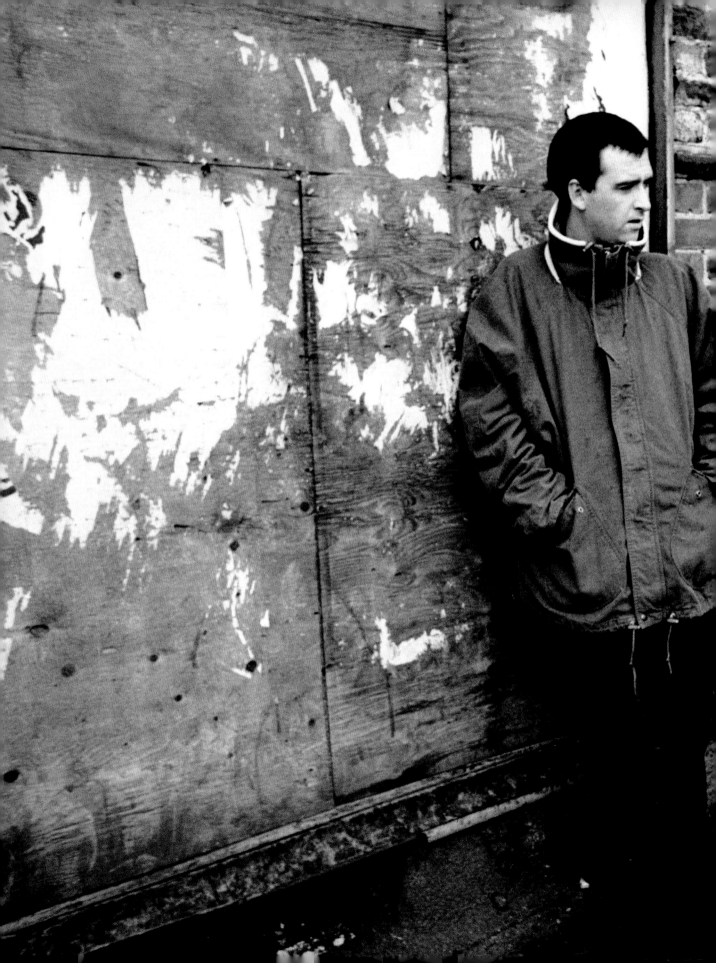

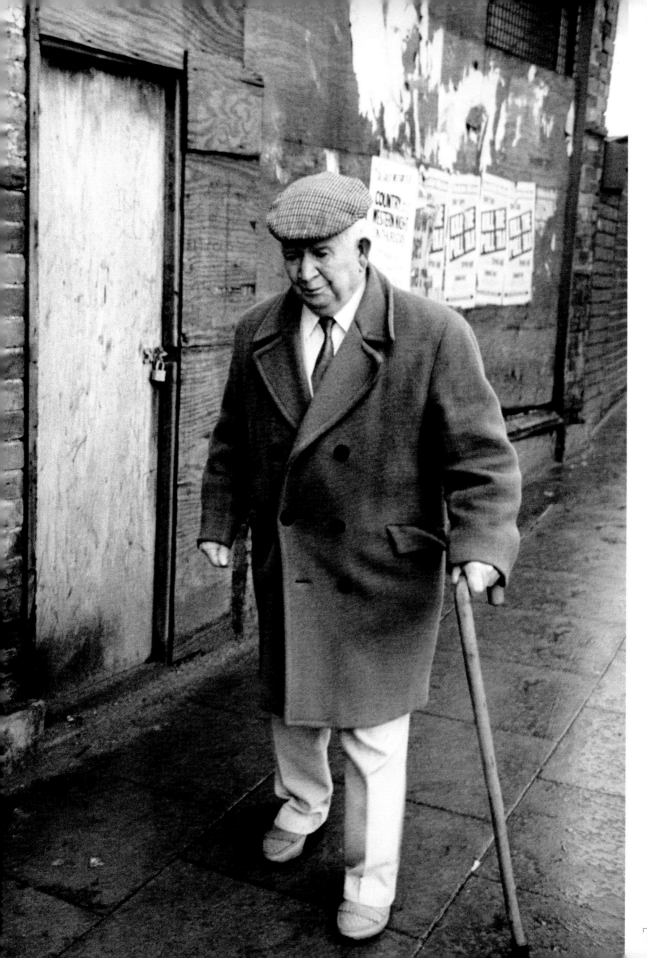

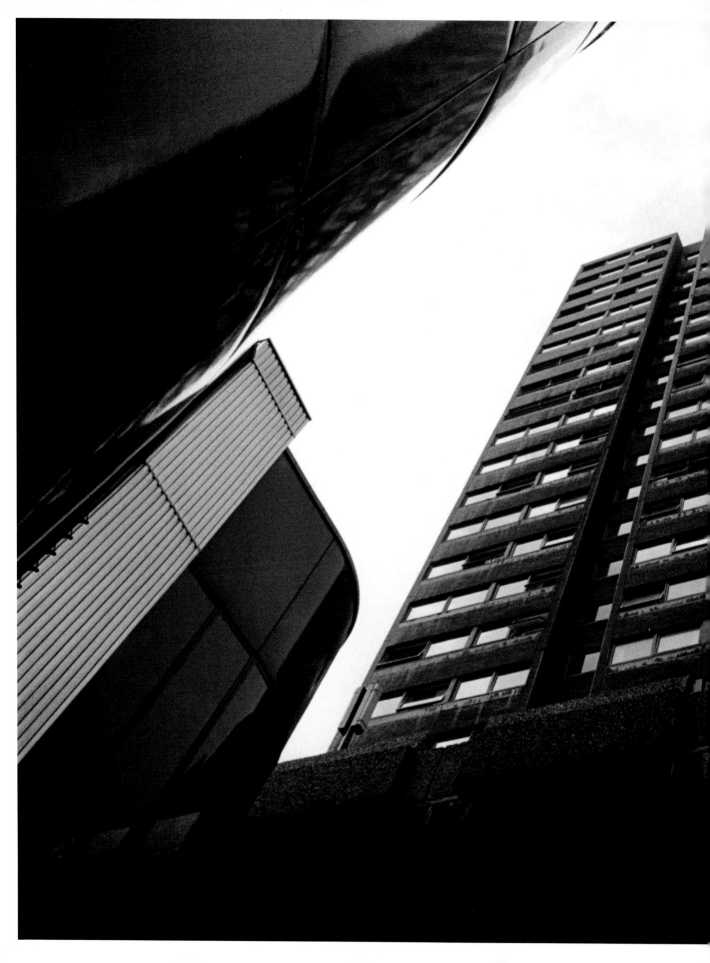

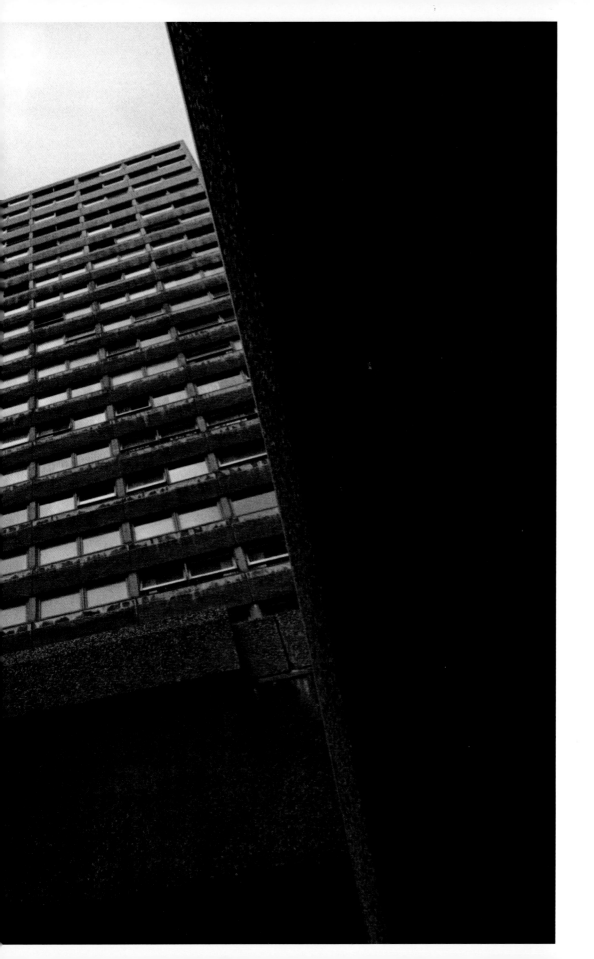

Morrissey (next page)
Tokyo
September 1991

Over: JOE DALLESANDRO, star of Andy Warhol's FLESH
and cover-star of the debut album by THE SMITHS; a
ROUGH TRADE record (Rough 61), issued on vinyl and
in cassette formats - released 24th February, 1984
Cunningly titled 'THE SMITHS' - and by THE SMITHS.

Dear Kevin,
    The "City Life"
cover moved me
dramatically. I
WANT THIS PICTURE
Can you oblige?
Let me know at
once!

Love etc,
MORRISSEY

SALES:(01) 727 1098/ENQUIRIES: (01) 727 6085
ROUGH TRADE RECORDS Ltd., 137 Blenheim Cres,
London W11. Distribution in UK by THE CARTEL

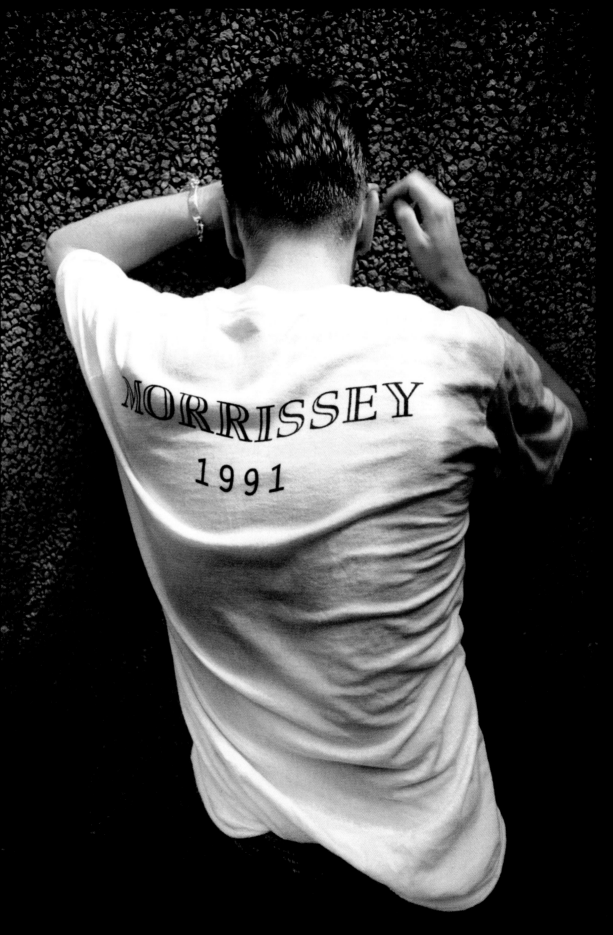

In September 2006, the British prime minister bade farewell to his party in a speech he gave at the railway terminus turned conference centre then called GMEX, these days known as the Manchester Central Convention Centre. Tony Blair would serve another nine months in office, but in keeping with his love of political theatre, this was one of a series of goodbyes, commemorated with no end of gravitas by an obliging media. 'You're the future now,' he told his audience. 'Make the most of it.' A motorcade duly whisked him away, tracked by the television cameras as if it was speeding him to the nearest airport, and from there to his favourite Caribbean holiday haunt, and into retirement, but no: he was simply on his way to London, back to his job.

This was, let us not forget, the first PM who had spent time as the lead singer with a college rock group; the only premier in history who had once made a speech paying tribute to The Clash, The Smiths and The Stone Roses; a statesman whose early months in office had included a Downing Street reception at which he had set great store by sharing a few minutes of small talk with the guitarist and songwriter with the biggest British rock group of the day. A Downing Street memo, prepared well in advance of his departure from office, had expressed the wish that in going, he should somehow leave with 'the crowds wanting more', like a 'star who won't even play the last encore'. Those hopes didn't come to much, but the Manchester speech fitted the general idea: in obeisance to the rock manual, a phoney farewell, so as to set the public up for the next one, and the one after that.

The arena in which Blair spoke had been opened in 1986, a spectacular memorial to the metropolitan council that had been abolished by the government led by that great centralising libertarian – a radical Conservative, no less – Margaret Thatcher. It had gone on to host exhibitions and sports tournaments and concerts by most of the rock groups who had symbolised Manchester's reinvention as the alleged heart of British pop culture. The same year it opened, by way of commemorating the tenth anniversary of the Sex Pistols' catalytic appearance at the Lesser Free Trade Hall, it had hosted what Tony Wilson grandly titled the Festival of the Tenth Summer, starring The Smiths and New Order. In subsequent years, GMEX concerts marked the arrival in rarefied commercial territory – if only, as in so many cases, for a brief instant – of such talents as Happy Mondays, James and the Inspiral Carpets. Oasis belatedly pitched up in 1997; nine years later, Morrissey's comeback was confirmed by a two-night stand that was celebrated by the local press – and received by twenty thousand people – as a magical homecoming.

And now there was this: the party conference as arena spectacular. Thanks to the political equivalent of metrosexuality, New Labour no longer wanted to congregate at the good old British seaside – and certainly not in Blackpool, a town so achingly trad that it would surely cause Blairites no end of grief – but in a compact modern metropolis, now full of cafés and bars, and café-bars, and a gay village, and bright lights, and the highest number of Anti-Social Behaviour Orders issued by any council in the country; looked at from a certain angle, as close to a New Labour utopia as the party had managed. 'What about Manchester?' Blair asked his audience. 'A city transformed. A city that shows what a confident, open, and proud people with a great Labour council can do.'

He was right; the *Rough Guide to Britain* said so. It paid tribute to Manchester's 'cultural renaissance' and 'an urban facelift unequalled in modern Britain'. 'The city today boasts a thriving social and cultural scene few, if any English cities, can rival,' it said. 'Its cutting-edge sports facilities, concert halls, theatres, clubs and café society are boosted by England's largest student population and a pioneering gay village.' Given such tributes, tourism was no longer a matter of those wide-eyed Smiths fans who could once be spotted excitedly making their way around Southern Cemetery and the Salford Lads' Club, but a new kind of visitor, drawn to the promise of high-end comfort and cutting-edge cultural attractions. If you Googled 'Manchester citybreak', up the recommendations came:

Mancunians may be too down-to-earth to say it themselves, but the capital of the northwest has come over all Manhattanchester . . . You're now as likely to come across loft-dwellers quaffing mojitos as you are flat-capped tradesmen nursing pints of Newton & Ridley ale in the Rover's. For the cosmopolitan weekender shopping for denim on Tib Street or dining in a converted cotton warehouse and bar-hop in the Northern Quarter, Manchester is as vibrant and immediate as any European capital . . . The Industrial Revolution has been succeeded by a Residential Revolution, with grand old mills and factories now housing apartments, restaurants and bars, and elegant new glass and steel inventions transforming the landscape by the week.

You can now go back to Manchester, and walk or drive around whole swathes of the city, and have only the vaguest clue about where exactly you might be going. The revelation hit me in 1999 or thereabouts, trying to navigate from the university end of Oxford Road to the old heart of Hulme, keeping my eye on the few sights that seemed familiar, but soon getting lost. The infamous crescents, high-rise leviathans in which the underclass shared space with countercultural squatters, had long gone. So too had the maze of jerry-built flats and covered walkways that once sat next to them. The road layout had changed beyond recognition; all you could do was point the car in roughly the right direction, and hope.

Can you write songs about the unsettling effects of urban redesign? One brave group had a go: Doves, the trio of sometime Haçienda regulars who had initially called themselves Sub Sub and managed a top-five hit in 1993 with a rubbery dance piece called 'Ain't No Love, Ain't No Use', but then reinvented themselves as a rock group (a little bit Talk Talk, a little bit Smiths). 'Some Cities' – which, accidentally echoing that 'Manhattanchester' hype, takes its lead from The Velvet Underground – is not the stuff of great poetry, but it's all there. 'I think I might have met you before,' goes its first line, addressing a place suddenly rendered alien. Streets have been re-routed; memories have gone; all that remains are ghosts, if you know where to look. 'Too much history coming down,' it moans. 'Another building brought to ground.' It's a song about history's onward march, and a quiet kind of bereavement.

Making your way around modern Manchester, one thought hits you more than most. Where is the old subterranea – that network of low-end property, shabby performance spaces and faded clubs and bars that formed the backdrop to just about all the city's musical glories? And is its apparent absence the reason why Manchester seems to have gone so quiet? On occasion, the difference between then and now becomes so pointed as to be almost painful. The Lesser Free Trade Hall is now part of a huge Radisson hotel. Most notably, the Haçienda is the name of an expensive apartment block – or, if you prefer, a cocktail served at the Hilton's Sky Bar on the twenty-third floor of the Beetham Tower, Britain's tallest building outside London, which towers over Deansgate as a talismanic embodiment of everything that has changed.

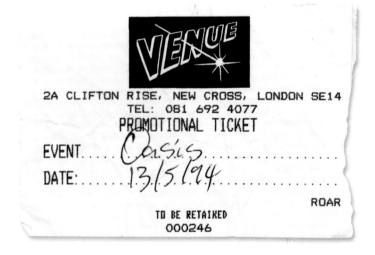

Before all this came to pass, one group of musicians emerged from the city and achieved success and wealth that their predecessors would have thought mind-boggling. Despite all kinds of limitations, they were initially excitement incarnate – though what they eventually came to represent perhaps mirrored the fate of their home city: hedonism teetering into conspicuous consumption; what once seemed bold and forward-looking peeled back to reveal comfy nostalgia. Theirs is a Manchester story, but not in the same thoroughgoing terms as many of the Mancunians who had preceded them. Not for them an excess of civic pride, or any imperative to somehow pay it all back. Oasis left town, headed south, and rarely came back – though in the British public's mind, they remain a giant byword for the place whence they came; and in that sense, perhaps the most Mancunian rock group of all.

So where to start? At Maine Road on 27 and 28 April 1996, when Oasis became an accredited stadium attraction, and local gangs reportedly threatened to kidnap Liam Gallagher? On 13 and 14 December 1997, when they came to GMEX in the slipstream of their third album – praised to the skies in the press, though eventually damned as an over-hyped travesty – to play a show that began with their exit from a giant red phone box? Or on 18 August 1991, when they played their first show – without Noel Gallagher – to a noncommittal half-crowd at the Boardwalk?

Or how about page 4 of the *New Musical Express*, on 5 March 1994? A Kevin Cummins portrait of a scowling Noel, arms folded, posing by a poster for the Sleepin Arena, Amsterdam, among whose current advertised attractions are Fischer Z, The Mekons, Sultans of Ping FC, Clusterfuck and Guzzard. The main headline reads, 'Dam busted!' 'Oasis were deported from Holland last week after they were involved in a drunken brawl,' says the story.

> The Creation act were forced to cancel their first show outside the UK when singer Liam Gallagher and bassist Paul McGuigan were arrested by Dutch police while travelling from Harwich to Amsterdam. After consuming large quantities of champagne and Jack Daniel's, Liam and Paul were involved in scuffles with security men and police. They were then handcuffed and locked in the brig.

Recounting the story in strait-laced terms that somehow make it even funnier – like *The Football Factory* meets *Carry On Abroad* – it goes on:

> The following morning, guitarist 'Bonehead' woke to find out that his room had been ransacked and his passport and clothes stolen . . . Four band members were placed in a dockyard cell upon the ferry's arrival and put on the first boat back to Harwich, leaving guitarist Noel Gallagher – who apparently slept through the whole incident – to make his way to the venue to call off the show.

A 'band spokesperson' sums up the intrigue thus: 'Several of the band members have never been abroad before and obviously got carried away with themselves. But their treatment at the hands of the police was particularly harsh. They were wrongly accused of all kinds of things, including handling counterfeit money.' Oasis, the story concludes, have 'no plans to return to the Dutch port in the near future'. Instead, they will soon be making their way around such English settlements as Bedford, Tunbridge Wells, Bath, Middlesbrough, Stoke and Kingston-upon-Hull.

Three years later, when all was six-figure pay cheques and Brit Awards, Noel Gallagher sat in an upscale rehearsal space in south London, and reflected on his group's early history. Back then, he said, Oasis did not approach the touring ritual with the kind of wearied insouciance that one associates with leather-trousered rock 'n' rollers; rather, in the conjunction of motorways, cheap hotels and what are still colloquially known as toilet venues, they glimpsed a joyous kind of liberation. 'Someone'd give us three hundred quid, put us in a van with all the gear and say, "You're playing Bath Moles tonight, and it's three hundred miles away,"' he said.

> The manager'd be going, 'Right, I'll see you tomorrow,' and we'd be like, 'If you're fucking lucky, mate.' And we'd just be off. Off. Turn up at the gig late. Give it to the monitor engineer: 'Oi! Speccy! Fucking turn it up!' And we'd just signed off. That was our first job.

Anyone who has seen this kind of life up close will know that its appeal never lasts long. These days, those who are lucky get quickly promoted to theatres, then arenas, then stadiums, and glory in a world in which luxury comes on tap and the bar is always open. For the less fortunate, the supposed romance of sticky-floored venues, boarding-houses and sore heads soon palls, and they either grimly continue, or quit.

If things are moving in the right direction, however, it is in this phase that you glimpse the ambition and excess that defines what some romantics still call The Rock Dream, and all at their most pure. In the Cummins portfolio, there is a slew of pictures taken on an early Oasis tour in which all this is crystallised, mostly by the younger Gallagher: Liam leaning against the microphone stand à la John Lydon, affecting the kind of vacant self-belief that was already his hallmark; Liam standing astride a table festooned with beer bottles, belligerently making some wee-hours point or another; most notably, Liam in a hotel bar in Newport, Gwent. Fortuitously, it was called the Oasis Bar, though that was not really the point: what was important was that even people who were sceptical about Oasis saw in that picture the kind of charismatic flash that, back then, British rock music had mislaid.

In April 1994, a very different image was meant to be on the cover of the *NME*: the two Gallaghers, clad in Manchester City shirts – home and away, both emblazoned with the amusingly apt logo of the electronics firm Brother. When the on-the-road pictures arrived in the *NME*'s office, however, the Newport picture instantly became The One. Via a Stone Roses song title and the paper's innate love of hyperbole, it did not take long to come up with the cover-line: 'Oasis: What the World Is Waiting For'.

Now, if all this sounds a little overblown, as if some of us were deludedly seeing Dionysian rites regularly re-enacted at the Sheffield Leadmill and Hull Adelphi, two points need making. First, on the rare occasions that everything perfectly coheres, rock music can do that to people. Second, a lot of Oasis's early music captures that self-same romance, as if Noel Gallagher was knowingly essaying their own story. Many of their best songs were founded on a keening desire for escape and the celebration of living in the moment, with music to match: fuzz-toned guitars, the most pared-down, piledriving drumming (poor Tony McCarroll, sacked from the group in 1995, only for people to realise that his punk-rock approach was a crucial part of that early magic), and Liam's bulgy-veined vocals, surely as perfect a vehicle for those songs as his brother could have wanted.

For proof of how winning that mixture was, listen to the song that starts their first album, *Defintely Maybe*, released in August 1994. 'Rock 'n' Roll Star' has a first line that nods to everything that Noel wants to leave behind ('I lived my life in the city/But there's no easy way out'), a chorus that seems to propel him and his group somewhere better by sheer force of will ('Tonight, I'm a rock 'n' roll star'), and a pile-up of a coda that salutes the simple glory of the music:

It's just rock 'n' roll
It's just rock 'n' roll.

From the off, there was not much nuance or light and shade about Oasis. They did not share the longstanding Mancunian fondness for such black forms as funk and soul. Despite Noel Gallagher's professed liking for some electronic dance music, none of it ever encroached on their abiding sound: thirty years of rock, mixed up and winningly simplified, with little room for anything resembling a groove. In his catch-all cultural history *Manchester, England*, the DJ and writer Dave Haslam recalls their habit of finishing Friday-night rehearsals in the bowels of the Boardwalk and then coming upstairs to a club night called Yellow – rock-free, and soundtracked by the pulse that then defined Mancunian clubland. In his recollection, 'Liam rarely moved from the cigarette machine.'

Surveying recent(ish) Mancunian history, one begins to wonder how to make sense of the fact that twenty-odd years of musical developments reached their climax with music so antediluvian. How to get from, say, the Haçienda's list of most-played records from 1982 – Marvin Gaye's 'Sexual Healing', Grandmaster Flash and the Furious Five's 'The Message', A Certain Ratio's 'Knife Slits Water', the Associates' 'Party Fears Two' – to stuff whose most obvious antecedent was the assuredly populist rock music once pioneered by the vaudevillian Slade? What links the Gallaghers' songs with the psychedelicised murk of the Mondays' *Bummed*, the spartan clatter of The Fall or the shadowy alchemy mastered by Joy Division? Noel Gallagher claims to have loved The Smiths – and Johnny Marr in particular – but took on little of their understanding of the necessity of space and understatement, let alone Morrissey's facility with words. Even The Stone Roses, the group the Oasis myth identifies as their forefathers, were always lithe and fluid – and at their best, endowed with an enigmatic magic that Oasis never tried to get near.

The central Oasis idea, honed during those long rehearsals at the aforementioned Boardwalk, was very simple. Two guitars, bass and drums were used to hammer home music built from brazenly rudimentary chord changes, thrumalong basslines and rigidly four-four rhythms. In place of the experimental impulse rooted in the British art-school experience and streaked through so much classic British music, from Pink Floyd to the Sex Pistols and beyond, there was a warm embrace of what more adventurous minds might have damned as cliché. With a guileless glee, Oasis rehabilitated the three-chord trick, gloried in sentimental balladry, and pilfered whatever they could from other people, usually without bothering to cover their tracks.

To those who liked music to push the envelope, their music could seem positively Neanderthal – a betrayal of the drive to experiment that had defined so much great British music, not least so much of the stuff created by Oasis's beloved Beatles. They had a point, not least when Oasis lapsed into lazy pastiche. But consider the case for the defence: how complex and pointy-headed are songs as great as 'Louie Louie', 'She Loves You', 'Whole Lotta Rosie' or 'Cum On Feel the Noize'? As one of their associates once put it, 'It's not Captain Beefheart. It's not Leonard Cohen. It's Oasis. It's a giggle; it's fun. Punch the air, get whacked, life's great. Sore head the next day.' To quote Noel himself, interviewed for the *Sunday Times* in the spring of 2008: 'What's great about great music is that you don't have to think about it. It just hits you, wham, and that's it.' Such was the irresistible spell they cast in their first two triumphant years. One encounter with what they did – for me, it happened at the 100 Club in London, only to be quickly repeated in Liverpool, Glasgow and a few places besides – and you instantly knew what Paul 'Bonehead' Arthurs had known when he first heard Noel's songs: 'Something'll happen with this.'

When they began, circumstances were not favourably aligned for a Mancunian rock group. Noel's first Oasis performance came in 1992, the year that Happy Mondays set off for the doomed sojourn in Barbados that would begin their demise, replete with crack, car crashes and an album put to tape without vocals. The Stone Roses were nowhere to be seen, cloistered in rural studios and getting nowhere fast, and ensnared by legal problems that would so sap their momentum that they wouldn't reappear until late 1994. The Haçienda, once the embodiment of all of Manchester's dazzle, was plagued by the city's drug gangs and apparently letting in anyone who turned up. Phil Saxe, the Factory label's chief talent scout, fleetingly considered signing Oasis – and a band from Sheffield called Pulp – but found out that the money had run out. Sped into extinction by the sky-high interest rates that had followed the Major government's bungling on Black Monday – who killed Factory? Norman Lamont! – the label closed its doors that November.

At this point, British rock music was in a state of washout. Thanks to the soul-scraping sound pioneered by Nirvana, the US seemed completely dominant. For reasons bound up with a somnambulant genre known as shoegazing and a smattering of groups from Oxford and Reading – Ride, Slowdive, Chapterhouse – the 'alternative' elements of the music industry briefly decided that the UK's musical centre of gravity lay, of all places, in the Thames Valley. The green shoots of recovery were about to appear, thanks chiefly to a London-based group called Suede, though until that summer you would never have known. Among the hotly tipped groups being written about in the weekly music press were Bivouac, Mint 400 and good old Swineherd.

Oasis carried on, to what seems to have been large-scale indifference. 'We had a song called "Rock 'n' Roll Star",' Noel recalled. '"Tonight, I'm a rock 'n' roll star." People were going, "Yeah, course you are mate – bottom of the bill at the Boardwalk on a Tuesday night." Pretentious arseholes is what they thought we were.'

In retrospect, however, things were starting to align – albeit subtly – in their favour. 1993 saw not only the decisive arrival of Suede, whose debut album arrived at the top of the charts that April, but a bold step forward by a group who had previously laboured in the long shadow of The Stone Roses, scored a solitary big hit, and then apparently floundered. Blur's second album, *Modern Life Is Rubbish*, was released in May, trailered by a single called 'For Tomorrow', a gorgeous conceit whereby the influence of David Bowie and Ray Davies was used to evoke the existential overload of modern London. They were a very different proposition from Suede, arch and playful whereas the latter were deadly serious, though both groups had broad outlines in common: an evident fondness for the kind of classic British rock that had recently fallen from fashion, and a proud fluency in the language of pop music. If it seemed unclear what place there might be for Oasis's music in a milieu still so completely dominated by Kurt Cobain and his musical offspring (*In Utero*, Nirvana's third album, was released that September), these records offered some kind of answer.

It is one of this period's more unfortunate facts that the arrival of what became known as Britpop was heralded in the grisliest way imaginable. Kurt Cobain shot himself in Seattle on 5 April 1994, thus ensuring that subsequent generations would see him as a kind of secular saint. In Britain, however, the wake of his death found the ensuing weeks of mourning colliding with a mood that was its complete opposite, thanks largely to the release of Blur's masterful *Parklife*. The week he died, the cover of the *NME* featured his portrait in bummed-out monochrome. Within a few weeks, its pages were full of altogether brighter colours, belatedly fulfilling one of Damon Albarn's claims-cum-prophecies from the previous year, uttered in the back seat of a vintage car en route to the Essex resort of Clacton: 'If punk was getting rid of hippies, then I'm getting rid of grunge. It's the same sort of feeling: people should smarten up, be a bit more energetic.'

The week after Cobain's suicide, Oasis released their first single: 'Supersonic', still one of their greatest achievements. In its mangled-up lyrics there lurked the apparent influence of Happy Mondays – 'guttersnipe surrealism', one of my colleagues later called that quality – though it transcended their influence from the opening moments: a boom-crash drum intro and spindly guitar noises that sounded like the last strains of something about to snap, and then the first words, which seemed to serve notice of what Oasis had come to avenge. 'I need to be myself,' sang Liam. 'I can't be no one else.'

'Music for me at the moment is dead,' said Noel, with characteristic understatement.

It's poncey and serious and everyone's got to make some sort of statement, whether it be about 'Parklife' or their feminine side or their politics. But we're a rock 'n' roll band – we say all you need is cigarettes and alcohol. Everyone's dead into analysing, but don't analyse our band. 'That's a good song, that is. What does it mean?' Who gives a fuck what it means?

Oasis's pronouncements drew on The Stone Roses' old habit of claiming to be among the best bands in the world, but with the latter's soft-spoken detachment replaced by the sense that the Gallagher brothers – and Noel in particular – could not stop talking. 'I get a buzz off giving new songs to Alan McGee,' he told me, ''cos he thinks we're the greatest band in the fucking world. He phones me up at four or five o'clock in the morning: I'll get out of bed and it's McGee on the other end going' – and here, the quote broke into block capitals, because that's what you did back then – '"I'M FEELING SUPERSONIC! GIVE ME GIN AND TONIC! WE'RE GONNA ANNIHILATE THE WORLD MAN!"'

That quote was hurled into my tape recorder at some time after midnight, the night

'Supersonic' was released. Oasis had just contributed to a live Radio 1 broadcast in Glasgow, and then gone back to the Forte Crest Hotel, an Alan Partridge-esque place that, for one night only, was a theatre of very modest dreams. Among the first people the Oasis party spotted was Andrew Roachford, still riding the small wave that had been stirred by a 1988 single called 'Cuddly Toy'. With no little enthusiasm, Liam Gallagher duly sprinted in his direction. '"Cuddly Toy", man!' he said. 'Tune of the eighties!'

An hour or so later, Noel and Liam – along with a couple of aides – were in the former's hotel room, sitting for their first proper feature in the *NME*. The highlights of the opening rounds, initially focused on the aforementioned pantomime en route to Holland, went like this:

(Note: accidentally, the *NME*'s old insistence on printing the word 'fucking' as 'f---ing' actually heightened the argument's comedy, softening what looks on paper like a belligerent bust-up, and thus heightening the air of slapstick.)

NME: How do you feel about your notoriety as . . . kind of . . . Rock 'n' roll animals?

Liam: I'm into it me, I'm into it. But at the end of the day, I go off home and I get a clip off me mam. And I *do*. She clips me round the ear and goes, 'What have you been doing, you little tinker?' But I like the way it's bubbling up. It's like the Roses all over again. I like that, me. I want to get two thousand people in a nice fucking gaff who are there to see *me* . . .

Noel: That's not what he's on about.

Liam: He is.

Noel: No, he's on about getting thrown off ferries. And the thing about getting thrown off ferries and getting deported is not summat that I'm proud about.

Liam: Well, I am, la.

Noel: Right then. Well, if you're proud about getting thrown off ferries, then why don't you go and support West Ham and get the fuck out of my band and go and be a football hooligan? We're *musicians*, right?

Liam: You're only gutted 'cos you were in bed, reading your fucking books.

Noel: Shut up! Shut up! This lot think it's rock 'n' roll to get thrown off a ferry. And do you know what my manager said to him? He said, 'Nah. Rock 'n' roll is playing in Amsterdam, coming back, and telling everyone you blew 'em away.' Not getting thrown off the ferry like some Scouse schlepper with handcuffs. I won't stand for it.

Some time later:

Liam: Look, all I've got to say is, I'm just having the crack. It's not doing anyone any harm. John Lennon used to do loads of mad things . . .

Noel: Do you *know* John Lennon?

Liam: Yeah, I do.

Noel: Well, you must be pretty old then. How old are you? Twenty-one?

Liam: No. About a thousand and five fucking one [*sic*].

Noel: You're twenty-two. And I watched you being born, so shut the fuck up about knowing John Lennon.

At the height of Oasis's success, a couple of books appeared that attempted to tell the story of the group's prehistory. One was co-authored by Chris Hutton, the luckless would-be singer who had been displaced by Liam Gallagher in 1990 and happily sent on his way by a band who had, so they later said, grown tired of his fondness for a rewrite of an old Troggs hit that went 'Wild thing/You smoke a draw'. The other was the work of Paul Gallagher, the third brother who surfaced in the wake of Oasis's success looking rather more damaged and sad than his two siblings – 'Bod', they called him – and had an unsuccessful stab at managing a couple of Manchester rock bands.

Both books featured plate sections in which the members of Oasis were pictured as adolescents, looking – with the notable exception of Noel – like the kind of people for whom rock music and its associated dress codes had precious little relevance. Even in the images of Liam, there were bumfluff moustaches and pleated trousers. These were, perhaps, not people too bothered about the more classical notions of cool.

Even in their pomp, you could draw much the same conclusion. Though Oasis were aspiring rock 'n' rollers, there was also something very un-rock 'n' roll about them, an impression only furthered by their outward presentation. On stage, they stood stock still. Most of their haircuts did not exactly reflect the standard rock archetypes: Noel, to quote a comparison used by one Mancunian musician, looked ever so slightly like the sometime *Blue Peter* presenter John Noakes. Paul 'Bonehead' Arthurs, as one of their London-based peers was heard to marvel, was bald (or, rather, balding).

Their singer, meanwhile, had sartorial tastes that placed him light years away from those icons who had once wrapped themselves in the kind of raffish finery they bought from King's Road boutiques. 'Liam wasn't fashionable,' one of their associates later marvelled. 'He used to shop in Marks and Spencer: he'd go in there and pull out the most fantastic garb. I remember him taking me into a Clarks shoe shop once and going, "Look at these – great shoes." He'd go to Dunn & Co and pull stuff out.' In April 1995, I was confronted by Liam at a soundcheck in Paris, where he had just taken delivery of a consignment of high-end leisurewear. He had quickly changed into what he obviously thought was the most choice item: a lime-green Lacoste two-piece, midway between thermal pyjamas and a jogging suit.

But there was something about the Oasis aesthetic that was exactly right. What they did was couched in terms of a kind of Mod-ish simplicity: the monochrome logo, like something clipped from the inside collar of a polo shirt; the Gallaghers' clothes, neat, primary-coloured and proudly high-street. They did not do encores, nor say much to their audience. Everything, like the music, was so reductive as to come out looking simple and strident and thereby unstoppable.

Their first album, however, was not the instinctive work of instant perfection that many might have expected. *Definitely Maybe* had been through two remakes, as the group and their associates had fretted over their seeming inability to capture their spark on tape. Their initial attempts, in fact, sounded like the work of a different band: thin and reedy, tentative instead of authoritative; the songs put to tape via the usual studio practice of insisting that each player was clinically recorded separately, whereas Oasis were surely best putting their Boardwalk groupthink to good use, and recording live.

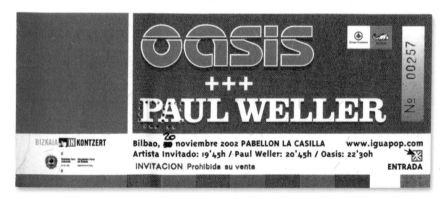

In the summer of 1994, it was rescued by a last-ditch spurt of remixes and overdubs, though listening to it, you would never have guessed. Just about all of it pulsed with the right stuff: not just brio and excitement and motion, but a brilliant sense of menace. 'Columbia' began, as one writer later pointed out, with 'a near-"Gimme Shelter" sense of there being something loud and vengeful coming round the corner', and then tumbled into Oasis's one and only take on the Mancunian sounds they had presumably imbibed in the late eighties, only with menace replacing Haçienda feelgoodery. The same sense of unease was streaked through 'Bring It On Down', such a potent piece that it had been considered as their first single. 'Slide Away' – for which millions fell at a stroke – confidently mined the same seam as 'Live Forever'. Perhaps best of all was 'Cigarettes and Alcohol': everyday excess melded to T. Rex's 'Get It On', and probably the last great dole lyric –

Is it worth the aggravation,
To find yourself a job when there's nothing worth working for?

The album closed with one of Oasis's most underrated songs, brimming with a wit that never really reared its head again. 'Married with Children' was a thumbnail sketch of Noel circa 1992, living in a flat just off Whitworth Street, bumping up against domesticity, and itching to make his move, with lyrics that seemingly quoted from yet another argument:

I hate the way that you are so sarcastic,
And you're not very bright.
You think that everything you've done's fantastic.
Your music's shite, it keeps me up all night.

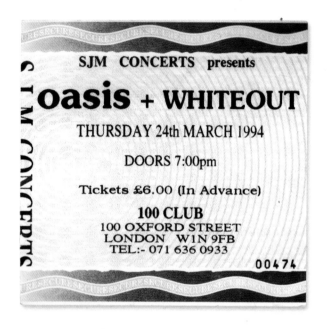

From lyrics like that to Liam's vowel sounds, you could make out Manchester in just about all of *Definitely Maybe* – and yet unlike just about all the groups that had preceded them, Oasis itched to get away. Noel in particular made a point of fleeing as soon as he could. 'As soon as I got some money,' he later recalled,

I was out of there. In Manchester, I was sick and tired of going into pubs I'd been going into since I was fifteen and everyone saying, 'Tight bastard!' if I didn't buy the drinks and 'Flash bastard!' if I did. I was sick and tired of young crackheads coming up to me in clubs, sticking a screwdriver in my back and saying, 'We're doing the merchandise on your next tour,' or 'We're going to be your security team.' I hate the way anyone from the working class who makes money, the working class turns on them.

From here on in, when Manchester made its way into its lyrics, it was characterised as either the backdrop to nostalgic japery (witness 'Round Are Way' – workaday northwestern life turned into a half-cocked nursery rhyme), or a grim place to be visited only when necessary, as on 'D'You Know What I Mean?':

Step off the train all alone at dawn
Back into the hole where I was born.

One episode in Oasis's early history captures all this perfectly. In September 1994, just after the first album had been released, they came back to Manchester and played at the Haçienda, a ghost of the place it had been circa 1989, and destined soon to close for good. The experience was recounted to me by Ian Robertson, the group's short-lived 'Head of Security', an officer-class alumnus of Sandhurst whose accent did not exactly suggest an archetypal member of the road crew. 'It was quite staggering,' he said.

These brain-dead thugs turned up, and – of course – they ended up backstage. It was, 'How did you people get back here?' And then we had the conversation: 'Oh, we're doing Oasis's security.' 'Really? As a matter of fact, you're not.' Whenever we did shows in Manchester, I took extra security on the road.

Among the backstage faces that night was Shaun Ryder, quietly marking time after the demise of Happy Mondays. In Robertson's *What's the Story?* – in its own gonzo way, the best Oasis book by some distance – he is somewhat imaginatively cast as a cowboy of the Wild North West school, outraged by a refusal to let him watch Oasis from the stage. 'My posse's here and you're a dead man,' he says. 'You won't leave Manchester alive.'

Noel had by then pitched up in Camden Town, the shabby north London enclave that quickly became the HQ of the musicians who would be hailed as the vanguard of Britpop. Much like Manchester circa 1989 – only with countercultural fizz replaced with the whiff of corporate chicanery – for a brief period, it often looked like a pop-cultural theme park: bands and their hangers-on routinely gathered in a handful of pubs, the shops and stalls blasted out the requisite hits, and ever-increasing numbers of pop-cultural tourists arrived there to stock up on clothes and records, and gawp.

If only for a fleeting moment, the stories that had brought them there were pretty much true. A clutch of musicians really did form a loose network variously based around rivalry, friendship and mutual admiration. There were occasions when it was possible to see a quite remarkable array of talent without shifting from the same spot: at the Sunday of 1994's Glastonbury, for example, I spent a day sitting in front of the *NME* stage and watched Oasis, Pulp, Radiohead and Blur (and, by way of a reminder of Noel's past, Inspiral Carpets, the Oldham band for whom he had once been a roadie-cum-'guru'). And for a brief time, there was some sense of common cause, as in February 1995, when an apparently magnanimous Damon Albarn held one of Blur's Brit Awards aloft and said, 'I think this should be shared with Oasis.' ('Yeah, much love and respect to them,' added Graham Coxon, though it wasn't clear whether he meant it.)

Two months before that, Oasis released a seven-minute song called 'Whatever', in which Noel used not only Beatles-esque descending chords and a faux-psychedelic middle eight, but a crisp string arrangement that instantly evoked Christmas. Now, it sounds a little too full of moon-in-June sentimentality, though at the end of 1994, it seemed perfect. With great singles arriving at speed, Radio 1 purged of its senile old guard, and the thrill that came from seeing rock groups springing up the charts, it was not hard to be seduced by the dewy-eyed optimism of 'Whatever'. Everything, after all, was going right.

At speed, all this was wrapped in red, white and blue and packaged up as a shining cultural renaissance that extended way beyond the rock groups who were its most obvious public face. Britpop soon became one aspect of what was fleetingly known as Cool Britannia. Restaurateurs, models, artists, designers and writers were held up as the exemplars of what the aforementioned Mr Blair called a 'young country', and he and his colleagues worked themselves into a lather about a short-lived project called 'the rebranding of Britain', whereby the UK might somehow dump the fusty, backward-looking, class-bound ways that had so held it back and become a primary-coloured, all-singing meritocracy. As is usually the case, the developments that so inspired them were most fulsomely documented at the point when the shine had begun to wear off – most notably in March 1997, when *Vanity Fair*'s front cover featured Liam Gallagher and Patsy Kensit posing amid pillows and a duvet fashioned from the Union Jack, and the magazine claimed that London was swinging with a confidence and brio not seen since the sixties. Indeed, their voluminous coverage occasionally suggested that this *was* the sixties, restaged and re-celebrated with all the camp that implied: an Austin Powers kind of fantasia, with Oasis's repeated claims to be the new Beatles fitting in just fine.

For *Vanity Fair*, Tony Blair was 'The Visionary', twenty-one points ahead of John Major in the opinion polls, and perfectly happy to talk about his own political story in the terms the magazine wanted:

> *I think the idea of a new and revitalised Labour Party saying, 'Britain can be better – we can do things and we can be more confident about our future' . . . I think these things interact with what's happening in culture and the arts and what's happening not just in*

London but in other cities. If you look in Glasgow, Manchester, Newcastle, similar things are happening.

He went on: 'I'm a product of my generation. I'm delighted at the success of British pop music.' And he was: in the carefree days when he had yet to be elected prime minister but was as close to premier-designate as any leader of the opposition has ever got, he made a habit of showing up at awards ceremonies and making the acquaintance not just of the musicians he had admired as a twentysomething longhair, but the groups positioned much closer to the supposed cutting edge. His first meeting with the new breed came in November 1994, when he ran into a visibly refreshed Noel Gallagher at the Q Awards on Park Lane; history records that the latter placed his arm round Blair's shoulders, clapped him on the chest, and warmly instructed the Labour leader to 'fuckin' do it for us man'.

What was this? These days, with Blair long gone and the nineties' giddy optimism replaced by anxiety and national self-doubt – focused on everything from Islamist terrorism and feral youths to the looming prospect of ecological disaster – it seems difficult to comprehend the surreal tenor of the end of the twentieth century: politics reduced to showbusiness, MPs fraternising with musicians, songwriters only too happy to pen swelling anthems to nothing in particular, and the abiding sense that whereas the eighties had seen Britons polarised and divided, the country now apparently shared a lot of the same appetites and instincts, reflected in everything from million-selling Britpop records to the ubiquity of football, crystallised by England's hosting of the 1996 European Championships – and, in a rather different sense, the mass hysteria that greeted the death of Diana, Princess of Wales. Events that fitted this new suggestion of unprecedented national unanimity were reported with a frenzied, almost delusional enthusiasm; the music press, perhaps for good and all, lost its old sense of chippy cynicism and often resorted to something close to cheerleading.

Yet something had definitely happened. For one thing, after eighteen years of misrule and strife, the Conservative Party was on its way out of office, a prospect which sowed a giddy euphoria, not least among a generation for whom life without a Conservative government had once seemed an impossible prospect (I was nine years old when the Tories came to power, twenty-seven when they fell). More grandly, the mid-nineties were surely the high point of that island of innocence that fell between the fall of the Berlin Wall and the events of 11 September, 2001, when plenty of wars and conflicts raged on, but loud voices claimed that the world had been stilled as never before, and there was now surprisingly little to worry about. In 1992 the American academic Francis Fukuyama published an endlessly discussed book entitled *The End of History and the Last Man*: 'What we may be witnessing is not just the end of the Cold War, or the passing of a particular period of post-war history,' he wrote, 'but the end of history as such: that is, the end point of mankind's ideological evolution and the universalisation of Western liberal democracy as the final form of human government.'

Getting from there to the collective mindset of rock groups might have looked like the stuff of hopeless pretentiousness, but it wasn't too hard. If the previous era's ideological charge had tended to cast the best music in terms of an underlying sense of confrontation and iconoclasm, its absence was reflected in music that often seemed to act as a kind of national balm. Among scores of musicians, there were no axes to grind. A blithe kind of hedonism ruled, and they seemed to want to create stuff that could be enjoyed by just about anybody. 'Who wants to be an indie noise-freak, alienating everybody?' asked Damon Albarn. 'We want to make music our grandmothers like.'

Rock music's old assumption of generational tension was nowhere to be seen. Albarn set great store by meeting Ray Davies; Noel Gallagher was more than honoured to share the company of Paul McCartney. In the midst of Britpop's wonders, The Beatles launched a decisive campaign to establish themselves as unassailable gods via a TV series and reissue project called *Anthology*, and – despite the questionable quality of a de facto comeback single entitled 'Free as a Bird', built around a polished-up cassette recording of John Lennon – easily succeeded. To a slightly less sentimental response, the Sex Pistols regrouped in 1996, recasting themselves as pantomimic rogues ('Who'd have thought it?' said John Lydon. 'Fat, forty and back!'). By way of completing the sense that the best parts of the past had been reawakened, in late 1994, after spending close to five years in apparent seclusion, The Stone Roses had appeared with an album they ill-advisedly decided to call *Second Coming*. Even better, the summer of 1995 saw the belated return of Shaun Ryder, now leading a group called Black Grape, who somehow took the fundamental aesthetic of Happy Mondays and nipped, tucked and sharpened it to a point of near-perfection. Seeing them on their first manoeuvres in the early summer of 1995 – I watched them in a packed hall at the student union at Manchester University, surrounded by people who looked as if they had not ventured out since the Mondays' demise – delivered an unsettling reminder that for all their winning qualities, the Gallaghers were in the habit of making music that was not nearly as adventurous.

Black Grape had a song called 'A Big Day in the North', which by then sounded almost sarcastic. What had happened to Manchester? The pre-eminence of London and the fallout from the city's gang strife seemed to render it strangely quiet, though events on the ground were of a piece with the mid-nineties' abiding spirit. It is perhaps some token of the period's underlying narrative of boundless opportunity – or, rather, opportunism – that the IRA bomb that tore up a whole swathe of the city centre in June 1996 has subsequently been scratched into Mancunian history as the event that sparked a revival that had less to do with music than bricks, cement and the decisive arrival of cutting-edge consumerism. In its wake, there came new shiny landmarks – most notably, a retail complex called the Triangle and the upscale exhibition space Urbis. One hesitates to link Situationist theory with 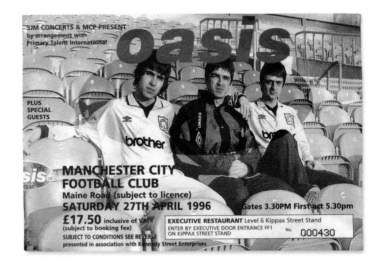 the opening of new shops, bars and apartments, but an old dream that had informed the bohemian utopianism of the Factory Records set – of Manchester reinvented as a kind of European city-state, peppered with spaces for creativity and play, so forward-looking as to make London look parochial – was in there somewhere, though it was hindered by one problem: the absence of a local soundtrack. The best Manchester could muster that year were four teenage faux-toughs from Heald Green who traded, somewhat comically, as Northern Uproar, and swiftly disappeared.

I have one particularly clear Manchester memory from this period. 1995 was the third year of In the City, the annual music business bunfight conceived by Tony Wilson and his partner Yvette Livesey, which successfully drew hundreds of people to the city to eat, drink, argue and watch scores of unsigned bands. Jimmy Cauty and Bill Drummond – the two provocateurs who had crashed into public view as the KLF, but now carried out their mischief as the K Foundation – arrived at the Holiday Inn Crowne Plaza, long known to Mancunians as the Midland Hotel. They brought with them an hour-long film that appeared to document their burning of a million pounds, claiming that they were engaged in a quest to discover why exactly they had done it. For the music business, they had one question: was what they had done 'rock 'n' roll'?

The ensuing conversation went nowhere much. Far more interesting was the way that the film chimed with the abiding atmosphere of spend-happy lunacy. It had not been that long since the prophets of dance music had declared, with some justification, that rock music had never looked so bereft and hopeless, and the future would essentially be electronic. And now there was all this: rock records selling in their millions, any group with guitars in with a shout, and expense accounts paid with no questions. Who would remember Powder, Pimlico (*Pimlico!*), Octopus, Livingstone, Silver Sun,

Laxton's Superb, Proper, and Sussed? There again, in the moment, who really cared? That year, the cocaine queues got ever longer, and there was always money to fund the dreams of yet another bunch of musicians. Watching Drummond and Cauty's film, you did not need to be a cultural studies specialist to spot the metaphor.

One of my favourite Oasis memories is of a balmy evening in April 1995, when they appeared on a short-lived British TV show called *The White Room*, on which the Mancunian DJ Mark Radcliffe bellowed enthusiastic introductions to each week's attractions, and the audience was always asked to wear black and white. The blessed Paula Yates was in attendance, apparently set on transcending the age gap and making a move on Liam, who paced around the studio in a deeply unfashionable brown flying jacket. Noel was readying himself for a slightly less sensational duet, singing a new ballad called 'Talk Tonight', accompanied by his hero and new friend Paul Weller.

The first song the band played was a B-side, arbitrarily given the title 'Acquiesce' (aimed, said the Creation Records press office, at 'stopping people like Damon out of Blur saying that Oasis aren't intelligent'). You can watch it on YouTube: Liam delivering a note-perfect delivery of words apparently written to capture his air of suppressed anger – 'I don't know what it is that makes me feel alive/I don't know how to wake the things that sleep inside' – and then circling the stage as his brother sings the chorus that many took, rightly or wrongly, as a tribute to the Gallaghers' mutual dependence:

Because we need each other
We believe in one another.

On the page, it looks a like cheap sentiment, but when that passage was played in front of huge audiences, it became one of the most euphorically received moments in their repertoire.

'Acquiesce' was one of four songs assembled on the single fronted by 'Some Might Say', along with the aforementioned 'Talk Tonight' – and a woefully overlooked song entitled 'Headshrinker', probably the best example of devil-may-care rock music they ever recorded, all spite, bitterness, and escape from some unspecified dead end, with echoes of the Sex Pistols' pitch-black 'Bodies'. It's worth playing if you ever doubt either their early brilliance, or the fact that the Gallagher brothers had an instinct for what so much great rock depends on: the kind of inchoate rage that Liam could sum up in his best vocal performances (in this song, the threat-level is reminiscent of Johnny Rotten's twelve-word manifesto, 'Don't know what I want, but I know how to get it'), and the way his brother could alchemise old ingredients into the stuff of rampaging excitement (which is to say that 'Headshrinker' was as traditional as rock gets, but also so energised as to come out sounding iconoclastic, and thrillingly so).

The single arrived in the charts at number one, which apparently caused Damon Albarn no end of annoyance, and thus sparked the episode that marked both Britpop's high point and the start of its long decline. It was realised via a combination of Blur design and Oasis accident, and ideally timed for the Silly Season, the weeks when parliament is in recess and the newspapers seize on anything – sharks off the coast of Cornwall, crop circles, killer turtles in the Thames – that might get them through a dry spell.

By July, it had become clear that Blur and Oasis would be releasing singles on the same day, and for the press, the prospect of the two groups locking horns was too good to be true. Thus began what some people characterised as a microcosm of the class war – the *Guardian* wrote up the contest as a matter of 'Working-class heroes' taking on 'Art school trendies' – and others saw as the music industry's tawdry and huckster-ish version of a meat raffle. As it turned out, the groups' respective singles were among the worst either had ever recorded. 'Country House' was a paper-thin, faux-music-hall example of what Graham Coxon called 'the Blur stomp'; 'Roll with It' a lame Xerox of The Beatles circa 1964, with lyrics that were absolutely unbearable ('You wanna be who you be, if you're coming with me'). Not that it mattered: so taken were the British public that 490,000 people bought one or both of the singles. While they were about it, they stocked up on other records as well; that week, sales in the singles market went up by an overall figure of 41 per cent. In the world of night-time radio, independent labels and guitar groups, the corporate music industry had once seen no potential for making big money; now, it was pointing the way to marketing feats hitherto undreamed of.

Thanks chiefly to their decision to put out two different versions of their single on compact disc, Blur won out, though by now Oasis were unstoppable. In October, they released (*What's the Story*) *Morning Glory?*, swiftly recorded in Wales during a two-week spurt, broken only by a ruck in which Noel Gallagher had attacked his brother with a cricket bat, briefly returned to London, and then come back to the studio to finish things off. It was not as consistent a record as *Definitely Maybe*, and a lot of it was lacking the urgent attack that had been Oasis's métier. It arrived at the offices of London's music magazines in the form of a cassette – which included 'Step Out', which stole so much from Stevie Wonder's 'Uptight' that it had to be temporarily withdrawn – and spread an uneasy feeling of anticlimax. 'They sound knackered,' said one reviewer, and he seemed to have a point.

That said, even if 'Hey Now' and 'She's Electric' sounded like mere makeweights, and 'Cast No Shadow' nudged Oasis perilously close to the middle of the road, there were enough masterstrokes to ratchet up Oasis's momentum. 'Don't Look Back in Anger' was built from a pretty much meaningless lyric and an arrangement that held nothing back, but it stood as a masterclass in gaudily great pop music. 'Morning Glory' and the irresistible 'Champagne Supernova', a wired cocaine night and deliriously hung-over morning conveyed with instinctive expertise, may well stand as the acme of Noel Gallagher's labours in the recording studio – and in any case, those songs paled into irrelevance next to the composition that truly glued Oasis into the national consciousness. On first hearing, 'Wonderwall' could easily sound a bit monotonous – 'a ballad and a "Live Forever" revisit that becomes a bit of a dirge,' as David Cavanagh from Q put it. To most listeners, however, it was quickly revealed as an anthem about redemption in difficult circumstances: a song with all the universality of a newspaper horoscope. Its wonders became evident a week after it was released as a single, when Noel delivered a wholly acoustic version to sell-out crowds at Earl's Court, and left the crowd to sing whole swathes of it. By the end of the year, Britain was in the midst of what Blur's Alex James later called 'the "Wonderwall" Christmas', sealed by a smugly unfunny 'easy listening' version by a short-lived sensation called The Mike Flowers Pops.

In its first week on sale, *What's the Story* had sold 346,000 copies. By the Christmas of 1995, the figure was nudging two million. It was simply omnipresent, blasting from every open car window and shop-front: a national soundtrack that spent eighteen months as the incidental music for millions of lives. As insane as this may sound, if you went a few days without hearing it, you felt its absence: the following summer, I made a habit of forgetting to pack it when I left town, and blithely bought replacements wherever I went: I still own four CDs, two cassettes and a vinyl copy that was barely played. It was of those rare collections of music that quickly slipped out of the control of its creators and became truly public property, and something about it made it seem fated to do so. The most obvious explanation was bound up not just with Noel's songs, but the way his brother sang them. Pete Townshend, long fascinated by the way that the divide between musicians and their audience can suddenly dissolve, said this: 'When we hear Liam's voice, it's our voice. It's everyone's voice.'

There was at least one occasion when Oasis's elevation to such heights seemed completely triumphant: the weekend of 27 and 28 April 1996, when they played two concerts at that Mancunian holy of holies Maine Road, and proved to be unlikely practitioners of the grandiloquent form known as stadium rock. Four months later came Knebworth, for which 2.6 million people – or one in twenty-four of the British population – applied for 250,000 tickets. Those lucky enough to be successful duly found themselves in a vast field near Stevenage, squinting at a distant stage, while the thousands included on the event's guest list made merry in a hospitality area that stretched into the distance, complemented by a sizeable golden circle in which pass-holders were guaranteed splendid views. 'We are the biggest band in Britain of all time, ever,' said the ever self-deprecating Noel, cloistered in his backstage trailer. 'The funny thing is that we were fucking mouthing off three years ago . . . and we actually went and did it. And it was a piece of piss.'

Among their other feats, Oasis had achieved the kind of fame that enshrined them as a permanent fixture of the British newsstand. When I worked at *Select* magazine, we made the requisite phone calls and amassed every tabloid front page that had featured Oasis over the previous six months. The best ran as follows: 'WHAT'S THE STORY, LIAM QUITS THE TOURY', 'PATSY'S GOT HIM BY THE WONDERBALLS', 'PATSY SENDS LIAM TO THERAPY', 'YUK AND ROLL' ('Supergob Liam spits on pop fans'), 'MY DRUG AND SEX HELL WITH LIAM', 'BLOWOASIS' ('Hotel fist-fight then Noel and Liam axe band'), 'OASIS LIAM: I WANT TO KILL MYSELF', 'OASIS LIAM IN DRUG BUST', 'WONDER BALD' ('Oasis Liam's new hairdo'), 'BETTER BED THAN WED' ('Liam and Patsy scrap ceremony for a lie-in'), 'OASIS STAR'S £4,000 A WEEK COCAINE SHAME'. This level of notoriety is a perilous business, in that the garish idiocy of such headlines can easily come to define the lives they describe. From a distance, that certainly seemed to be the fate that befell Liam Gallagher.

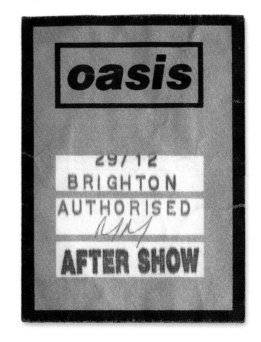

Soon after Knebworth – and initially without their singer, who left his colleagues on an aeroplane, claiming that he had to buy a new home and thus being portrayed by the red-tops as a house-trained wimp – they set off on a decisive American tour, calling at such places as Long Island, Chicago and Philadelphia, before they arrived in Charlotte, North Carolina. There, the show was cancelled, Noel mysteriously flew home – on Concorde, he later assured me – and there was a brief assumption that Oasis had split up, a possibility that the news media accorded all the importance of a major international incident. There were whispers that an unexpected downgrading from a 12,000-capacity arena to a facility that held a mere 3,500 had been too much for them – though as it turned out, the ructions were down to that longstanding syndrome whereby one or other Gallagher would eventually tire of the other's company, and everything would temporarily implode.

The following year, I interviewed Oasis over a long summer's day at a plush rehearsal facility in Bermondsey, where Liam split his time between watching instrumental renditions of the songs and distractedly flicking through a Sotheby's catalogue, ticking off the Beatles memorabilia he fancied while also taking delivery of yet another batch of expensive leisurewear. The band rehearsed without him, making much the same piledriving noise that they ever had, each song apparently delivered with minimal effort and at the loudest possible volume.

'What it was, as far as I'm concerned . . . Well, we'd done Knebworth, yeah? Big gig,' said Liam. '*Really* big gig. After Knebworth, we should've gone on holiday for a couple of months. Chilled right out. It was a big high and all that tackle. Then a week later we were on a plane to fucking America, playing in front of ten thousand people, which is not good for your ego.'

'No one ever said that,' Noel shot back. 'If anyone'd have said that, they'd have got the sack . . . I'll play to twelve people, let alone twelve thousand.'

There was also a response, of sorts, to the predominantly negative tone of their coverage in the American press ('Few bands put out so little and expect so much,' said the *New York Times*). 'Oh, they're wankers,' said Liam. 'They want grungey fucking people, stabbing themselves in the head on stage. They get a bright bunch like us, with deodorant on, and they don't get it.'

For an hour or so, I sat in blazing sunshine with Noel Gallagher. We talked about Manchester, and when he had last been back. 'About three months ago, to see me mam,' he said. 'It's easier to bring her down here. As soon as you go back there, someone's on the phone to the *Manchester Evening News* and they come round saying, "Oooh, what are you doing back in Manchester?"' The mention of his home town, it quickly transpired, could still prompt even more fretful thoughts. 'I always think a load of thugs from Moss Side are going to be driving past, going, "There's that cunt out of Oasis,"' he said. 'And they'll get out and beat your head in, pinch your watch or shoot you in the foot or summat. That's what worries me about that city.'

He went on to briefly explain the third album that had long been finished but no one but the closest Oasis aides was allowed to hear. That day, the voice that had previously couched even average Oasis efforts in terms of unimpeachable triumph sounded uncharacteristically hesitant.

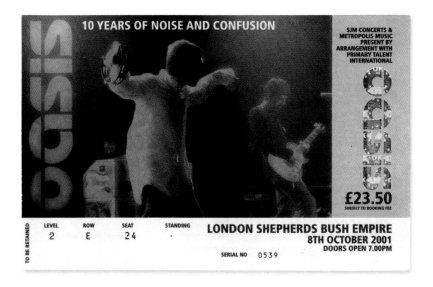

> *I'm proud of the songs, but I think me and Owen [Morris, producer] got a bit lazy in the studio. That's my opinion, and I'm allowed to say it – no one else is . . . I'm getting a bit bored of the 'Roll with It'-type song, the 'Wonderwall'-type song and summat in the middle. That's why I was saying, years ago, about doing three albums and having a big rethink . . . I like the songs, but the production's a bit bland . . . There's a song called 'I Hope, I Think, I Know', which is a bit [makes fart noise] a bit like 'Roll with It' – pie-in-the-sky fucking shit, really. 'All Around the World' – that's a bit cheesy.*

He was not wrong, though he was not quite right either. *Be Here Now*, released to a huge fanfare on 21 August 1997, was a bit more of a calamity than even Noel's momentary self-criticism suggested: on the whole, a bilious mistake that captured long cocaine nights, new wealth and ridiculous hubris. Some of it, to be fair, is better than its reputation suggests: despite the fact that it sounds a little like the Texan gonzo-rock trio ZZ Top, the title track holds fast to the same basic magic of their best early stuff; so too, despite all the caked-on overdubbing, do 'My Big Mouth' and 'It's Getting Better (Man!!)'. There again, anyone who has ever wondered what a hybrid of Oasis and Bon Jovi would sound like should listen to the inexplicable 'Fade In/Out' – and as an example of what happens when the sentimental populism of a song like 'Whatever' is all but wrecked by too big a recording budget and the simple failure to know when to stop, 'All Around the World' is grimly perfect. A good deal of *Be Here Now*, in fact, remains borderline unlistenable, a quality best (worst?) exemplified by a baffling song entitled 'Magic Pie', stuffed with non-sequiturs and bursts of self-aggrandising nonsense, and given the decisive ring of awfulness by the fact that one of its lines was taken from a Tony Blair speech.

Perhaps inevitably, the same brazen enthusiasm that had once powered Oasis around fag-end B&Bs and tiny venues was now curdling into an unbecoming oafishness. No award seemed truly worthy of them; aside from a clutch of dull groups blessed with the older Gallagher's approval and thereby grouped into a genre known as 'Noelrock' –

Cast, Kula Shaker, Ocean Colour Scene – their contemporaries attracted little more than withering contempt. What was particularly striking was the fact that wealth and success did not encourage the Gallaghers to widen their horizons – simply to carry on listening to The Beatles and get back to their drinks. Metaphorically at least, Liam never did stray too far from that cigarette machine at the Boardwalk.

One particular episode embodies not just this phase of Oasis's career, but the flatly strange place at which British music – and, indeed, the wider culture – had arrived. On Wednesday 29 July 1997, Noel Gallagher made his way to Downing Street, to toast the new Labour government and share the company of a rum array of stars whose presence was designed to confirm the idea that Britain had been pulled into a new era of shiny self-confidence. The prospect of his visit – arranged at the behest of Blair's chief of staff Jonathan Powell – was enough to cause jitters at the very top, as evidenced by a panicked entry in Alastair Campbell's diary:

> I spoke to Alan McGee at Creation Records, who was coming to the No. 10 reception with Noel Gallagher, and said can we be assured he would behave OK. Alan said he would make sure he did. He was not going to mess around. He said if we had invited Liam, it might have been different. Gallagher arrived with his wife Meg, McGee and his girlfriend, loads of photographers outside, then Cherie met them and took them upstairs to see Kathryn and Nicky, who was very gobsmacked when Gallagher walked in. He said he thought Number 10 was 'tops' [sic], said he couldn't believe there was an ironing board in there. He was very down to earth, very funny. I took them up to do pictures with TB, then Lenny Henry, Maureen Lipman, a few others.

As it turned out, Noel was there at the behest of his mother, and entertained no thoughts of misbehaviour: 'She said it was a great honour for her to say one of her sons was going to see the Prime Minister – she told me to go.' If the rock 'n' roller was thereby revealed as a deferential softie, it was later revealed that during an exchange about the night of the general election, the PM had affected an unexpected licentiousness. Noel said,

> We were chatting away and I said, 'Oh, it was brilliant man, because we stayed up till seven o'clock in the morning to watch you arrive at the headquarters. How did you manage to stay up all night?' And this is his exact words: he leant over and said, 'Not by the same means you did.' And at that point, I knew he was a geezer.

By now, Noel had set up home in a north London pile he understatedly named Supernova Heights and began a two-year reign as a monarchical socialite, forever inviting whoever he and Meg Mathews scooped up on their West End rounds back for ad hoc parties that would stretch over whole days. Where once their press coverage had been about the kind of hi-jinks that could be enjoyed on limited means, now their cuttings file bulged with stories about high-end clubbing and shopping in Bond Street. Eventually, Noel's life was partly documented in a short-lived *Sunday Times* column credited to Meg Mathews and entitled 'Yeah!'. The instalment on 10 January 1999 ran as follows:

> You wouldn't think that Noel and I could still be starstruck about anyone, but while we were staying in the French alps we bumped into Zinedine Zidane . . . Back home in the country over the New Year, former Scary Spice Mel B came round to swap presents. Her mansion is only about 15 minutes away, which comes in very handy when I run out of Fendi croissants . . . Anna Friel (I suppose she is today's Julie Christie) was also staying, and she had us in stitches regaling us with stories about her new life as a starlet in Los Angeles . . . I've dyed my hair platinum blonde again . . . I feel more co-ordinated when my hair matches my credit card.

Liam, meanwhile, had married the aforementioned Patsy Kensit, and commenced three years of gossip-column domination. To begrudge the Gallaghers their new life could easily seem churlish, though there was something not quite right about it all, particularly given that Oasis had recently been hailed as the definitive People's Band. No longer, it seemed. Their essential condition-cum-predicament was cruelly sent up by one of their old associates at Creation Records: 'Oasis are raw art turned to shit. They came down [to London] as little matchstick men and turned into a Jeff Koons.'

Of the group's original membership, only Noel and Liam now remain. There is now a small mountain of Oasis songs, unloved and unlistened-to, that will never be played in concert or included on any compilation album. They sit in much the same place as the later work of any number of once great musicians, my generation's equivalent of, say, the Rolling Stones' *Black and Blue* or *Emotional Rescue*, or the run of Paul McCartney music that followed *Band on the Run*. Some song titles prove the point: 'Put Yer Money Where Yer Mouth Is', 'I Can See a Liar', 'Gas Panic!', 'Roll It Over', 'Force of Nature', '(Probably) In My Mind', 'She Is Love', 'Born on a Different Cloud', 'Better Man'. Shuffling iPods must occasionally alight on them; some of Oasis's more hard-bitten disciples presumably still drag them out from time to time. As part of the Gallagher brothers' story, they matter only in so far as they represent the passage from their imperial phase to life as a rather more ordinary phenomenon: a very popular rock group, forever associated with a short and dizzying moment in modern British history, who resurface every few years, playing much the same music as ever – straight-ahead rock, proudly in thrall to classic archetypes, and usually saved from generic tedium by the magnetic presence of Liam Gallagher.

Their penultimate album, *Don't Believe the Truth*, recovered some of what they lost a decade ago, and sold handsomely. The record that eventually followed it, *Dig Out Your Soul*, rather paled by comparison, but was another success. In 2008, for what these things are worth, the *NME* testified to Oasis's invincibility by awarding a group with an average age not much under forty its Best British Band award. They remain a stadium attraction, delivering performances that lean heavily on their first two albums and thereby allow the older parts of their audience to tap back into a time when the world seemed so much simpler, and younger recruits – of whom there are plenty – to lap up songs that now count as the stuff of Classic Rock: 'Supersonic', 'Live Forever', 'Some Might Say', 'Wonderwall'. When they were written, no one had seen airliners being piloted into tall buildings, nor fretted much about the planet breathing its last. Revive the right spirit, and there you are: Punch the air, get whacked, life's great. Sore head the next day.

And Manchester? Since the ascent of Oasis, the city has not produced anything properly comparable to them, or their musical forebears – although, to be fair, the glacial rise to fame of Elbow (who are originally from Bury, but rightly understood as a Manchester group) has returned some attention to the place, and often involved music with a rich sense of loss – Mancunian tristesse, to be pretentious – that captures what has happened to the city. After all, much of the urban expanse that spawned Manchester's most celebrated musicians has largely disappeared, replaced by towering new buildings, and regenerated housing developments, and a retail sector and leisure industry that would have you believe that it has created an urban idyll. To paraphrase Little Richard, perhaps Manchester got what a lot of people wanted but lost what it had. It remains a fine city in which to spend time, and for those moneyed enough, a great place to live. But where has its noise gone?

If Oasis remain the last era-defining Mancunian rock group, that may feel rather unsatisfactory, fixing a city whose best music – indeed, whose history – was once the stuff of invention and iconoclasm as a byword for conservatism and nostalgia. There again, maybe such thoughts amount to a denial of the Gallaghers' essential glory, summed up in the first song on that first album:

It's just rock 'n' roll,
It's just rock 'n' roll . . .

Here, anyway, is a coda. Tony Wilson died a tragically untimely death on 10 August 2007, aged fifty-seven. The flag above Manchester Town Hall was lowered to half mast, and the *NME* put his image on the cover. Paul Morley, Peter Saville, Richard Madeley and Stephen Morris paid tribute on *Newsnight*; Manchester's Labour council quickly resolved to put up a permanent memorial. In the newspapers, there was a lot of talk about the lines to be drawn from Wilson's civic pride and urban dreams to Manchester's ongoing renewal. The *Guardian* claimed that 'his record label's pioneering approach to design and architecture helped kick-start Manchester's transformation into a European cultural centre'; according to the *Sunday Times*, his death saw him 'lionised as the biggest single influence on Manchester's regeneration'. Their coverage went on: 'As a counterweight to *Coronation Street*, his bars, Haçienda club and Factory record label helped bumpstart the loft-living and nightclub scene that changed Manchester's image from a gritty industrial city to a cool, happening place.'

If that was true – and to my mind, it seems incontestably so – there was surely an uneasy irony at work. Wilson's visions had influenced and inspired the Mancunian renaissance, but the latter had eventually so altered the city that the places which gave rise to so much of what he loved had been wiped from the map. In that sense, his death merited the clichéd talk about the 'end of an era', and rather confirmed that the story he turned into a legend – of a Sex Pistols concert catalysing fifteen or so years of music and associated creativity that eventually fed into the city's reinvention – now threatened to be the stuff of history. That said, as Wilson would always ferociously point out, pop music is cyclical, naysayers tend to be the wrong side of thirty, and there may – who knows? – already be young Mancunians plotting the next brilliant phase of this story.

A couple of days after his passing, sent back to dozens of records by the Wilson obituaries and in search of inspiration for the last of the words you have just read, I spent a morning idly playing some of the music that informs this book. I put on *Closer*, and *Unknown Pleasures*, and *Low-Life*, and the glowingly great *Bummed*. I eventually flicked through *The Queen Is Dead*, *The Frenz Experiment* and *Definitely Maybe* – but quite randomly, I began with A Certain Ratio's 'Do the Du', put to tape in 1980, released by Factory, and destined to tumble out of the Haçienda's sound system on just about every Thursday night I ever went there.

On it came: two sharp percussive stabs and the rattling sound of the future. My partner, who was born and raised in southern England, was listening in. 'What's this?' she said. 'Is it new?'

Manchester: home of living causes. What Manchester thinks today, England thinks tomorrow. Manchester has always been more critical than creative. The city looks as if it has been built to withstand foul weather.

J. B. Priestley

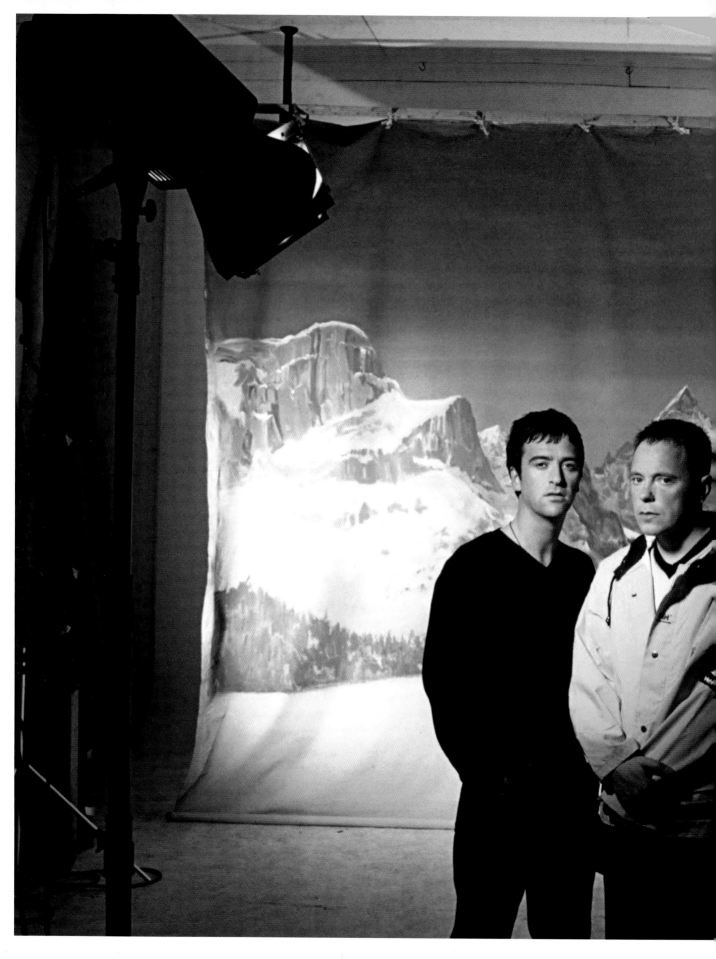

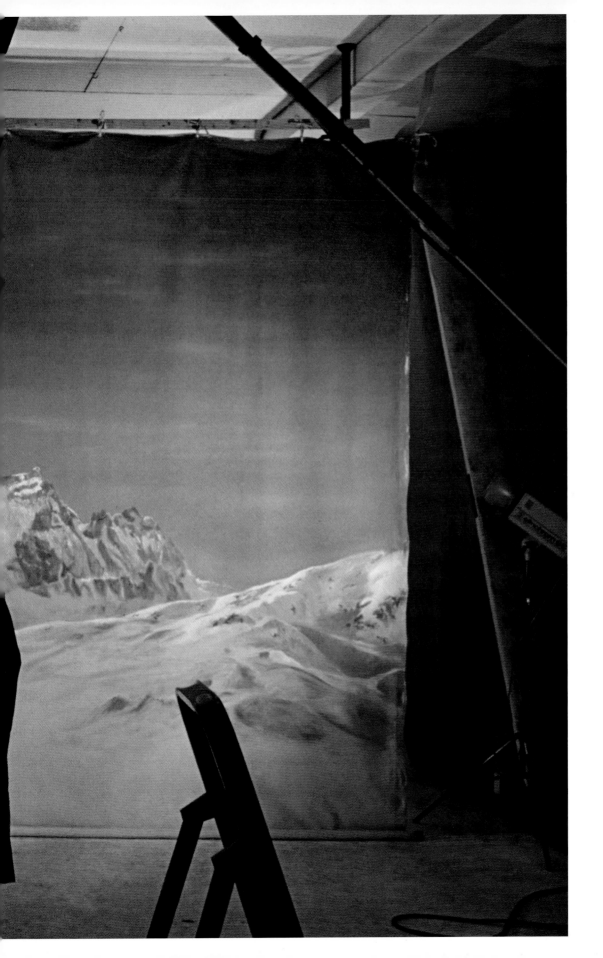

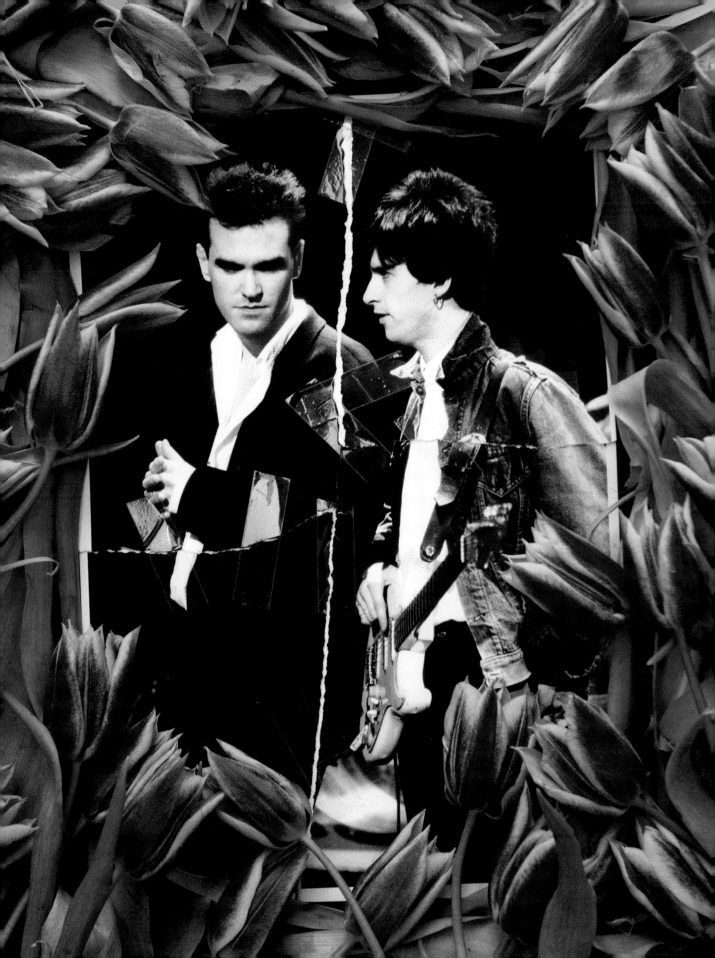

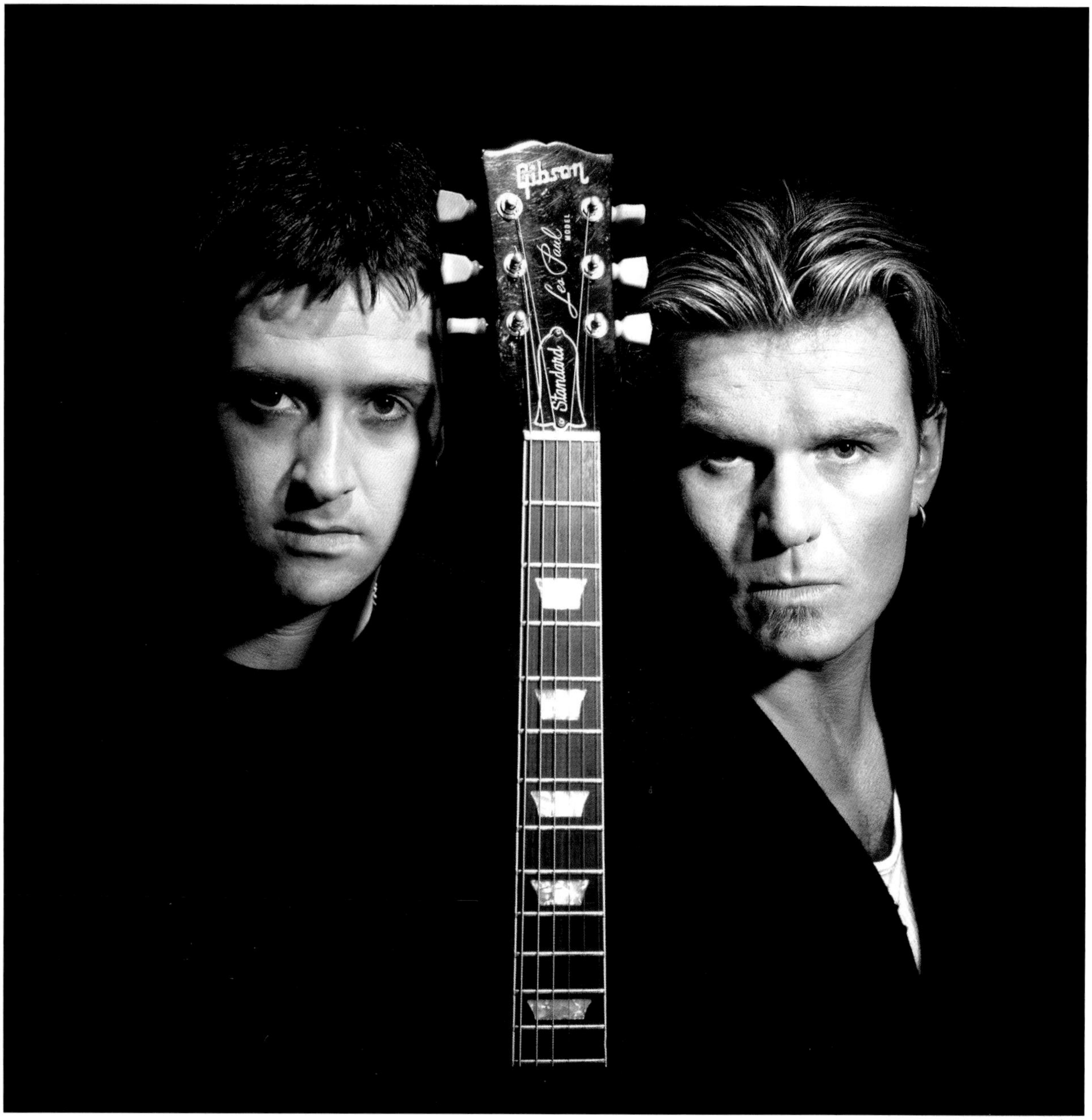

Johnny Marr, Billy Duffy
Studio, east London
June 1992

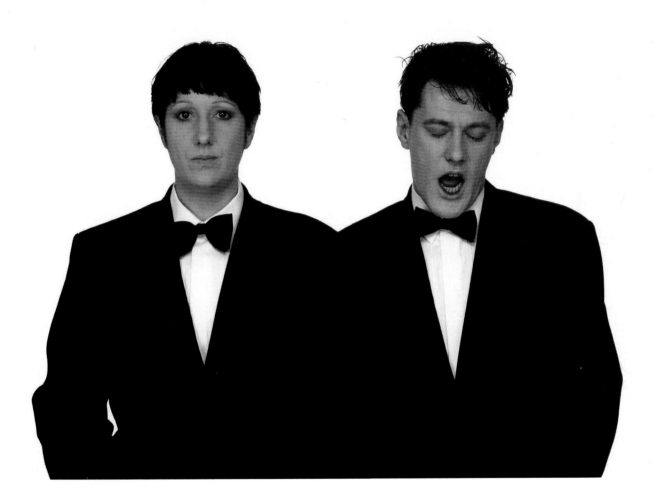

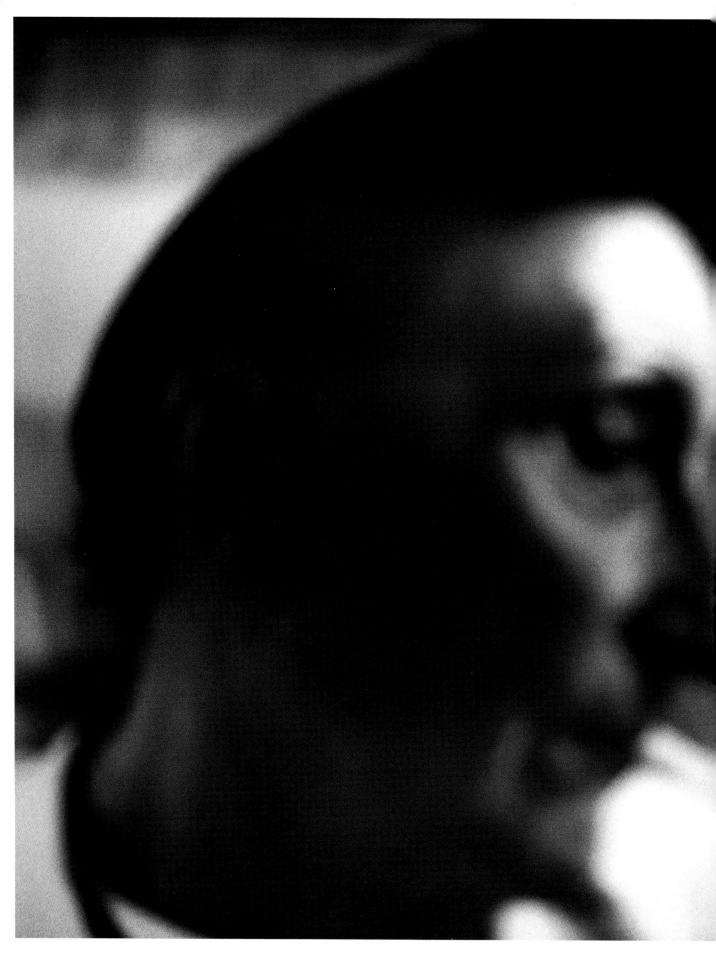

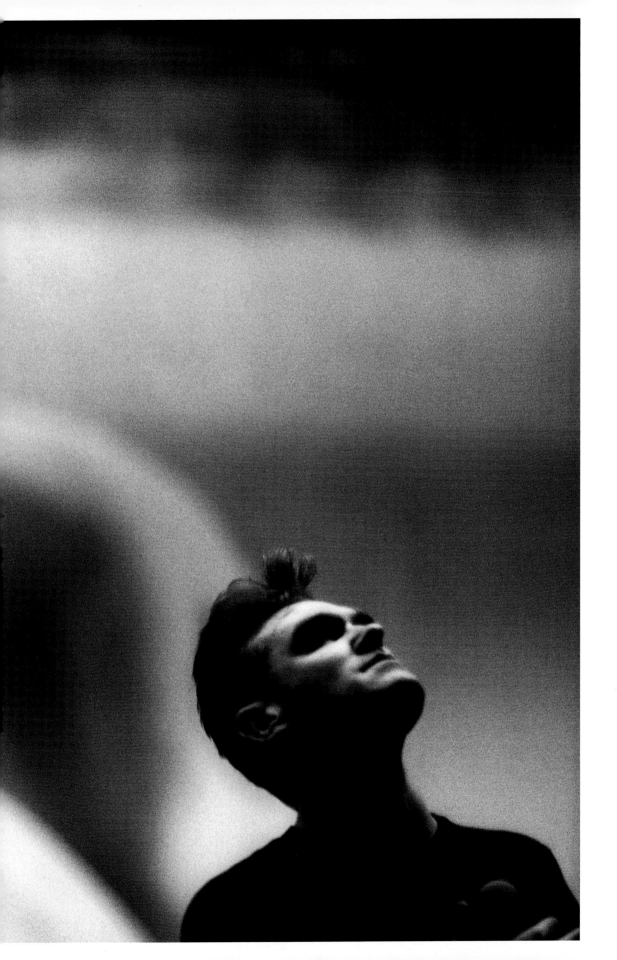

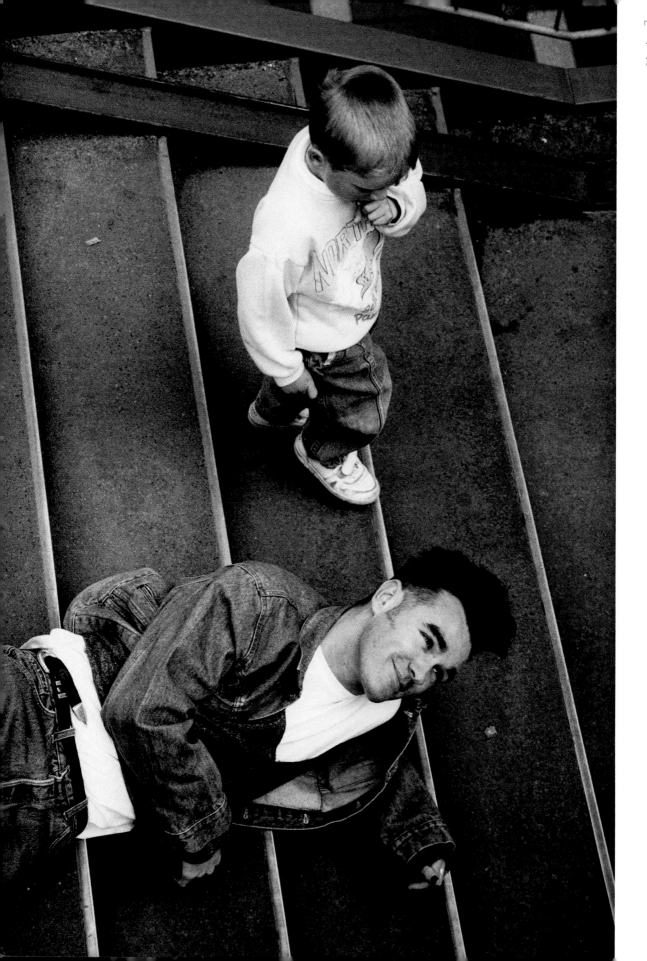

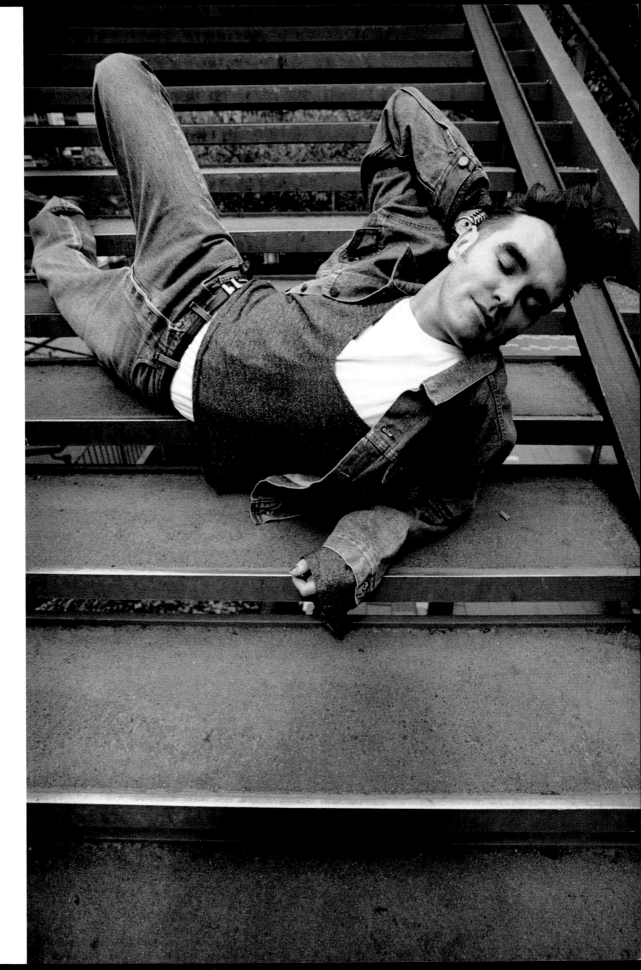

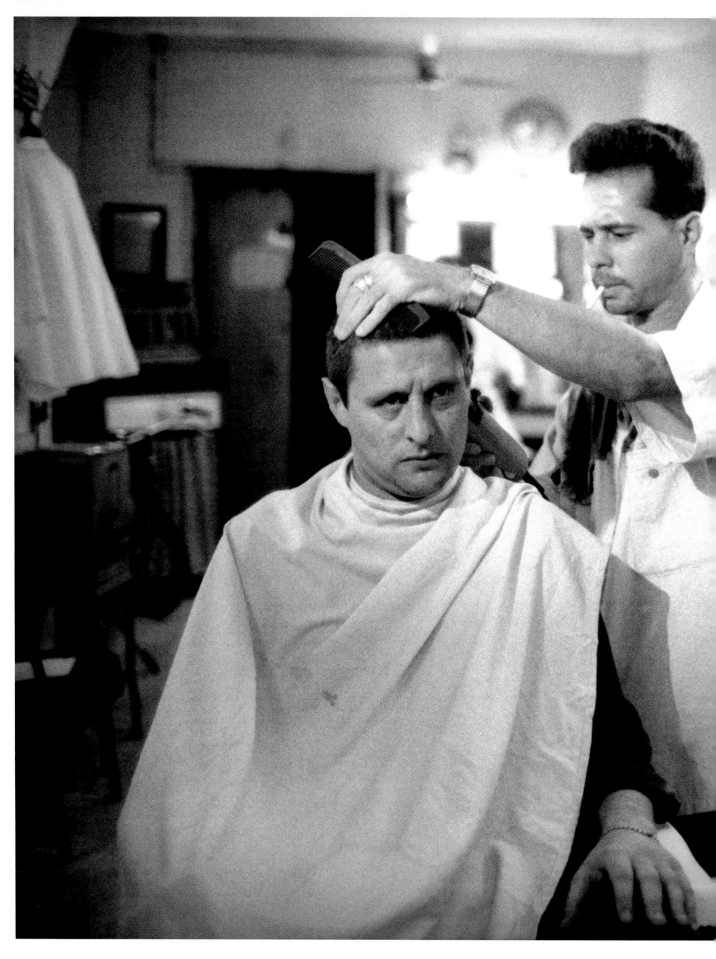

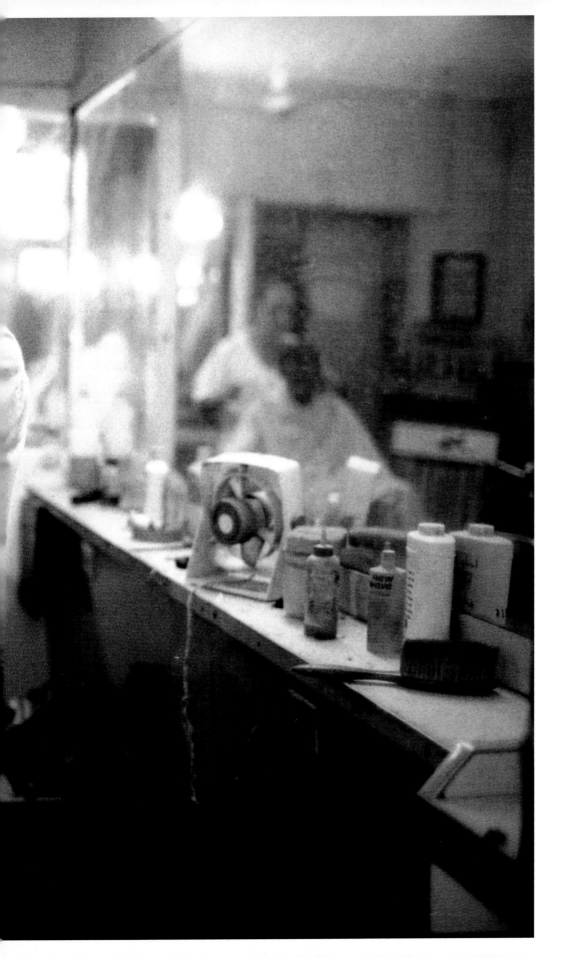

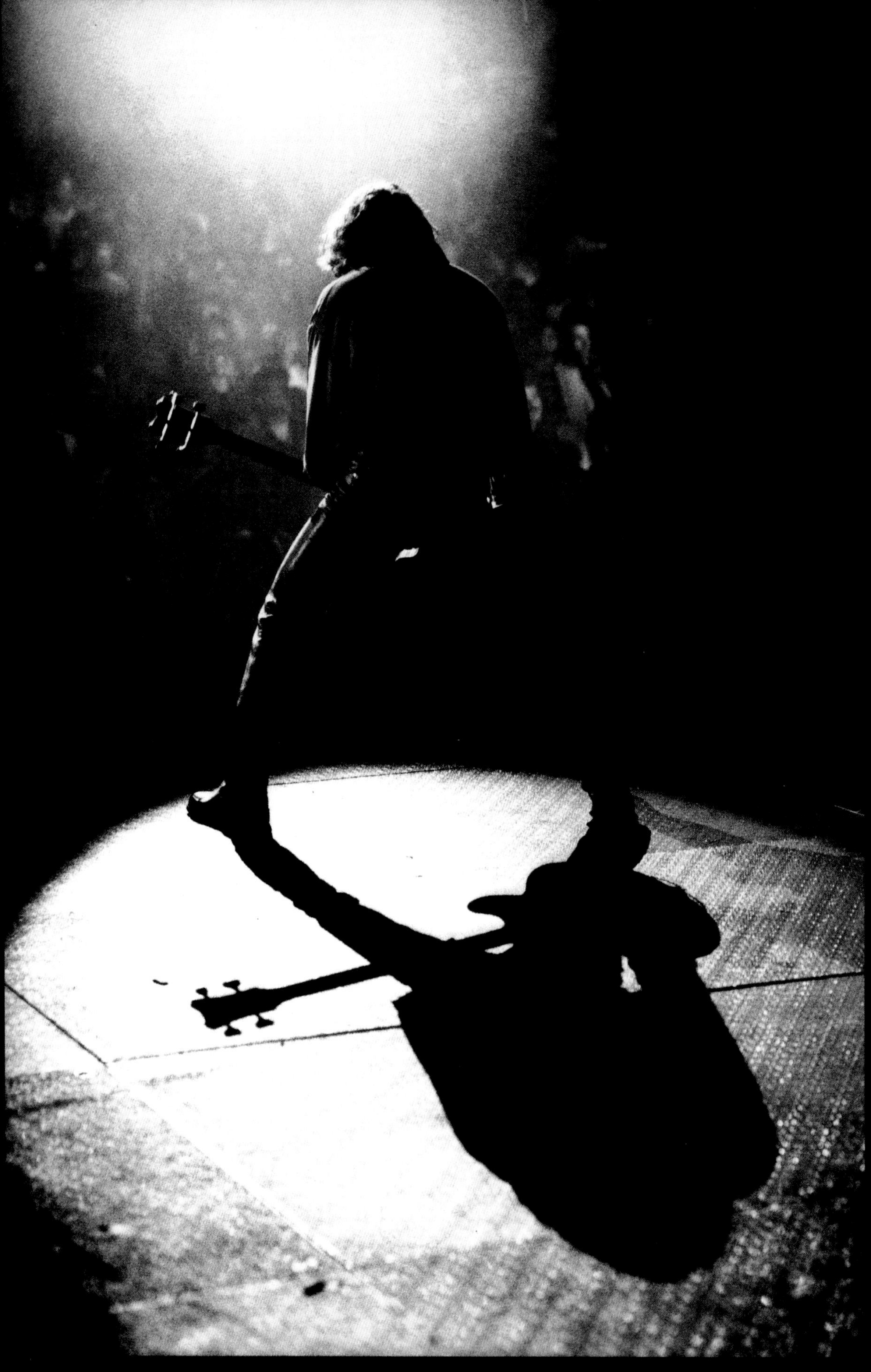

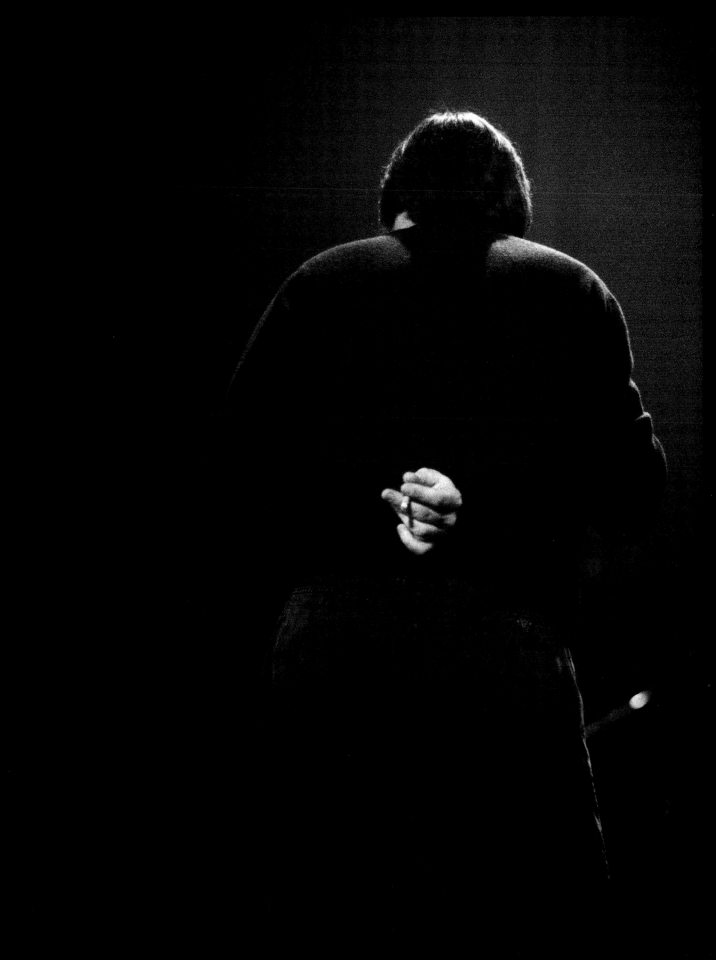

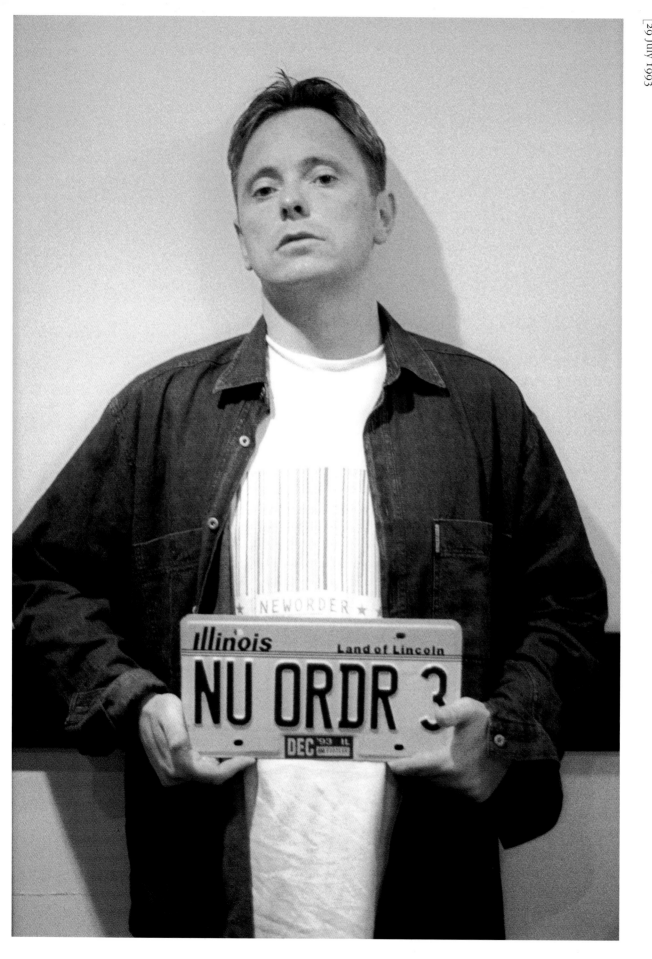

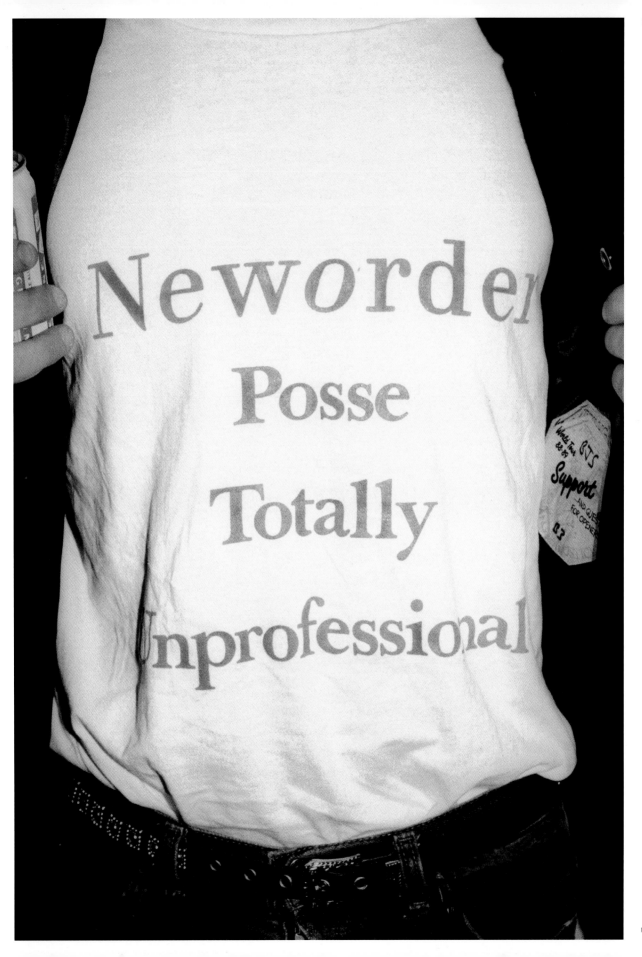

On this waterlogged landscape . . . are scattered palaces and hovels . . .
It is here that the human spirit becomes perfect, and at the same time brutalised, that civilisation produces its

marvels and that civilised man returns to the savage.

Alexis de Tocqueville

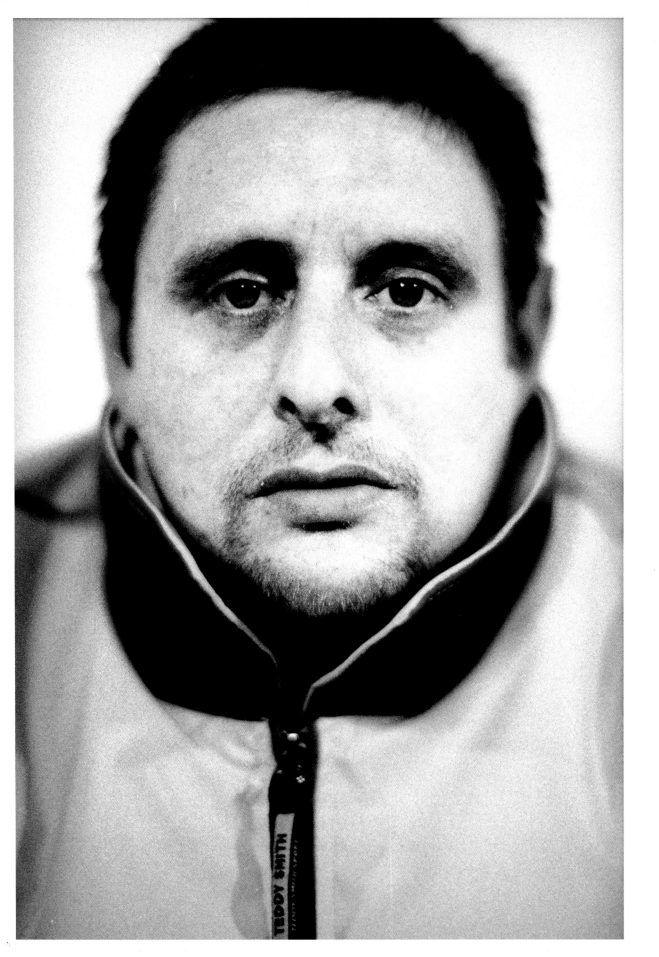

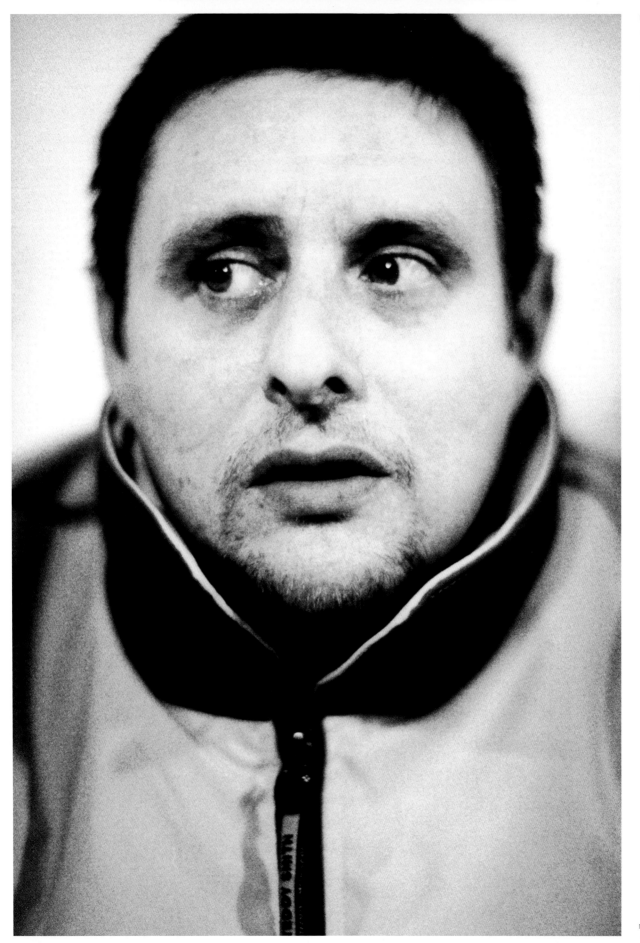

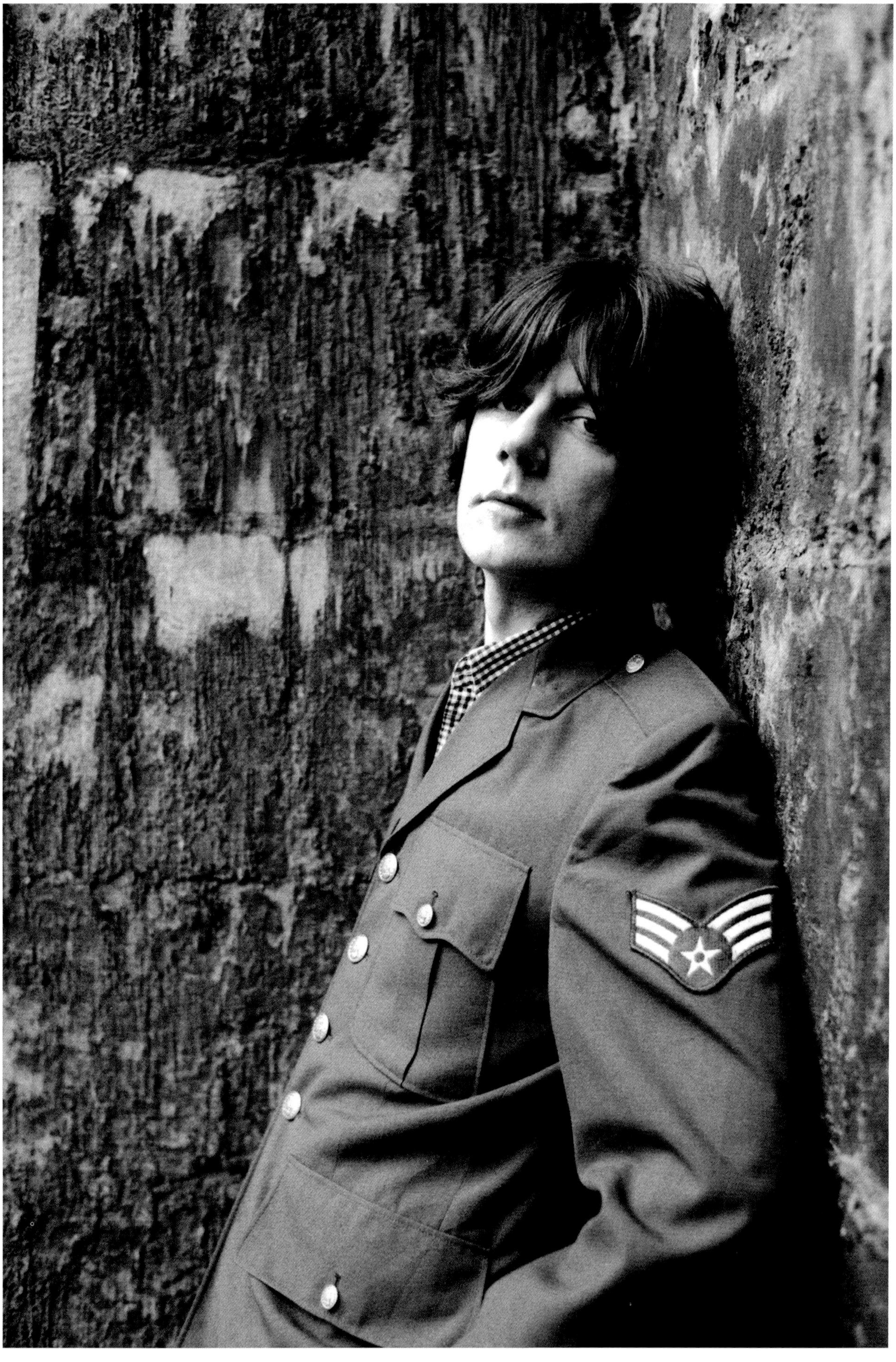

John Squire, The Seahorses
York
April 1997

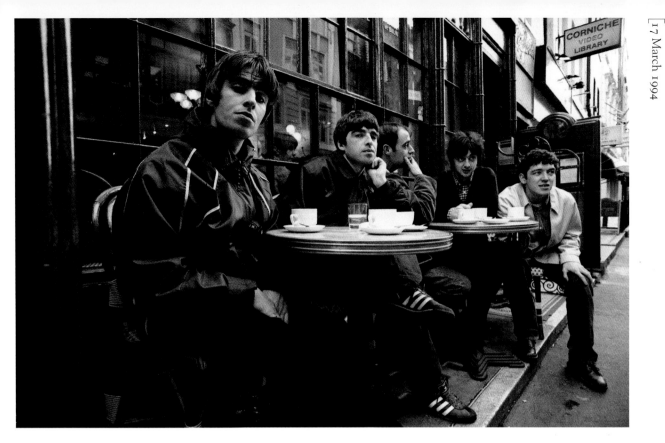

[Mancunians] make an affectation of candour and trade a little on their county's reputation for uncouthness.

Harold Brighouse

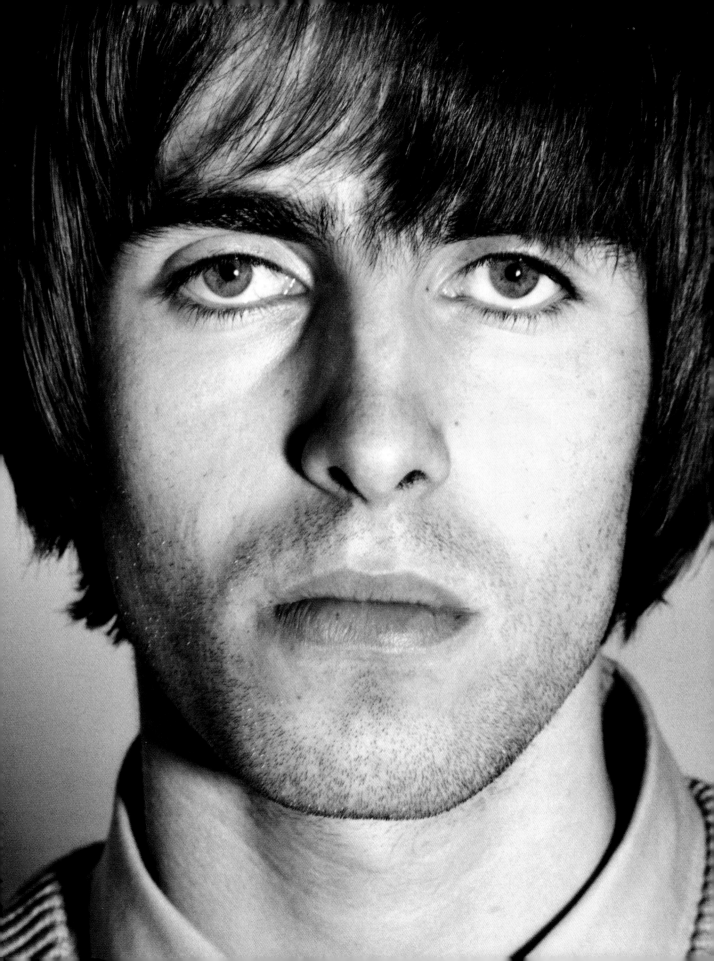

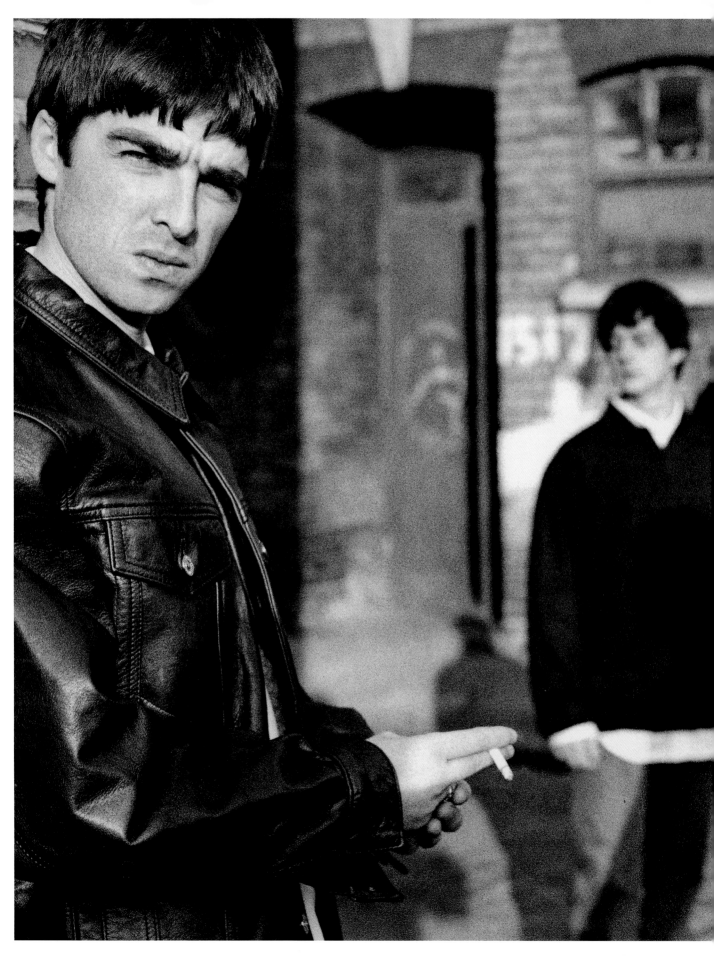

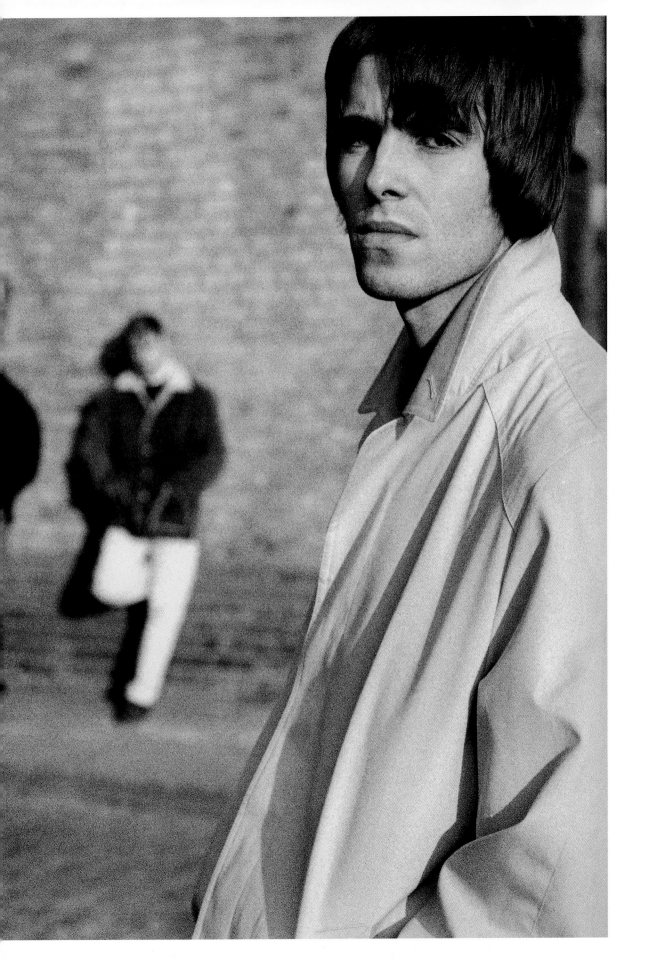

Oasis
Sly Street, east London
21 February 1994

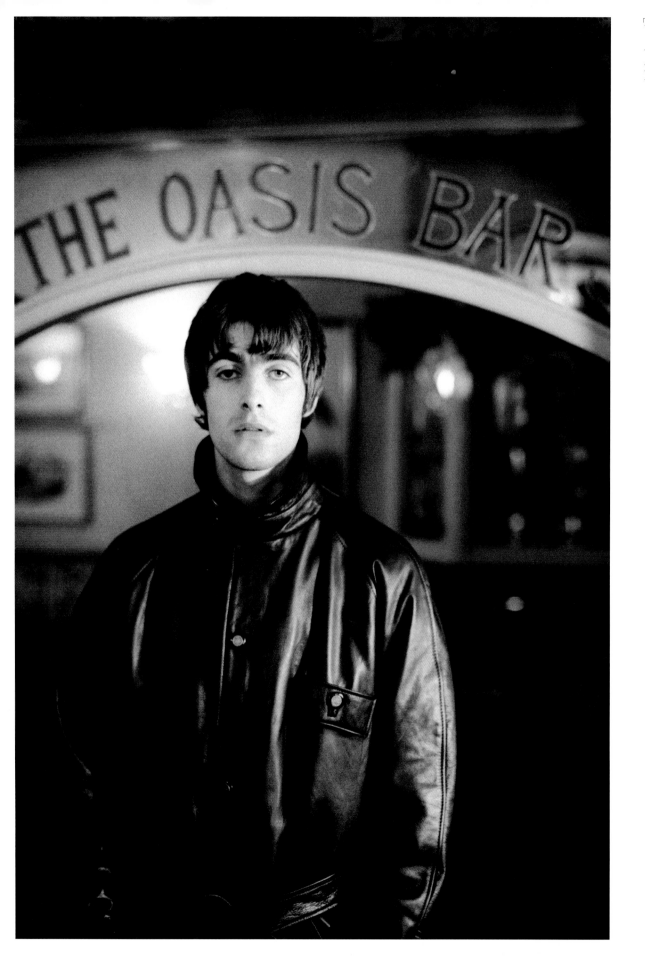

Liam Gallagher
The King's Hotel, High Street, Newport, Gwent
4 May 1994

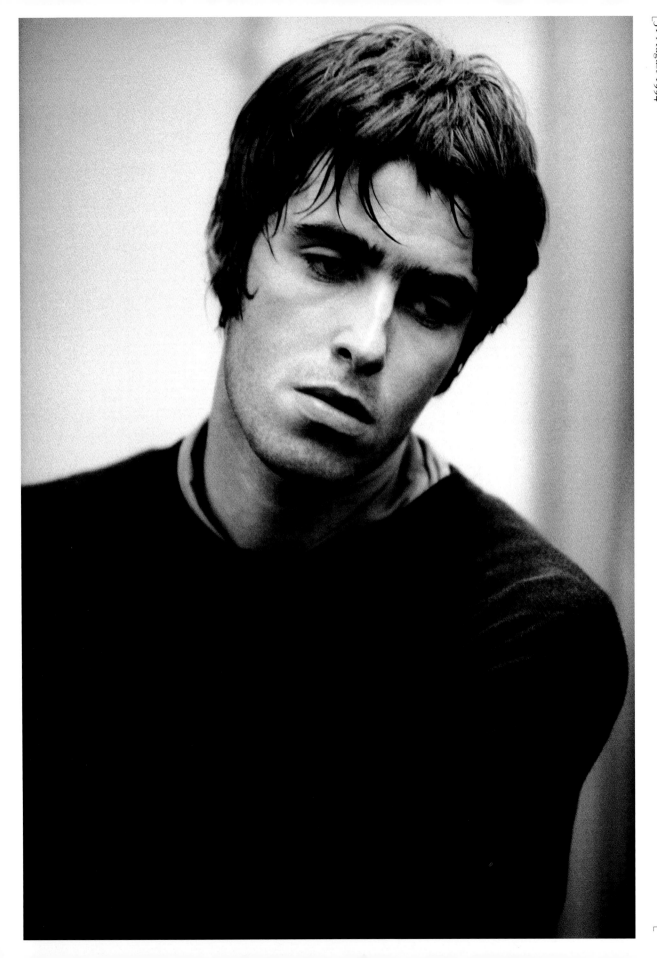

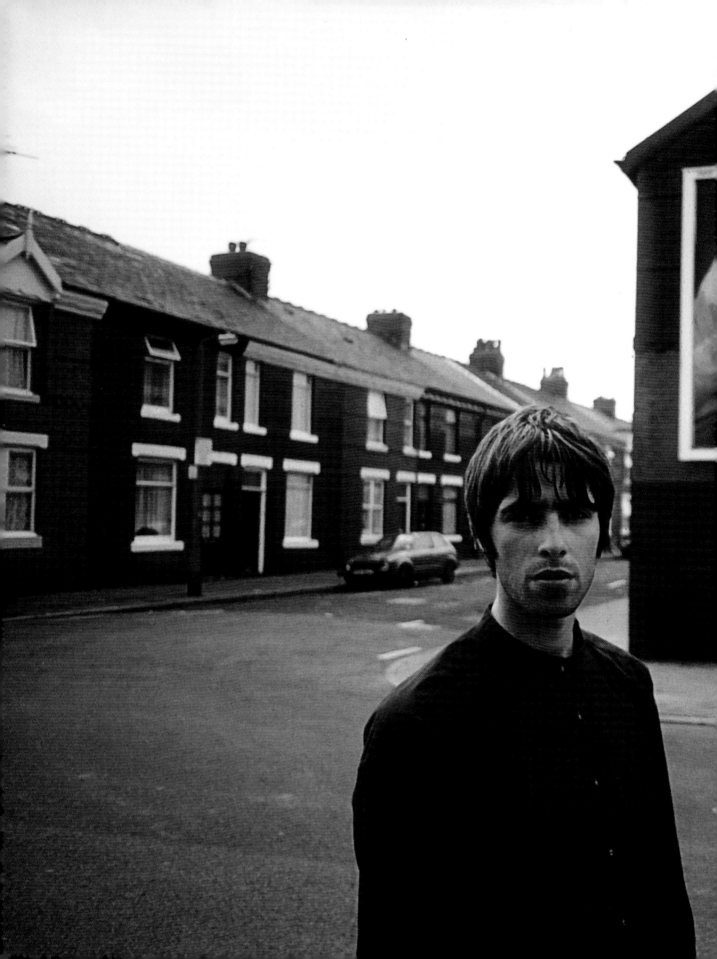

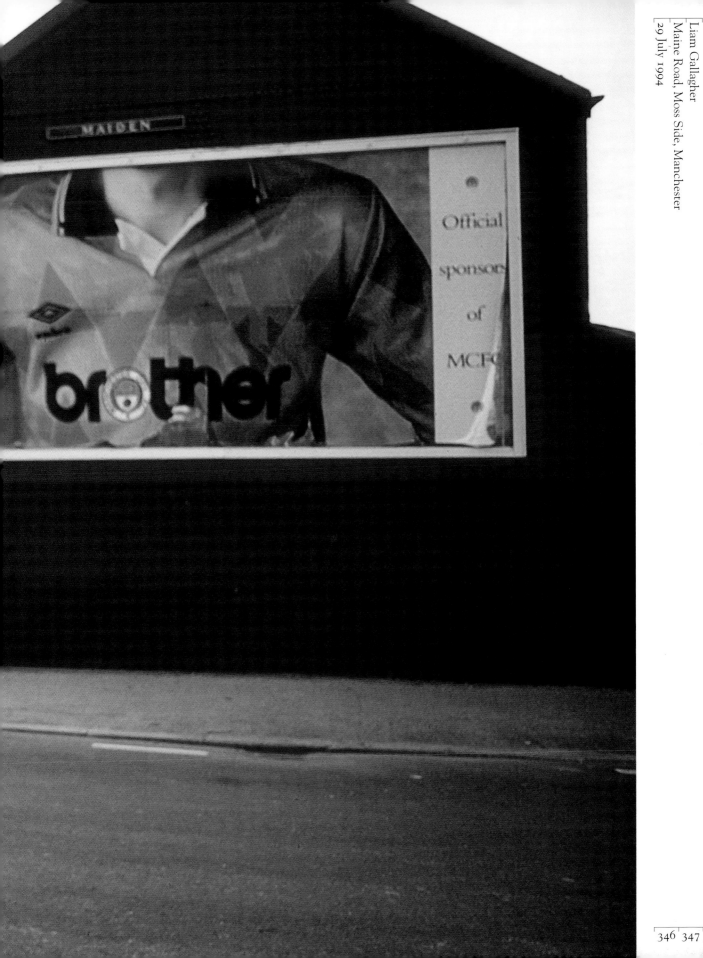

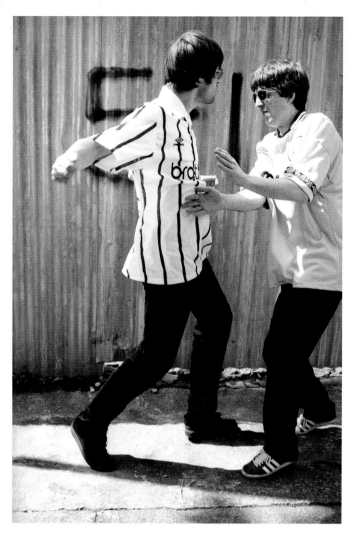
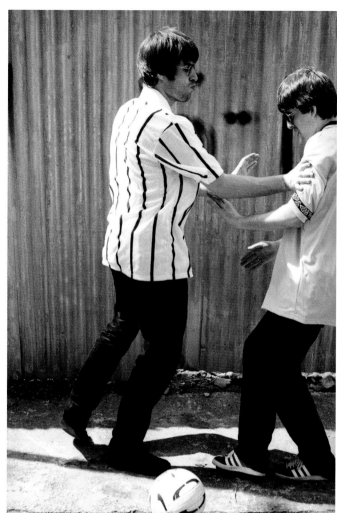

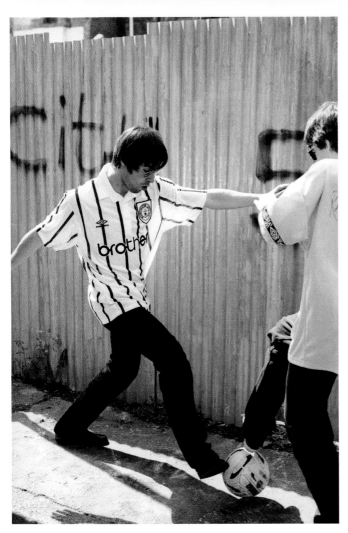
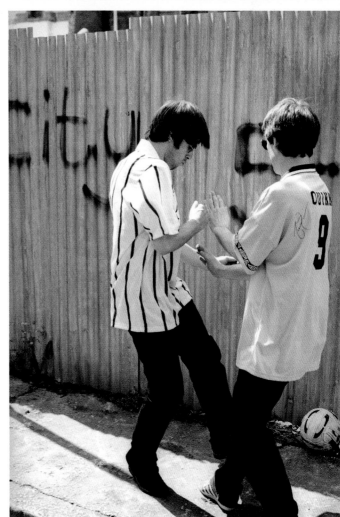

Liam and Noel Gallagher
Rampart Street, east London
8 May 1994

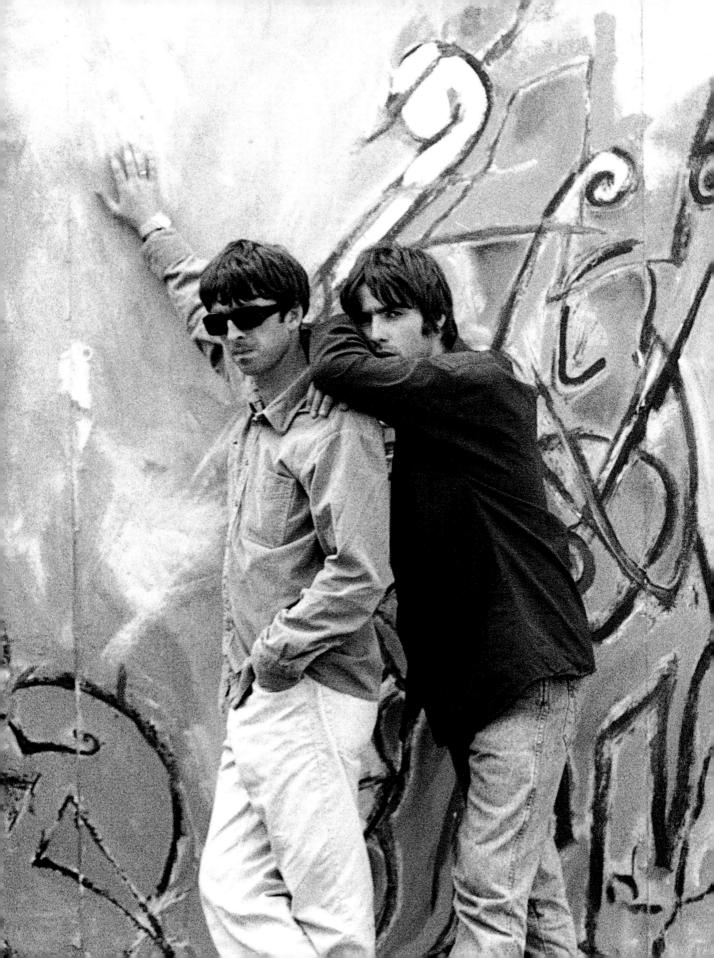

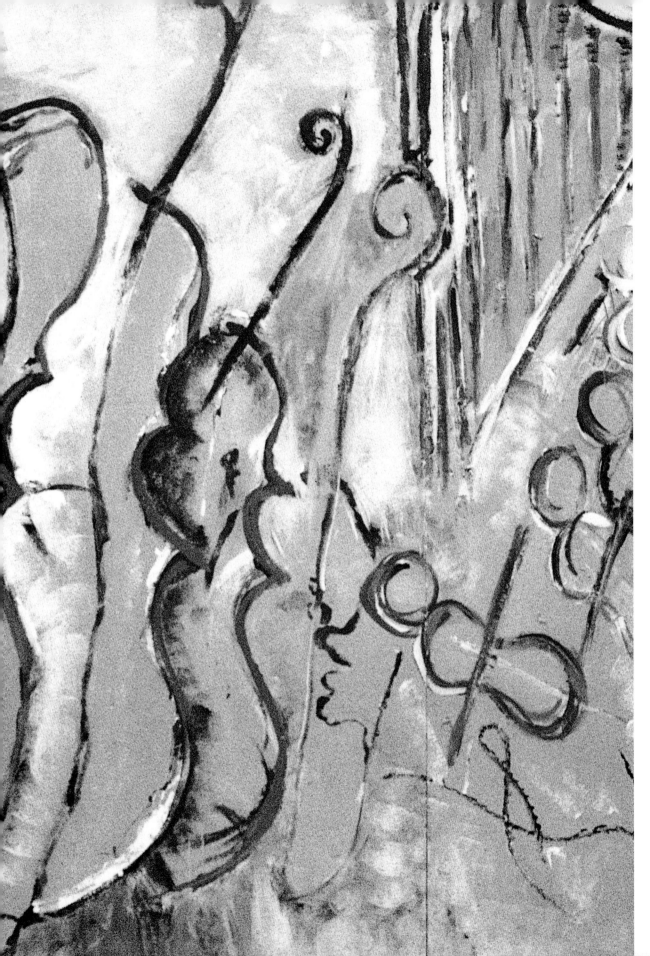

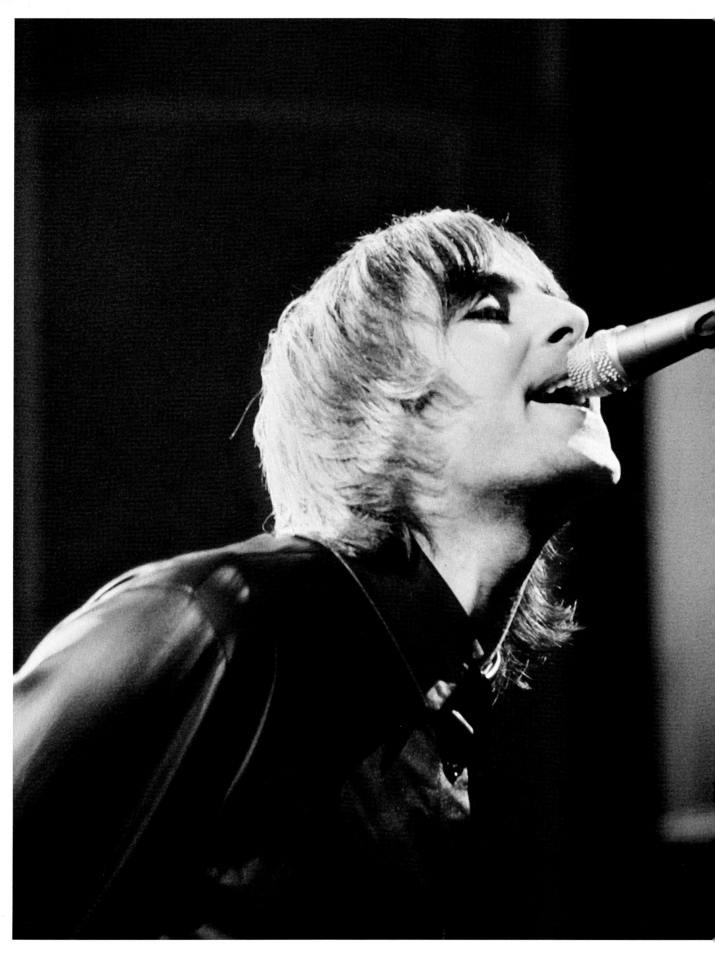

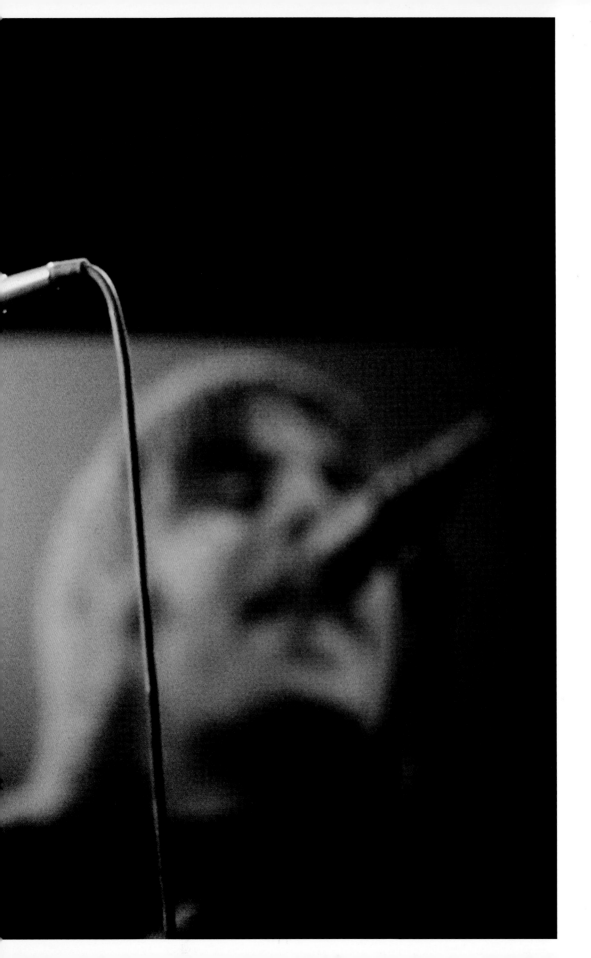

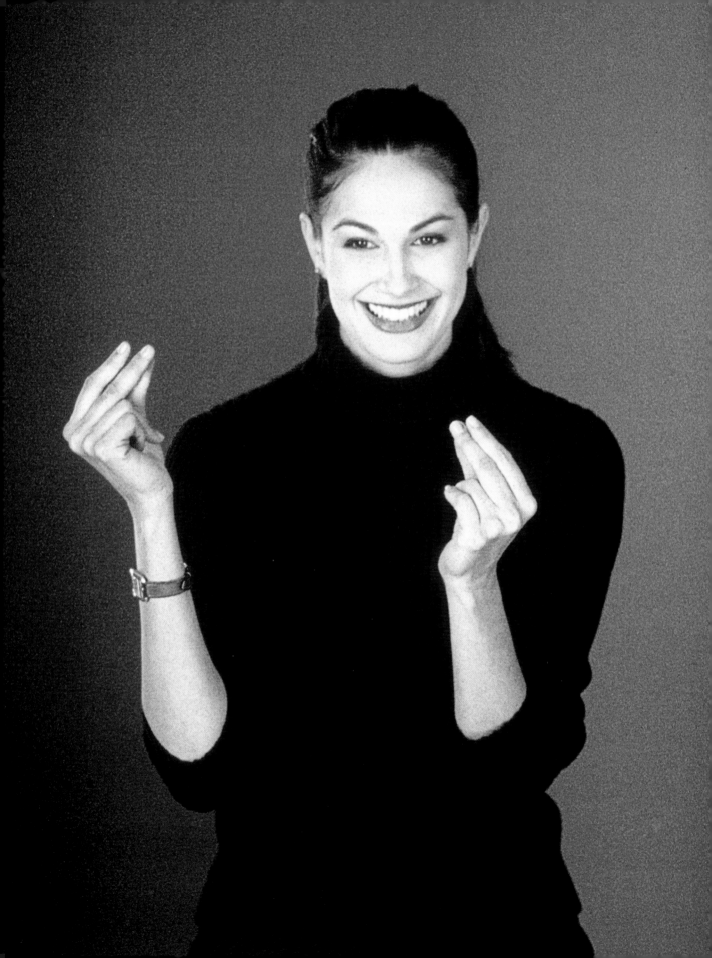

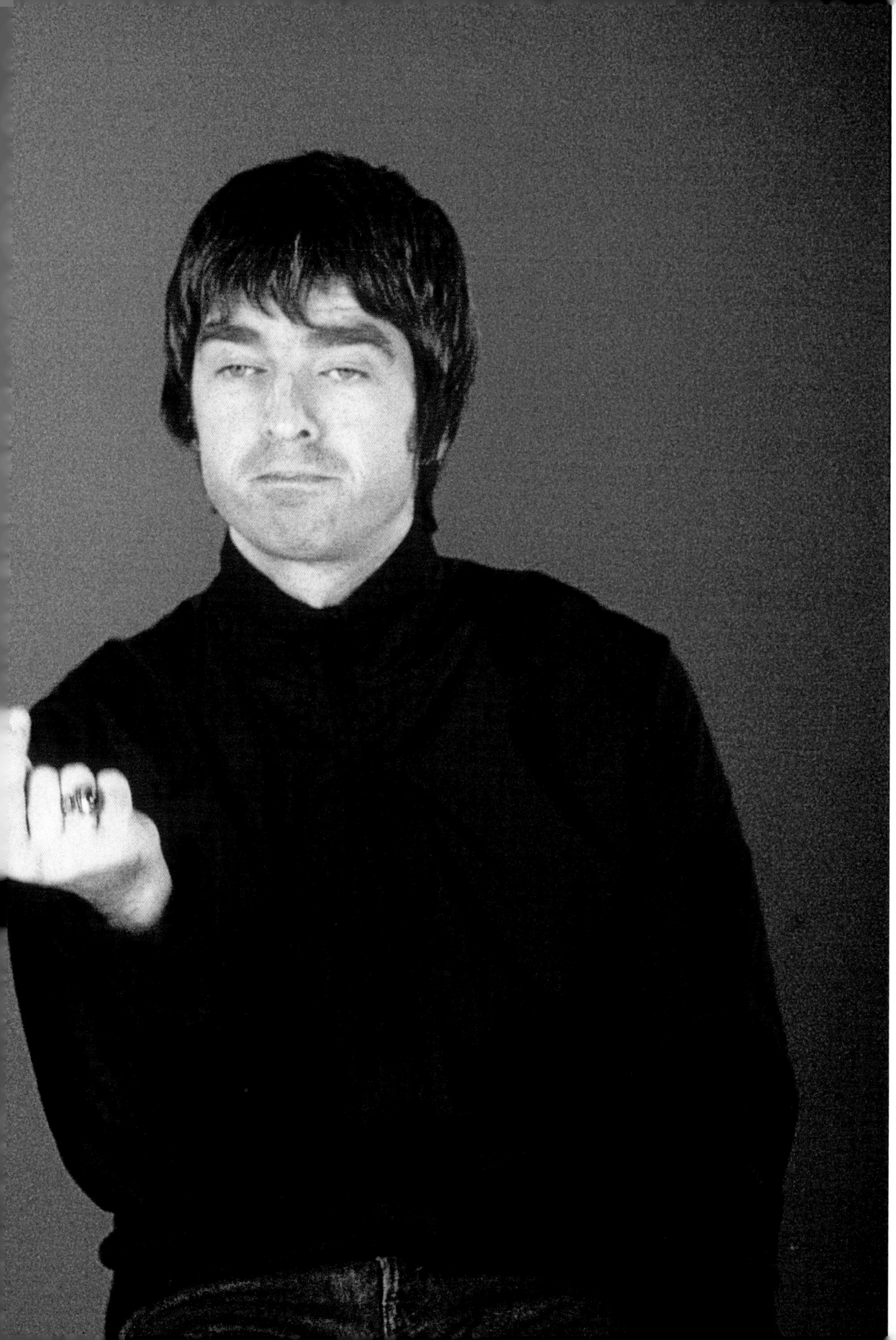

Helena Noguerra and Noel Gallagher
TV Studio, Paris
23 February 2000

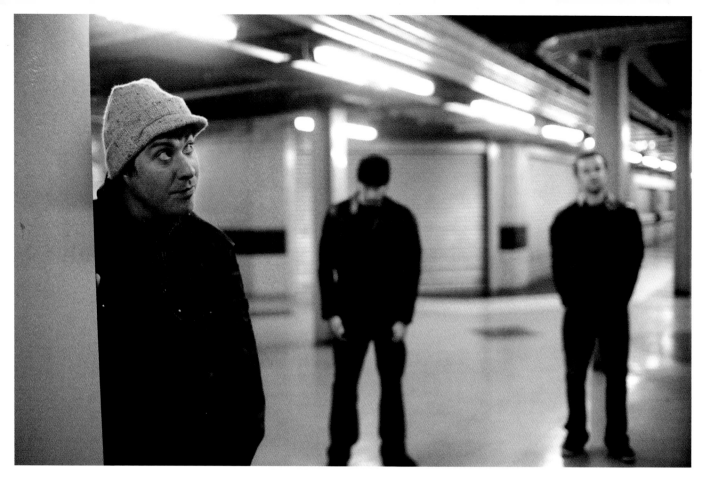

Doves
Maine Road, Kippax Street Stand
May 2003

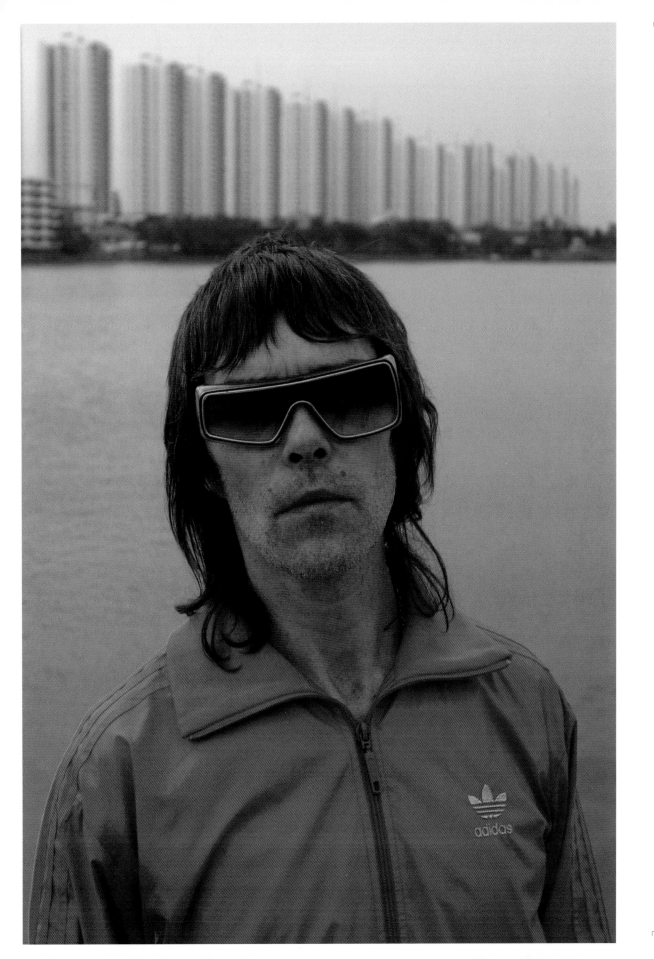

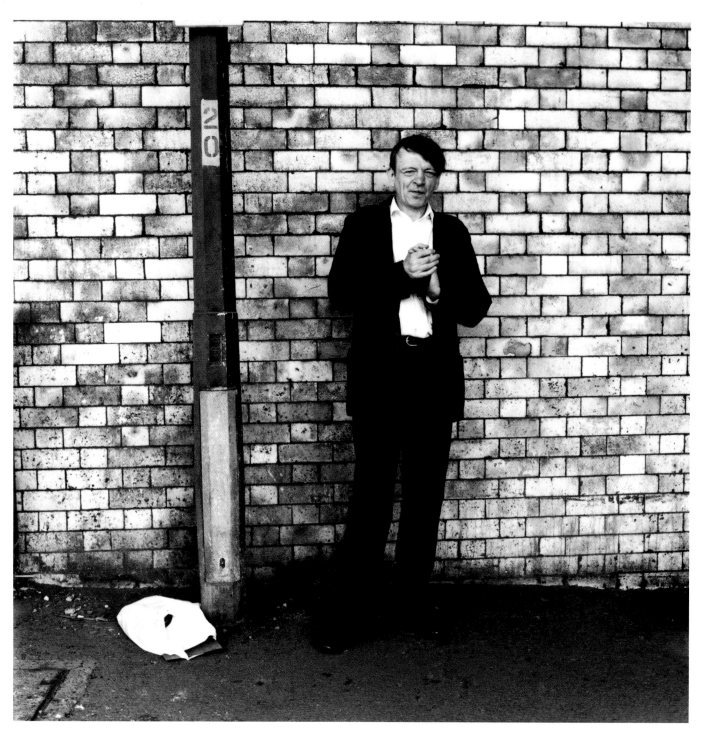

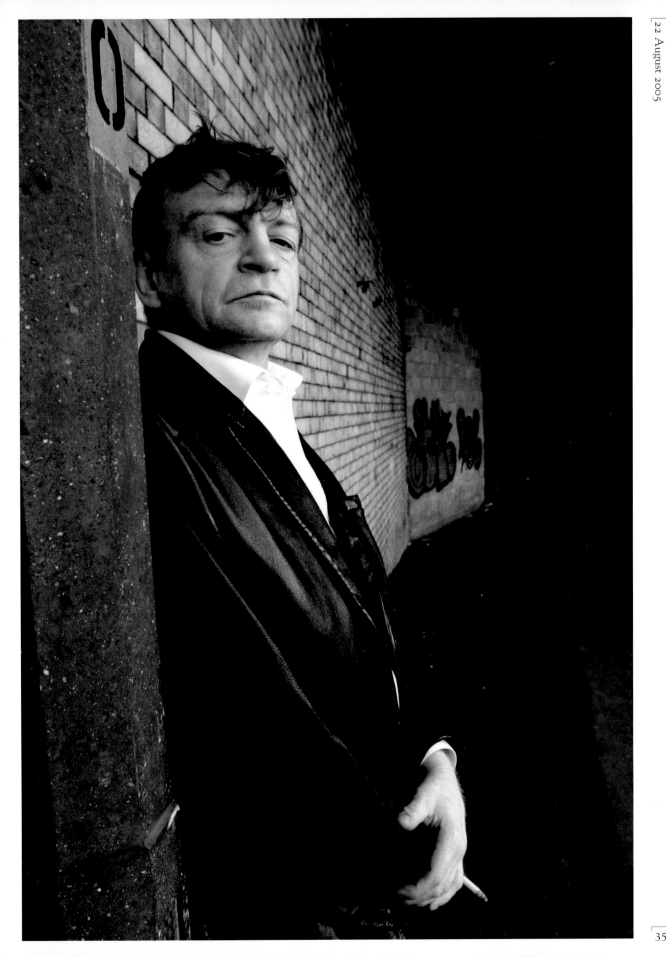

Manchester ... the belly and guts of the Nation.

George Orwell

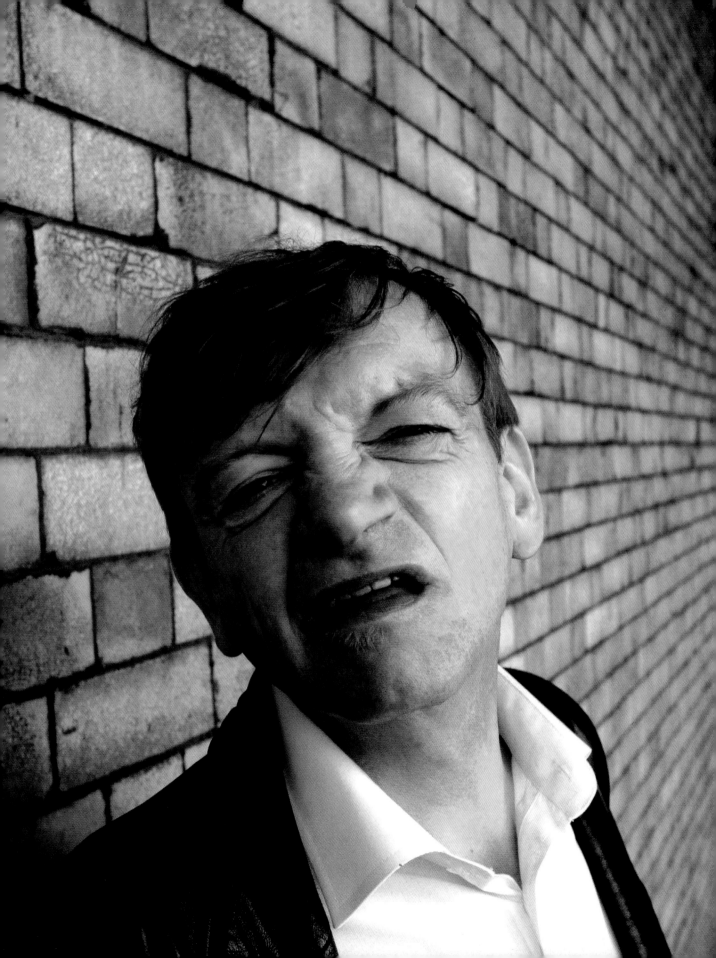

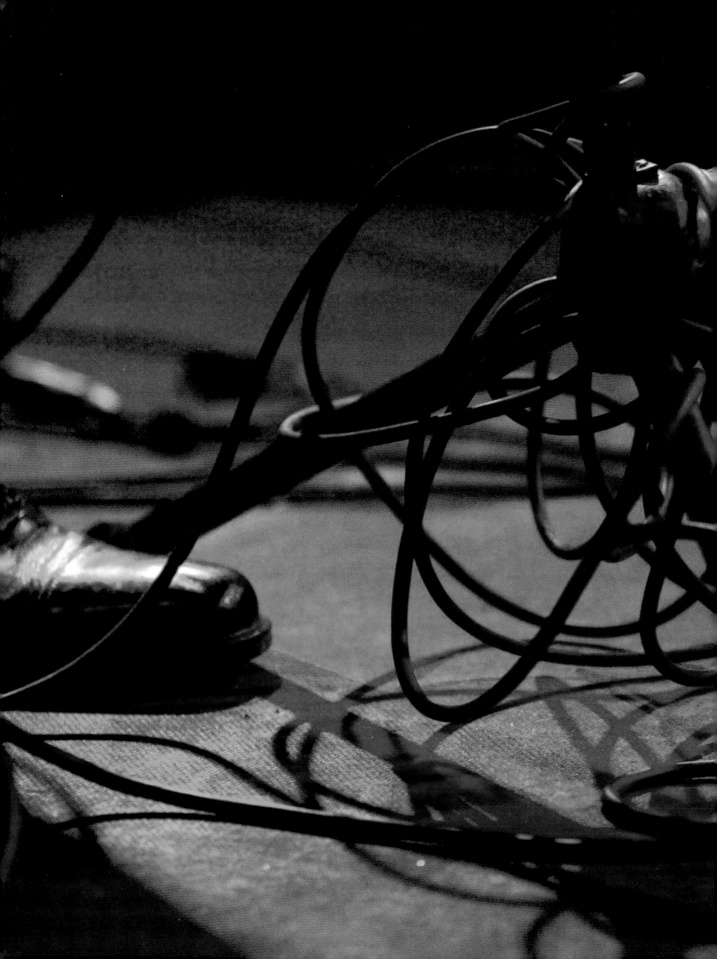

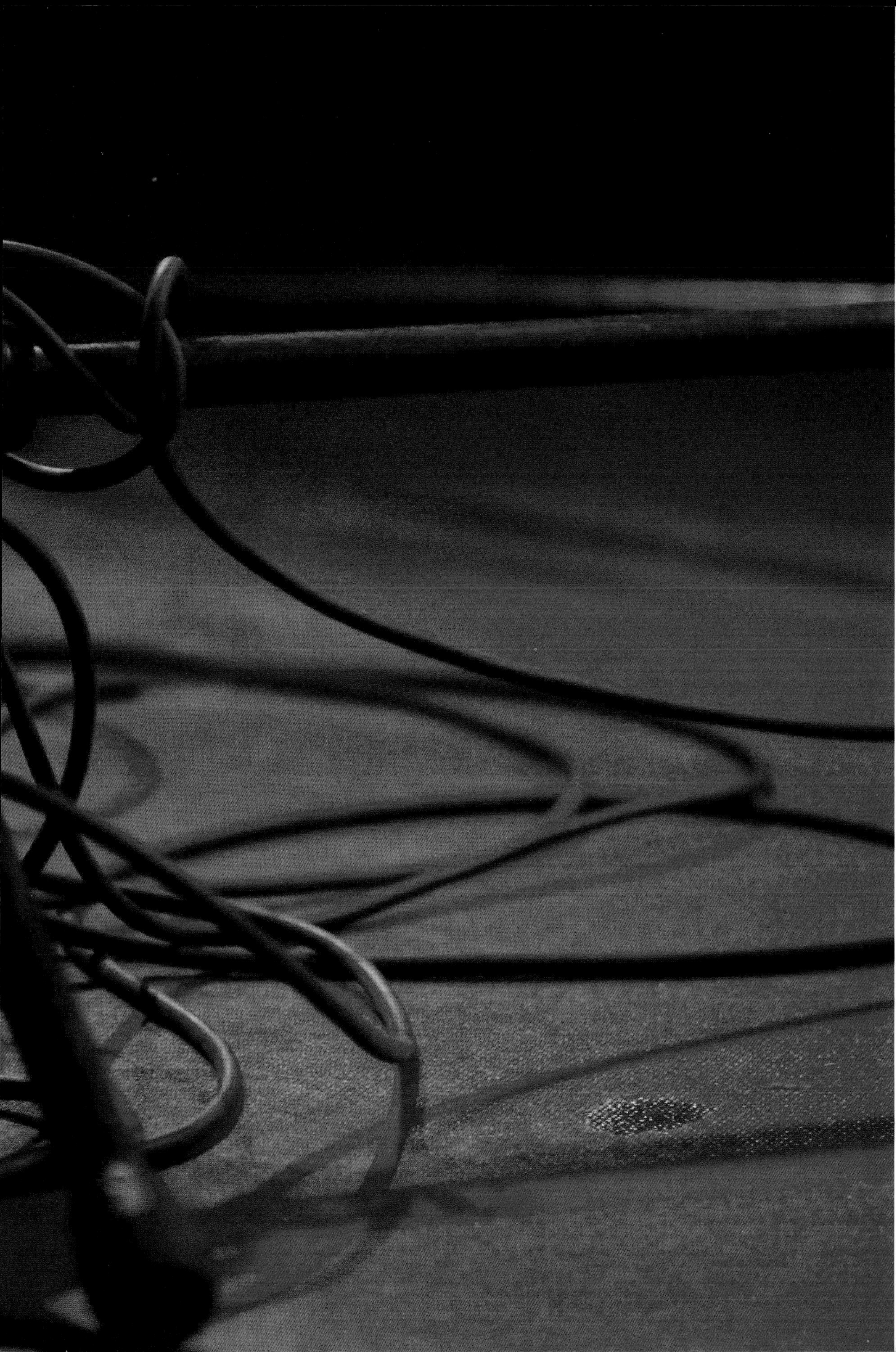

The Fall
Maria am Ostbahnhof, Berlin
21 April 2006

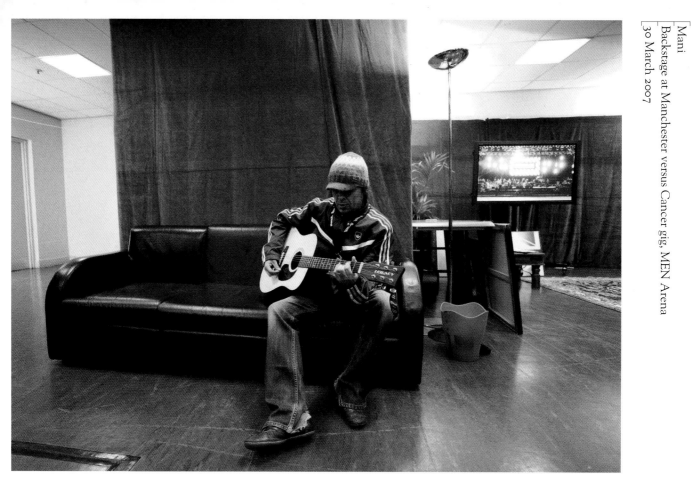

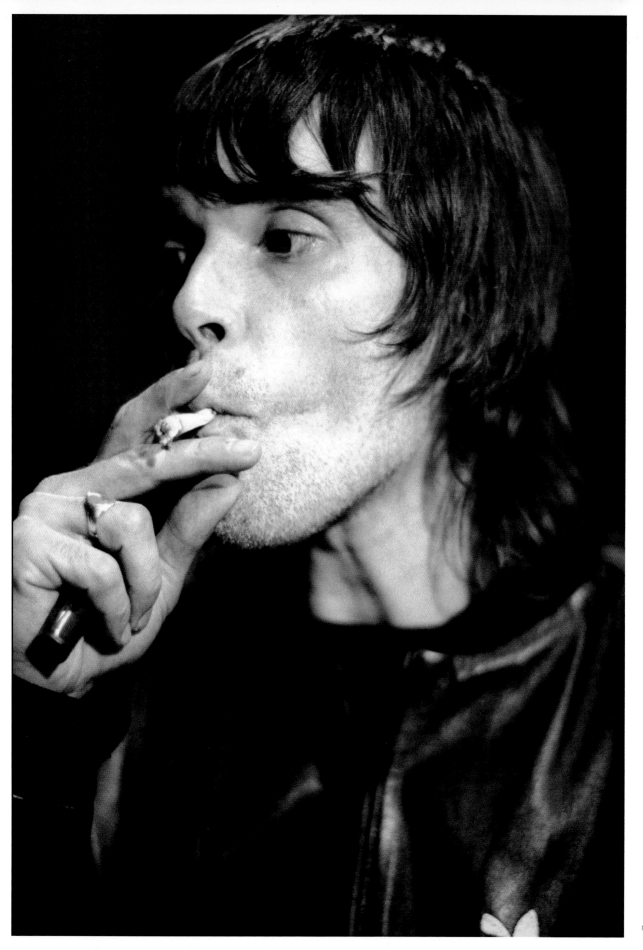

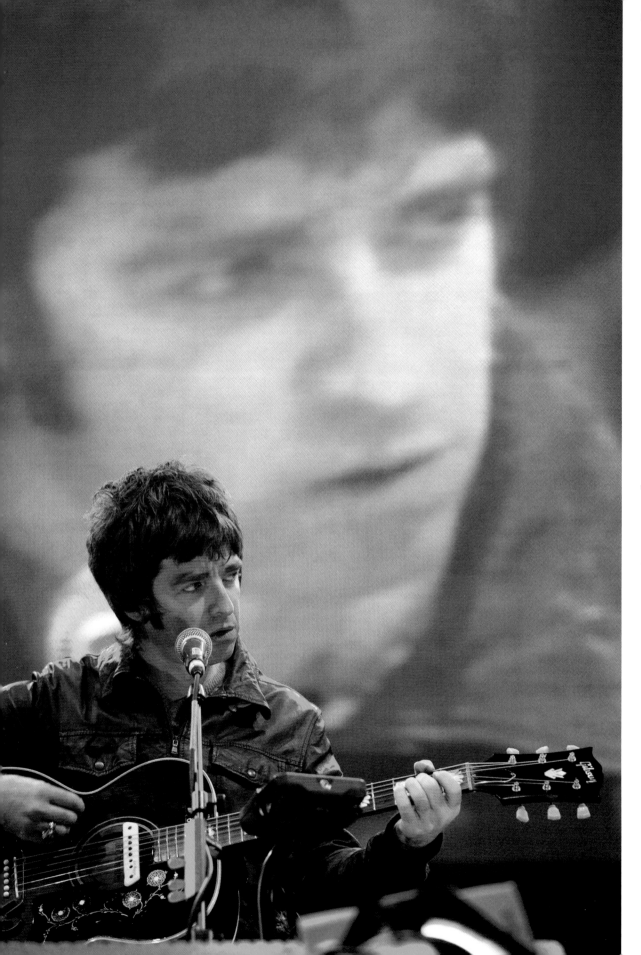

Noel Gallagher
Manchester versus Cancer gig, MEN Arena
30 March 2007

Ian Brown
Manchester versus Cancer gig, MEN Arena
30 March 2007

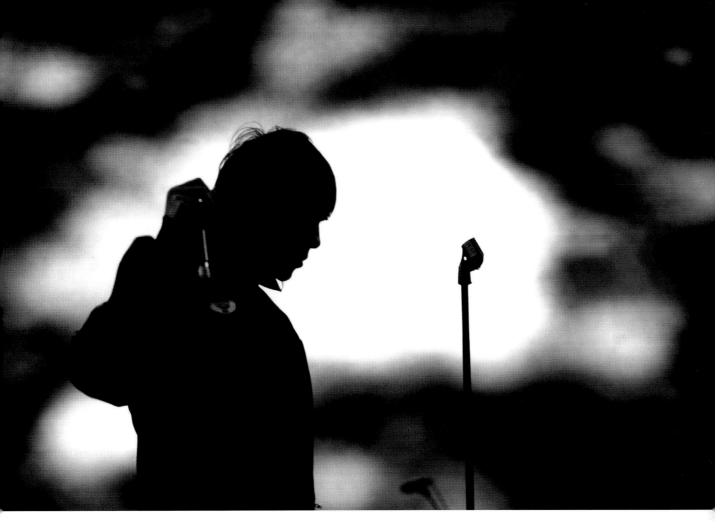

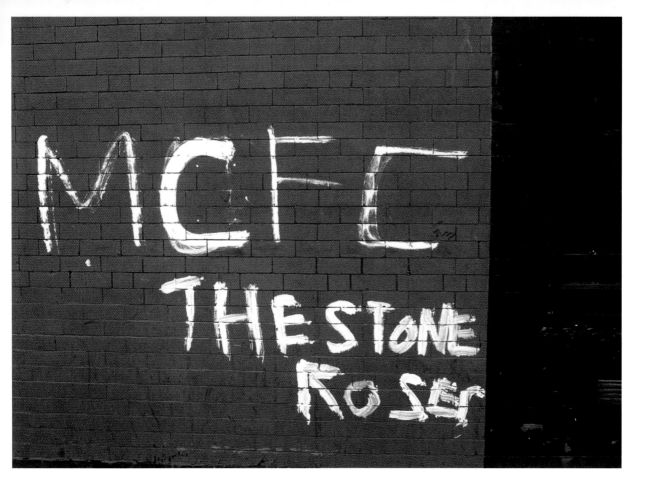

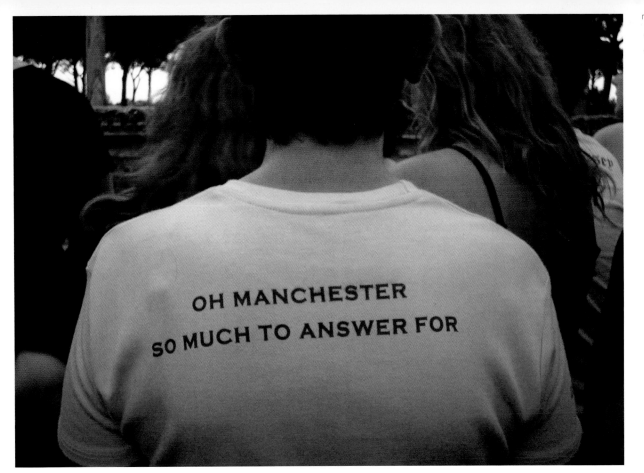

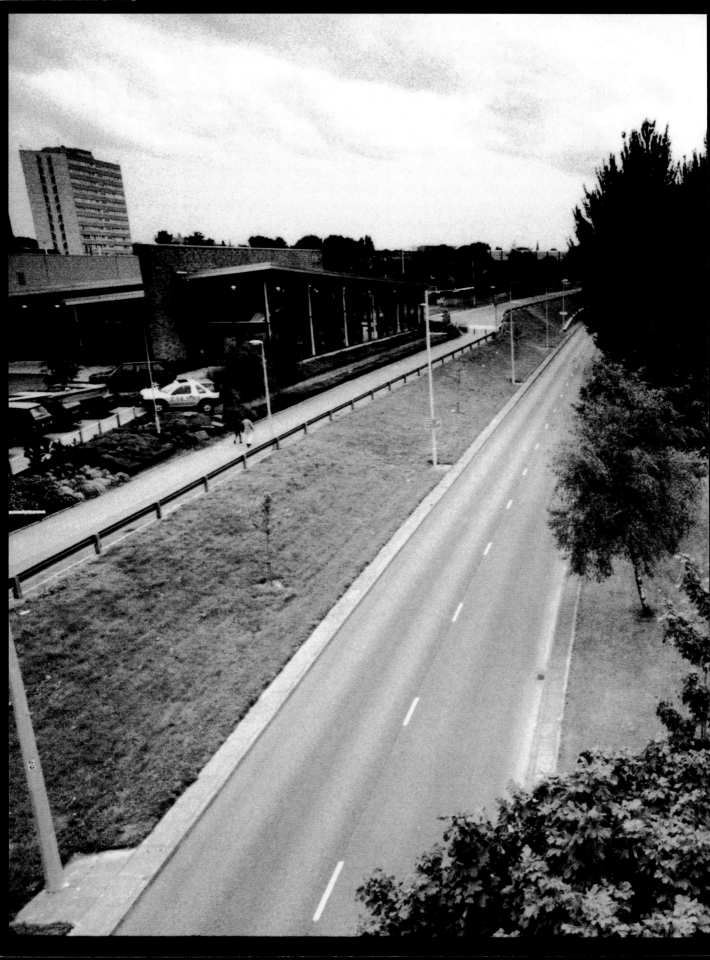

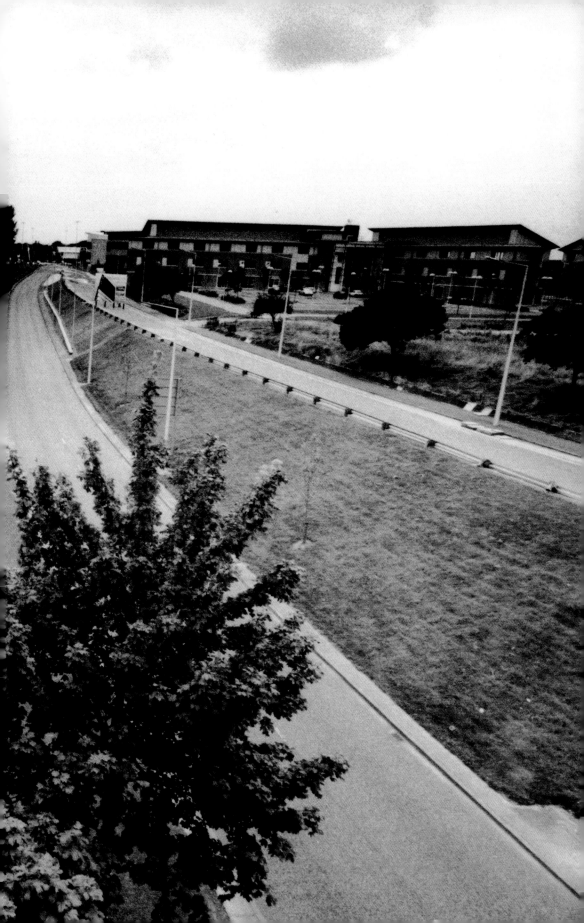

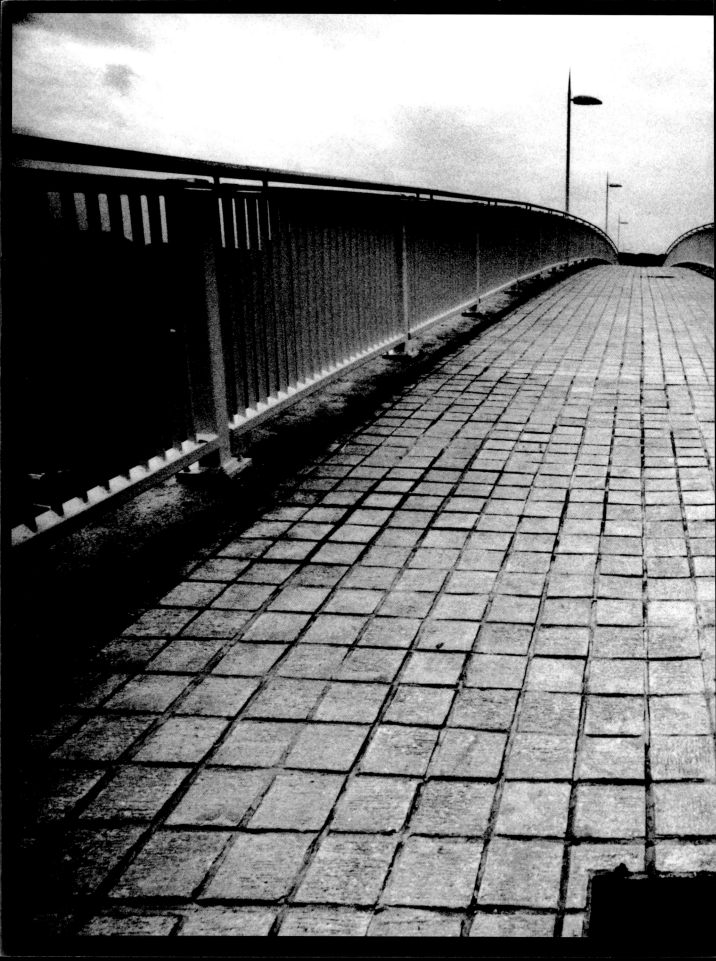

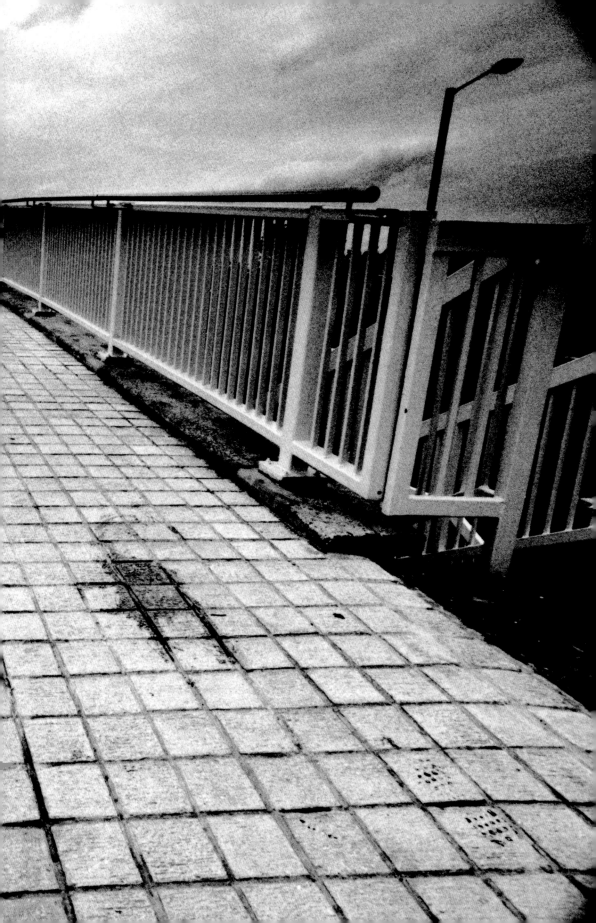

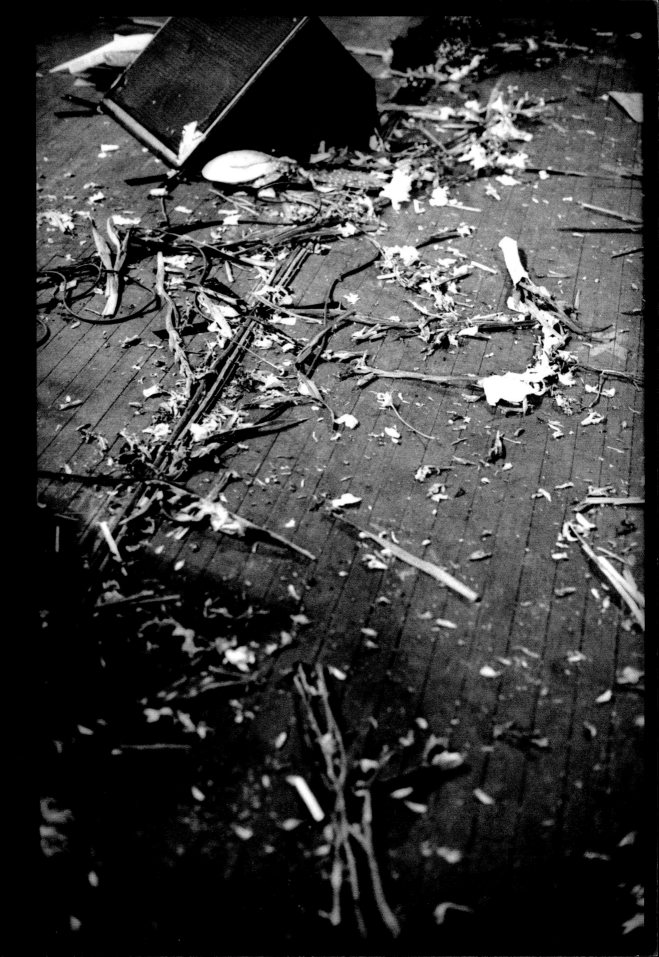

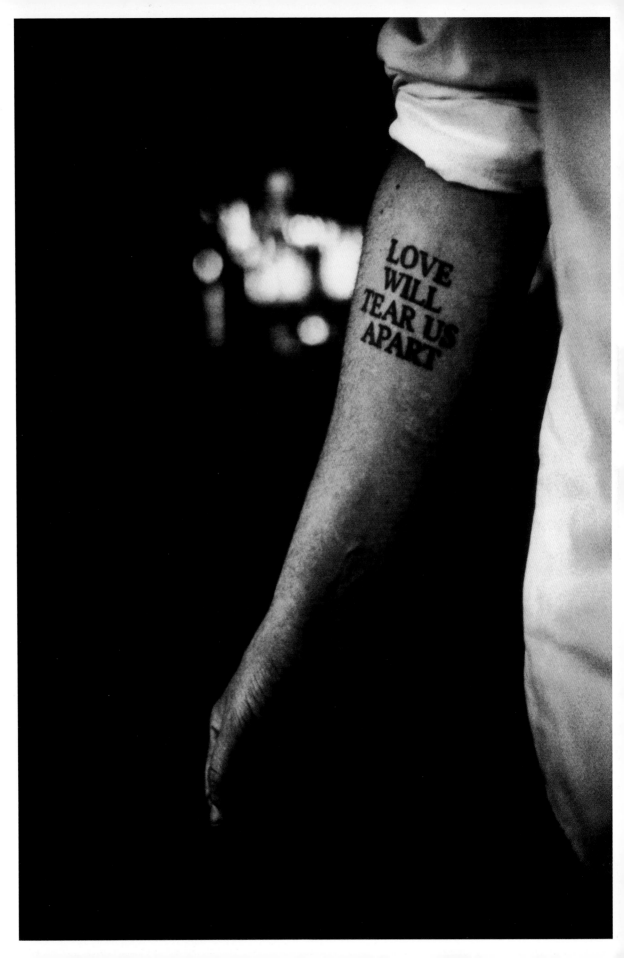

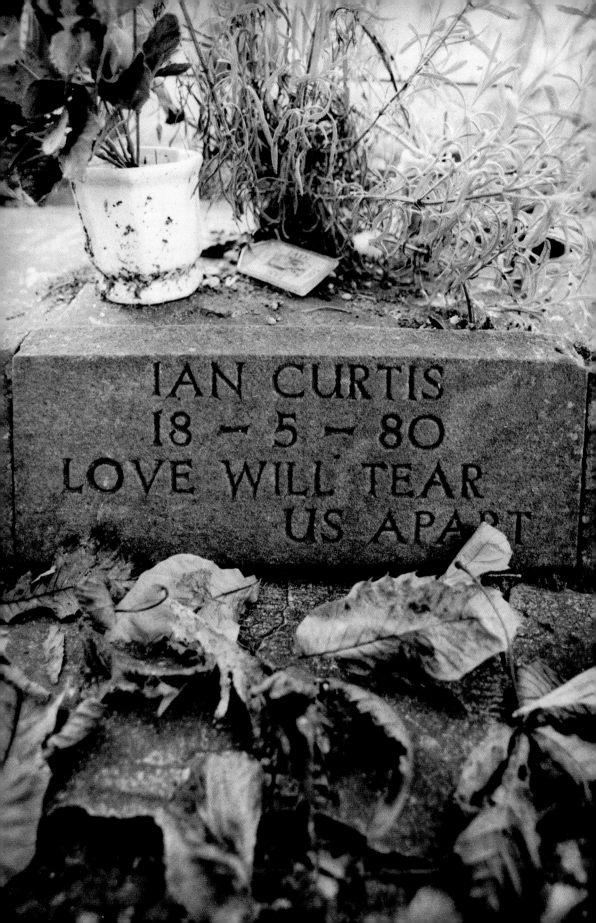

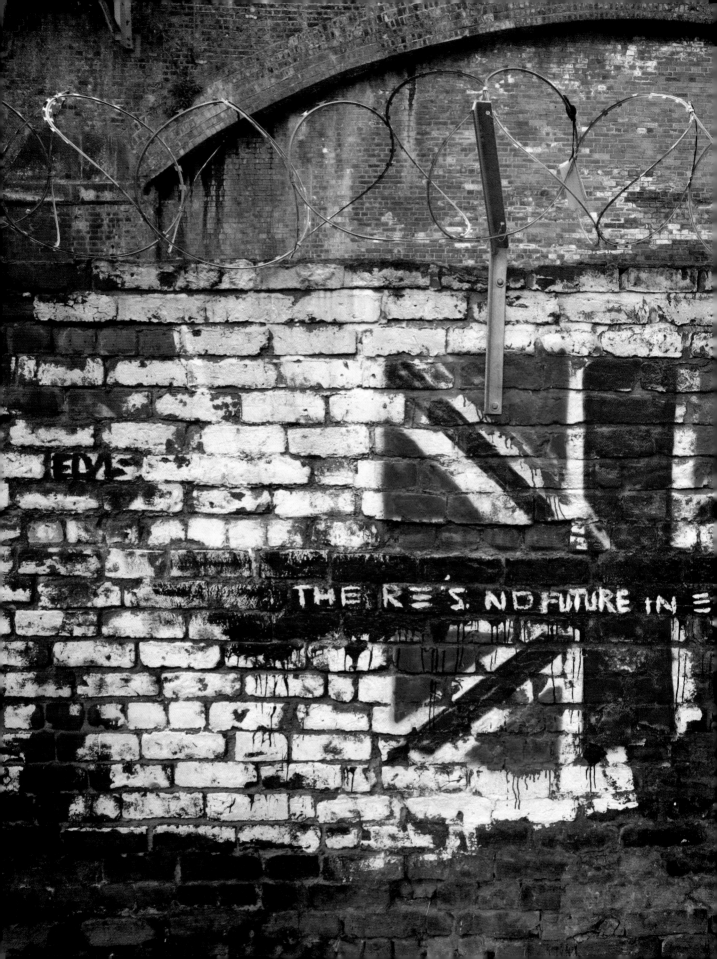

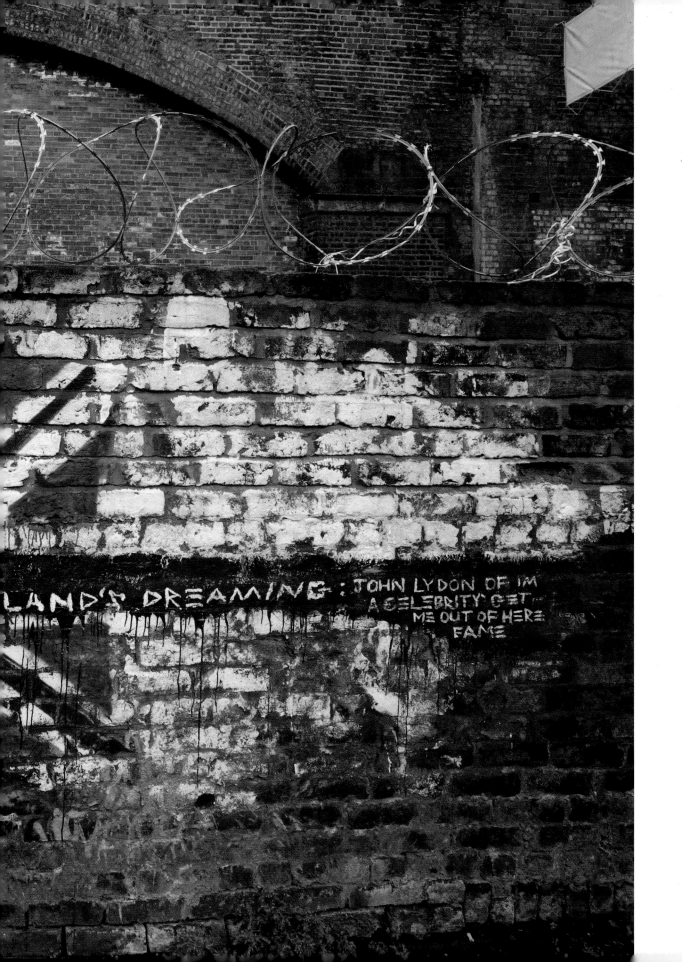

[Afterword – Tony Wilson]

'Kevin, sweetheart. Sorry I haven't sent the piece to you yet. I've just had to go back into hospital. It's all in my head though, darling. I'll download it as soon as I come out.'

He died three days later: 10.08.07

Kevin Cummins was born in Manchester and was the *NME*'s chief photographer for over a decade. Revered worldwide as one of the finest music photographers of our time, he is the author of the acclaimed book of Joy Division photographs, *Juvenes*, and *We're Not Really Here: Manchester City's Final Season at Maine Road*.

John Harris was raised fourteen miles south of Manchester in the Cheshire suburbs, and has written about music since he was nineteen, for such publications as *Sounds*, *NME*, *Q* and *Mojo*. He now writes about politics and culture for the *Guardian*, and is a regular panelist on BBC2's *Newsnight Review*. He first worked with Kevin Cummins in 1993.

Stuart Maconie is a writer and broadcaster best known for his work on BBC radio and for the bestselling books *Cider With Roadies*, *Pies and Prejudice* and *Adventures on the High Teas*. He was formerly deputy editor for the *NME* where he first met and travelled the world with Kev 'Mate' Cummins.

Gavin Martin was born in Belfast and his first publication, *Alternative Ulster*, was printed by Richard Boon in Manchester in 1977, before Stiff Little Fingers used the fanzine title for a song. He has been a writer ever since – for *NME*, *The Times*, *Uncut*, *Independent*, *Guardian*, *Observer* and is currently Music Critic at the *Daily Mirror*. Gavin lives in London where he remains open to suggestions – particularly if they involve a trip to Manchester.

Richard Milward is the author of the acclaimed novels *Apples* and *Ten Storey Love Song*, and recently graduated from Central St Martins with a Fine Art degree. He was born in Middlesbrough in 1984.

Paul Morley is the author of *Words and Music: The History of Pop in the Shape of a City* and *Nothing*. He is currently at work on a biography of Tony Wilson.

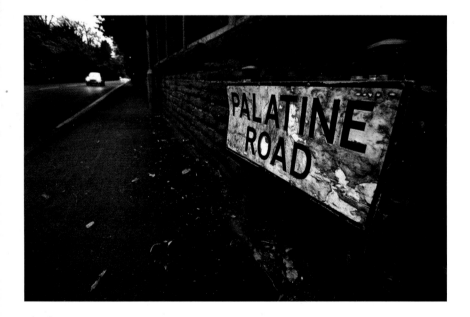